DIMENSIONS OF
STATE & URBAN
POLICY MAKING

General Editors **Richard H. Leach**
Timothy G. O'Rourke

Editors David P. Lindquist
Regis Koslofsky

DUKE UNIVERSITY

Dimensions of State & Urban Policy Making

MACMILLAN PUBLISHING CO., INC.
New York
Collier Macmillan Publishers
London

Printed in the United States of America

Macmillan Publishing Co., Inc.
866 Third Avenue
New York, New York 10022

Collier-Macmillan Canada, Ltd.

Library of Congress Cataloging in Publication Data

Leach, Richard H comp.
Dimensions of state and urban policy making.

Includes bibliographies.
1. State governments—Addresses, essays, lectures.
2. Municipal government—United States—Addresses, essays, lectures. I. O'Rourke, Timothy G., joint comp. II. Title.
JK2431.L4 350'.0008 74–3805
ISBN 0–02–369000–3

Printing: 1 2 3 4 5 6 7 8 Year: 5 6 7 8 9 0

Preface

Although this book may have wider applicability, it is intended for use in college political science courses in state and urban government.

It has become customary for both students and their professors to deplore the so-called "textbook" treatment of government. The object of criticism is not so much the textbook *per se* as the approach of particular textbooks. The standard approach encompasses the identification of the major institutions of government and a description of their functions; it may also involve case studies illustrating the activities of public agents working within the institutions of government. While college text writers in the field of state and local government have not been able to avoid entirely the pitfalls of this descriptive type approach, most recent texts in the area do reflect a more sophisticated concern with the analysis of state and local government. In brief, the writers have begun to give attention to the need to place state and local policy formation in comparative perspective, to view governmental activity in the wider socioeconomic setting, and to use political science as a tool for prescription as well as description.

Within this perspective, books of readings have had an ambiguous role. In some instances, readers in state and local governments have been collections of case studies designed to complement the generalized discussions of textbooks. Such case studies were often mere chronological accounts of incidents, devoid of broader interpretative analysis. The reaction to the obvious weaknesses of the case study reader has been the emergence of readers incorporating material that is broadly comparative in nature. Often through more or less sophisticated statistical examination, the comparative approach has led to significant generalizations based on data from all fifty states or a larger number of communities. Much of the comparative work, however, fails to convey the feeling of actual government at work.

Yet another pitfall of books of readings has been the tendency for them to contain material selected either according to structural criteria (something on the governor, something on the legislature, etc.) or along problem lines (finances, welfare, education, etc.). To choose the structural approach alone is to ignore key areas of policy concern to emphasize the mechanics of policy formation rather than the policies themselves. Focusing solely on problem areas neglects the often vital and intriguing aspects of the institutions as they actually operate.

Thus it would seem that the ideal book of readings on state and local government would be one that is both specific and comparative, as well as structurally and problem oriented. Of course, no book of readings can satisfy all of these demands within a reasonable space limitation. There are, however, some considerations that make the task of selecting material somewhat less overwhelming. First, the nature of the intended audience for the book limits the amount of material that could conceivably be a part of the book. Not without justification, we have limited our selection to writings of social scientists. Second, we attempted to enact our belief that a collection of material encompassing concerns of both institutional and problem-oriented analysis is needed. However, these concerns were not overriding in the sense that we felt that we had to include something on *every* governmental institution and problem. Third, we hoped to find material focused on particular institutions or problem areas but at the same time comparative in outlook. Operationally, this meant abandoning the case study approach in favor of a comparative bias. Nevertheless, we continually sought comparative material with a "real-world" relevance to policy making and to particular kinds of policies. Finally, we tried to select the best material available—best in the sense of meeting the previous three guidelines; best in the sense of being essentially informative and useful in the study of state and urban government; best in the sense of being eminently readable; and best in some rather esoteric qualitative senses. In sum, we attempted to illustrate a range of important considerations in an overall analysis of state and urban policy making.*

Each group of readings is followed by suggested readings designed to introduce the curious student to further valuable readings on the given topic. The selections themselves are entirely in the authors' words, though some deletions and simplifications have been made. Footnotes have been omitted unless they are integral to the text or make reference to important correlative reading. The contribution by James Lee appears in print for the first time.

* We may point out that this collection of readings on state and urban policy making grew out of a bibliography on state and local government initially prepared in connection with an advanced graduate seminar in political science at Duke University. The state government portion of the original bibliography has subsequently been published as *A Selected Bibliography on State Government* (Lexington, Ky.: Council of State Governments, 1972).

Contents

Part I

The Policy-Making Environment

While it is obvious that public officials perform the formal policy-making functions of governmental units, it is equally true, if not so apparent, that the shape of public policy also depends on such factors as public opinion and the social and economic pattern within the particular communities. In short, the nature of each political environment helps to determine the kinds of policies enacted by a given governmental unit. A major area of this environment embraces public attitudes toward the government and its policies; in a broad sense, this area is public opinion, or more narrowly defined, voter opinion. The form of government within whose structure policy decisions must be made is of obvious importance. Still another component of the policy-making environment encompasses the distribution of political power and influence among individuals and groups in and out of government; the character of elites and interests in the particular community has special importance for governmental policy. The readings in Part 1 address these aspects of the policy-making environment. The bibliographies suggest other readings on the same subject.

M. Kent Jennings and L. Harmon Zeigler

The Salience of American State Politics

In a day of increasing centralization—of continentalism, some argue—the emphasis on the decentralized exertions of power common to federal systems is called into question, both on theoretical grounds and in terms of performance. In the United States, state and local governments have been assailed for failing to provide their citizens with the kinds of action on public problems which are required for the continued public welfare. In former Governor Terry Sanford's apt phrase, there has resulted a "storm over the states," which will subside only when a large number of steps to improve and modernize state and local government are taken.

Those steps will not be taken, however, regardless of the nation's commitment to federalism, unless the people of the states appreciate the problem and support the necessity of remedial action. What do we know about popular attitudes toward state and local government? On the surface, it would seem that mobility, nationalized communications, and a nationwide job pool on the one hand, and wars and rumors of war on the other, have so focused American public attention at the national and international levels that little room is left for concern about state and local government and politics.

Jennings and Zeigler demonstrate conclusively that such a surface judgment is incorrect. State and local government and politics are important to the American people. A sound basis for effective state and local policy outcomes thus exists.

Reprinted from *American Political Science Review*, **64**:523–35 (June 1970) by permission of the authors and the publisher. Some descriptive and bibliographical footnotes have been omitted for considerations of space and textual format.

Research emphasizing the correlates of state policy outputs and the performance of particular institutions has overshadowed the role of the citizenry in the drama of state politics. One question of basic concern is the relevance of state government and politics for the inhabitants of a state. At the level of public policy and institutional performance the answer to this is factual and straightforward. The nature, amount, distribution, and to some extent the quality of a state's services and policies can be specified. Since states perform most of the traditional functions of governmental units and since these functions affect the fortunes of the citizens, state politics has an obvious, tangible, objective relevance for a state's inhabitants. At another level, however, the answer is not so clear-cut. Here we are dealing with the idea of what is subjectively relevant. Large numbers of people apparently pass their lives being touched by political institutions in a variety of ways without becoming particularly interested in or involved with these institutions. Other people become intensely, purposively related to these same institutions. Still others fall along a continuum between these two poles. If substantial variations exist in the general salience of politics, there is little reason to doubt that the same conditions may be found in particular subsets of political matters. In the case at hand this subset consists of the cluster of institutions, actors, and processes known as state political systems.

I. The Concept of Salience Maps

It may be assumed that for every individual at a given point in time some aspects of politics are more salient than are others. These varying degrees of salience result in cognitive maps yielding surfaces with divergent contours and topographies. Analytically, at least two kinds of mapping operations can be visualized. One is laid out according to issue domains. For some people civil rights issues are most salient, for others tax and fiscal issues, for still others questions of foreign affairs predominate, while education may be the prominent part for yet another cluster of people. Some individuals may place equal stress—ranging from high to low—on a host of disparate issues, but given the opportunity costs involved it seems likely that at any point in time the mapping operations result in an ordering of issue salience.

More germane for present purposes is a salience map arranged according to geopolitical units. A variety of investigations have suggested that people do, in fact, develop such maps. Perhaps the most noted shorthand expression of this differentiation is the local-cosmopolitan dimension. Important ramifications for political systems stem from differentiated salience maps. One has only to think of the stresses and strains in the emergent countries or the separatist enclaves in established polities to grasp these possibilities. The difficulties encountered by national governments as a partial consequence of sub-national loyalties are impressive. Proclivities toward independence in the Canadian province of Quebec, the Nigeria-Biafra confrontation, the uneasy federalism of India, and the failure of the American South to be incorporated fully into the mainstream of American politics testify to the magnitude of these difficulties.

As with salience maps oriented around issues, the maps dealing with levels of government could in fact attach equal relevance to the component parts. That is, a person could be equally interested (or uninterested) in international, national, state, and local public affairs and politics. Yet this would seem to be an inefficient mode of operation if nothing else, and as we shall see momentarily it is a deviant pattern.

Upon what basis would a person distinguish among these four levels of politics? Assuming that he had equal information about all of them, or at least access to equal information, two dimensions can be suggested. First, he may arrange them according to his interest in the policy outcomes involved. Whereas some find local outcomes about services and amenities of greatest subjective relevance, others are more intrigued by the results of military encounters and diplomatic skirmishes at the international level. A second dimension rests not so much with outcomes as with the demands and conversion processes at work within a given system. Here the interest comes from watching how the game is played rather than in what the final scores are. Charismatic political leaders, factional fights, and broader societal cleavages are kinds of forces which can lead to differential salience along this dimension. Attention to outcomes and conversions may operate simultaneously and feed upon each other. Interest generated by a strong, personable governor might be combined with concern over a state tax program to produce a heightened salience for state politics. Should such convergences occur, the two types of salience maps begin to merge. That is, the overlay of the issue salience map on the system salience map begins to produce a single topography. Although the question of overlap between issue and system maps is an important one, our major concern is with the system map arrangement.

II. The Place of the States Versus Other Levels

For a variety of reasons one could predict that the states generate but a modicum of interest amongst their residents. Many of these reasons are either explicit or implicit in a statement by Dahl, made in the context of a discussion about optimum units for popular democratic government:

> Yet in the perspective I am suggesting the states do not stand out as important institutions of democratic

> self-government. They are too big to allow for much in the way of civic participation—think of California and New York, each about as large in population as Canada or Yugoslavia and each larger than 80 per cent of the countries of the world. Yet an American state is infinitely less important to citizens of that state than any democratic nation-state to its citizens. Consequently the average American is bound to be much less concerned about the affairs of his state than of his city or country. Too remote to stimulate much participation by their citizens, and too big to make extensive participation possible anyway, these units intermediate between city and nation are probably destined for a kind of limbo of quasi-democracy. . . . It cannot even be said that the states, on the whole, can tap and strong sentiments of loyalty or likemindedness among their citizens.[1]

In a sense the states are caught between the immediacy of the local system and the glamour and importance of the national and international systems. Without wishing to become embroiled in the question of the appropriate units for a democratic polity, we can nevertheless introduce some material which will clarify the location of the states in the salience maps of Americans.

Our data are drawn primarily from the University of Michigan Survey Research Center's 1966 election study, which utilized a national probability sample of the adult population. In order to obtain the interest accorded various levels of politics a series of questions was put to the respondents, beginning with an initial question designed to filter out those people (17 per cent) who barely attend to matters of the body politic.[2] The remainder rank-ordered which kinds of public affairs they follow most closely—international, national, state, and local.[3]

One immediate result of the ranking operations is that it reveals the

[1] Robert A. Dahl, "The City in the Future of Democracy," *American Political Science Review* **61**:968 (December 1967).

[2] This question ran: "Some people seem to follow what's going on in government and public affairs most of the time, whether there's an election going on or not. Others aren't that interested. Would you say that you follow what's going on in government and public affairs most of the time, some of the time, only now and then, or hardly at all?" Those selecting one of the first three alternatives are considered to be members of the attentive public.

[3] After handing the respondent a card showing the four levels of public affairs, he was asked to rank them in this fashion: "Which one of these kinds of public affairs do you follow most closely?" "Which one do you follow most (next) closely?" (sic) "Which one do you follow least closely?" With first, second, and fourth ranks thus determined the residual level automatically occupied the third rank.

TABLE 1 *Rank Order Distributions for Salience of Governmental Affairs at Four Levels*

Level of governmental affairs	Rank of how closely followed: First	Second	Third	Fourth	Total[a]	N
International	20%	16%	20%	42%	100	983
National	32	31	26	10	99	983
State	17	33	27	22	99	983
Local	30	20	25	25	100	983
	99%	100%	100%	99%		
	N = 983	983	983	983		

[a] Total percentages do not equal 100% due to rounding. Cases involving tied ranks or missing data have been deleted in this table. Their inclusion in any rows or columns would have a maximum effect of but 1 per cent on any cell value. The total number of cases for analysis will be 1,008.

readiness of Americans to distinguish among the four levels. All but 6 per cent of the sample (excluding the inattentive) gave complete orderings. The ease with which the rankings were obtained as well as the meager proportions declining to give complete orderings indicates that people at least believe they have salience maps characterized by a rugged terrain rather than a smooth plain.

It is apparent that, while some respondents place state affairs above all other levels, the majority share of first rank attention is devoted to national and local affairs, such as Dahl predicted (Table 1). If one wants to consider international affairs a mental extension of America's role in world affairs (which some respondents undoubtedly did), then state affairs is even more clearly in last place. Taking only the leading rankings demonstrates that the attentive public for state politics is not particularly large.

The danger in closing the argument on the basis of first ranks is nicely demonstrated in two ways. Looking at fourth ranks, for example, reveals that state affairs has next to the lowest proportions in this category. More compelling evidence is provided by moving to the second ranks. State affairs has strong second-place strength, being in fact the level selected most often at that rank. The contrast with the fate of international affairs is the most striking, since it too (compared with national and local affairs) had abundant opportunity to pick up second place strength. The result of combining first and second ranks finds one-half of the sample placing state matters either first or second, thereby moving it to an equal footing with local affairs, well ahead of international affairs, but still to the rear of national affairs. While the states may not be uppermost in the political thoughts of their residents, they do occupy a secure niche.[4]

What are the risks in using the respondents' rank orderings of interest in the four levels of politics as a way of deriving their interest in state politics alone? Three immediate justifications for the measure can be offered. First, it should be reemphasized that these orderings reflect those of the national sample *minus* an apolitical stratum, the 17% who avowed they paid no attention to public affairs and politics. Thus we have eliminated at least a substantial proportion of those people who might have contributed idiosyncratic, error-prone estimates of the differential salience of various levels of politics. Second, these kinds of rank-orders have been subjected to a spatial scaling technique which indicates the prominence of at least one major dimension running through the rank orders, *viz.,* that of the geo-political domain encompassed by given governmental levels. Essentially, this means that the ranking of state politics nestles reasonably well within an overall, multi-level salience framework.

A third argument is perhaps the most persuasive. It could be charged that the *relative* salience of state politics bears but little correspondence to its *absolute* salience. Illustratively, a politically passive person ranking state politics first might actually pay less attention to it than a political activist ranking it third or fourth. While the plentiful presence of such inconsistencies could be overlooked on the grounds that one is primarily interested in the workings of individual preference orders regardless of intensities, our concept of salience maps will acquire an extra dimension if it can be shown that this is not the common pattern. The 1966 election study did not ascertain absolute levels of interest in politics at multiple levels, but the 1968 election study did this as well as obtaining the rank orderings of interest.[5] A moderately satisfying result would take the form of little association between relative and absolute salience. This would at least allow for the play of relative salience across a spectrum of people having about the same absolute interest in state politics. A much more gratifying result, of course, would be a clear positive relationship between the two dimensions.

The cross-tabulation of the two measures (Table 2) is unequivocal in demonstrating a moderate correspondence between absolute and relative

[4] It should be recognized that we are not merely playing with numbers in order to make a case for the saliency of state politics. There is no logical necessity, given the nature of the questions used, that state affairs attract any second rankings. All respondents after making their first choice could have ranked state affairs third or even last had they been so inclined.

[5] In the 1968 study the respondents were, as in 1966, first put through a screening question which eliminated the apoliticals. They then replied to questions about their attention to the four levels of politics. For state politics the question read: "And how about affairs here in (STATE WHERE R LIVES); do you pay a great deal, some, or not much attention to state affairs?" Rank orders of relative interest were obtained after these questions.

TABLE 2 *Relative Versus Absolute Levels of Interest in State Politics*[a]

Rank of how closely state politics followed	Attention paid to state politics			Row totals	Marginal totals	N
	Great deal	Some	Not much			
First	58%	39%	04%	101%	15%	(166)
Second	44	50	06	100	38	(407)
Third	27	55	18	100	28	(307)
Fourth	22	56	22	100	19	(204)
Marginal Totals	37	51	12		100%	(1084)

[a] Data are drawn from the Survey Research Center's 1968 national election study.

salience, in terms of self-reports. We can say with some confidence that, on the average, those who attend relatively more often to state affairs also tend to pay more absolute attention. By the same token (if the table is percentaged vertically) it is clear that the attentive public in absolute terms comes disproportionately from the ranks of those for whom the state is relatively more salient. There is little reason to suspect that different results would have been obtained from the 1966 respondents, had they been asked the additional questions. One indirect piece of evidence, for example, is that the marginals for the rank-ordered interest in state politics are remarkably similar across the two samples.[6]

Given previous work with the local-cosmopolitan dimension, a positive association between rank orderings for state and local affairs would be hypothesized. Rank order interrelationships can be demonstrated in a fairly straightforward way without the added refinement of spatial or scaling techniques. The respondents' rankings of state politics were crossed against their rankings of each of the other three levels of politics. From these matrices were extracted the sum of respondents who allocated either a first

[6] Since we have both relative and absolute measures for the 1968 sample, it might be asked why we do not utilize that sample rather than the earlier one. The reasons are two-fold: (1) in order to capture a "purer" reflection of the salience of American state politics it seems desirable to base the analysis on data gathered during a period relatively uncontaminated by the forces of a national election, for much the same reasons that studies of state voting turnout, division of the vote, and party strength often separate the off-year from presidential year statistics; (2) a number of questions of direct relevance for state politics were asked in the 1966 study, but not in 1968. On the other hand, subsequent work in this general area might well utilize both absolute and relative measures of salience in order to arrange people in a multi-dimensional mode.

or second rank to each of the other three levels. These proportions are as follows:

First or second rank given to:	State affairs ranked First	Second	Third	Fourth
International	5	9	30	40
National	43	38	42	37
Local	52	52	28	23
	100%	99%	100%	100%

Without doubt, the higher the salience of state affairs the higher is that of local matters and, on the other hand, the lower is that of international affairs.

An easy transition between and intermixing of state and local politics creates a sizable cluster of people who are state and locally oriented. Another way of viewing these rankings is to think of people living in the same geographical area, but focusing their attention upon different political objects. There is a state public—overlapping in great part with the local—and a more cosmopolitan public. Both cosmopolitan and state-local political processes operate simultaneously within a given area; but the "separate" publics of each level probably filter out to varying degrees the information about processes less relevant for them.

Having set forth the concept of salience maps and the place of the states in such maps, we can now turn to two major sets of questions. First, we are interested in the attitudinal and behavioral corollaries or consequences of differential state salience. Other things being equal, the various psychological theories of balance, congruence, and consonance would suggest a probable linkage between high state salience and the favorable evaluation of objects associated with states, and a negative evaluation of objects foreign to the states. Similarly, high salience should be associated with greater behavioral activity in the domain of state politics.

Second, we are concerned with the determinants of distinctive state salience maps. These may be presumed to flow from two sources, one social and the other political. A variety of social experiences are ordinarily associated with narrower, more provincial perspectives. These lead us to predict that state salience will vary with the nature of these experiential historics. The strictly political factors to be considered are state-specific. Although theoretical underpinnings are less apparent here, we will take as a point of departure the progressive, "good government" model of politics. This model would suggest that the more the state political system conforms to the tenets of progressive democracy, the more interested will be the citizenry in the state as a political institution. That is, salience maps will vary with (good) systematic properties, *ceteris paribus*.

In the analysis to follow we have collapsed the four rankings of state politics into two by combining ranks one and two into "high," and three and four into "low."

III. Salience, Attitudes, and Behavior

While one can argue that determining the distribution of differential salience maps is important in and of itself, the subject will be more compelling if it can be shown that certain attitudes and behaviors accompany the different configurations. For instance, it can be demonstrated that there is a connection between salience levels and affective orientations. Those following state affairs could, in fact, be responding to negative impressions about the state's institutions and leaders. Given the need for consonance rather than dissonance in the human psyche, it seems more likely that there would be a "strain toward congruity." Attention and favorable dispositions do, indeed, occur together. One example is that those who pay more attention to state politics accord higher prestige to the occupation of governor than do those paying less attention ($\gamma = .32$).[7] That is, there is greater identification with a symbol (role) connected with the more salient level of government.

By drawing upon data from the 1968 election study it is possible to show more precisely the connection between salience and affect. Respondents rank ordered their faith and confidence in the three levels of the American federal system—national, state, and local.[8] Comparing salience and confidence levels reveals that as the salience of a state's politics rises so does the evaluation of that government's performance. Just as people tend to pay more attention to candidates they like, and vice versa, so too they seem to operate in a selective fashion with respect to political units such as the states. Again, there is no particular reason to suppose that this pattern would not hold for the 1966 sample with which we have been dealing.

Inferentially, the relatively more attentive public for state politics

[7] The question read: "Now we're interested in learning what kinds of work Americans respect mostly highly. Which of these occupations do you respect the most?" Three choices were made. The list included, in this order: "U.S. Senator, Bishop or other church official, general or admiral, famous doctor, justice of the U.S. Supreme Court, atomic scientist, professor at a large university, President of the U.S., well-known athlete, president of a large corporation like General Motors, governor of your state." Altogether governor was the fourth-most choice, being tabbed by 29% of the sample. The correlation in the text is based on first choices.

[8] The questions ran: "We also find that people differ in how much faith and confidence they have in various levels of government in this country. In your case, do you have more faith and confidence in the national government, the government of this state, or in the local government around here?" "Which level do you have the least faith and confidence in—the (——) or the (——)?"

would seem to provide sources of political support for the ongoing performance of state officials. While the overlap of attention and support is a pleasing state of affairs for state officials, it also raises the possibility of a tacit exchange between these officials and the supportive public. The convergence between support and favorable perception suggests that the values of the attentive public are echoed and legitimized by the state's elites. In any event, if people for whom state politics is highly salient have socio-political views differing from those of the less attentive public, and if there is meaningful interaction between and among elites and attentive publics, then it should follow that the state's political life would vary according to the mix of people more closely attuned to state affairs. It becomes relevant, then, to assess the political values of this attentive public.

We may begin by noticing that people who pay more attention to state politics are basically less trusting of the world about them. They are more likely than others to say that one can't be too careful when dealing with other people rather than affirming that most people can be trusted ($\gamma = .31$). They are also more inclined to think that their fellow man is primarily looking out for himself rather than trying to be helpful to others ($\gamma = .19$). By ranking state politics higher than national and international affairs an individual has given a hint that he may be suspicious of larger, more remote environments. His more distrustful orientation toward other people rests comfortably in this outlook.

Attitudes more manifestly political give some glimpse into the way state-oriented individuals view national government and its role in their own lives. Those inclined toward state affairs avow more often that what Washington does makes less of a difference in their personal lives ($\gamma = .30$). In one sense this is a confirmation of our earlier speculation that a system-level salience map reflects in part an issue salience map, since state-oriented citizens see less subjectively important outcomes at the highest level of the federal structure.

Given the subjectively lesser importance of Washington decisions, it would be anticipated that the special public of the states is concerned about the increasing erosion of state decision-making by the federal government. Such concern is present, though not as visible as might be expected. Those attuned to state matters more often say that the federal government is playing too powerful a role in society ($\gamma = .16$). By the same token they more often oppose Washington's taking a strong role in integrating the nation's schools ($\gamma = .21$). The lack of stronger relationships may proceed from the fact that such people may simply not feel threatened by an actor (Washington) which is of lesser importance to them in general.

It should be noted, incidentally, that the prominent political orientation of party identification bears almost no overall relationship to state salience: ($\gamma = .08$), using the S.R.C. seven-point party identification measure which runs from strong Democrat to strong Republican. This is so despite the fact that, nationally, the Republican party is often linked with a states' rights position. Actually the only region in which party identification has an observable connection with state salience is the South, where Democrats more often rank state affairs higher ($\gamma = .21$). For the other regions the relationship is nil.

Although virtually all the above relationships persist within each category of the control variables employed,[9] they are more marked among some strata. The prime example is not socio-economic or spatial; rather, it is by political strata. Non-voters in the 1966 general election (and to a lesser extent non-voters in the 1966 primary contests) exaggerate the original correlations. Thus the relationships are heightened for non-voters versus voters when salience is related to a disavowal of Washington's impact (.54 vs .15); belief that the federal government is too powerful (.30 vs .11); and being against federal intervention in school integration (.28 vs .17)[10]

Identification with the state is as much or more symbolic than active for the non-voters. Denying the relevance of a disliked national government, they interpose the state as a symbolic barrier between the national government and themselves. These and other variations denote a multiplicative effect, whereby salience maps are especially linked to views about the federal government among citizens with certain characteristics. Consequently, the practical, political effects of varying proportions of state-oriented residents in the state depend upon other traits of these residents.

Perhaps the most acute test of the impact of differential attention toward state politics comes in examining overt behaviors. If the concept of diverse salience maps is to have viability, some behavioral manifestations are in order. Should these be found, it would suggest that the fabric of a state's politics is further mediated by or informed by the distribution of interest orderings.

It may be stated at the outset that close followers of state politics are, in many respects, slightly less participative than are those less devoted to state politics. For example, they report following public affairs and politics often ($\gamma = -.20$), they vote less often in presidential elections ($\gamma = -.16$), they had less interest in the 1966 congressional campaign ($\gamma = -.13$), and knew a little less about the candidates ($\gamma = -.10$), and were just a shade less likely to vote in the congressional election ($\gamma = -.08$). These relationships seem at first glance to cast doubt on our earlier demonstration (with the 1968 sample) that relative interest in state politics was linked to absolute interest. However, the declining magnitude of these correlations as one moves from a general interest in politics on through to activities

[9] Controls include region, urbanization, education, subjective social class, interest in public affairs, voting regularity, and party identification.

[10] The results obtained when controlling for voting participation are not artifactual or differential turnout rates by region or urbanization.

reflecting participation in congressional races contain a hint that the closer the activity is to state and local matters the more likely will this pattern be erased or even possibly reversed.

Such proves to be the case. There is absolutely no difference in turnout for the gubernatorial election in those states where that office was at stake. Furthermore, those most interested in state politics more often reported voting in the 1966 primaries ($\gamma = .15$). Finally, an indirect indicator of a linkage between state-level salience and forms of participation is that the more attention paid to state matters the greater is the likelihood of voting a straight party ticket in the 1966 state and local elections ($\gamma = .17$).[11] The general drift of these admittedly modest correlations over a range of behavioral phenomena suggests that a higher focus on state affairs may depress participation within nationally oriented politics but enhance it at state and local levels. Thus the concept of attentive publics is given a behavioral as well as attitudinal dimension.

These overall relationships disguise some fascinating interplay between state level salience and other factors associated with political participation. It is well-known, for example, that education is positively related to both spectator and participatory levels of politicization. Since—as shall presently be demonstrated—education is inversely related to the attention paid state politics, it might be assumed that the generally negative relationships between state level salience and political participation are a function of education. If this were so, it would not account for the absence of a relationship with turnout in the gubernatorial election and the presence of a positive association with turnout in the primary balloting. Nevertheless, it is true that at least some portion of the meager relationships are a fuction of the confounding influence of educational attainment. What is much more intriguing, though, is that education and the attention directed toward state affairs interact with each other to produce strikingly divergent patterns of political behavior.

This process is best illustrated with three measures: interest in the 1966 congressional campaign, voting in the 1966 general election, and voting in the 1966 primary. It will be recalled that the bivariate correlations between interest in state politics and affirmative respones to these three items were either slighly negative (for the first two) or positive (for the latter). By noting the correlations at each of four educational levels it is possible to see the profound interaction effects between education and state interest. There is considerable deviation around the aggregate bivariate correlations. This is shown in Figure 1, which contains plottings by educational level for each of the three measures. Among the less educated, following state politics is marked by less interest and voting. As education rises these negative relationships either decline or move to the positive side. Finally, among the

[11] This holds true among Democrats and Independents, but not for Republicans.

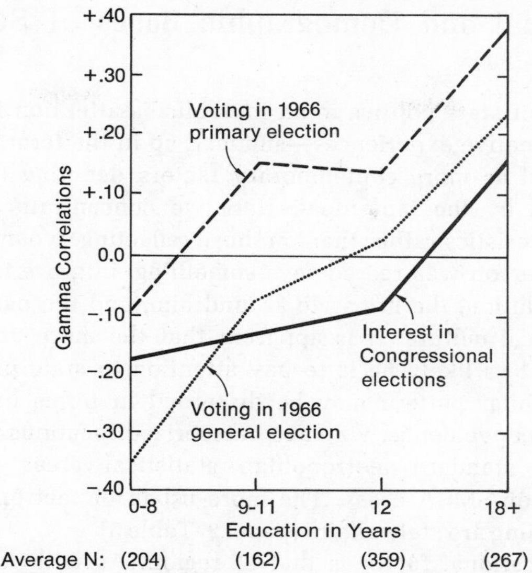

FIGURE 1 Relationship between salience of state politics and state-level participation, by education.

well-educated being attuned to state politics exerts a very positive effect. A similar pattern holds among the subsample located in states with a gubernatorial contest in 1966.

These changing relationships are not easily accounted for. One line of explanation is that the salience of state politics for the poorly educated and the well educated attentive publics rests upon different bases of psycho-political orientations. For the poorly educated, who have much less factual knowledge about state politics, the attachment is primarily affective, a buffer against a fearsome intruder. For the better educated, high interest in state politics takes a more instrumental form, whereby participation becomes more meaningful. If, indeed, the better educated transform their attention levels into more participation via an instrumental orientation, then it should follow that the participation levels in state (and local) elections would be higher for those paying more attention to state politics. As we observed, this is precisely the case.

It is more difficult to say why the attention level is inversely related to participation among the poorly educated. Perhaps their more affective orientation, when combined with a higher interest in state politics, results in a perspective that voting accomplishes relatively little. High affective symbolic orientations may reduce the need for participation. Inner gratification flows from withdrawal and non-participation.

IV. Individual and Demographic Bases of State-Level Salience

The place of state politics in an individual's attention frame will be a function of formative experiences—summed up in the term political socialization—as well as more contemporary factors denoting the type of life space occupied by the individual. Here we concentrate on the various "static" characteristics rather than on those reflecting dynamic elements.

Where a person was reared says something, in gross terms, about his family of orientation, the life style around him, and the nature of the surrounding political culture. It is apparent that the more urban a person's upbringing the less likely he is to pay attention to state politics (panel 1, Table 3). A similar pattern may be discerned in terms of contemporary residence. For convenience, we have categorized locations in terms of the twelve largest standard metropolitan statistical areas (SMSA), other SMSA's, and non-SMSA areas. The more urban or metropolitan the area the less compelling are state affairs (panel 2, Table 3).

A third locational factor is that of region. As with the other spatial variables, region is a summary construct. That is, it often captures (imperfectly to be sure) a set of historical experiences, socialization patterns, life styles, and political culture differences which are relevant to certain political phenomena. Two recent illustrations of "regionalism" are the findings that the adoption of policy innovations and the patterns of state expenditures have distinct, independent regional components. It can also be argued that, even if region as a term simply disguises the "real" underlying dimensions at work, this still does not alter the fact that the distribution of opinion and behavior within a region—hence the states in that region—is different, and that these differences may either reflect or produce different political processes. In the case at hand it turns out that the salience of state politics does vary among the regions, with Southerners being most attuned to state matters. Westerners next, and Midwesterners and Northeasterners least (panel 3, Table 3).[12] Similar proportions emerge by taking the individual's region of birth instead of current region.

A slight diversion is necessary here to comment on the possible historical and contemporary reasons for these regional divergencies. In one cluster are the Southern states, bound by the pains, memories, and dislocations of an historical trauma. To say that the states have a unique place in past and present Southern politics is to repeat a commonplace. At the other

[12] Regional groupings follow Census Bureau classifications: Northeast = New England and Middle Atlantic states; Midwest = East North Central and West North Central states; South = South Atlantic, East South Central, and West South Central states; and West = Mountain and Pacific states. Other regional combinations were employed, but with less rewarding outcomes.

TABLE 3 *Social and Demographic Correlates of State Politics Salience*

Proportion of people paying first or second most attention to state affairs, by:				gamma[a]
WHERE REARED				
Farm	Small town	Small city	Large city	
65% (323)[b]	50% (256)	42% (169)	40% (240)	−.30
CURRENT RESIDENCE				
Non-SMSA	Medium SMSA	Large SMSA		
62% (359)	51% (357)	38% (292)		−.31
CURRENT REGION				
South	West	Midwest	Northeast	
62% (288)	54% (167)	46% (310)	43% (243)	—[c]
EDUCATION				
0–8 grades	Some high school	High school graduate	Some college or more	
64% (208)	59% (164)	52% (362)	34% (269)	−.32
SUBJECTIVE SOCIAL CLASS				
Working	Middle			
59% (543)	41% (441)			−.34
LENGTH OF RESIDENCE IN STATE				
0–19 years	20 years or more, but less than entire life	Entire life		
42% (120)	47% (236)	54% (620)		.17

[a] These represent the correlation between the overall high-low salience dichotomy and the accompanying social and demographic characteristics.

[b] These are the N's upon which the percentages are based.

[c] Gamma computation inappropriate because region is a nominal variable.

extreme is the cluster of Northeastern and Midwestern states, those states generally considered most cosmopolitan in outlook, the major repositories of the great economic, cultural, social, and political institutions of the nation. Between these two clusters are those states which may be characterized as Western and hybrid in nature. Settled in large part by immigrants from other states, carved in part out of the former federal territories, ushered into statehood at a time when the trend was toward stronger state government, and physically remote from the centers of national power, these states have neither the high cosmopolitanism of the Northeastern-Midwestern tier, nor the scars and ethnocentrism of the South. It remains to be seen whether these regional patterns persist in the light of various controls which shall subsequently be applied.

To the locational factors may be added those characteristics reflecting a person's social status and life style. The higher a person's formal education and subjective social class the less interest he evinces in state politics (panels 4 and 5, Table 3). This pattern echoes the well-known propensity of the better off and better educated to be more concerned than lower status people with broader environments. In view of this it is not surprising that those from the working class and lower educational strata are more likely to form a portion of the attentive public for state politics.

While the demographic and social strata components supply a substantial amount of differentiation, there are also temporal factors at work. One of these is simply the individual's length of residence in his state. The commonsense hypothesis that the longer a person resides in a state the higher the salience of that state's politics for him is borne out by the data (panel 6, Table 3). At this aggregate level the differences are not marked, but are clearly in the hypothesized direction.

We now know that the amount of attention devoted to state affairs differs according to several social and spatial characteristics. Of additional importance is whether the observed patterns hold under a variety of control conditions and whether there are cumulative effects at work. The answer to the first query is unequivocal. With only one exception[13] the original bivariate associations are maintained when controls are exerted for each of several other variables. For example, the basic negative relationship between SMSA size and state level salience persists regardless of rearing site, region, education, social class, and length of state residence. With some confidence one can say that the social and locational factors cited above have an independent impact on the probable occurrence of divergent salience maps.

Although the staying power of the various characteristics constitutes an important aspect of the analysis, it is significant that there are also cumulative processes at work. Two examples will depict what is, for the most

[13] The deviant case is that of length of residence controlled by region. Interest in state affairs does not increase with length of residence in the West (−.05), a finding no doubt occasioned by the continued Westward migration of the populace. Correlations for the other three regions are South = .39; Northeast = .26; Midwest = .16.

part, a common form of behavior when two of the predisposing factors are combined and then related to state politics salience. One instance of this process comes by combining educational attainment and the site where the individual was reared. It was established previously that the higher one's education and the more urban the rearing site environment the less salient is state politics. Now if these two factors operate in an additive fashion when combined it should mean, for example, that the highly educated from urban areas would be especially prone to rank state affairs low. Without doubt this is the case. Only 28 percent of the college educated persons reared in a city placed state politics high. On the other hand, 74 per cent of the elementary educated respondents who were reared on farms gave high prominence to state affairs. Percentages between these two poles tended to reflect very faithfully the operation of additivity principles.

A second example of the cumulative processes at work merges education and region. In addition to knowing that education is negatively related to following state affairs and that pronounced regional variations exist, we also know that educational differences persist within each of the four regions (α: South = − .32; West = − .34; Midwest = − .34; Northeast = − .23). Under such conditions it should come as no surprise to find that by categorizing people in terms of both education and region the range of high interest in state affairs is elongated. Furthermore, the elongation conforms remarkably well to the predicted values, assuming additivity.

Figure 2 contains two lines, one showing the predicted order of values under an additivity model, and the other showing the actual values attached to those predicted for each region-education combination. While the lines do not follow the same precise path, the actual proportions adhere rather nicely to the predicted ones.[14] That is, given four overall regional means, the effects of education are roughly similar across each region. Conversely, given different educational strata means, the effects of region are approximately the same across each educational strata.

Because we are dealing with a national sample, none of the foregoing results would apply with certainty to particular states. Yet to the extent that the nationally-based findings provide state-specific clues it is clear that salience maps possess quite different configurations according to some well-defined individual and demographic properties. Short of dramatic events, the states thus seem destined to be populated by unequal propor-

[14] The monotonic ordering and predicted values for given combinations were constructed by taking the marginal values from the appropriate column and row intersected by the cell (combination), and adding these row and column effects to the grand mean. The intercorrelation problem was handled by utilizing Multiple Classification Analysis, a program which helps remove the intercorrelation effects. Nearly identical results were obtained by using James Coleman's partitioning formulas. See his *Introduction to Mathematical Sociology* (New York: The Free Press of Glencoe, 1964), Ch. 6.

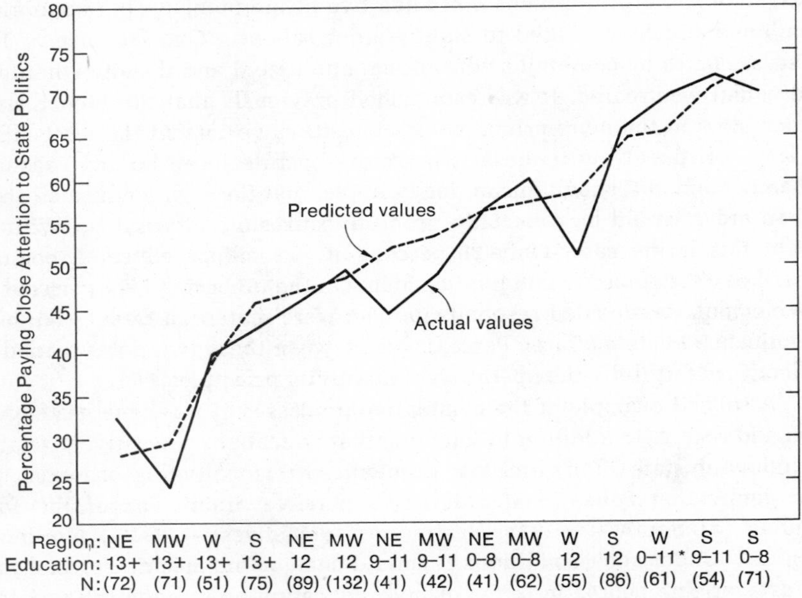

FIGURE 2 Predicted and actual values of high state level salience for region-education combinations.

tions of state-attentive publics.[15] How much and in what ways these inequalities affect the state's political life cannot be answered here, nor are they easily solved questions. Their solution, however, should enrich our comprehension not only of intra-state politics but also that of the linkages among the various levels of politics in the federal union.

V. Systemic Bases of State-Level Salience

Each state comprises a set of distinctive social and political phenomena. Assuming individual-system interaction, the question is whether the individual's salience map will vary with the particular kind of political system in which he finds himelf. To some extent, of course, the summary variable "region" freights a political element; but here we wish to treat specific political indicators. In particular we will introduce a number of systemic properties which should be positively linked to state-level sali-

[15] The sheer rates of interstate mobility impose a strong restraint on change. Contrary to popular impressions Americans do not change state of residence with great frequency. For the present sample 63% had lived their entire lives in one state and another 24% had spent at least 20 years there.

ence according to the good government, healthy competition, active citizenry view of politics.

One of the more significant and obvious aspects of a state's political life is the level of malapportionment in the state legislature. It might be thought that the better the apportionment, the more interested would people be in state politics: such is the "good government" view of the political world. That it is a false view is demonstrated by the negative relationship (− .27) between following state affairs and the fairness of apportionment—using the 1960 David-Eisenberg Index.[16] This association shows a remarkable persistence under a variety of control conditions. Region is an especially critical control to impose here since the South, which is relatively malapportioned, is also the area containing the largest number of state-oriented respondents. Nevertheless, with Southerners removed from the sample, the negative association persists (− .21); and in no region does a positive trend emerge.

Much the same conclusion can be reached about the degree of inter-party competition. Let contests for the governorship and Hofferbert's omnibus inter-party competition index serve as indicators of state-level competition.[17] While it might be expected that the more spirited the competition between the parties the more salient would be the politics of the state, the opposite is true. Regardless of which measure is used the relationships are negative, even though not strong (− .24 and − .22 for the governorship and Hofferbert's index, respectively). Again the pattern tends to persist under a variety of control conditions, including region.

Another common variable used to characterize the state's political culture is that of election turnout. In general it is argued that the higher the turnout the more vigorous the level of politics. Turnout for gubernatorial

[16] From Paul T. David and Ralph Eisenberg, *Devaluation of the Urban and Suburban Vote,* Vol. I (Charlottesville, Virginia: Bureau of Public Administration, University of Virgina, 1961). Although widespread reapportionment has occurred since the *Baker v. Carr* decision of 1962, most occurred after 1964. Indeed the latest reapportionment of *both* legislative houses occurred as late as 1965–66 for thirty states and 1967–69 for eight states. Given the time lag between legal changes of this sort and their imprint on the mass public, it seems advisable to use the 1960 malapportionment figures for our 1966 sample. To utilize this measure and the ones to follow the respondents have been allocated into roughly equal quartiles or quintiles according to the scores of the state in which they resided. It can be shown that the distribution of the sample across *groups* of states with varying score ranges approaches the distribution for the universe.

[17] The gubernatorial measure is based on contests from 1946–62, and is taken from Dennis Riley and Jack Walker, "Problems of Measurement and Inference in the Study of the American States," (unpublished paper, University of Michigan, 1968). Hofferbert's index is reported in Richard I. Hofferbert, "Classification of American State Party Systems," *Journal of Politics,* 26 (August, 1964), esp. pp. 562–563. More recent single elections were also used in our analysis; these produced results similar to those for the above two measures.

and U.S. senatorial contests will be used as a safe guide to the state-specific forces activating differential turnout. The common-sense hypothesis is that the higher the voting participation the higher the salience of state politics for the state's inhabitants. Such is not the case, however. There is, in fact, a small tendency (−.12) for salience levels to decline as turnout rises. Whatever forces are acting to develop a high following for state matters, they are not very well described by the differential participation of the electorate.

It has become apparent that for many people the affairs of government are wrapped up in what a few of the very visible political office-holders do. Accordingly, it might be advanced that the stronger the office the more salient would be the institutions, activities, and processes surrounding that office. While it is obviously true that a personable, aggressive governor can capture a substantial amount of attention regardless of the statutory limitations in his power, it seems reasonable to suppose that the same sort of governor with an arsenal of legal powers could do even more to make himself and the state government topics of conversation. As it turns out people living in states with powerful governors are no more likely to follow state affairs than are people living in a state with weak chief executives. What correspondence exists is actually on the negative rather than the positive side (−.12).

As noted earlier, many of the recent investigations about state politics have treated the determinants of public policy outputs. Because the great share of operational measures so far developed for assessing state policy outcomes are based on expenditure items, we are restricted in examining the connection between salience and state performance. The "good government" advocate would argue that the more active the state government, the more salient it would be for its residents. There is but meager support for that proposition. Trivial, positive relationships (ranging from .02 to .14) exist between high salience and the number of state government employees per one thousand population, state expenditures per $1,000 income, and state expenditures per capita. Slight negative associations are found between salience and state aid to cities and recent (1950–1960) changes in general state expenditures. These are all single indicators. Employing a ranking of the states based on Crittenden's "Scope of Government" factor[18] —which has very high loadings on tax level per capita, tax level per income unit, spending level per capita, and governmental employment—again produces an extremely modest positive correlation (.08). Regional controls reveal the association to be slightly higher in the Midwest and West.

Walker, among others, has argued that it is essential that non-expenditure policies be included in any attempt to explicate the articulation be-

[18] John Crittenden, "Dimensions of Modernization in the American States," *American Political Science Review* **61**:989–1001 (December 1967).

tween state performance and socio-economic and political characteristics. In response to his own admonition he developed a set of policy innovation scores for the several states, stretching from the late nineteenth century to mid-twentieth century. The "good government" position is that the innovative states would command more interest from their residents than would the laggardly ones. This is hardly the case, however, for the association is but slightly above zero. Unfortunately, few other reliable indicators of state performance are at hand. If we are to judge by the innovative pattern, non-expenditure performance measures are no more likely to affect salience maps of state residents than are those based on expenditures.

Most of the associations involving the foregoing political characteristics exhibit an exaggerated mode among non-voters. For better or worse, the less participative citizens react to the political culture in a more severe fashion than the more participative. That is, if a system manifestation such as malapportionment accompanies greater interest in state affairs, it is especially prone to do so among the less participative. One can picture them as less autonomous and self-assured than their more participative fellows. Environmental forces thus come to have more impact on them. There would seem to be a certain perversity about this, but apparently the less active citizens are, in effect, bolstered by these aberrations from what the reformers and democratic theorists see as progressive democracy.

Concluding Remarks

The concept of salience maps has been used to explore the relationship of the citizenry to their state governments as a particular set of institutions in the American political system. People do organize their cognitive views of the political world such that some system levels assume more prominence than others. There are indications that cognitive and affective dimensions of state salience are inter-locked. Attidudinal and behavioral corollaries of differentiated salience maps depend in part upon one's social and political status. One of the most emphatic though somewhat puzzling findings is the degree to which these corollaries are exaggerated among less participative citizens. Correspondingly, the salience of state politics among these less active people varies more according to environmental forces than is true for the more active.

Broadly speaking, the forces which contribute to following state politics can be grouped into two categories. On the one hand, there are those factors which are essentially "given" or uncontrollable. On the other hand, there are other factors which are more subject to elite manipulation and political change. Place of residence, education, social class, and the like are —to a greater or lesser extent—set for the individual. To a similar extent, the states have limited control over these aspects of a person's life.

Asserting that these factors are given is not to adopt a crudely deterministic stance. Rather, it is to hold them in contrast to another set of variables that are substantially more malleable. State outputs, such as program expenditures or policy innovations, are more amenable to the short-run persuasive efforts of elites and the occasional demands of masses. These are the areas of a state's political life that attract a good deal of attention from political scientists and specialized publics, but have precious little positive impact upon the salience maps of individuals. The contours of such maps are determined largely by the individual's life experiences and the characteristics of his immediate life space.

We have suggested (though not demonstrated) that a state's policies are determined by the attitudes and behaviors of its attentive public. However, the obverse of this proposition is not necessarily correct: the attitudes and behaviors of the attentive state public reflect dimly, at best, the quality of a state's public policy. Arguments that a vigorous, strong, and innovative state government produces an interested public are open to question. So, too, are the emphases placed on such touchstones of liberal democracy as interparty competition, equal representation, and enthusiastic electoral participation.

Whatever the correlates of state-level salience, it is apparent that the states still loom large in the perspectives of the American public. Any attempted juggling of political units involving the states would probably confront a reservoir of mass attachments to the states as political entities. Coupled with the historic traditions, legal preserves, and political utility of the states, this salience helps assure the continued prominence of the several states within the federal system.

Brian R. Fry and Richard F. Winters

The Politics of Redistribution

Public policy research has tried to find those variables that have the greatest influence on policy outcomes. Until this research, it appeared that political variables mattered little, most policy outcomes seeming to be factors of socioeconomic forces. This study also speaks importantly to certain aspects of state finance. It is in both ways a pioneering study.

A comparatively new line of research in political science involves the systematic investigation of political, social, and economic factors important in the formation of public policy. So far, such research has yielded temptingly persuasive evidence that political variables exert little or no independent influence on policy outcomes; that policy outcomes are governed overwhelmingly by socio-economic factors. Stated more succinctly, these findings have raised the question: Does politics make a difference in the policy formation process?

We suggest in the following analysis that these prior findings have been the result of the examination of a measure of public policy in which the influence of the political system is likely to be negligible, that is *levels* of public revenues and expenditures. To examine this proposition empirically, our study shifts attention to the allocation of the burdens and benefits of

Some of the data used in this analysis were taken from information made available by Thomas R. Dye. Computation time was provided by Stanford Computation Center, Stanford University. Machine and secretarial assistance were provided by the Hoover Institution on War, Revolution and Peace, Stanford University, as well as by the Institute of Political Studies, Stanford University. Our thanks also go to Raymond E. Wolfinger, Heinz Eulau, Hubert Marshall, and William Paisley for their encouragement and criticism.

Reprinted from *American Political Science Review,* **64**:508–22 (June 1970) by permission of the authors and the publisher. Some descriptive and bibliographical footnotes have been omitted for considerations of space and textual format.

state revenue and expenditure policies across income classes. In redirecting analysis to allocations rather than levels of state revenues and expenditures, we focus on a province we believe to be more predictably political.

We have taken as our dependent variable the net redistributive impact of revenues and expenditures as represented by the ratio of expenditures as represented by the ratio of expenditure benefits to revenue burdens for the three lowest income classes in each state. The major hypothesis of our study is that, in regard to the allocation of the burdens and benefits of state government revenues and expenditures, political variables will have a stronger influence on policy outcomes than will socio-economic variables.

I. Literature Review

The literature of the systematic analysis of public policy was launched with the publication in 1952 of Solomon Fabricant's *The Trend of Government Activity in the United States since 1900.*[1] As part of his analysis, Fabricant used a multiple regression statistical model to examine interstate variations in levels of per capita state and local expenditure in the United States in 1942. He found that more than 70% of the variance in these levels could be explained by the impact of differences in per capita income, urbanization, and population density. Both Fabricant's focus and his method have inspired subsequent research.

For example, a number of studies published in the *National Tax Journal*[2] have elaborated on Fabricant's initial findings within the basic framework of the multiple regression approach and with continued reliance on socio-economic independent variables. These efforts were directed mainly at extending Fabricant's analysis over time and breaking down the dependent variable to determine the edifferential impact of his three independent variables on various components of expenditures. What the studies indicated was, briefly, that the explanatory power of the independent variables has decreased since 1942, accounting for little more than half the variance in levels of state expenditures in 1957, and for only 18% of the *changes* in levels of state expenditures between 1957 and 1960. Further, these studies demonstrated that the effect of this set of independent variables varies with different facets of expenditures, having its least influence on welfare expenditures in the states. Probably the most impressive overall findings of these studies, however, is the consistently high explanatory

[1] Solomon Fabricant, *The Trend of Government Activity in the United States Since 1900* (New York: National Bureau of Economic Research, 1952), ch. 6.

[2] Glenn W. Fisher, "Determinants of State and Local Government Expenditures: A Preliminary Analysis," *National Tax Journal,* XIV (December 1961), 349–355; Roy W. Bahl and Robert J. Saunders, "Determinants of Changes in State and Local Government Expenditures," *National Tax Journal,* XVIII (March 1965), 50–57.

power of the socio-economic variables employed relative to absolute lveels of expenditures.

In 1963, Dawson and Robinson, through the explicit introduction of political variables, initiated an exploration of the political dimension of public policy outcomes.[3] Drawing their inspiration from a V. O. Key hypothesis,[4] they examined the relationship between interparty competition and welfare policies as evidenced by an amalgam of state tax and expenditure measures which they labeled "welfare orientation." They found that interparty competition is indeed fairly closely related to welfare orientation in the states, but this relationship disappears when controls for per capita income are introduced.

Subsequent research into the impact of political variables has tended to confirm Dawson's and Robinson's initial findings. For instance, Hofferbert followed Dawson's and Robinson's lead, but refined the definition of welfare orientation and added divided party control, malapportionment, and regional controls (South vs. non-South) to interparty competition as independent variables.[5] He reported low zero-order correlations[6] for divided party control and malapportionment, and no independent impact for any of the political variables considered.

Thomas Dye reported a veritable catalog of results in his book *Politics, Economics, and the Public: Policy Outcomes in the American States.*[7] He employed the multiple regression model to analyze the relationship between certain socio-economic variables (urbanization, industrialization, income, and education) and political variables (division of party control, interparty

[3] Richard E. Dawson and James A. Robinson, "Inter-Party Competition, Economic Variables and Welfare Policies in the American States," *The Journal of Politics,* XXV (1963), 265–289.

[4] V. O. Key, *Southern Politics* (New York: Random House, 1949), pp. 298–311.

[5] Richard I. Hofferbert, "The Relation Between Public Policy and Some Structural and Environmental Variables in the American States," *American Political Science Review,* LX (March 1966), 73–82.

[6] Four statistical terms used in this paper might be unfamiliar to some of the readers. A *zero-order correlation coefficient* is the simple, bivariate correlation coefficient. It is a summary measure of association. A *partial correlation coefficient* is a measure of association or the strength of a relationship between two variables—e.g., urbanization and redistribution—controlled for a third or more variables. Thus, it is a measure of the unique portion of the association after the common portion has been controlled. The *multiple-partial coefficient* is a summary measure of the "explanatory" power of a group of variables. It states the unique portion of the variance attributed to one set of variables—e.g., political variables—after another variable or set of variables—e.g., economic variables—has been controlled. The *coefficient of determination* associated with any of the three above measures is the square of the coefficient of correlation (simple or multiple) which is equal to the portion of variance explained by the measures.

[7] Thomas R. Dye, *Politics, Economic, and the Public: Policy Outcomes in the States* (Chicago: Rand McNally, 1966).

competition, voter participation, and malapportionment) on the one hand, and a wide variety of expenditure and tax measures on the other. Dye's findings were generally consistent with those of his predecessors: for forty-seven of fifty-four tax and expenditure measures, socio-economic variables had more influence on policy outcomes than did political variables. As Dye states:

> . . . correlation analysis reveals that these [political] system characteristics have relatively little *independent* effect on policy outcomes in the states. Economic development shapes both the political systems and political outcomes, and most of the association that occurs between system characteristics and policy outcomes can be attributed to the influence of economic development. Differences in the policy choices of states with different types of political systems turn out to be largely a product of different socio-economic levels rather than a direct product of political variables.[8]

But a few more positive results have appeared in the literature. Lineberry and Fowler shifted the level of analysis to American cities to determine the impact of reformism (reformed cities are defined as those having city manager government with nonpartisan and at-large elections) on tax and expenditure policy.[9] The authors ran separate multiple regression analyses in reformed and unreformed cities and found that socio-economic variables accounted for less of the variance in tax and expenditure levels in reformed cities. They saw the difference as an effect of reformism. Unfortunately, however, their methodology did not permit an assessment of the relative impact of political and socio-economic variables on policy outcomes. Grumm developed a new independent variable, an index of legislative professionalism, which he found to have an independent relationship with public welfare expenditures.[10] Sharkansky and Hofferbert factor analyzed a number of variables and discovered that the "political" factor positively correlated with welfare-education policies after controlling for their socio-economic factor.[11]

Two authors have followed a different approach, alterations in the dependent variable, in arriving at their more positive results concerning polit-

[8] Ibid., p. 293.

[9] Robert L. Lineberry and Edmund P. Fowler, "Reformism and Public Policies in American Cities," *American Political Science Review*, LXI (September 1967), 701–716.

[10] John G. Grumm, "Structural Determinants of Legislative Output"; paper delivered at Conference on the Measurement of Public Policies in the American States, Ann Arbor, July 28–August 3, 1968.

[11] Ira Sharkansky and Richard I. Hofferbert, "Dimensions of State Politics, Economies, and Public Policy," *American Political Science Review*, LXIII (September 1969), 867–879.

ical variables. Sharkansky proposed that a distinction be drawn between public policy (expenditures and other indicators of official concern) and policy outputs (the results of those policies).[12] He examined the relative impact of environmental variables and policy variables on high school attendance and completion (output measures). Sharkansky found policy measures more closely related than environmental variables to levels of attendance and rate of graduation, though that relationship was reversed in regard to dropouts. Walker, on the other hand, devised a non-monetary measure of public policy: his innovation index measures the extent and rapidity of adoption of eighty-eight policies among the states.[13] Walker found that, although each of a number of political variables (party competition, party turnover, legislative apportionment, and legislative professionalism) correlated fairly closely with innovation, the relationship disappeared when socio-economic controls were introduced for all but the malapportionment-innovation correlation (a finding of no mean significance in itself).

This brief literature review highlights a number of findings relevant to the present analysis. First, socio-economic variables have relatively high explanatory value in terms of policy as it is measured by levels of taxes and expenditures in the states. Second, where political variables have been examined in relation to tax and expenditure levels their effect has usually been overshadowed by that of socio-economic variables, and often have shown no independent impact whatsoever. Third, the relationship between socio-economic variables and fiscal policies varies according to the specific components of these policies, and the relationship is particularly weak in reference to welfare policies.

The first two findings suggest that the political analyst may have to look beyond levels of taxes and expenditures to find politics having an independent or dominant influence on policy outcomes in the states. The third finding indicates that, as Key originally hypothesized, a fruitful area of search for such influence may be the redistributive policies of state governments.

Accordingly, as stated earlier, this analysis takes as its dependent variable the net redistributive impact of state revenues and expenditures. The political relevance of this variable has been suggested by Jacob and Lipsky in a review of research on public policies:

> The distribution of benefits or sanctions is perhaps the most significant output dimension for political scientists, since much of the conflict preceding adoption of a program

[12] Ira Sharkansky, "Problems of Theory and Method: Environment, Policy, Output, and Impact"; paper delivered at Conference on the Measurement of Public Policies in the American States, Ann Arbor, July 28–August 3, 1968.

[13] Jack L. Walker, "The Diffusion of Innovations among the American States," *American Political Science Review,* LXIII (September 1969), 880–899.

> is not about whether it should be embarked upon but who will pay and who will benefit. Even programs that apparently benefit most of the population—such as education and highway construction—have a variable incidence of benefits.[14]

Implicit in this statement and in our analysis is a conception of politics as a bargaining process in which trade-offs are made at the margins in deciding among alternative policies. The product of this process is embodied in the final configuration of penalties and rewards, which we are measuring in terms of the net redistributive impact of state revenues and expenditures. In sum, though one would expect that environmental conditions would largely determine at what *level* revenues and expenditures will be set, politics is likely to be pivotal in establishing the *allocations* of rewards and benefits at that level.[15]

Our purposes in this study are twofold: (1) to develop a statistical model that has a fairly high degree of explanatory power in regard to the redistributive policies of American states, and (2) to examine the relative importance of political and socio-economic variables within that model. We shall use multiple regression analysis as an instrument for accomplishing those purposes.

II. Dependent Variable

The obvious first requirement of this analysis is to devise a satisfactory measure of the net redistributive impact of revenues and expenditures. We use as a basis for this derivation the Tax Foundation study, *Tax Burdens and Benefits of Government Expenditure by Income Class, 1961 and 1965.*[16] This study, as the title implies, distributes revenue burdens and expenditure benefits across income classes. To do this, Foundation researchers selected a number of allocation bases which appeared to describe the incidence of revenue burdens and expenditure benefits by income class and applied these bases to revenue and expenditure totals. For instance, elementary and secondary education expenditure benefits were assumed to be distributed according to the number of children under 18 in families in each income

[14] Herbert Jacob and Michael Lipsky, "Outputs, Structure and Power: An Assessment of Changes in the Study of State and Local Politics," *Journal of Politics,* XXX (May 1968), 510–538.

[15] Dawson and Robinson attempted to get at the concept of redistribution in the article already cited, but their perspectives were restricted by the measure of welfare orientation they chose and a concntration on levels of taxes and expenditures. See Dawson and Robinson, op. cit. We proposed a considerably more comprehensive measure addressed specifically to allocations of benefits and burdens.

[16] Tax Foundations, Inc., *Tax Burdens and Benefits of Government Expenditure by Income Classes, 1961 and 1965* (New York: Tax Foundation, Inc., 1967).

class, so that if 20% of children under 18 were in families with an income of $4,000 to $4,999, 20% of expenditures on elementary and secondary education were assigned as benefits to that income class. Similarly on the revenue side, if 20% of total expenditures on alcoholic beverages were made by families with an income of $6,000 to $7,499, it is assumed that 20% of the alcoholic beverage tax was paid by families in that income class. This process, with an appropriate allocation base for each revenue and expenditure category, was repeated for all federal government revenues and expenditures and for aggregate category totals of state and local government revenues and expenditures. Expenditure totals by level of government were taken from Department of Commerce, Office of Business Economics reports, and the allocation bases from Department of Labor data.

For our study we have calculated by revenue and expenditure category the percentage distributions of state revenue burdens and expenditure benefits from the Tax Foundation study. However, since Office of Business Economics expenditure and revenue figures, which are the basis for the Tax Foundation study, are not available on a state-by-state basis, we have used Census Bureau expenditure and revenue state totals as the base to which allocation factors are applied.[17]

Our analysis is restricted to revenues and expenditures for state governments only, rather than a combination of state and local totals, for several reasons. First, it would appear that the state-local combination is more a statistical construct than a coherent governmental jurisdiction. As Sharkansky put it:

> . . . the fusion of state and local government activities confuses the efforts of politically-distinct units. The state-plus-local aggregate is artificial, and not the arena in which policy-makers decide about the size of their budgets or the allocation of funds.[18]

Second, the state level has traditionally been a level at which redistribution has been sought both in an attempt to overcome regional differences in tax bases and expenditure policies and in the name of equity. Third, previous research has indicated that state and local levels are analytically distinct,

[17] This shift raises a procedural problem, since the Census Bureau and the Office of Business Economics define revenue and expenditure categories somewhat differently. To counter this difficulty, we have either grouped the Census Bureau figures into categories at least nominally equivalent to those set up by the Office of Business Economics or we have used allocation bases which appear to be appropriate to the Census Bureau categories. A number of technical differences prevent a direct comparison between the categories to derived and the Office of Business Economics data, but comparability is not a major consideration, since it is only necessary to assume that the allocation bases are appropriate for the revised categorization of the Census Bureau figures.

[18] Sharkansky, op. cit., p. 4.

responding in different ways to different influences.[19] Fourth, and in a more practical vein, there is a potential ecological problem in analyzing statewide political, social, and economic indicators in relation to local output measures. Were local outputs to be included in the analysis, the prudent but difficult course to follow would be to collect data on the independent variables at the local level. The theoretical case for the state-local separation is not clear-cut, but we feel that the above considerations are sufficiently persuasive to justify that separation in this analysis.

A number of additional factors should be noted in our development of the dependent variable. First, we have included intergovernmental revenues and expenditures in state revenue and expenditure totals. This inclusion was made on the assumption that political and socio-economic conditions within a given state are related to both the level and nature of intergovernmental revenues and expenditures in that state. We have distributed intergovernmental expenditure benefits across income classes according to the distribution of each category of intergovernmental expenditures. We have distributed intergovernmental revenues in proportion to the distribution of the burden of all federal revenues. Second, we have treated unemployment compensation as a state program.[20] Finally, though the Tax Foundation analyzed revenues and expenditures for 1965, we have used their revised data for 1961 because both their allocation bases and the information used in our independent variables are based on figures for the earlier period. Expenditure and revenue totals, and the allocation bases for each revenue and expenditure category, are shown in Tables 1 and 2. Tables 3 and 4 display the percentage distribution of revenue burdens and expenditure benefits by income class for each type of revenue and expenditure.

Given the revenue and expenditure totals and the allocation factors, the remaining steps in the calculation of the dependent variable are relatively simple:

1. Apply the allocation factors to the amounts collected and the amounts spent in each revenue and expenditure category in each state. This computation yields the amounts paid in revenue and received in benefits by income class for each category of revenues and expenditures in each state.
2. Sum the benefits received and revenues paid for each income class. The sums are the total revenue burden and expenditure benefit for each income class in each state.

[19] Ibid.

[20] This classification is somewhat ambiguous since the federal government levies a tax on employers but allows a credit for state taxes up to 90% of the amount of the federal tax. Since most states have adopted a tax to take advantage of the credit, and in accordance with the Tax Foundation classification, we have considered unemployment compensation to be a state program.

TABLE 1 *State Government Expenditures (1961)*

Category	Amount (millions)	Basis for allocation
DIRECT EXPENDITURES	$24,578	
Education	3,792	
Elementary & Secondary	226	Number of Children under 18
Higher and Other	3,566	Higher Education Expenditures of Families
Highways	6,230	Half Auto Operation Expenditure and Half Total Current Consumption
Public Welfare	2,311	Income from Public Social Assistance and Private Relief
Agriculture[1]	435	Farm Money Income Before Taxes
Liquor Store	873	Alcoholic Beverage Expenditures
Insurance Trust[2]	4,701	Public Unemployment & Soc. Security Benefits
Interest[3]	584	Interest Income
Other—General	5,652	Half Family Money Income Before Taxes & Half Number of Families and Unrelated Individuals
INTERGOVERNMENTAL	10,114	
Education	5,963	Combined Allocation for all Education Expenditures
Highways	1,266	Same as Direct Highway Expenditures
Welfare	1,602	Same as Direct Welfare Expenditures
General	1,283	Same as Direct General Expenditures
TOTAL EXPENDITURES	$34,693	

Sources: U.S. Dept. of Commerce, Bureau of the Census, *State Government Finances in 1961.* Washington, D.C., U.S. Government Printing Office; and Tax Foundation, Inc., *Tax Burdens and Benefits of Governmental Expenditures By Income Class, 1961 and 1965.* New York, Tax Foundation, Inc., 1967, pp. 11 and 12.

1 Prorated share of nonseparable intergovernmental expenditures deducted.

2 Unemployment compensation classified as a state program.

3 Interest paid.

3. Calculate the ratio of expenditure benefits received to revenues paid for each income class in each state.

The summary measure of the net redistributive impact of revenues and expenditures in each state is simply the ratio derived in step 3 for the lowest three income classes in each state. This gives us a directional measure of

TABLE 2 *State Government Revenues (1961)*

Category	Amount (millions)	Basis for allocation
TAXES	$20,175	
Sales and Gross Receipts	14,328	
Alcoholic Beverage[1]	1,893	Alcoholic Beverage Expenditures
Tobacco	1,001	Tobacco Expenditures
Motor Vehicle[2]	4,948	Automobile Operation Expenditures
All Other[3]	6,486	Total Current Consumption
Individual Income	2,355	Personal Taxes
Corporation[4]	1,712	Half Total Current Consumption and Half Dividend Income
Property Tax	613	Half Housing Expenditures and Half Total Current Consumption
Death and Gift	501	Completely to the $15,000 and Over Income Class
All Other	648	Total Current Consumption
Severance	451	
Other	197	
SOCIAL INSURANCE CONTRIBUTIONS[5]	4,067	Combination of Social Security, Railroad, and Government Retirement Contributions and Total Current Consumption
CHARGES AND MISCELLANEOUS	2,854	Total Current Consumption
INTERGOVERNMENTAL[6]	6,412	Distribution of All Federal Taxes
TOTAL REVENUE	$33,508	

Sources: Same as Table 1.

1 Includes alcoholic beverage tax, alcoholic beverage license fee, and liquor store revenues.

2 Includes motor fuel tax and motor vehicle license fee.

3 Includes general sales and gross receipts tax, other license fees, and other sales and gross receipts taxes.

4 Includes corporation net income tax and corporation license fees.

5 Excludes earnings on investments.

6 From federal government only.

TABLE 3 *Distribution of Expenditure Benefits by Income Class (1961)*

Expenditure category	Under $2,000	$2,000 –2,999	$3,000 –3,999	$4,000 –4,999	$5,000 –5,999	$6,000 –7,999	$7,500 –9,999	$10,000 –14,999	$15,000 & over	Total[1]
DIRECT										
Elem. and Sec. Education	5.0%	8.0%	10.1%	14.3%	15.6%	19.9%	17.1%	8.1%	1.9%	100.0%
Higher and Other Education	1.4	2.1	3.4	6.6	10.0	15.7	20.6	25.3	14.7	99.8
Highways	3.2	5.1	8.2	11.4	13.7	19.4	20.5	13.5	4.9	99.9
Public Welfare	49.7	24.8	8.1	5.3	5.1	2.8	1.8	2.2	—	99.8
Agriculture	5.5	8.6	11.6	11.1	12.6	14.5	15.1	11.5	9.4	99.9
Liquor Store	2.4	3.7	8.0	9.8	11.6	18.8	22.3	17.0	6.3	99.9
Insurance Trust	21.4	20.0	17.2	9.7	9.2	9.3	7.8	4.7	0.6	99.9
Interest	4.8	9.9	10.1	8.9	8.2	11.5	16.4	14.9	15.1	99.8
Other—General	8.6	7.8	9.1	11.2	12.4	16.3	17.4	11.3	5.5	99.9
INTERGOVERNMENTAL										
Education	4.5	7.1	9.1	13.1	14.7	19.3	17.6	10.7	3.9	100.0
Highways	3.3	5.1	8.2	11.4	13.8	19.4	20.5	13.4	4.9	100.0
Public Welfare	49.8	24.8	8.1	5.3	5.1	2.8	1.7	2.2	—	99.8
Other—General	8.6	7.8	9.1	11.2	12.4	16.6	17.4	11.3	5.5	99.9

Source: Tax Foundation, Inc., *Tax Burdens and Benefits of Government Expenditures by Income Class, 1961 and 1965.* New York, Tax Foundation, Inc., 1967, pp. 48–51.

[1] Rows may not total 100.0% due to rounding.

TABLE 4 *Distribution of Revenue Burden by Income Class (1961)*

Revenue category	Under $2,000	$2,000 –2,999	$3,000 –3,999	$4,000 –4,999	$5,000 –5,999	$6,000 –7,499	$7,500 –9,999	$10,000 –14,999	$15,000 & over	Total[1]
Alcoholic Beverage	2.4%	3.7%	8.0%	9.9%	11.6%	18.9%	22.3%	17.0%	6.3%	100.1%
Tobacco	4.9	7.5	9.8	12.6	14.2	19.3	19.0	9.5	3.3	100.1
Motor Vehicle	1.9	4.4	8.2	12.0	14.5	20.6	21.0	13.4	4.1	100.1
All Other Sales & Gross Receipts Taxes	4.6	5.8	8.1	10.9	13.0	18.2	20.1	13.5	5.6	99.8
Individual Income	0.6	1.7	3.6	7.6	10.1	17.1	22.6	18.8	17.8	99.9
Corporation	2.7	4.2	7.7	7.5	10.2	13.2	15.5	17.7	21.3	100.0
Property	5.2	6.1	8.2	10.8	13.1	18.1	19.7	13.1	5.7	100.0
Death and Gift	—	—	—	—	—	—	—	—	100.0	100.0
All Other Taxes	4.7	5.9	8.2	10.9	13.0	18.2	20.0	13.5	5.6	100.0
Social Insurance Contribs.	3.7	5.2	7.7	11.1	13.5	19.0	20.8	14.0	5.1	100.1
Charges and Miscellaneous	4.6	5.9	8.1	10.9	13.0	18.2	20.1	13.5	5.6	99.9
Intergovernmental	1.8	3.2	5.7	8.6	11.1	16.6	20.1	16.8	16.1	100.0

Source: Same as Table 3.

1 Rows may not total 100.0% due to rounding.

TABLE 5 *Redistributive Ratios for 48 States*[1]

	Ratio[2]		Ratio[2]		Ratio[2]
1. Massachusetts	3.320	17. Arkansas	2.212	33. Maryland	1.923
2. Missouri	2.712	18. Idaho	2.205	34. Michigan	1.920
3. New York	2.644	19. Vermont	2.199	35. North Carolina	1.900
4. Oklahoma	2.567	20. Delaware	2.190	36. Florida	1.850
5. Connecticut	2.486	21. New Jersey	2.135	37. North Dakota	1.845
6. Rhode Island	2.482	22. Georgia	2.127	38. New Hampshire	1.830
7. Colorado	2.464	23. Pennsylvania	2.107	39. Nevada	1.826
8. Oregon	2.446	24. Minnesota	2.098	40. Nebraska	1.813
9. Kentucky	2.428	25. Washington	2.093	41. Texas	1.800
10. Illinois	2.376	26. Maine	2.060	42. Indiana	1.793
11. Wisconsin	2.340	27. Tennessee	2.031	43. South Carolina	1.775
12. California	2.322	28. West Virginia	2.011	44. New Mexico	1.720
13. Mississippi	2.274	29. Iowa	2.001	45. South Dakota	1.715
14. Alabama	2.267	30. Kansas	1.998	46. Arizona	1.694
15. Louisiana	2.252	31. Montana	1.962	47. Wyomiing	1.660
16. Ohio	2.242	32. Utah	1.954	48. Virginia	1.620

[1] Alaska and Hawaii have been excluded from the analysis because data for some of the independent variables were not available for the time period considered.

[2] The ratio of expenditure benefits to tax burdens for the three lowest income classes.

redistribution (assuming, as is the case, that the ratios are higher in the lowest three income classes than in the remaining income classes), with higher summed ratios indicating more redistribution to the lowest income groups. Since it is commonly believed that the lowest income groups are denied access to the decision-making chambers of government, the limitation of our analysis to redistribution to the three lowest income groups poses a rigorous test for hypotheses involving political variables. The ratios for the lowest three income classes in each state are shown in Table 5.

There are a number of problems in this explication of the net redistributive impact of revenues and expenditures which should be kept in mind in interpreting the results of this study. First, the Tax Foundation analysis was not done for each state, but only for aggregate state and local revenues and expenditures, with nationwide allocation bases. In applying these allocation bases to state-by-state revenue and expenditure totals we have necessarily assumed that the allocation base distributions are constant in all the states. Thus, for instance, in apportioning the burden of the cigarette tax, we assume that cigarette expenditures in each state are distributed across income classes in the same manner as in the nation as a whole. This is clearly an unrealistic assumption, but one necessitated by restrictions on available data. To the extent that these distributions diverge among the states, of course, the data will be in error. Second, in the interest of simplification, the Tax Foundation study embodies a number of assumptions about the incidence of revenue burdens and expenditure benefits in allocating burdens and benefits to income classes. Perhaps the most controversial are the assumptions concerning the incidence of the corporation income tax and general expenditures. In recognition of this problem, the Tax Foundation has offered alternatives in both of these areas. In the present study, in deference to arguments among economists concerning the incidence of the corporation income tax, we have adopted the alternative which assumes that half the corporate taxes and fees are borne by stockholders and half are shifted to the consumer. We have also followed a middle course concerning general expenditures, assuming that half of these benefits are distributed in proportion to family money income before taxes and half in proportion to the number of families and unrelated individuals in each income class. The relevant question, in terms of this analysis, is whether or not these assumptions accord with the perceptions of fiscal policy-makers. We feel that our assumptions do no great violence to those perceptions, but this, of course, is a matter for empirical investigation. Third, some of the allocation bases employed in the Tax Foundation study would appear to be more applicable to federal revenues and expenditures than to those of the states, particularly in regard to income taxes (allocated according to the federal income tax burden) and insurance trust revenues and expenditures (both allocated in part according to the distribution of the burdens and benefits of social security taxes and expenditures). The practical effect of the choice of these allocation bases is probably to reduce our level of measurement from an interval to an ordinal scale. Here we assume that the *order* of the relative redistributive impact of the revenue and expenditure categories is preserved despite the fact that the relative *degree* of redistribution is probably distorted. For instance, we assume that state income taxes have a higher redistributive impact than most other state revenue sources although the relative degree of redistribution is probably overstated because of the Tax Foundation assumption that the distribution of the burden of state income taxes is the same as that of the federal income tax. Finally, in our consideration of only revenues and expenditures, the deficit of the states has been ignored; therefore revenue burdens are understated. To the extent that this omission has an equal impact in all the states, there will be no distortion in the regression analysis.

III. Independent Variables

Consonant with our first objective, developing a model with relatively high explanatory power, we have embarked on a frankly exploratory expedition in choosing independent variables. Hofferbert provided the general structure for this exploration when he suggested that independent variables be drawn from several dimensions: historic-geographic conditions, socio-economic composition, mass political behavior, governmental institutions, and elite behavior.[21] We have attempted to draw variables from all of these dimensions save that of historic-geographic conditions, though our classification is admittedly arbitrary.

The socio-economic variables used in this analysis are median family income, industrialization,[22] urbanization,[23] education,[24] percentage of families with less than $3,000 annual income, and the Gini index of income inequality.[25] The first four variables—income, industrialization, urbanization, and education—were chosen because of the high explanatory power they have exhibited in previous studies as correlates of levels of revenues and expenditures. We hypothesize that as a state develops economically and more completely fulfills basic service functions, a larger portion of its resources becomes available for other functions which tend to be more redistributive in character. The use of these variables also allows a direct comparison between the results of this and previous studies. The percentage of the population with income under $3,000 and the Gini index were both added on the assumption that the greater the inequality of income in a state and/or the larger the proportion of low income families in that state, the greater the perceived need for redistribution through state revenue and expenditure policies.

[21] Richard I. Hofferbert, "Elite Influence in Policy Formation: A Model for Comparative Inquiry"; paper delivered at 1968 Annual Meeting of the American Political Science Association, Washington, D.C., September 2–7, 1968, p. 8.

[22] Industrialization is measured by one minus the per cent of the work force engaged in farming, fishing and forestry work; drawn from ibid., p. 1–249.

[23] Urbanization is measured by the per cent of the population living in urban areas; from U.S. Department of Commerce, Bureau of the Census, *U.S. Statistical Abstract, 1968* (Washington, D.C.: U.S. Government Printing Office, 1968), p. 367.

[24] Education is defined as the median school year completed by persons 25 years of age; drawn from *U.S. Census of the Population, 1960,* p. 1–248.

[25] The Gini index is a summary measure of the inequality of income in a given population. It is derived from a Lorenz curve on which the percentage of total income is arrayed along the y-axis and percentage of consumer units is arrayed along the x-axis. A line drawn at a 45-degree angle across the graph describes perfect equality, since a given percentage of the consumer units will claim an equal percentage of total income at points on this line (e.g., the lowest 10 per cent of the consumer units have 10 per cent of total income). The Gini index describes, roughly, the area between the 45-degree line and the line representing the actual distribution of income. The larger the area—the higher the Gini index—the more unequal the distribution of income in the population. The Gini index used in this study is from David Verway, "A Ranking of States by Inequality Using Census and Tax Data," *Review of Economics and Statistics,* XLVIII (1966), p. 314.

Political participation,[26] Democratic vote,[27] interparty competition,[28] and legislative inducements to participation[29] are used as indicators of mass political behavior. First, we hypothesize that the participatory aspect of the political system will have a positive impact on state redistributive policies. Both overall measures of political participation and legislative inducements to participate are related to this hypothesis. Our decision to consider political participation, as measured by the average rate of voter participation in gubernatorial races between 1954 and 1962, was prompted by the well-established proposition that lower income groups are less likely to vote than higher income groups. Thus we assume that the higher the voter participation, the more likely it is that voters in the lower income groups have participated in the election. With more electoral participation by the lower income groups, we further assume there will be increased pressure for measures favorable to those groups. Our use of the Millbrath index of legislative inducements to vote was based on much the same rationale. On the premise that legal barriers to participation have a differentially greater effect on lower income groups, we assume that removal of these barriers—or positive encouragement to vote—will have its greatest impact on the lowest income groups.

We are also concerned with the partisan component of mass political behavior: interparty competition and Democratic vote are employed to measure this dimension. The inclusion in our analysis of the Hofferbert index of interparty competition follows a hypothesis posed by V. O. Key in *Southern Politics*—that interparty competition promotes the distribution of benefits to lower income groups.[30] Key asserted that interparty competition leads to the organization and subsequent representation of lower income groups as the "outs" replace the "ins" and policies favorable to the new

26 The participation index is defined as the votes cast for the state's Governor as a percent of voting age population. See U.S. Department of Commerce, Bureau of the Census, *U.S. Statistical Abstract, 1963* (Washington, D.C.: U.S. Government Printing Office, 1968), p. 367.

27 Measured in terms of average Democratic vote for Governor as in *U.S. Statistical Abstract, 1968*, p. 367.

28 The measure of interparty competition is a rank order measure integrating the state's competition in the presidential, senatorial and gubernatorial races. For more detail on the measure, see Richard I. Hofferbert, "Classification of American State Party Systems," *Journal of Politics*, XXVI (1964), 550–567.

29 The legislative inducements to participation index is a summed measure noting the extent to which each state has legal measures facilitating participation, e.g., absence of literacy tests and residency requirements, permanent registration, etc. See Lester Milbrath, "Political Participation in the States," in Herbert Jacob and Kenneth Vines (eds), *Politics in the American States* (Boston: Little, Brown, 1965), p. 46.

30 Key, op. cit., pp. 298–311.

analysis of party behavior a step further. Here we attempted to probe the groups result. With the introduction of Democratic vote, we have taken the programmatic content of partisan behavior. We assume that the Democratic party propounds programs more favorable to lower income groups than does the Republican party. Hence we hypothesize, the greater the electoral support for the Democratic party in a given state, the more directionally redistributive will be the revenue and expenditure policies of that state. Democratic vote is measured by the average percentage of votes received by Democrats in gubernatorial elections between 1954 and 1964.

We have selected four variables to represent Hofferbert's next dimension, governmental institutions: legislative apportionment, legislative party cohesion,[31] gubernatorial powers and gubernatorial tenure.[32] Malapportionment has been a subject of considerable interest and analysis, and despite generally negative findings, the suspicion lingers that it has an important political impact. This suspicion is based on persuasive theoretical arguments which, in terms of redistribution, can be summed up rather simply: since malapportionment usually reflects underrepresentation of urban areas, and since the strongest demand for redistributive policies is likely to emanate from these urban areas, it is assumed that the degree of mallapportionment will vary inversely with the extent of redistribution in a state.

Governor's tenure and power were included in the analysis on the basis of two assumptions. First, we assume that governors are likely to press for redistributive measures in response to the varied pressures of the broad-based constituency required for their election. Second, we assume length of time in office, re-election possibilities, and structural sources of power will provide the governor with the tools necessary for the accomplishment of his purposes. Legislative party cohesion is used on much the same rationale. Here we assume that the accommodation of the varied interests necessary to produce party cohesion will lead to the enactment of redistributive measures.

The final dimension suggested by Hofferbert is elite behavior. The variables we have chosen to represent aspects of elite behavior are interest-group strength, percentage of state employees under civil service coverage,

[31] The measures of party cohesion and interest-group strength were derived from a questionnaire "sent to two or more competent persons in each state, including political scientists . . . , director of . . . research, agencies or bureaus, legislative officers and politicians. At least one reply was received from each of the 48 states—in most cases two or three." See Belle Zeller, *American State Legislatures* (New York: Thomas Crowell, 1954), pp. 190–192.

[32] The measure of gubernatorial tenure is an index combining the gubernatorial length of term and the legal possibilities for re-election. The gubernatorial power index combines evaluative indices of budget powers, appointive powers, and veto powers. See Joseph Schlesinger, "The Politics of the Executive," in Jacob and Vines, op. cit., pp. 220, 222, 226–27, 229.

Grumm's index of legislative professionalism,[33] and Walker's innovation index.[34] In regard to interest-group strength, we hypothesize that redistribution to the lowest income groups is *negatively* related to the strength of interest-groups in a state. This hypothesis is based on Schattschneider's contention that a society with many interest groups incorporates a bias against the lower income groups, which typically are not represented in the interest-group system.[35] We would expect that the stronger the interest-group system, the lower the probability of success for political strategies based on the mobilization of the lower income classes. The inclusion of the percentage of employees covered by the civil service system can be justified in two ways. The more conventional explanation, expounded by such authors as Herring and Key, is that as civil service appointments replace political appointments, state services (in this case measured by revenue and expenditure policies) replace patronage as an inducement or a reward for party loyalty. The allocation of these rewards or inducements is here assumed to be redistributive in character in response to the broad-based coalitions which form political parties. An alternative formulation links civil service coverage with the indexes of legislative professionalism and innovation as measures of what may be termed the "progressive" character of the state political system. Fenton contends that as civil service coverage expands in state offices, "job-oriented" employees are succeeded by "issue-oriented" employees who perceive rewards more in terms of service than in terms of employment security, and that redistribution results.[36] The high incidence of professionalism in the legislature and policy innovation in the states can be taken as indicators of the same type of emphasis on "equitable, efficient, issue-oriented politics" that is associated with the progressive tradition in American politics.

IV. Hypotheses

Our basic hypothesis in this study, as indicated earlier, is that political variables are more closely related to the net redistributive impact of state revenues and expenditures than are socio-economic variables. However, in

33 Grumm, op. cit., p. 25. The index combined four important qualities of legislative life: (a) compensation of legislators, (b) total length of sessions in 1963–64, (c) expenditures for legislative services and operations, (d) a "legislative services" score.

34 Walker, op. cit., pp. 882–883. The innovation index measures the rapidity and extent of adoption within the states of eighty-eight different programs. Such programs ranged from "the establishment of highway departments and the enactment of civil rights bills to the creation of state councils on the performing arts and the passage of sexual psycopath laws."

35 E. E. Schattschneider, *The Semi-Sovereign People* (New York: Holt, Rinehart and Winston, 1960), pp. 30–33.

36 John Fenton, *People and Parties in Politics* (Glenview, Ill.: Scott, Foresman, 1966), pp. 46–49, 50–78.

our attempts to develop an explanatory model of redistribution in the states, we have suggested a number of subsidiary hypotheses which can be tested in this analysis. These subsidiary hypotheses are listed below.

I. Socio-Economic Variables
   A. Redistributive policies of the states vary directly with the level of economic development in the state.
      1. Redistribution varies directly with median family income in the states.
      2. Redistribution varies directly with the degree of industrialization in the states.
      3. Redistribution varies directly with the degree of urbanization in the states.
      4. Redistribution varies directly with the level of education in the states.
   B. Redistributive policies of the states vary directly with the perceived need for such policies in the states.
      1. Redistribution varies directly with the degree of income inequality in the states.
      2. Redistribution varies directly with the proportion of families with less than $3,000 annual income.

II. Mass Political Behavior Variables
   A. Redistributive policies of the states vary directly with the extent of participation of lower income classes in the electoral process.
      1. Redistribution varies directly with the overall rate of political participation.
      2. Redistribution varies directly with legislative inducements to political participation.
   B. Redistributive policies of the states vary directly with the nature of partisan activities in the states.
      1. Redistribution varies directly with interparty competition in the states.
      2. Redistribution varies directly with the extent of the support for the Democratic party in the states.

III. Governmental Institution Variables
   A. Redistributive policies of the states vary directly with the quality of apportionment in the states.
   B. Redistribution varies directly with the degree of the governor's power in the states.
   C. Redistribution varies directly with the extent of the governor's tenure in the states.
   D. Redistribution varies directly with legislative party cohesion in the states.

IV. Elite Behavior Variables

A. Redistributive policies of the states vary inversely with the degree of interest-group strength in the states.

B. Redistribution varies directly with the extent of the coverage of the civil service system in the states.

C. Redistribution varies directly with the degree of legislative professionalism in the states.

D. Redistribution varies directly with the degree of innovative tendencies in the states.

V. Findings

To test the hypotheses, we have run separate multiple regression analyses in 48 states and for non-Southern states.[37] We will examine the overall coefficients of multiple correlation and determination as indicators of the explanatory power of our model, zero-order and partial coefficients of correlation to test the relationship between each independent variable and redistribution in the states, and multiple-partial coefficients of determination to assess the relative importance of political and socio-economic variables in determining interstate variations in redistributive fiscal policies. Our statistical findings are summarized in Table 6.

As Table 6 indicates, we have achieved a measure of success in our efforts to develop a fairly powerful explanatory model. For all 48 states, the multiple coefficient of determination (R^2) is .55, indicating that the model "explains" 55% of the variance in interstate redistributive fiscal policies.[38] When separate regression analyses are run for the socio-economic and political variables included in this analysis, we find that socio-economic variables alone account for 17% of the variance in redistribution in the 48 states, and that political variables account for 38% of that variance.

The importance of the regional distinction (South separated from non-South) is indicated by the multiple coefficient of determination derived from a separate regression analysis performed for non-Southern states. For these states, the multiple coefficient of determination for all independent variables increases to .67, with both socio-economic variables ($R^2 = .28$) and political variables ($R^2 = .46$) accounting for more variance than in the 48 states as a whole.[39]

[37] For the purposes of this study, the following states were considered to be in the "South"; Alabama, Arkansas, Florida, Georgia, Kentucky, Louisiana, Mississippi, North Carolina, South Carolina, Tennessee, Texas. and Virginia.

[38] We have not used tests of statistical significance in this analysis, since all 48 states have been included.

[39] Analysis of the impact of political variables in the 12-state area of the South is proscribed by limitations on the degrees of freedom. However, regression analysis of the lesser number of socio-economic variables permits some

The subsidiary hypotheses generated with the introduction of the independent variables in the analysis will receive only perfunctory attention since they are of secondary importance in this study. Table 6 provides a listing of zero-order and partial coefficients of correlation for each independent variable with redistribution for both the 48 states and the non-Southern states. In general the independent variables selected bear the hypothesized relationships to redistribution in both the 48 states and the non-Southern states.

In terms of zero-order correlations in the 48 states, all relationships are as hypothesized with the exception of education, Democratic vote, interparty competition, the Gini index of income inequality, and the proportion of families with less than $3,000 in annual income. As one would expect, Democratic vote is redeemed when Southern states are excluded from the analysis, with a positive correlation between Democratic vote and redistribution for non-Southern states. The same reversal occurs for the Gini index of income inequality.

Shifting our attention to partial coefficients of correlation, a measure of independent impact of each independent variable on redistribution, we find somewhat longer lists of contrary correlations. For the 48 states, the partials for median income, industrialization, interparty competition, proportion of families with less than $3,000 annual income, and legislative party cohesion are all related to redistribution in a direction opposite to that hypothesized. For non-Southern states, all of the same reverse relationships persist and the index of governor's power is added.

Two of these variables—interparty competition, and proportion of

---

speculation about the South-non-South differences: the multiple coefficient of determination for the socio-economic variables in the South is .74 higher than for either the 48 states as a whole or for the non-Southern states. Thus, in this analysis we have a situation in which the socio-economic variables account for more of the variance in each region examined than in the 48 states as a whole. Though a precise investigation of this anomaly is not possible within the statistical confines of the present study, we presume that the 48-state analysis contains a number of suppressed relationships which become statistically apparent only in the regional breakdown. The fragmentary data available to us support this presumption. An examination of the zero-order correlations between the socio-economic variables and redistribution in the South reveals that median income, industrialization, urbanization, and education have a strong *negative* relationship with redistribution. On the other hand, both the Gini index and the percentage of families with less than $3,000 in annual income have a strong positive relationship with redistribution. In short, redistribution varies inversely with what appear to be measures of ability to pay and directly with perceived need for redistribution. Since we would expect federal aid to vary in the same manner, with assistance provided to those states most in need and least able to pay, we assume that South-non-South differences in redistribution can be accounted for largely by differences in the impact of federal aid, and that this differential impact produces relationships obscured in the 48-state data. This conclusion can only be considered tentative and in need of more direct substantiation, but it suggests a fruitful area for future research.

TABLE 6 *Summary of Findings*

	48 States		Non-South	
	Zero-order	Partial	Zero-order	Partial
I. Variables				
Socio-Economic Variables				
Ability to pay				
Median Income	.18	−.27	.23	−.40
Industrialization	.29	−.02	.33	−.05
Urbanization	.34	.15	.42	.23
Education	−.01	.17	−.08	.19
Need (demand)				
Gini Index	.00	.22	.13	.47
% under $3,000	−.14	−.07	−.21	−.23
Political Variables				
Mass political behavior				
Political Participation	.14	.37	.06	.36
Democratic Vote	−.06	.11	.11	.17
Interparty Comp.	−.21	−.14	−.16	−.19
Leg. Inducements	.03	.07	.11	.33
Government insts.				
Apportionment	.04	.01	.10	.09
Leg. Party Cohesion	.24	−.05	.25	.00
Governor Power	.26	.12	.24	−.04
Governor Tenure	.17	.12	.12	.17
Elite Behavior				
I. G. Strength	−.04	−.17	−.01	−.07
Civ. Ser. Coverage	.33	.34	.35	.48
Leg. Professionalism	.51	.28	.56	.14
Innovation Index	.46	.07	.50	.17
II. Multiple Coefficients of Correlation and Determination				
	R	R^2	R	R^2
All Variables	.75	.55	.82	.67
Socio-Economic Variables	.42	.17	.53	.28
Political Variables	.62	.38	.67	.46
III. Multiple-Partial Coefficients of Determination				
Political Variables Controlled for Socio-Economic Variables	.46		.54	
Socio-Economic Variables Controlled for Political Variables	.27		.39	

families with less than $3,000 annual income—are related to redistribution in a direction opposite to that hypothesized for both zero-order *and* partial coefficients of correlation and regardless of regional breakdown. For these two variables, then, the statistical evidence is most convincing for rejecting the assertion that they are correlated as hypothesized with the degree of redistribution in the states. For interparty competition, our data lead us to reject the venerable Key hypothesis that an increased level of interparty competition will increase the level of redistribution in the states. The negative relationship between the proportion of families with less than $3,000 annual income and the extent of redistribution should be evaluated in light of the positive relationships between redistribution and both legislative inducements to participate and the overall rate of participation. If we are correct in assuming that the latter two measures indicate the extent of electoral participation by lower income groups, we can tentatively conclude that, as might be expected, redistribution to the lowest income classes is more a function of participation by these classes than of their size.

The most interesting and significant finding in this study, however, concerns the relative importance of political and socio-economic variables in determining redistributive fiscal policies in the states. As indicated in the introductory section, previous studies of policy outcomes in the states have been hard pressed to find an independent impact for the political variables considered, and where the relative impact of political and socio-economic variables has been examined the socio-economic variables have predominated. In the present analysis, these findings are reversed. Not only do the political variables have an independent impact on redistributive policies in the states; they also account for considerably more of the variance in redistribution than do socio-economic variables. The relative explanatory power of the political and socio-economic variables is indicated by the multiple-partial co-efficients of determination displayed in Table 6. For the 48 states the multiple-partial for political variables is .46 while the multiple-partial for the socio-economic variables controlled for the political variables is only .27. For the non-Southern states, the results are similar. The multiple-partial for political variables controlled for economic variables in the non-South is .54 while the multiple-partial for the socio-economic variables controlled for political variables is only .39. In other words, in the 48 states and in the non-Southern states, the political variables included in our analysis are considerably more powerful than the socio-economic variables in explaining variance in state redistributive policies.

Two objections which can be raised about the above interpretation of the multiple-partial coefficients of determination are: (A) the finding may be an artifact of the number of political variables used in the analysis (12) relative to the number of socio-economic variables employed (6); and (B) there may be variables not yet considered which could alter the observed relative impact of the political and socio-economic variables. The first objection is susceptible to a direct statistical confrontation. Taking only the five most powerful political variables (measured in terms of sums of squares reduction) versus the five most powerful socio-economic variables, the multiple-partial for the political variables controlled for the socio-economic variables is .42, while the multiple-partial for the socio-economic variables controlled for the political variables is .20 for the 48 states. Making the same comparison in the non-Southern states, we find the multiple-partial for political variables controlled for socio-economic variables is .47, while the multiple-partial for socio-economic variables controlled for political variables is .34. Thus, our finding concerning the relative impact of political and socio-economic variables is not simply the product of the number of each type of variable incorporated in this study. The second objection, the possibility that a variable not considered in this analysis could alter the observed relationships, cannot be answered definitively. We have attempted to minimize this possibility by developing a model with a high degree of explanatory power. Our findings, of course, are only tentative and subject to modification by future research.

VI. Conclusion

The foregoing analysis has been specifically addressed to an investigation of the determinants of variations in the net redistributive impact of revenues and expenditures in American states. In a broader sense, however, this study has been concerned with the more general question of whether or not the political system exercises an independent impact on public policy outcomes, and with the specification of an arena in which such an impact is likely to be found.

Previous analyses of policy outcomes have generally indicated that socio-economic variables have a dominant influence on those outcomes, with few reported instances of political variables exerting an independent impact. We have contended that these results have been the product of a continuing concentration on policy outcomes as measured by levels of taxes and expenditures. Accordingly, we have shifted the focus of our analysis to an examination of allocations of burdens and benefits in state systems of revenues and expenditures.

Our statistical results indicate that the shift in focus has been fruitful. First, we have been able to develop a statistical model that accounts for more than half the variance in redistribution among the 48 states included in the analysis and more than two-thirds of the variance in non-Southern states. Second, and more significantly, we have found that the political variables employed in the model are considerably more powerful than the socio-economic variables in explaining interstate variations in redistributive patterns. Thus, our data not only support the assertion that politics makes a difference, they suggest that politics plays a dominant role in the allocation of the burdens and benefits of public policies.

It is obvious that this study represents only a preliminary exploration of the theoretical utility of the concept of the net redistributive impact of revenues and expenditures as a dependent variable. The summary measure of redistribution employed in this analysis (the ratio of expenditure benefits to revenue burdens for the lowest three income groups) is only one of many possible measures with a variety of political implications. The complex interrelationships among the independent variables used in this analysis are susceptible to more systematic treatment. Longitudinal analysis could avoid the dangers inherent in the present research design of drawing dynamic inferences from a cross-sectional model of analysis. Our effort is meant to be but a first step in an intensive analysis of a dependent variable whose value we feel has been demonstrated.

Robert L. Lineberry and Edmund P. Fowler

Reformism and Public Policies in American Cities

Not only must there be popular support for state and local governments to act effectively in solving problems, there must be an effective framework for action. States have begun recently to pay attention to organization and structure, and a good deal of revision is taking place in state government. In any case, it is simpler for the states in that they can take cues from the national government, even as they did in introducing executive reorganization.

It is not so simple for local governments. Basically (except for a few New England towns), Americans deal with local problems through three kinds of government structure: mayor-council, manager, and commission forms of government, the last two being "reform" deviants from the traditional mayor-council form.

What effect does reformed structure have on the ability of local governments to attack problems, that is, to make effective public policy? Despite a swelling literature on local government and politics, this vital question had not been answered until Lineberry and Fowler wrote the following analysis.

A decade ago, political scientists were deploring the "lost world of municipal government" and calling for systematic studies of municipal life which emphasized the political, rather than the administrative, side of urban political life. In recent years, this demand has been generously answered and urban politics is becoming one of the most richly plowed

Reprinted from *American Political Science Review*, **61**:701–16 (September 1967) by permission of the authors and the publisher. Some descriptive and bibliographical footnotes have been omitted for considerations of space and textual format.

fields of political research. In terms originally introduced by David Easton,[1] political scientists have long been concerned with inputs, but more recently they have focused their attention on other system variables, particularly the political culture and policy outputs of municipal governments.

The present [study] will treat two policy outputs, taxation and expenditure levels of cities, as dependent variables. We will relate these policy choices to socioeconomic characteristics of cities and to structural characteristics of their governments. Our central research concern is to examine the impact of political structures, reformed and unreformed, on policy-making in American cities.

Political Culture, Reformism, and Political Institutions

The leaders of the Progressive movement in the United States left an enduring mark on the American political system, particularly at the state and municipal level. In the states, the primary election, the referendum, initiative and recall survive today. The residues of this *Age of Reform*,[2] as Richard Hofstadter called it, persist in municipal politics principally in the form of manager government and at-large and nonpartisan elections. The reformers were, to borrow Banfield and Wilson's phrase, the original embodiment of the "middle class ethos" in American politics. They were, by and large, White Anglo-Saxon Protestants reacting to the politics of the party machine, which operated by exchanging favors for votes.

It is important that we understand the ideology of these reformers if we hope to be able to analyze the institutions which they created and their impact on political decisions. The reformers' goal was to "rationalize" and "democratize" city government by the substitution of "community oriented" leadership. To the reformers, the most pernicious characteristic of the machine was that it capitalized on socioeconomic cleavages in the population, playing on class antagonisms and on racial and religious differences. Ernest S. Bradford, an early advocate of commission government with at-large elections, defended his plans for at-large representation on grounds that

> . . . under the ward system of governmental representation, the ward receives the attention, not in proportion to its needs, but to the ability of its representatives to 'trade' and arrange 'deals' with fellow members. . . . Nearly every city under the aldermanic system offers flagrant examples of this vicious method of 'part representation.' The

[1] David Easton, "An Approach to the Analysis of Political Systems," *World Politics*, IX (April, 1957), pp. 383–400.

[2] Richard Hofstadter, *Age of Reform* (New York: Alfred A. Knopf, 1955).

> commission form changes this to representation of the city as a whole.[3]

The principal tools which the reformers picked to maximize this "representation of the city as a whole" were the commission, and later the manager, form of government, the nonpartisan election and the election at-large. City manager government, it was argued, produced a no-nonsense, efficient and business-like regime, where decisions could be implemented by professional administrators rather than by victors in the battle over spoils. Nonpartisan elections meant to the reformer that state and national parties, whose issues were irrelevant to local politics anyway, would keep their divisive influences out of municipal decision-making. Nonpartisan elections, especially when combined with elections at-large, would also serve to reduce the impact of socioeconomic cleavages and minority voting blocs in local politics. Once established, these institutions would serve as bastions against particularistic interests.

Banfield and Wilson have argued that the "middle class ethos" of the reformers has become a prevalent attitude in much of political life. The middle class stands for "public-regarding" virtues rather than for "private-regarding" values of the ethnic politics of machines and bosses. The middle class searches for the good of the "community as a whole" rather than for the benefit of particularistic interests.[4] Agger, Goldrich, and Swanson, in their study of two western and two southern communities, have documented the rise of a group they call the "community conservationists," who "see the values of community life maximized when political leadership is exercised by men representing the public at large, rather than 'special interests.' "[5] Robert Wood has taken up a similar theme in his penetrating analysis of American suburbia. The "no-party politics of suburbia" is characterized by "an outright reaction against partisan activity, a refusal to recognize that there may be persistent cleavages in the electorate and an ethical disapproval of permanent group collaboration as an appropriate means of settling disputes." This ideological opposition to partisanship is a product of a tightly-knit and homogeneous community, for "nonpartisanship reflects a highly integrated community life with a powerful capacity to induce conformity."[6]

Considerable debate has ensued over both the existence and the consequences of these two political ethics in urban communities. Some evidence

[3] Ernest S. Bradford, *Commission Government in American Cities* (New York: Macmillan, 1911), p. 165.

[4] Edward C. Banfield and James O. Wilson, *City Politics* (Cambridge: Harvard University Press, 1963), p. 41.

[5] Robert Agger, Daniel Goldrich, and Bert E. Swanson, *The Rulers and the Ruled* (New York: Wiley, 1964), p. 21.

[6] Robert C. Wood, *Suburbia: Its People and Their Politics* (Boston: Houghton Mifflin, 1959), pp. 154, 155.

has supported the view that reformed governments[7] are indeed found in cities with higher incomes, higher levels of education, greater proportions of Protestants, and more white-collar job-holders. Schnore and Alford, for example, found that "the popular image of the manager city was verified; it does tend to be the natural habitat of the upper middle class." In addition, manager cities were "inhabited by a younger, more mobile population that is growing rapidly." [8]

More recently, Wolfinger and Field correlated socio-economic variables—particularly ethnicity and region—to political structures. They concluded that "the ethos theory is irrelevant to the South . . . inapplicable to the West . . . fares badly in the Northeast . . . " and that support for the theory in the Midwest was "small and uneven." [9] Region proved to be a more important predictor of both government forms and of policy outputs like urban renewal expenditures than did the socio-economic composition of the population.

In our view, it is premature to carve a headstone for the ethos theory. It is our thesis that governments which are products of the reform movement behave differently from those which have unreformed institutions, even if the socio-economic composition of their population may be similar. Our central purpose is to determine the impact of both socio-economic variables and political institutions (structural variables) on outputs of city governments. By doing this, we hope to shed some additional illumination on the ethos theory.

Research Design

VARIABLES

The independent variables used in this analysis, listed in Table 1, constitute relatively "hard" data, mostly drawn from the U.S. census.[10] These variables were selected because they represent a variety of possible social

[7] We refer to cities characterized by commission or manager government, nonpartisan elections, and at-large constituencies as "reformed." Our use of the term is historical and no value position on reformism's merits is intended. To refer to reformed cities as "public-regarding" or "middle class" is, it seems, to assume what needs to be proved.

[8] Leo Schnore and Robert Alford, "Forms of Government and Socio-Economic Characteristics of Suburbs," *Administrative Science Quarterly,* VIII (June, 1963), pp. 1–17.

[9] Raymond Wolfinger and John Osgood Field, "Political Ethos and the Structure of City Government," *American Political Science Review,* LX (June, 1966), pp. 325–326.

[10] The source for the first nine variables is *The City and County Data Book* (Washington: United States Bureau of the Census, 1962). For the last three variables, the source is Orin F. Nolting and David S. Arnold (eds.), *The Municipal Yearbook, 1965* (Chicago: International City Managers' Association, 1965), p. 98 ff.

TABLE 1 *Independent Variables*

1. Population, 1960
2. Per cent population increase or decrease, 1950–60
3. Per cent non-white
4. Per cent of native population with foreign born or mixed parentage
5. Median income
6. Per cent of population with incomes below $3000
7. Per cent of population with incomes above $10,000
8. Median school years completed by adult population
10. Per cent of population in white collar occupations
11. Per cent of elementary school children in private schools
12. Per cent of population in owner-occupied dwelling units

cleavages which divide urban populations—rich vs. poor, Negro vs. White, ethnic vs. native, newcomers vs. old-timers, etc. We assume that such social and economic characteristics are important determinants of individual and group variations in political preferences. Data on each of these independent variables were gathered for each of the two hundred cities in the sample.[11]

Our principal theoretical concern will be with the consequences of variations in the structural characteristics of form of government, type of constituency, and partisanship of elections. The variable of form of government is unambiguous. Except for a few small New England towns, all American cities have council-manager, mayor-council, or commission government. There is, however, somewhat more ambiguity in the classification of election type. By definition, a "nonpartisan election is one in which no candidate is identified on the ballot by party affiliation." The legal definition of nonpartisanship conceals the wide variation between Chicago's and Boston's nominal nonpartisanship and the more genuine variety in Minneapolis, Winnetka, and Los Angeles. We will quickly see, though, that formal nonpartisanship is not merely an empty legal nicety, but that there are real differences in the political behavior of partisan and nonpartisan cities, even though we are defining them in legal terms only.[12]

Our classification of constituency types into only two groups also conceals some variation in the general pattern. While most cities use either the

[11] We used a random sample of 200 of the 309 American cities with populations of 50,000 or more in 1960. All information on the forms of government and forms of election are drawn from *The Municipal Yearbook, 1965,* op. cit.

[12] At least one other variable may produce a given institutional form in a city—the legal requirements of a state government, which vary from state to state and may even vary for different kinds of cities within the same state. We have not taken account of this variable because systematic information on comparative state requirements in this area was unavailable to us. However, Wolfinger and Field consulted several experts and eliminated cities which are not given free choice over their institutions. Nevertheless, a comparison of our figures with theirs revealed no important differences.

at-large or the ward pattern of constituencies exclusively, a handful use a combination of the two electoral methods. For our purposes, we classified these with district cities.

The dependent variables in this study are two measures of public policy outputs. A growing body of research on local politics has utilized policy measures as dependent variables. The present research is intended to further this study of political outputs by relating socio-economic variables to expenditure and taxation patterns in cities with varying political structures.

The dependent variables are computed by a simple formula. The measure for taxation was computed by dividing the total personal income of the city into the total tax of the city, giving us a tax/income ratio. Similarly, dividing expenditures by the city's aggregate personal income gave us an expenditure/income ratio as the measure for our second dependent variable. These measures, while admittedly imperfect,[13] permit us to ask how much of a city's income it is willing to commit for public taxation and expenditures.

HYPOTHESIS

Much of the research on city politics has treated reformed institutions as dependent variables. Although we shall briefly examine the social and economic differences between reformed and unreformed cities, our principal concern will be to explore the *consequences* for public policy of political institutions. From our earlier discussion of the political culture of cities, we hypothesized that:

1. The relationship between socio-economic cleavages and policy outputs is stronger in unreformed than in reformed cities.

This hypothesis focuses on the intention of the reformers to minimize the role of particularistic interests in policy making.

Reformed and Unreformed Cities: A Comparison

The economic and social contrasts between reformed and unreformed cities have been the subject of much research, and for our purposes we may be brief in our treatment. We divided independent variables into three

[13] We recognize that these are only rough indicators of city finance policies. Definitions of taxation vary from city to city and what may be financed from taxes in one city may be financed from fees in another. Expenditures present a more complex problem because the types and amounts of state transfer payments vary from state to state according to state laws, the division of government labor in a state, the incomes and sizes of cities, not to mention political factors at the state level. We think it important, however, that our independent variables explain a large proportion of the variation in municipal outputs as we measured them. No doubt one could explain an even larger

TABLE 2 *Comparison of the Means (and Standard Deviations) of Socio-economic Characteristics of Reformed and Unreformed Cities*

Independent variable	Mayor-council		Manager		Commission	
	Government type					
Population						
Population (10^3)	282.5	(858.6)	115.7	(108.0)	128.6	(115.2)
Per cent change, 1950–1960	34.4	(118.8)	64.1	(130.4)	18.5	(36.7)
Class						
Median income	$6199	(1005.0)	$6131	(999.6)	$5425	(804.4)
Per cent under $3000	15.3	(7.0)	17.3	(6.9)	21.5	(7.9)
Per cent over $10,000	16.9	(7.2)	17.5	(6.7)	12.5	(3.7)
Per cent high school graduates	40.7	(10.8)	48.1	(8.9)	41.6	(10.4)
Median education (yrs.)	10.7	(1.1)	11.4	(.89)	11.0	(2.1)
Per cent owner-occupied dwelling units	54.9	(15.1)	57.3	(13.6)	54.6	(13.7)
Per cent white collar	44.1	(9.0)	48.1	(7.1)	44.2	(7.6)
Homogeneity						
Per cent nonwhite	10.6	(11.5)	11.6	(10.8)	16.5	(14.9)
Per cent native with foreign born or mixed parentage	19.7	(9.9)	12.4	(8.3)	11.7	(10.7)
Per cent private school attendance	23.5	(11.9)	15.3	(11.8)	16.6	(11.8)
	$N = 85$		$N = 90$		$N = 25$	

Independent variable	Partisan		Nonpartisan	
	Election type			
Population				
Population (10^3)	270.8	(1022.1)	155.8	(198.7)
Per cent population increase 1950–1960	17.1	(40.1)	58.3	(136.1)
Class				
Median income	$5996	(904.5)	$6074	(1045.5)
Per cent under $3000	16.8	(7.1)	17.2	(7.2)

groups, one measuring population size and growth, a second containing social class indicators, and a third including three measures of social homogeneity. The means and standard deviations for each variable by institutional category are found in Table 2.

---

proportion of the variation in measures which specify different functional responsibilities of cities. At least these measures constitute a starting point, and we hope others will improve on them. The source of our output measures was the *City and County Data Book,* op. cit.

Independent variable	Election type			
	Partisan		Nonpartisan	
Class				
Per cent over $10,000	16.1	(6.1)	16.7	(7.0)
Per cent high school graduates	40.5	(9.2)	45.3	(10.6)
Median education (yrs.)	10.6	(1.1)	11.2	(1.2)
Per cent owner-occupied dwelling units	51.5	(14.4)	57.7	(13.8)
Per cent white collar	43.5	(7.5)	46.7	(8.3)
Homogeneity				
Per cent nonwhite	13.0	(11.9)	11.5	(11.8)
Per cent native with foreign born or mixed parentage	17.5	(10.7)	14.7	(9.6)
Per cent private school attendance	24.1	(13.6)	16.9	(11.3)
	$N = 57$		$N = 143$	

Independent variable	Constituency type			
	District		At-Large	
Population				
Population (10^3)	246.9	(909.8)	153.6	(191.2)
Per cent population increase 1950–1960	23.1	(36.4)	59.1	(143.7)
Class				
Median income	$6297	(965.2)	$5942	(1031.9)
Per cent under $3000	14.7	(6.5)	18.2	(7.6)
Per cent over $10,000	17.7	(7.1)	16.0	(6.6)
Per cent high school graduates	43.6	(10.9)	44.4	(10.4)
Median education (yrs.)	10.9	(1.1)	11.2	(1.2)
Per cent owner-occupied dwelling units	55.1	(14.4)	56.9	(14.5)
Per cent white collar	45.2	(9.4)	46.3	(7.5)
Homogeneity				
Per cent non white	9.8	(10.6)	13.0	(12.3)
Per cent native with foreign born or mixed parentage	18.9	(9.4)	13.4	(9.7)
Per cent private school attendance	23.2	(12.5)	16.6	(11.7)
	$N = 73$		$N = 127$	

It should initially be noted that population size and growth rate fairly clearly separate the reformed from the unreformed cities. . . . The larger the city, the greater the likelihood of its being unreformed; the faster its growth rate, the more likely a city is to possess manager government, nonpartisan and at-large elections. These differences are largely accounted for by the fact that very large cities are most likely to (1) have unreformed institutions and (2) be stable or declining in population. Since neither of these variables emerged as particularly important predictors of our output variables, we relegated them to secondary importance in the rest of the analysis.

The data in Table 2 indicate that reformed cities (at least those over 50,000) do not appear to be "the natural habitat of the upper middle class." While reformed cities have slightly more educated populations and slightly higher proportions of white collar workers and home ownership, unreformed cities have generally high incomes. In any case, whatever their direction, the differences are not large. What is striking is not the differences between the cities but the similarities of their class composition.

Homogeneity is easily one of the most ambiguous terms in the ambiguous language of the social sciences. We have followed Alford and Scoble who used three measures of homogeneity: for ethnicity, the per cent of population native born of foreign born or mixed parentage; for race, the per cent nonwhite; and for religious homogeneity, the per cent of elementary school children in private schools. The last measure, while indirect, was the only one available, since data on religious affiliation are not collected by the Census Bureau.

With the exception of race, reformed cities appear somewhat more homogeneous than unreformed cities. While the differences in homogeneity are more clear-cut than class differences, this hardly indicates that reformed cities are the havens of a socially homogeneous population. Although the average nonpartisan city has 16.9 per cent of its children in private schools, this mean conceals a wide range—from 2 to 47 per cent.

Our findings about the insignificance of class differences between reformed and unreformed cities are at some variance with Alford and Scoble's conclusions. There is, however, some support for the argument that reformed cities are more homogeneous. While we used cities with a population of over 50,000, their sample included all cities over 25,000; and varying samples may produce varying conclusions. The only other study to analyze cities over 50,000 was Wolfinger and Field's and our conclusions are generally consistent with theirs. We differ with them, however, on two important questions.

First, Wolfinger and Field argued that what differences there are between unreformed and reformed cities disappear when controls for region are introduced: "The salient conclusion to be drawn from these data is that one can do a much better job of predicting a city's political form by knowing what part of the country it is in than by knowing anything about the composition of its population."[14] Since regions have had different historical experiences, controls for region are essentially controls for history and, more specifically, historical variation in settlement patterns. The problem with this reasoning, however, is that to "control" for "region" is to control

[14] Wolfinger and Field, op. cit., p. 320.

not only for history but for demography as well: to know what region a city is in *is* to know something about the composition of its population. Geographical subdivisions are relevant subjects of political inquiry only because they are differentiated on the basis of attitudinal or socio-economic variables. The South is not a distinctive political region because two surveyors named Mason and Dixon drew a famous line, but because the "composition of its population" differs from the rest of the country.

It is therefore difficult to unravel the meaning of "controlling" for "region" since regions are differentiated on precisely the kinds of demographic variables which we (and Wolfinger and Field) related to reformism. Cities in the Midwest, for example, have a much higher proportion of home ownership (64%) than cities in the Northeast (44%), while Northeastern cities have more foreign stock in their population (27%) than the Midwest (16%). Hence, to relate ethnicity to political reformism and then to "control" for "region" is in part to relate ethnicity to reformism and then to control for ethnicity. Consequently, we have grave reservations that the substitution of the gross and unrefined variable of "region" for more refined demographic data adds much to our knowledge of American cities. "Controlling" for "region" is much more than controlling for historical experiences, because region as a variable is an undifferentiated *potpourri* of socio-economic, attitudinal, historical, and cultural variations.[15]

We also differ with Wolfinger and Field in their assertion that their analysis constitutes a test of the ethos theory. As we understand it, Banfield and Wilson's theory posits that particular attitudes are held by persons with varying sociological characteristics (ethnic groups and middle class persons, in particular) and that these attitudes include preferences for one or another kind of political institution. But relating the proportion of middle class persons in a city's population to its form of government says nothing one way or another about middle class preferences. An important part of understanding, of course, is describing and it is certainly useful to know how reformed cities differ from unreformed cities.

In our view, however, such tests as Wolfinger and Field used cannot logically be called explanations, in any causal sense. The most obvious reason is that they violate some important assumptions about time-order: independent variables are measured with contemporary census data, while

[15] In statistical parlance, the problem with "region" as an independent variable might be described as treating a complicated background variable as the first variable in a specific developmental sequence. But, as Blalock argues, "... *one should avoid complex indicators that are related in unknown ways to a given underlying variable.* Geographical region and certain background variables appear to have such undesirable properties." Hubert M. Blalock, *Causal Inferences in Nonexperimental Research* (Chapel Hill: University of North Carolina Press, 1964), p. 164 (italics in original).

the dependent variables are results of decisions made ten to fifty years ago. Moreover, this problem is multiplied by the difficulty of inferring configurations of political power from demographic data. Presumably, their assumption is that there is a simple linear relationship between sheer numbers (or proportions) of, say, middle class persons and their political power: the larger the size of a group in the city's population, the easier it can enforce its choice of political forms. At least one prominent urban sociologist, however, has found empirical support for . . . the opposite proposition . . . that the smaller the proportion of middle class persons in a city, the greater their power over urban renewal policies.[16] Similarly, it may also be dubious to assume that the size of an ethnic population is an accurate indicator of influence of ethnic groups. Although we recognize the importance of describing the socio-economic correlates of political forms, the logical problems involved suggest the need for a good deal of caution in interpreting these differences as explanations.

In any case, the question of why the city adopts particular structures is of less interest to us than their consequences for public policy. It is to this analysis that we now turn.

Policy Outputs and the Responsiveness of Cities

We are now in a position to take three additional steps. First, we can compare the differences in policy outputs between reformed and unreformed cities. Second, we can assess the cumulative impact of socio-economic variables on these policy choices. Finally, we can specify what variables are related in what ways to these output variables. In essence, we can now treat political institutions, not as dependent variables, but as factors which influence the *level* of expenditures and taxation and the relationship between cleavage variables and these outputs.

DIFFERENCES BETWEEN REFORMED AND UNREFORMED CITIES' OUTPUTS

Contrary to the situation in the Chicago suburbs, our data indicate that reformed cities both spend and tax less than unreformed cities, with the exception of expenditures in partisan and nonpartisan cities. It appears that partisan, mayor-council, and ward cities are more willing to commit their resources to public purposes than their reformed counterparts. What is of more importance than the difference in outputs, however, is the relative responsiveness of the two kinds of cities to social cleavages in their population.

[16] Amos Hawley, "Community Power and Urban Renewal Success," *American Journal of Sociology,* LXVIII (January, 1963), pp. 422–431.

TABLE 3 *Mean Values of Tax/Income and Expenditure/Income Ratios, by Structural Characteristics*

Structural Variables	Per cent	
	Taxes/income	Expenditures/income
Election type		
Partisan	.032	.050
Nonpartisan	.030	.053
Government type		
Mayor-council	.037	.058
Manager	.024	.045
Commission	.031	.057
Constituency type		
Ward	.036	.057
At-large	.027	.049

THE RESPONSIVENESS OF CITIES

We have argued that one principal goal of the reform movement in American politics was to reduce the impact of partisan, socio-economic cleavages on governmental decision making, to immunize city governments from "artificial" social cleavages—race, religion, ethnicity, and so on. As Banfield and Wilson put their argument, the reformers "assumed that there existed an interest ('the public interest') that pertained to the city 'as a whole' and that should always prevail over competing, partial (and usually private) interest." The structural reforms of manager government, at-large, and nonpartisan elections would so insulate the business of governing from social cleavages that "private-regarding" interests would count for little in making up the mind of the body politic. But amid the calls of the reformers for structural reforms to muffle the impact of socioeconomic cleavages, a few hardy souls predicted precisely the opposite consequence of reform: instead of eliminating cleavages from political decision-making, the reforms, particularly the elimination of parties, would enhance the conflict. Nathan Matthews, Jr. a turn-of-the-century mayor of Boston, issued just such a warning:

> As a city is a political institution, the people in the end will divide into parties, and it would seem extremely doubtful whether the present system, however illogical its foundation be, does not in fact produce better results, at least in large cities, than if the voters divided into groups, separated by property, social or religious grounds.[17]

[17] Quoted in Banfield and Wilson, op. cit., p. 154.

Matthews recognized implicitly what political scientists would now call the "interest aggregation" function of political parties. Parties in a democracy manage conflict, structure it, and encapsulate social cleavages under the rubric of two or more broad social cleavages, the parties themselves. "Parties tend to crystallize opinion, they give skeletal articulation to a shapeless and jelly-like mass . . . they cause similar opinions to coagulate. . . ." The parties reduce effectively the number of political opinions to manageable numbers, bring order and focus to the political struggle, simplify issues and frame alternatives, and compromise conflicting interests. Since parties are the agencies of interest aggregation, so the argument goes, their elimination makes for greater, not lesser, impact of social cleavages on political decisions.

Political scientists have recently confirmed Matthews' fears, at least with regard to electoral behavior in partisan and nonpartisan elections. Evidence points to the increased impact of socio-economic cleavages on voting when a nonpartisan ballot is used than when the election is formally partisan. Gerald Pomper studied nonpartisan municipal elections and compared them with partisan elections for the New Jersey State Assembly in Newark. He concluded that the "goal of nonpartisanship is fulfilled, as party identification does not determine the outcome. In place of party, ethnic affiliation is emphasized and the result is 'to enhance the effect of basic social cleavages.' "[18] If (1) this is typical of other American cities and if (2) electoral cleavages can be translated effectively into demands on the government in the absence of aggregative parties, then we might assume that the reformed institutions would reflect cleavages more, rather than less, closely than unreformed ones.

Essentially, then, there are two contrasting views about the consequences of municipal reform. One, the reformers' ideal, holds that institutional reforms will mitigate the impact of social cleavages on public policy. The other argues that the elimination of political parties and the introduction of other reforms will make social cleavages more, rather than less, important in political decision-making.

THE MEASUREMENT OF RESPONSIVENESS

We have hypothesized that socio-economic cleavages will have less impact on the policy choices of reformed than of unreformed governments. Thus, one could do a better job of predicting a city's taxation and expenditure policy using socio-economic variables in partisan, mayor, and ward cities than in nonpartisan, manager, and at-large cities. Operationally, we

[18] Gerald Pomper, "Ethnic and Group Voting in Nonpartisan Municipal Elections," *Public Opinion Quarterly*, XXX (Spring, 1966), p. 90; see also, J. Leiper Freeman, "Local Party Systems: Theoretical Considerations and a Case Analysis," *American Journal of Sociology*, LXIV (1958), pp. 282–289.

FIGURE 1 Proportion of variation explained (R^2) in taxation policy with twelve socio-economic variables, by institutional characteristics (in the total sample, the twelve independent variables explained 52% of the variation in taxes).

INDEPENDENT VARIABLES	STRUCTURAL VARIABLES (per cent)		DEPENDENT VARIABLE
	Reformed institution		
	Government: commission	62	
	Government: council manager	42	
	Election: nonpartisan	49	
	Constituency: at-large	49	
Twelve socio-economic variables			Tax/income ratio
	Unreformed institution		
	Government: mayor-council	52	
	Election: partisan	71	
	Constituency: ward/mixed	59	

FIGURE 2 Proportion of variation explained (R^2) in expenditure policy with twelve socio-economic variables, by institutional characteristics (in the total sample, the twelve independent variables explained 36% of the variation in expenditures).

INDEPENDENT VARIABLES	STRUCTURAL VARIABLES (per cent)		DEPENDENT VARIABLE
	Reformed institution		
	Government: commission	59	
	Government: council-manager	30	
	Constituency: at-large	36	
	Elections: non-partisan	41	
Twelve socio-economic variables			Expenditure/income ratio
	Unreformed institution		
	Government: mayor-council	42	
	Constituency: ward/mixed	49	
	Elections: partisan	59	

will test this hypothesis by using multiple correlation coefficients. Squaring these coefficients, called "multiple R's," will give us a summary measure of the total amount of variation in our dependent variables explained by our twelve independent variables.[19] The results of the correlation analysis are summarized in Figures 1 and 2.

[19] It is possible that the difference between any two correlations may be a function of very different standard deviations of the independent variables. A quick look at Table 2, however, suggests that this is not likely to affect the relationships we find.

On the whole, the results of the correlation analysis strikingly support the hypothesis, with the exception of commission cities. Thus, we can say, for example, that our twelve socio-economic variables explain 71 per cent of the variation in taxation policy in partisan cities, and 49 per cent of the variation in nonpartisan cities. In commission cities, however, socio-economic variables predict substantially more variations in both taxes and expenditures than in the unreformed mayor-council cities. The anomaly of commission governments is an interesting one, for they present, as we will see, marked exceptions to virtually every pattern of relationships we found. The substantial explanatory power of these socio-economic variables is not altered, but confined, by examining the variables independently. The rest of the correlations show a consistent pattern: reformed cities are less responsive to cleavages in their population than unreformed cities.

If one of the premises of the "political ethos" argument is that reformed institutions give less weight to the "private-regarding" and "artificial" cleavages in the population, that premise receives striking support from our analysis. Our data suggest that when a city adopts reformed structures, it comes to be governed less on the basis of conflict and more on the basis of the rationalistic theory of administration. The making of public policy takes less count of the enduring differences between White and Negro, business and labor, Pole and WASP. The logic of the bureaucratic ethic demands an impersonal, apolitical settlement of issues, rather than the settlement of conflict in the arena of political battle.

To Spend or Not to Spend

If efforts to expand or contract the scope of government stand at the core of municipal political life, they are nowhere better reflected than in the taxation and expenditure patterns of cities. A generation ago, Charles Beard wrote that, "In the purposes for which appropriations are made the policies of the city government are given concrete form—the culture of the city is reflected. Indeed, the history of urban civilization could be written in terms of appropriations, for they show what the citizens think is worth doing and worth paying for." [20] Pressures to expand and contract government regulations and services are almost always reflected one way or another in the municipal budget. Labor, ethnic groups, the poor, and the liberal community may press for additional services and these must be paid for; the business community may demand municipal efforts to obtain new industry by paring city costs to create a "favorable business climate"; or businessmen may themselves demand municipal services for new or old

[20] Charles A. Beard, *American Government and Politics* (New York: Macmillan, 1924, 4th ed.), p. 727.

business. In any case, few political conflicts arise which do not involve some conflict over the budget structure.

CLASS VARIABLES AND PUBLIC POLICIES

Part of the political rhetoric associated with the demand for a decrease in the scope of the national government is the argument that the initiative for policy-making should rest more with the state and local governments. Opposition to federal spending levels, as V. O. Key has demonstrated, is found more often among persons with middle class occupations than among blue-collar workers.[21] It is not inconceivable that the middle class argument about state and local responsibility might be more than political rhetoric, and that at the local level, middle class voters are willing to undertake major programs of municipal services, requiring large outlays of public capital. Wilson and Banfield have argued that the "public-regarding" upper-middle class voters in metropolitan areas are often found voting for public policies at variance with their "self-interest narrowly conceived," and that "the higher the income of a ward or town, the more taste it has for public expenditures of various kinds." Similarly a longitudinal study of voting patterns in metropolitan Cleveland found that an index of social rank was positively correlated with favorable votes on welfare referenda. If these data reflect middle-class willingness to spend on a local level, they might indicate that the "states' rights" arguments was more than ideological camouflage: middle class voters stand foursquare behind public expenditures at the local level even when they oppose those expenditures from the national government. Therefore, we hypothesized that:

2a. The more middle class the city, measured by income, education, and occupation, the higher the municipal taxes and expenditures.

In line with our general concern of testing the impact of political structures on municipal policies, we also hypothesized that:

2b. Unreformed cities reflect this relationship more strongly than reformed cities.

With respect to hypothesis *2a*, the data in Table 4 on three middle class indicators are unambiguous and indicate a strong rejection of the hypothesis. However we measure social class, whether by income, education, or occupation, class measures are negatively related to public taxes and expenditures.

It is possible, however, that income does not have a linear, but rather

[21] V. O. Key, *Public Opinion and American Democracy* (New York: Alfred A. Knopf, 1961), p. 124.

TABLE 4 *Correlations Between Middle Class Characteristics and Outputs in Reformed and Unreformed Cities*

	Government type			Election type		Constituency type	
Correlations of	Mayor-council	Manager	Commission	Partisan	Nonpartisan	Ward	At-large
Taxes with							
Median income	−.13	−.24	−.19	.03	−.19	−.17	−.22
White collar	−.23	−.12	−.62	−.21	−.33	−.30	−.32
Median education	−.36	−.22	−.08	−.45	−.24	−.48	−.18
Expenditures with							
Median income	−.19	−.32	−.43	−.04	−.32	−.23	−.34
White collar	−.24	−.23	−.58	−.18	−.39	−.32	−.35
Median education	−.32	−.36	−.26	−.36	−.38	−.44	−.32

a curvilinear relationship with municipal outputs. Banfield and Wilson argue that "In the city, it is useful to think in terms of three income groups—low, middle, and high. Surprising as it may seem to Marxists, the conflict is generally between an alliance of low-income and high-income groups on one side and the middle-income groups on the other." If the relationship between income and expenditure is curvilinear, then we should expect to find that proportions of both low- and high-income groups are positively correlated with outputs. Our data, however, lend no support to this notion of a "pro-expenditure" alliance. Rather, the proportion of the population with incomes below $3000 is positively correlated with expenditures in all city types (although the relationships are small) and the proportion of the population in the above $10,000 bracket is negatively correlated with expenditures. Summing the two measures and correlating the combined measure with outputs produced no correlation greater than .15 and the relationships were as likely to be negative as positive. Tests for nonlinearity also suggested that no such coalition exists in the cities in our analysis.

To be sure, aggregate data analysis using whole cities as units of analysis is no substitute for systematic survey data on middle-class attitudes, but it is apparent that cities with larger middle class population have lower, not higher expenditures. As we emphasized earlier, the "ethos theory" deals with attitudes and the behavior of individuals, while our data deal with cities and their behavior. The coalition suggested by Banfield and Wilson, however, is not discernible at this level of aggregation in these cities.

Hypothesis 2*b* is not consistently borne out by the data. In fact, the

TABLE 5 *Correlations Between Owner Occupancy and Government Outputs in Reformed and Unreformed Cities*

Correlations of owner occupancy with:	Government type			Election type		Constituency type	
	Mayor-council	Manager	Commission	Partisan	Nonpartisan	Ward	At-large
Taxes	−.57	−.31	−.73	−.64	−.45	−.56	−.48
Expenditures	−.51	−.23	−.62	−.62	−.40	−.50	−.40

relationship between middle class variables and outputs are, if anything, stronger in the reformed than in the unreformed cities. One would not want to make too much out of the data, but a large body of literature on city politics, which we discuss below, suggests that reformed institutions maximize the power of the middle class.

We originally assumed that the proportion of owner-occupied dwelling units constituted another measure of middle class composition, but it soon became apparent that it was only weakly related to income, occupation, and education measures. Nevertheless, it emerged as the strongest single predictor of both expenditure and taxation policy in our cities. We hypothesized that:

3*a*. Owner-occupancy and outputs are negatively correlated, and
3*b*. Unreformed cities reflect this relationship more strongly than reformed cities.

Hypothesis 3*a* is consistently borne out in the data presented in Table 5. These relationships were only slightly attenuated when we controlled for income, education, and occupation. No doubt self-interest (perhaps "private-regardingness") on the part of the home owner, whose property is intimately related to the tax structure of most local governments, may account for part of this relationship. Moreover, home ownership is correlated (almost by definition) with lower urban population density. High density, bringing together all manner of men into the classic urban mosaic, may be itself correlated with factors which produce demands for higher expenditures—slums, increased needs for fire and police protection, and so on.

In confirmation of hypothesis 3 *a*, the unmistakable pattern is for unreformed cities to reflect these negative relationships more strongly than the manager, nonpartisan and at-large cities, although commission cities show their usual remarkably high correlations.

TABLE 6 *Correlations Between Ethnicity and Religious Heterogeneity and Outputs in Reformed and Unreformed Cities*

	Government type			Election type		Constituency type	
Correlations of	Mayor-council	Manager	Commission	Partisan	Nonpartisan	Ward	At-large
Taxes wtih							
Ethnicity	.49	.26	.57	.61	.43	.56	.40
Private school attendance	.38	.15	.37	.33	.37	.41	.25
Expenditures with							
Ethnicity	.36	.02	.21	.48	.21	.44	.13
Private school attendance	.34	—.01	.07	.25	.24	.40	.05

HOMOGENEITY VARIABLES AND PUBLIC POLICIES

Dawson and Robinson, in their analysis of state welfare expenditures, found strong positive relationships between the ethnicity of a state's population and the level of its welfare expenditures.[22] If this is symptomatic of a generalized association of ethnic and religious minorities with higher expenditures, we might find support for the hypothesis that:

4*a*. The larger the proportion of religious and ethnic minorities in the population, the higher the city's taxes and expenditures.

And, if our general hypothesis about the impact of political institutions is correct, then:

4*b*. Unreformed cities reflect this relationship more strongly than reformed cities.

The correlations between ethnicity, religious heterogeneity, and outputs (see Table 6) are, with one exception, positive, as predicted by hypothesis 4*a*. These associations may reflect the substantial participation by ethnic groups in municipal politics long after the tide of immigration has been reduced to a trickle. The relatively intense politicization of ethnic groups at the local level, the appeals to nationality groups through "ticket balancing" and other means, and the resultant higher turnout of ethnic

[22] Richard E. Dawson and James A. Robinson, "The Politics of Welfare," in Herbert Jacob and Kenneth Vines, eds., *Politics in the American States* (Boston: Little, Brown and Co., 1965), pp. 398–401.

groups than other lower status groups, may produce an influence on city government far out of proportion to their number.

We found when we related all twelve of our independent variables to outputs in various city types that the associations were much weaker in cities we have labeled reformed. The correlations for ethnicity and religious homogeneity show a generally similar pattern, with commission cities exhibiting their usual erratic behavior. The data, then, show fairly clear support for hypothesis 4*b*.

The third variable of our homogeneity indicators—per cent of population nonwhite—had almost no relationship to variation in outputs, regardless of city type. We found the same weak correlations for the poverty income variable, which was, of course, strongly related to the racial variable. An easy explanation suggests that this is a consequence of the political importance of Negroes and the poor, but one should be cautious in inferring a lack of power from the lack of a statistical association.

We have dealt in this section with factors which are positively and negatively related to spending patterns in American cities. While social class variables are associated negatively with outputs, two measures of homogeneity—private school attendance and ethnicity—are positively related to higher taxes and spending. Examining the strengths of these correlations in cities with differing forms, we found some support for our general hypothesis about the political consequences of institutions, especially for the homogeneity variables and the home ownership variable. Interestingly, however, this was not the case with class variables.

Reformism as a Continuous Variable

The central thrust of our argument has been that reformed governments differ from their unreformed counterparts in their responsiveness to socio-economic cleavages in the population. Logically, if the presence of one feature of the "good government" syndrome had the impact of reducing responsiveness, the introduction of additional reformed institutions should have an additive effect and further reduce the impact of cleavages on decision-making. We therefore decided to treat "reformism" as a continuous variable for analytic purposes and hypothesized that:

5. The higher the level of reformism in a city, the lower its responsiveness to socio-economic cleavages in the population.

We utilized a simple four-point index to test this hypothesis, ranging from the "least reformed" to the "most reformed." The sample cities were categorized as follows:

1. Cities with none of the reformed institutions (i.e., the government is mayor-council, elections are partisan and constituencies are wards).

TABLE 7 *Correlations Between Selected Independent Variables and Output Variables by Four Categories of Reformism*

Correlations of	Reform scores 1 (Least reformed)	2	3	4 (Most reformed)
Taxes with				
Ethnicity	.62	.41	.50	.34
Private school attendance	.40	.32	.28	.25
Owner-occupancy	—.70	—.39	—.54	—.44
Median education	—.55	—.27	—.32	—.13
Expenditures with				
Ethnicity	.51	.27	.41	.05
Private school attendance	.46	.23	.16	.08
Owner-occupancy	—.67	—.30	—.54	—.38
Median education	—.49	—.19	—.38	—.37

2. Cities with any one of the reformed institutions.
3. Cities with two of the reformed institutions.
4. Cities with three reformed institutions (i.e., the government is either manager or commission, elections are nonpartisan and constituencies are at-large).

We cannot over emphasize the crudity of this index as an operationalization of the complex and abstract concept of "reformism." Nonetheless, we think some of the relationships we found are strongly suggestive that reformism may in reality be a continuous variable.

To test this hypothesis, we took four variables which had moderate to strong correlations with our dependent variables and computed simple correlations in each reform category. If our hypotheses is correct, the strength of the correlations in Table 7 should decrease regularly with an increase in reform scores. While there are some clear exceptions to the predicted pattern of relationships, there is some fairly consistent support for the hypothesis. Even when the decrease in the strength of the correlations is irregular, there is a clear difference between cities which we have labeled "most reformed" and "least reformed."

Again, we would not want to attach too much importance to the results of this rough-and-ready index. But the patterns support our previous argument about the impact of reformism: the more reformed the city, the less responsive it is to socio-economic cleavages in its political decision-making.

A Causal Model and an Interpretation

A CAUSAL MODEL

The implicit, or at times explicit, causal model in much of the research on municipal reformism has been a simple one: socio-economic cleavages cause the adoption of particular political forms. A more sophisticated model would include political institutions as one of the factors which produce a given output structure in city politics. We hypothesize that a causal model would include four classes of variables: socio-economic cleavages, political variables (including party registration, structure of party systems, patterns of aggregation, strength of interest groups, voter turnout, etc.), political institutions, (form of government, type of elections, and type of constituencies), and political outputs. Figure 3 depicts one possible causal model.

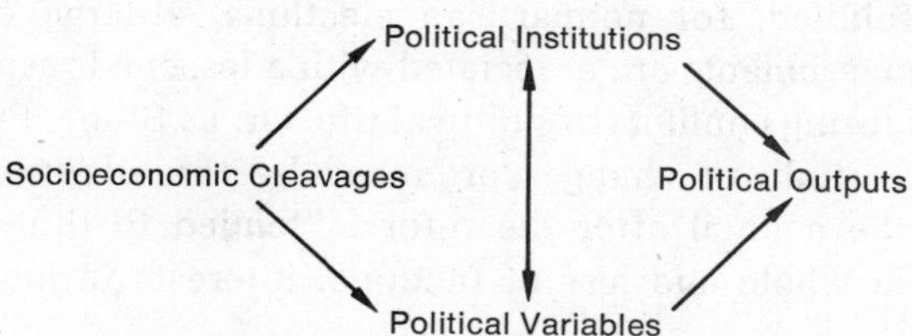

FIGURE 3 A hypothesized causal model.

This study has of necessity been limited to exploring the linkages between socio-economic cleavages, political institutions, and political outputs. We found that political institutions "filter" the process of converting inputs into outputs. Some structures, particularly partisan elections, ward constituencies, mayor-council governments, and commission governments, operate to maximize the impact of cleavage indicators on public policies. We conclude by discussing some of the reasons that different structures have varying impacts on the conversion process.

AN INTERPRETATION

Three principal conclusions may be derived from this analysis.

1. Cities with reformed and unreformed institutions are not markedly different in terms of demographic variables. Indeed, some variables, like income, ran counter to the popular hypothesis that reformed cities are havens of the middle class. Our data lent some support to the notion that reformed cities were more homogeneous in their

ethnic and religious populations. Still, it is apparent that reformed cities are by no means free from the impact of these cleavages.

2. The more important difference between the two kinds of cities is in their behavior, rather than their demography. Using multiple correlation coefficients, we were able to predict municipal outputs more exactly in unreformed than in reformed cities. The translation of social conflicts into public policy and the responsiveness of political systems to class, racial, and religious cleavages differ markedly with the kind of political structure. Thus, political institutions seem to play an important role in the political process—a role substantially independent of a city's demography.
3. Our analysis has also demonstrated that reformism may be viewed as a continuous variable and that the political structures of the reform syndrome have an additive effect: the greater the reformism, the lower the responsiveness.

Through these political institutions, the goal of the reformers has been substantially fulfilled, for nonpartisan elections, at-large constituencies, and manager governments are associated with a lessened responsiveness of cities to the enduring conflicts of political life. Or, as Stone, Price and Stone argued in their study of changes produced by the adoption of manager governments, the council after the reform "tended to think more of the community as a whole and less of factional interests in making their decisions." [23]

The responsiveness of a political institution to political conflicts should not be confused with the "responsibility" of a political system as the latter term is used in the great debate over the relative "responsibility" of party systems. In fact, the responsiveness of political forms to social cleavages may stand in sharp contrast to "responsible government" in the British model. Presumably, in American cities, partisan elections, ward constituencies, and mayor-council governments maximize minority rather than majority representation, assuring greater access to decision-makers than the reformed, bureaucratized, and "depoliticized" administrations.

Partisan electoral systems, when combined with ward representation, increase the access of two kinds of minority groups: those which are residentially segregated and which may, as a consequence of the electoral system, demand and obtain preferential consideration from their councilmen; and groups which constitute identifiable voting blocs to which parties and politicians may be beholden in the next election. The introduction of at-large, nonpartisan elections has at least five consequences for these groups. First, they remove an important cue-giving agency—the party—from the electoral scene, leaving the voter to make decisions less on the

[23] Harold Stone, Don K. Price and Kathryn Stone, *City Manager Government in the United States* (Chicago: Public Administration Service, 1940), p. 238.

policy commitments (however vague) of the party, and more on irrelevancies such as ethnic identification and name familiarity. Second, by removing the party from the ballot, the reforms eliminate the principal agency of interest aggregation from the political system; hence, interests are articulated less clearly and are aggregated either by some other agency or not at all. Moreover, nonpartisanship has the effect of reducing the turnout in local elections by working class groups, leaving officeholders freer from retaliation by these groups at the polls. Fourth, nonpartisanship may also serve to decrease the salience of "private-regarding" demands by increasing the relative political power of "public-regarding" agencies like the local press. And when nonpartisanship is combined with election at-large, the impact of residentially segregated groups, or groups which obtain their strength from voting as blocs in municipal elections is further reduced. For these reasons, it is clear that political reforms may have a significant impact in minimizing the role which social conflicts play in decision-making. By muting the demands of private-regarding groups, the electoral institutions of reformed governments make public policy less responsive to the demands which arise out of social conflicts in the population.

The structure of the government may serve further to modify the strength of minority groups over public policy. It is significant in this respect to note that commission governments, where social cleavages have the greatest impact on policy choices, are the most decentralized of the three governmental types and that manager governments are relatively the most centralized. From the point of view of the reformer, commission government is a failure and their number has declined markedly in recent years. This greater decentralization of commission and of mayor-council governments permits a multiplicity of access points for groups wishing to influence decision-makers. It may also increase the possibilities for collaboration between groups and a bureaucratic agency, a relationship which has characterized administrative patterns in the federal government. As a result of this decentralization, group strength in local governments may be maximized.

It is important in any analysis of reformism to distinguish between the factors which produce the *adoption* of reformed institutions and the *impact* of the new political forms once they have been established. We can offer from our data no conclusions about the origins of reformed structures, for it is obviously impossible to impute causation, using contemporary census data, to events which occurred decades ago. Once a city has institutionalized the reformers, . . . however, a diffused attitude structure may be less helpful in explaining the city's public policy than the characteristics of the institutions themselves. With the introduction of these reforms, a new political pattern may emerge in which disputes are settled outside the political system, or in which they may be settled by the crowd at the civic club at the periphery of the system. If they do enter the political process, an impersonal, "non-political" bureaucracy may take less account of the conflicting interests and pay more attention to the "correct" decision from the point of view of the municipal planner.

These conclusions are generally consistent with the ethos theory developed by Banfield and Wilson. If one of the components of the middle class reformer's ideal was "to seek the good of the community as a whole" and to minimize the impact of social cleavages on political decision-making, then their institutional reforms have served, by and large, to advance that goal.

Thomas R. Dye and L. Harmon Zeigler

Elites in States and Communities

Social scientists have clearly demonstrated in recent years that policy making is more a function of the elites than of the masses. Since the United States is a federal union, having according to the latest (1967) Census of Governments some 80,000 units of government, the number of elites involved in policy making is enormous. Although there is little doubt that the national elites wield great power, even at the height of their influence they do not touch all areas of American life. Decentralization is an outstanding feature of American government and politics, and decentralization, as Dye and Zeigler point out, means decision making by sub-elites.

The issues settled by sub-elites are to a large extent, then, kept out of the national political arena, so that national elites are relieved of the necessity of dealing with them. Moreover, policy made by sub-elites lessens the possibility of having to battle over the development of a single national policy to be adopted uniformly throughout the nation. Finally, sub-elites are probably more responsive to local needs than national elites would be—at least, the people seem to feel that this is the case. Thus sub-elites play a continuing and very likely expanding role in the governance of the American people and so warrant the kind of analysis Dye and Zeigler give them here.

Elite structures vary among the fifty states, but observers generally agree that economic elites are the most influential. The authors of *The Legislative System* interviewed state legislators in four states, asking them

---

Reprinted from *The Irony of Democracy: An Uncommon Introduction to American Politics*, 2nd edition, by Thomas R. Dye and L. Harmon Zeigler. Footnotes have been renumbered.

which interests were perceived as most powerful.[1] In all four states, business interests were named the "most powerful groups" more often than any other interests; educational and labor interests, although important, were ranked below business interests in perceived influence. Agricultural interests, government interests (associations of city, county, and township governments, and government employee associations), ethnic interests, and religious, charitable, and civic interests were given only minor mention by state legislators.

It is difficult to measure the relative strength of economic interests in all fifty states. The strength of any interest group is a function of many factors, including resources, organization, leadership, prestige, "cohesion" (unity), and "access" (contacts) to decision makers. Some years ago, the American Political Science Association questioned social scientists in the several states, asking them to judge whether interest groups in their state were strong, moderately strong, or weak.[2] Their judgments are open to challenge, but they are probably the best testimony of interest group strength in the states. This classification of the states in terms of the strength of their interest groups does not focus exclusively upon economic interests; but it is reasonable to assume that the judgments of these observers were heavily influenced by economic factors.

Table 1 shows the relationship between the perceived strength of interest groups in the states, the level of inter-party competition, the degree of party cohesion, and the socioeconomic environments in the states. States with stronger interest groups are more likely to be (1) one-party states, rather than competitive two-party states; (2) states in which parties in the legislatures show little cohesion and unity; (3) states which are poor, rural and agricultural. Wealthy, urban, industrial states may have *more* interest groups, but it is difficult for a single interest to dominate the political scene. In contrast, the poorer, rural, agricultural states with relatively backward economies may have fewer interest groups, but the interest groups are stronger and may exercise considerable power over public policy. "These findings lend some empirical support to James Madison's belief [expressed in *Federalist* no. 10] that "the smaller the society, the fewer the number of interests, and the greater the likelihood that a single interest will dominate." Madison believed that the larger the political society, the less likely a single elite was to dominate its politics.

Let us divide the state elite systems into types to facilitate the identification of elite patterns in state politics. First, in the *single unified elite* system, usually found in a state with a non-diversified economy and weak,

[1] John Wahlke, *et al.*, *The Legislative System* (New York: John Wiley, 1964).

[2] See Belle Zeller, *American State Legislatures* (New York: Thomas Y. Crowell Co., 1954), pp. 190–191.

TABLE 1 *The Strength of Pressure Groups in Varying Political and Economic Situations*

Social conditions	Type of pressure system[a] Strong (24 states)†	Moderate (14 states)‡	Weak (7 states)§
Party competition			
One-party	33.3%	0.0%	0.0%
Modified one-party	37.5%	42.8%	0.0%
Two-party	29.1%	57.1%	100.0%
Cohesion of parties in legislature			
Weak cohesion	75.0%	14.2%	0.0%
Moderate cohesion	12.5%	35.7%	14.2%
Strong cohesion	12.5%	50.0%	85.7%
Socioeconomic variables			
Urban	58.6%	65.1%	73.3%
Per capita income	$1,900.	$2,335.	$2,450.
Industrialization index	88.8	92.8	94.0

From L. Harmon Zeigler and Hendrik van Dalen, "Interest Groups in the States" in *Politics in the American States: A Comparative Analysis*, Second Edition, edited by Herbert Jacob and Kenneth N. Vines, p. 127. Copyright © 1971 by Little Brown and Company (Inc.). Reprinted by permission.

[a] Alaska, Hawaii, Idaho, New Hampshire, and North Dakota are not classified or included.

† Alabama, Arizona, Arkansas, California, Florida, Georgia, Iowa, Kentucky, Louisiana, Maine, Michigan, Minnesota, Mississippi, Nebraska, New Mexico, North Carolina, Oklahoma, Oregon, South Carolina, Tennessee, Texas, Washington, Wisconsin.

‡ Delaware, Illinois, Kansas, Maryland, Massachusetts, Nevada, New York, Ohio, Pennsylvania, South Dakota, Utah, Vermont, Virginia, West Virginia.

§ Colorado, Connecticut, Indiana, Missouri, New Jersey, Rhode Island, Wyoming.

non-competitive parties, a cohesive group of economic interests dominate state politics. A good example of this type of elite system is Maine, of which Duane Lockard writes: "In few American states are the reins of government more openly, more completely in the hands of a few leaders of economic interest groups than in Maine.[3] Specifically, power, timber, and manufacturing—"the big three"—have combined into a cohesive economic elite, due to their key position in the economy of the state. Over three fourths of the state is woodland, and most of this land is owned by a handful of timber companies and paper manufacturers. The timber interests, combined with

[3] Duane Lockard, *New England State Politics* (Princeton, N.J.: Princeton University Press, 1959), p. 79.

power companies and textile and shoe manufacturers, "control" Maine politics to protect their own economic well being. The "predominant authority" of the big three is rarely challenged with a significant degree of organization or sustained effort.

The deep South states also display the cultural homogeneity and unified elites characteristic of non-diversified agricultural economies. In addition, Southern elites have traditionally benefited from the general consensus among the white masses that the Negro must be "kept in his place," and that any efforts by national elites to rearrange racial patterns must be met by a unified white community. Competition among Southern elites is considered particularly dangerous, since a split might contribute to Negro political influence. Occasionally, "populist" candidates have arisen from the masses to challenge temporarily the dominance of the planting, landowning, and financial elites in Southern states. But once in power, the demagogues have seldom implemented populist programs; more frequently they have become instruments of the established elites whom they castigated in campaign oratory.

A second type of elite structure we shall label *a dominant elite among lesser elites*. This structure is also found in states with a non-diversified economy, although the states may display a reasonably competitive party system, with moderate party cohesion in the legislature. The distinct feature of the dominant elite among lesser elites structure is the prevailing influence of a single company or industry. A classic example of this elite structure is Montana, where the Anaconda Company has exercised unparalleled influence for almost a century. In a state in which the extraction of minerals is the major non-agricultural source of personal income, Anaconda is the largest employer. In Montana politics, Anaconda is known simply as "the company." The immensity of the Anaconda empire is described by Thomas Paine:

> Its strength rests not only in its wealth and resources but also in its elaborate network of relationships with key citizens, banks, legal firms and business organizations throughout the state. Rare is that unit of local government —county, city, or school district—that does not have among its official family an associate, in some capacity, of the Anaconda Company.[4]

However, some leaders, such as Burton K. Wheeler, have built a political career out of opposition to the company, and the company has been forced to accept defeat on certain occasions when faced with a strong combination of lesser elites. In 1959, Anaconda sold its chain of newspapers in the

[4] Thomas Paine, "Under the Copper Dome: Politics in Montana," in Frank H. Jonas (ed.), *Western Politics* (Salt Lake City: University of Utah Press, 1961), pp. 197–198.

state and assumed a somewhat less visible role in electoral politics. In recent years, Anaconda has remained as quiet as possible, confining itself to legislation directly affecting its economic interests.

The position of Anaconda in Montana is roughly parallel to the position of single dominant economic interests in other states, such as oil in Texas, or DuPont in Delaware. Doubtless the reputation of these interests for absolute control of a state far exceeds their actual exercise of control over public policy; there are many issues in Delaware, for instance, in which the DuPont Corporation and the DuPont family do not become actively involved. Yet it is unlikely that the state of Delaware would ever enact legislation adversely affecting the DuPont Corporation. Likewise, the reputation for oil control of Texas politics is exaggerated. The chairman of the Texas Democratic Executive Committee once said: "It may not be a wholesome thing to say, but the oil industry today is in complete control of state politics and state government." [5] This is an overstatement that one frequently hears in political circles; many issues in state politics are of little concern to the oil interests. However, it is unlikely that Texas politicians will ever oppose the oil depletion allowance in the federal tax structure, for this is a matter of direct and vital concern to the oil producers.

A *bipolar elite* structure is most likely to be found in an industrial, urban, competitive state with strong and cohesive political parties. Michigan is the prototype of this form of elite structure. While Michigan's economy is industrial rather than agricultural, it is non-diversified and heavily dependent upon the automotive industry; the automobile manufacturers are the largest single employer. But automobile manufacturers do not dominate Michigan politics, because organized labor has emerged as an effective counter-elite to the automobile manufacturers. Walter Reuther, president of the United Automobile Workers, and George Romney, former president of American Motors, are both influential members of Michigan's bipolar elite system. Joseph La Palombara concludes that "no major issues of policy (taxation, social legislation, labor legislation, etc.) are likely to be decided in Michigan without the intervention, within their respective parties and before agencies of government, of automotive labor and automotive management." [6] Labor and management elites in Michigan each have "their own" political party, and polarization in the elite system is accompanied by strong competition between well-organized, cohesive, and disciplined Democratic (labor) and Republican (management) party organizations.

A *plural elite* structure is typical of a state with a highly diversified

[5] Robert Engler, *The Politics of Oil* (New York: Macmillan Co., 1961), p. 354.

[6] Joseph La Palombara. *Guide to Michigan Politics* (East Lansing: Michigan University. Bureau of Social and Political Research, 1960), p. 104.

economy. California may have the most diversified economy of any state in the nation, with thriving agricultural interests, timber and mining resources, and manufacturing enterprises that run the gamut from cement to motion pictures. The railroads, the brewers, the race tracks, the motion pictures, the citrus growers, the airplane manufacturers, the insurance companies, the utilities, the defense contractors, and a host of other economic interests co-exist in this state. No one economic interest or combination of interests dominates California politics. Instead, a variety of elites govern within specific issue areas; each elite concentrates its attention on matters directly affecting its own economic interest. Occasionally, the economic interests of elites may clash, but on the whole co-existence, rather than competition, characterizes the relationships among elites. Political parties are somewhat less cohesive and disciplined in the plural elite system. Economic elites, hesitating to become too closely identified with a single party, even make financial contributions to opposing candidates to insure that their interests will be protected regardless of which party or candidate wins office.

Single Elites in American Communities

One of the earliest studies of community elites was the classic study of Middletown, conducted by Robert and Helen Lynd in the middle 1920s, and again in the mid-1930s.[7] In Muncie, Indiana, the Lynds found a monolithic power structure dominated by the owners of the town's largest industry, the "X" family. Community power was firmly entrenched in the hands of the business class, which controlled the economic life in the city, particularly through its ability to control the extension of credit. The city was run by a "small top group" of "wealthy local manufacturers, bankers, the local head managers of . . . national corporations with units in Middletown, and . . . one or two outstanding lawyers." Democratic procedures and governmental institutions were window dressing for business control. The Lynds described the typical city official as a "man of meager caliber" and as a "man whom the inner business control group ignores economically and socially and uses politically." Perhaps the most famous passage from the Lynds' study was a comment by a Middletown man made in 1935:

> If I'm out of work, I go to the X plant; if I need money I go to the X bank, and if they don't like me I don't get it; my children go to the X college; when I get sick I go to the X hospital; I buy a building lot or house in the X subdivision; my wife goes downtown to buy X milk; I drink X beer, vote for X political parties and get help from X charities;

[7] Robert S. and Helen M. Lynd. *Middletown* (New York: Harcourt, Brace & World, 1929); and *Middletown in Transition* (New York: Harcourt, Brace & World, 1937).

> my boy goes to the X YMCA and my girl to their YWCA; I listen to the word of God in a X subsidized church; if I'm a Mason, I go to the X Masonic temple; I read the news from the morning paper; and, if I'm rich enough, I travel via the X airport.[8]

W. Lloyd Warner, who studied Morris, Illinois, in the 1940s, describes a power structure somewhat similar to that encountered by the Lynds in Muncie. About one third of all of the city's workers had jobs in "The Mill," which Warner says dominated the town:

> The economic and social force of the mill affects every part of the life of the community. Everyone recognizes its power. Politicians, hat in hand, wait upon Mr. Waddell, manager of The Mill, to find out what he thinks on such important questions as "Shall the tax rate be increased to improve the education our young people are getting?"—"Should the city support various civic and world enterprises?"—"Should new industries enter the town and possibly compete with The Mill for the town's available labor supply?" They want to know what Mr. Waddell thinks. Mr. Waddell usually lets them know.[9]

Hollingshead studied the same town (sociologists seem to prefer to disguise the names of towns they are studying: Warner called the town Jonesville, Hollingshead called it Elmtown), and his findings substantially confirmed Warner's.[10] And in sociologist Floyd Hunter's influential study of Atlanta, Georgia[11] (presented in Chapter 1 of this book as a prototype of the "ruling elite" model of power), community policy is described as originating in a group composed primarily of business, financial, religious, and education leaders rather than from the people of the community.

Business approval of community projects is considered essential, especially on proposals involving great change in the community—metropolitan area government, urban renewal, public housing, freeway construction, and other massive public works requiring bond issues, condemnation of properties, and increased tax burdens. Business support bestows great prestige on a proposal, and the low prestige of municipal officials helps to explain why businessmen are needed to help promote any major community project. Moreover, middle-class people, whose vote is important in local politics, tend to respect the views of businessmen more than the views of city officials. Peter B. Clark quotes a Chicago attorney who has long been involved in civic affairs:

[8] Lynd and Lynd, *Middletown in Transition,* p. 74.

[9] W. Lloyd Warner, *Democracy in Jonesville* (New York: Harper & Row, 1949), p. 10.

[10] August B. Hollingshead, *Elmtown's Youth* (New York: John Wiley, 1949).

[11] Floyd Hunter, *Community Power Structure* (Chapel Hill: University of North Carolina Press, 1953).

> By and large, those with strong business backgrounds command greater respect . . . than those with the same skills who don't have that background. And the same is true of a lawyer versus the president of General Motors. They both could say the same thing . . . but the president would be listened to more. They transfer part of their business achievement into their public life.[12]

The views of businessmen are also respected because the community's economic growth and prosperity are linked to business firms and the men who head them. A community that depends upon the businessmen for employment must seriously consider the suggestion that a particular proposal might "hurt business" or "slow down the economy." Only occasionally is a firm required to threaten to close down and move elsewhere in order to get its way in policy matters. Business support lends a "conservative" image to community proposals. Businessmen are expected to be sound guardians of the status quo, who oppose "radical" sweeping changes in governmental structure, tax programs, and public services. Thus, the endorsement by these conservatives of any new program helps to assure the community that the program does not represent a radical break with the past.

In addition to the respect and prestige it lends, business support is also sought because so many community projects—public works, urban renewal, schools, streets, auditoriums, and hospitals—require financial investment; and banks and investment firms must underwrite the bond issues. Businessmen also have technical information that local governments, normally operating without a large professional staff, cannot themselves provide. Finally, business support often disarms potentially influential businessmen who might oppose a proposal if they were not consulted about it in its earliest stages.

The influence of businessmen can be felt even in matters in which they are not directly involved. Many government officials and civic organization workers admit that they anticipate the views of big businessmen in policy decisions, even when the businessmen are not directly consulted. Peter Clark quotes a civic staff man who explained why a particular community project failed: "This thing wasn't done right. It was just announced. The power structure and the newspaper people weren't checked out. All hell broke loose." Another staff man revealed both his style and his motives when he said: "My method of operation is to touch base early before I raise a question. I do my homework thoroughly to get the controversy out of it. Either revise it or throw it out. I have never proposed anything that hasn't been accepted. I don't want to propose anything that would fail."

[12] Peter B. Clark, *The Businessman as a Civic Leader* (New York: Free Press, 1964), pp. 6, 11.

Plural Elites in American Communities

Pluralist models of community power stress the fragmentation of authority, the influence of elected public officials, the importance of organized group activity, and the roles of public opinion and elections in determining public policy. Who, then, rules in the pluralist community? Different small groups of interested and active citizens rule in different issue areas with some overlap, if any, by public officials, and occasional intervention by a larger number of people at the polls. Citizens' influence is felt not only through organized group activity, but also through elites anticipating the reactions of citizens and endeavoring to satisfy their demands. Leadership in community affairs is exercised not only by elected public officials, but also by interested individuals and groups who confine their participation to one or two issue areas. The pluralist model regards interest and activity, rather than economic resources, as the key to elite membership. Competition, fluidity, access, and equality characterize community politics.

Perhaps the most influential of the pluralist community studies was Robert Dahl's *Who Governs?*, a detailed analysis of decision making in New Haven, Connecticut. Dahl's description of New Haven is presented in Chapter 1 as an example of a polycentric and dispersed system of elites. But Aaron Wildavsky's study of Oberlin, Ohio, revealed, if anything, an even more pluralistic structure of decision making than Dahl found in New Haven. Oberlin was a reaffirmation of small-town democracy, where "the roads to influence . . . are more than one; elites and non-elites can travel them, and the toll can be paid with energy and initiative as well as wealth." [13]

Wildavsky studied eleven community decisions in Oberlin, including such diverse issues and events as the determination of municipal water rates, the passage of the fair housing ordinance, the division of United Appeal Funds, and a municipal election. He found "that the number of citizens and outside participants who exercise leadership in most cases is an infinitesimal part of the community," but that no person or group exerted leadership on *all* issue areas. To the extent that overlap among leaders in issue areas existed, the overlap involved public officials—the city manager, the mayor, and city councilmen—who owed their positions directly or indirectly to "expressions of the democratic process through a free ballot with universal suffrage." Leaders often competed among themselves and did not appear united by any common interest. Persons exercising leadership were of somewhat higher social status than the rest of the

[13] Aaron Wildavsky, *Leadership in a Small Town* (Totowa, N.J.: Bedminster Press, 1964), pp. 8, 217, 265.

community, but it was not status or wealth that distinguished leaders from non-leaders; it was their degree of interest and activity in public affairs.

Edward Banfield's excellent description of decision making in Chicago also fails to reveal a single "ruling elite," although the structure of influence is centralized. Banfield finds that Mayor Daley's political organization, rather than a business or financial elite, is the center of Chicago's influence structure. According to Banfield:

> Civic controversies in Chicago are not generated by the efforts of politicians to win votes, by differences about ideology or group interest, or by the behind-the-scenes efforts of a power elite. They arise, instead, out of the maintenance and enhancement needs of large formal organizations. The heads of an organization see some advantage to be gained by changing the situation. They propose changes. Other large organizations are threatened. They oppose, and a civic controversy takes place.[14]

It is not usually business organizations that propose changes in Chicago; "in most of the cases described here the effective organizations are public ones, and their chief executives are career civil servants." Though business and financial leaders played an important role in Chicago politics, they did not constitute a single elite.

After studying seven major decisions in Chicago, Banfield concluded that political heads such as Mayor Daley, public agencies, and civic associations employed top business leaders to lend prestige and legitimacy to policy proposals. The "top leaders" of Chicago—the Fields, McCormacks, Ryersons, Swifts, and Armours—and the large corporations—Inland Steel, Sears Roebuck, Field's Department Store, and the Chicago Title and Trust Company—were criticized less for interfering in public affairs than for "failing to assume their civic responsibilities." Few top leaders participated directly in the decisions studied by Banfield. Banfield admits that this fact is not proof that the top business leadership did not influence decisions behind the scenes; and he acknowledges the widespread belief in the existence of a ruling elite in Chicago. He quotes the head of a Negro civic association as saying: "There are a dozen men in this town who could go into City Hall and order an end to racial violence just like you or I could go into a grocery store and order a loaf of bread. All they would have to do is say what they wanted and they would get it." Banfield states that top business leaders in Chicago have great "potential for power"—"Indeed, if influence is defined as the *ability* to modify behavior in accordance with one's intentions, there can be little doubt that there exist 'top leaders' with aggregate influence sufficient to run the city"—but he maintains that these

[14] Edward Banfield, *Political Influence* (New York: Free Press, 1961), pp. 263, 289, 290.

top leaders do not, in fact, run the city. Business leaders, divided by fundamental conflicts of interest and opinion, do not have sufficient unity of purpose in community politics to decide controversial questions. They have no effective communication system that would enable them to act in concord; and they lack the organization to carry out their plans, even if they could agree on what should be done.

Sub-Elites: A Comparative View

Differing descriptions of the structures of power in American communities may be a product of the differences among social scientists in theory and methods of research. It is likely, however, that community power structures in the United States range from monolithic elites to very dispersed pluralistic elites. Unfortunately, we do not yet know enough about community power structures across the nation to estimate the frequency of different structures.

The key to understanding community power is relating the types of power structure to local social, economic, and political conditions. For example, we may find that large communities with a great deal of social and economic diversity, a competitive party system, and a variety of well-organized, competing interest groups have pluralist elite systems. On the other hand, small communities with a homogeneous population, a single dominant industry, non-partisan elections, and few competing organizations may be governed by a single cohesive elite.

One of the most important comparative studies of community power was made by Agger, Goldrich, and Swanson, an intensive study of "power and impotence" in four American communities during a fifteen-year period.[15] These scholars identified four types of power structure based upon the degree of citizen participation and influence and the degree of competition and conflict among political leaders (Table 2). If many citizens shared political influence and two or more leadership groups competed with each other, the community was said to have a "competitive mass" power structure. If many citizens shared political influence, but little disagreement or conflict occurred among leaders, the community's power structure was termed "consensual mass." If few citizens shared political influence and leaders rarely disagreed among themselves, the power structure was said to be "consensual elite." If few citizens shared political influence but leaders divided into competing groups, the community was said to have a "competitive elite" structure.

The "consensual elite" structure most closely resembles the monolithic or single elite model described earlier, because citizen influence is limited

[15] Robert Agger, Daniel Goldrich, and Bert Swanson, *The Rulers and the Ruled* (New York: John Wiley, 1964).

TABLE 2 *Types of Power Structures*

Political leadership	Distributions of political power among citizens	
	Broad	Narrow
Convergent	Consensual mass	Consensual elite
Divergent	Competitive mass	Competitive elite

Source: Robert Agger, Daniel Goldrich, and Bert Swanson, *The Rulers and the Ruled* (New York: John Wiley, 1964), p. 73. Reprinted by permission of the publisher.

and leaders share a single ideology. The "competitive mass" structure most closely resembles our pluralist model, inasmuch as many citizens share power and competitions occurs among leadership groups. The "ideal" community is probably the "consensual mass" type, in which influence is widely shared among the citizens and little conflict occurs among leaders. The municipal reform movement envisions such a community, in which democracy prevails and "reasonable men" agree to govern in "the public interest."

The authors also proposed a typology of community "regimes" based upon the recognized "rules of the game" in community politics and the degree to which people believe that citizens can be politically effective (Table 3). When the "rules of the game" are followed by political leaders, the regime is labeled a "developed democracy" if citizens believe they can influence policy, and an "undeveloped democracy" if they believe they cannot. If leaders frequently resort to illegitimate means—including loss of employment, discrimination, or severe social ostracism—to curtail political participation or free expression, the regime is labeled either a "guided democracy," if public confidence remains high, or an "oligarchy," if people no longer feel they can affect policy.

The Rulers and the Ruled study produced many interesting findings about community power. The "competitive mass" type of power structure (pluralist) is related to a "developed democracy" regime. A sense of political effectiveness among citizens and adherence to the rules of games by leaders is essential for the development of broad citizen participation in community affairs and the emergence of competitive leadership groups. A lack of political confidence among residents and a widespread belief that political activity is useless often result in a monopoly of political leadership and a "consensual elite" (monolithic) power structure.

If leadership changes from competitive to consensual, the distribution of power changes from mass to elite. In other words, with the disappearance of competition among leadership factions, citizen participation declines, fewer issues are submitted to popular referenda, and the power distribution becomes more elitist. Conversely, when the distribution of power changes

TABLE 3 *Types of Regimes*

Sense of political effectiveness	Probability of illegitimate sanctions being used	
	Low	High
High	Developed democracy	Guided democracy
Low	Undeveloped democracy	Oligarchy

Source: Robert Agger, Daniel Goldrich, and Bert Swanson, *The Rulers and the Ruled* (New York: John Wiley, 1964), p. 183. Reprinted by permission of the publisher.

from elite to mass—that is, when an increasing number of people begin to "crack" the power structure—political competition is likely to increase.

A "competitive mass" (pluralist) type of power structure will be more stable through time if the competing leadership groups represent high and low socioeconomic classes than if the competitors represent the same socioeconomic class. Pluralism depends in part upon socioeconomic cleavages in the community being represented by separate leadership groups. When competitive leaders represent the sam socioconomic class, competition can easily disappear over time, and the power structure can become "consensual" rather than "competitive."

Agger, Goldrich, and Swanson also find that "developed democracy" regimes and "competitive mass" power structures are less likely to occur in communities in which the major industries are home-owned. Economic leaders of home-owned industries tend to be members of a single group of political leaders that discourage competition. The prominence of these people influences some groups in their communities to refrain from political activity because they fear illegitimate political sanctions, even though the actual use of these sanctions is relatively infrequent. Interestingly, Agger, Goldrich, and Swanson found no relationship between community size or growth rate and either the type of regime or the nature of the power structure in the four communities they studied.

SUGGESTED READINGS

The Policy-Making Environment

For a broader understanding of the subjects discussed in the preceding readings, the following bibliographical comments may prove helpful.

The most important general work in the field of electoral behavior is still Angus Campbell et al, *The American Voter*, available also in abridged form (New York: Wiley, 1964). For a concise examination of political participation at the state level, see Lester C. Milbrath, "Individuals and Government," in Herbert Jacob and Kenneth N. Vines, eds., *Politics in the American States*, 2nd ed. (Boston: Little, Brown, 1971), 27–81. Of further interest is M. Kent Jennings and Richard Niemi's "Party Identification at Multiple Levels of Government," *American Journal of Sociology,* **72** (July 1966), 86–101, and Howard D. Hamilton's "The Municipal Voter: Voting and Nonvoting in City Elections," *American Political Science Review,* **65** (December 1971), 1135–1140.

See also:

Alford, Robert R., and Eugene C. Lee. "Voting Turnout in American Cities," *American Political Science Review,* **62** (September 1968), 796–813.

Banfield, Edward C., and James Q. Wilson. *City Politics.* Cambridge, Mass.: Harvard University Press, 1965.

Boskoff, Alvin, and L. Harmon Zeigler. *Voting Patterns in a Local Election.* Philadelphia: Lippincott, 1964.

Boynton, G. R., Samuel C. Patterson, and Ronald D. Hedland. "The Structure of Public Support for Legislative Institutions," *Midwest Journal of Political Science* **12** (May 1968), 163–180.

Burnham, Walter Dean. "The Changing Shape of the American Political Universe," *Americal Political Science Review,* **59** (March 1965), 7–28.

Burnham, Walter Dean, and John Sprague. "Additive and Multiplicative Models of the Voting Universe: The Case of Pennsylvania: 1960–1968," *American Political Science Review,* **64** (June 1970), 471–490.

Campbell, Angus, Donald E. Stokes, Warren Miller, and Philip Converse. *Elections and the Political Order.* New York: Wiley, 1966.

Eulau, Heinz, ed. *Political Behavior in America.* New York: Random House, 1966.

Jennings, M. Kent, and L. Harmon Zeigler, eds. *The Electoral Process.* Englewood Cliffs, N.J.: Prentice-Hall, 1966.

Levin, Murray B., ed. *The Alienated Voter: Politics in Boston.* New York: Holt, Rinehart and Winston, 1960.

Milbrath, Lester C. *Political Participation.* Chicago: Rand McNally, 1966.

Patterson, Samuel C., John C. Wahlke, and G. R. Boynton. "Dimensions of Support in Legislative Systems," in Allan Kornberg, ed., *Legislatures in Comparative Perspective.* New York: McKay, 1973, 282–313.

Williams, Oliver P., and Charles R. Adrian. *Four Cities.* Philadelphia: University of Pennsylvania Press, 1963.

Zikmund, Joseph. "A Comparison of Political Attitude and Activity Patterns in Central Cities and Suburbs," *Public Opinion Quarterly,* **31** (Spring 1967), 69–75.

Policy outcomes analysis, examples of which are the readings by Fry and Winters and Lineberry and Fowler, has generated an extensive literature in recent years. The most controversial aspects of such analysis have involved the procedures for quantifying variables (such as industrialization or party competition) and the conclusions regarding the relative impact of socioeconomic variables (e.g., urbanization, per capita income) versus political system variables (e.g., party competition, malapportionment) on policy outcomes. For a critical review of this literature, see John H. Fenton and Donald N. Chamberlayne, "The Literature Dealing with the Relationship Between Political Process, Socioeconomic Conditions and Public Policies in the American States: A Selected Bibliographic Essay," *Polity,* **1** (Spring 1969), 383–404. A particularly insightful critique of policy outcomes studies as applied to the examination of the impact of reapportionment is William H. Bicker's "The Effects of Malapportionment in the States—A Mistrial," in Nelson W. Polsby, ed., *Reapportionment in the 1970s* (Berkeley: University of California Press, 1971).

With regard to policy outcomes in the states, the major works are Thomas R. Dye's *Politics, Economics and the Public: Policy Outcomes in the American States* (Chicago: Rand McNally, 1968) and Ira Sharkansky's *Spending in the American States* (Chicago: Rand McNally, 1968). At the urban level, a standard work is Alan K. Campbell and Seymour Sacks, *Metropolitan America* (New York: Collier-Macmillan, 1967).

See also:

Bahl, Roy H., and Robert J. Saunders. "Factors Associated with Variations in State and Local Government Spending," *Journal of Finance* (September 1966), 523–534.

Clarke, James W. "Environment, Process and Policy: A Reconsideration," *American Political Science Review,* **63** (December 1969), 1172–1182.

Crudde, Charles, and Donald J. McCrone. "Party Competitors and Welfare Policies in the American States," *American Political Science Review,* **63** (September 1969), 858–866.

Dawson, Richard E., and James A. Robinson. "Inter-party Competition, Economic Variables and Welfare Policies in the American States," *Journal of Politics,* **25** (May 1963), 265–289.

Dye, Thomas R. "Malapportionment and Public Policies in the States," *Journal of Politics,* **27** (August 1965), 586–601.

Eulau, Heinz, and Robert Eyestone. "Policy Maps of City Councils and Policy Outcomes: a Developmental Analysis," *American Political Science Review,* **62** (March 1968), 124–143.

Hawkins, Brett W. "A Note on Urban Political Structure, Environment, and Political Integration," *Polity,* **2** (Fall 1969), 32–48.

Hofferbert, Richard I. "The Relation Between Policy and Some Structural and Environmental Variables in the American States," *American Political Science Review,* **60** (March 1966), 73–82.

Hofferbert, Richard I. "Socioeconomic Dimensions of the American States: 1870–1960," *Midwest Journal of Political Science,* **12** (August 1968), 401–418.

Jacob, Herbert, and Michael Lipsky. "Outputs, Structures, and Power: An Assessment of Chances in the Study of State and Local Politics," *Journal of Politics,* **30** (May 1968), 510–538.

Morss, Elliot R. "Some Thoughts about the Determinants of State and Local Expenditures," *National Tax Journal,* **19** (March 1966), 75–103.

Sharkansky, Ira. "Economic Development, Regionalism and State Political Systems," *Midwest Journal of Political Science,* **12** (February 1968), 41–61.

Sharkansky, Ira, and Richard I. Hofferbert. "Dimensions of State Policy," in Herbert Jacob and Kenneth N. Vines, eds., *Politics in the American States,* 2nd ed. Boston: Little, Brown, 1971, 315–353.

Walker, Jack L. "The Diffusion of Innovation Among the American States," *American Political Science Review,* **63** (September 1969), 867–879.

The structure of power in states and communities continues to be one of the most controversial areas in political science literature. Most of the power structure analyses focus on national or local elite structures rather than on elites at the state level. However, H. H. Dalen and L. Harmon Zeigler's "Interest Groups in the States," in Herbert Jacob and Kenneth N. Vines, eds., *Politics in the American States,* 2nd ed. (Boston: Little, Brown, 1971), 122–162, and Richard I. Hofferbert's "Elite Influence in State Policy Formation: A Model for Comparative Inquiry," *Polity,* **2** (Spring 1970), 316–344 are major efforts to analyze state elite structures.

At the urban level, Norton Long's "The Local Community as an Ecology of Games," *American Journal of Sociology,* **64** (November 1958), 251–261, is a pioneer study of the problem, while Robert Dahl's study of New Haven, *Who Governs?* (New Haven: Yale University Press, 1961) is still the leading example of the pluralist thesis, and Floyd Hunter's Atlanta study, *Community Power Structure* (Chapel Hill: University of North Carolina Press, 1953), is the basic statement of the pyramidal view. A recent case study of community power is Edward C. Hayes' *Power Structure and Urban Politics: Who Rules in Oakland?* (New York: McGraw-Hill, 1972).

See also:

Agger, Robert, Daniel Goldrich, and Bert Swanson. *The Rulers and the Ruled.* New York: Wiley, 1964.

Aiken, Michael, and Paul E. Mott, eds. *The Structure of Community Power.* New York: Random House, 1970.

Bachrach, Peter, and Morton S. Baratz. "Two Faces of Power," *American Political Science Review,* **56** (December 1962), 947–952.

Fox, Douglas M. "Methods Within Methods: The Case of Community Power Studies," *Western Political Quarterly,* **24** (March 1971), 5–11.

Gilbert, Claire W. "Communities, Power Structures and Research Bias," *Polity,* **4** (Winter 1971), 218–235.

Jennings, M. Kent. *Community Influentials: The Elites of Atlanta.* New York: Free Press, 1964.

Mills, C. Wright. *The Power Elite.* Fairlawn, N.J.: Oxford University Press, 1956.

Polsby, Nelson W. *Community Power and Political Theory.* New Haven: Yale University Press, 1963.

Salisbury, Robert H. "Urban Politics: The New Convergence of Power," *Journal of Politics,* **26** (December 1964), 775–797.

Wolfinger, Raymond E. "Nondecisions in the Study of Local Politics," *American Political Science Review,* **65** (December 1971), 1063–1080.

Part II

Policy Making and State Government

For many years after the establishment of the Union, government policy making was minimal, as most of the people's needs were met by their own efforts and our contacts with other nations were few and limited. It has only been in the 20th century that the role of government—and particularly that of state and local government in the domestic area—has become so critically important to the quality of American life. In Walter Heller's words,

> A very large part of what we do through government is through state and local units. They are the ones to whom we usually turn as we seek to maintain and upgrade our educational efforts, improve our physical and mental health, redevelop decaying urban areas, build safer and better highways, overcome air and water pollution, and equip our suburbs with water systems, sewers, roads, parks schools, and the like.
>
> Walter Heller, *New Dimensions of Political Economy* (Cambridge, 1967), pp. 121–22

Thus it is not surprising that studies of how state and local policies are made were slow in developing. Recently, however, a great deal of attention has been devoted to facets of state policy making; the selections that follow deal with four important variables therein: the governor, state executives, state legislatures, and the courts as factors in policy determination. It should be noted that policy analyses of state government are still young, and that with fifty states, we are still a long way from having achieved a full understanding of the policy process in the states.

J. Stephen Turett

The Vulnerability of American Governors, 1900–1969

The governor stands in an awkward position in state policy making. As J. Stephen Turett points out, he seems to be the state officer primarily responsible for the state's achieving its policy goals, yet in fact he lacks many of the considerable powers that are available to the President of the United States. Most students of state executive power agree with former Governor Terry Sanford of North Carolina that "governors [are] often unable to carry out the mission and the problem of the states" and that for them to do better their positions as policy makers need to be strengthened considerably.

First, however, it is necessary to analyze the position of the governor from a number of points of view in order to obtain the hard data on which to base recommendations for change. Turett employs four measures of gubernatorial vulnerability to test the proposition that governors have become increasingly vulnerable over the years.

A number of scholars have held that American governors are more politically vulnerable now than was true in earlier years, and, furthermore, that this increasing vulnerability is related to characteristics inherent in the office and not shared by other major elected officials. This has occurred, we are led to believe, concurrently with—and despite—the continuous growth of gubernatorial power. Most significant among the several supporting

Reprinted from the *Midwest Journal of Political Science,* Vol. 15, No. 1 (February 1971), pp. 108–132, by permission of the Wayne State University Press and the author. Some descriptive and bibliographical footnotes have been omitted for considerations of space and textual format.

elements upon which the thesis is based are these: (1) The states have inadequate revenue sources, but (2) their populations demand more and more public services, because (3) increasingly they are urbanized and industrialized. Voters more frequently are making extravagant and sometimes impossible demands on the governor. Or, put somewhat differently, voter expectations have begun to run far ahead of any reasonable level in action or accomplishment. The governor, therefore, is placed in the unenviable and precarious position of being held responsible for that over which he has little or no control. "A governor today," warned Malcolm Jewell,

> is caught in the crossfire between growing demands for services and a chorus of protests against rising taxes, between the problems of the sprawling metropolis and the stubborness of a rural legislature. He is a victim of midcentury federalism, with local governments demanding state aid faster than the national government . . . can expand its grants to the states. The governor is blamed for the lagging economy, depressed areas, and spreading unemployment, none of which he can control, and every move on his part to expand state services and revenues is criticized on the grounds that it will drive industry away.[1]

The governor, then, whether or not he has the formal authority or power, is forced to fight on all fronts—and is expected to emerge victorious. The disorders at the public university, a rise in tax rates, or a drop in employment are visible problems of importance; but they are only a fraction of the total. Governors are faced with a whole galaxy of problems, all of which are within their sphere of influence, few within their orbit of command. As the population has grown and the problems of a complex society proliferate, the solutions of an earlier era become mere palliatives. . . . As a result, the argument goes, more governors are being sent into involuntary retirement. Incumbents suffer; challengers benefit.

The governor whose continuance in office is doubtful must act differently than one whose tenure is secure. Any approaching election may turn the former into a lame duck: his hand in policy-making, legislative leadership, and administrative management could be seriously impaired. Those seeking re-election might hesitate to alienate even small segments of the population; instead, they would go slow, let things ride—or, at worst, do nothing. A pall of uncertainty might straitjacket even the most ambitious of governors.

And certainly not least in importance is the impact this would have

[1] "State Decision-Making: The Governor Revisited," in *American Governmental Institutions*, ed. by Aaron Wildavsky and Nelson W. Polsby (Chicago: Rand McNally & Company, 1968), pp. 545–546.

on the recruitment of qualified and talented individuals to serve in the office. The challenge might not be worth the time, effort, and money; the office itself could decline in prestige. While probably not the principal cause, high electoral vulnerability could contribute to the decline of governors as presidential timber. In earlier years the governorship was looked upon as a stepping-stone to the Presidency. Since 1876 thirteen governors—two via the Vice-Presidency—have become national standard-bearers of their party. Recently, however, governors have lost out to Senators as presidential candidates. . . . Eleven of the thirteen governors who became their party's candidate were nominated prior to 1940; and it has been almost 40 years since the state capitals produced a White House winner. Moreover, since 1952 the vice-presidential nominees of both major parties have, with only two exceptions, come exclusively from the Congress.

For the ambitious office-seeker the prospects for advancement are not particularly appealing. Today governors encounter many of the same problems—only usually on a more intensified scale—as faced by big city mayors. And the latter . . . face poor prospects for advancement. . . .

The plight of a governor is even more complicated given the fact that consistency and coherence in attitudes and activities by state voters can easily deteriorate into contradiction. Thus, taxation to finance welfare programs meets opposition among those who favor welfare programs even more frequently than among those who oppose them. The same people simultaneously want increased expenditures and reduced taxes. High spending, then, may provide only an evanescent protection to the charge of high taxes.

Given that the proposition concerning vulnerability is verifiable, it is surprising that little empirical evidence can be gathered in its support. Three salient questions will therefore be examined. (1) Have governors, in fact, become more vulnerable? (2) Does vulnerability vary with certain economic and demographic factors? (3) How do presidential elections impinge upon gubernatorial races?

I

Several criteria of vulnerability have been employed in this analysis: (1) the election outcome, (2) the change in a governor's winning margin, (3) the relative change in a governor's winning margin, and (4) a compared margin of victory. Each measures a slightly different aspect of vulnerability.

At the lowest level, vulnerability can be measured by the election outcome itself—that is, the victory or defeat of an incumbent. A comparison of the defeat rate over time is revealing, but hardly decisive: fluctuations in turnout or a popular head of the ticket can too easily spell the difference between winning and losing. Under these circumstances, it becomes more difficult to measure vulnerability accurately.

More importantly, a "winning percentage" [2] can be computed. We can then compare the governor's current margin of victory to his margin in the election immediately preceding. If the winning percentage for the two successive elections is the same, the change in the winning percentage is zero; if the previous winning margin exceeds the present one, the change is negative.[3] These electoral margins are, in a sense, a measure of vulnerability as a potential for defeat. Shrinking pluralities, in other words, can plausibly be equated with higher vulnerability.

National or statewide movements should also be taken into account in measuring gubernatorial vulnerability. In some elections it might be misleading, indeed incorrect, to consider a governor more vulnerable simply because there was a decline in his winning margin. What we need in effect is to compare the change in his party's fortune in general. If they vary together, the governor per se is not becoming more vulnerable. Free from the contamination of distracting trends and movements, the relative change in a governor's winning margin will enable us to determine the extent to which the electorate singles out the governor for special treatment. The resulting figure is a comparison of changes and, as such, may be considered the "critical change." [4] For example, when the change in a governor's winning percentage stands at − 5 per cent and that for his party at − 7 per cent, the critical change is + 2 per cent.

Since the governorship is more competitive than other state offices, voting for the latter cannot be expected to yield a valid indicator of general party strength. As V. O. Key observed:

> The special role of the governor in our politics accounts in part for the divergence between results of elections of governors and elections of other officials. The prominence of the governor in the field of public attention and the tendency of popular discontent and hope to center upon him often make candidates for that office either weaker or stronger than the general strength of the party, if such a generalized party following may be supposed to

[2] The concept is defined as "the difference between the percentage of total votes gained by the victor and that gained by the candidate with the next largest number of votes."

[3] The figure is calculated by subtracting the previous winning margin from the present one. The former will always be positive. Should a governor be defeated, however, in his bid for re-election, his current "winning" margin will be negative, and the change in this margin will, of course, be an even lower negative number.

[4] The critical change may be thought of simply as the relative change in a governor's winning percentage. It can, of course, take on both positive and negative values.

> exist. Crusades tend to form behind personalities, not parties.[5]

To approximate the political milieu of an incumbent governor after an election the statewide congressional (U.S. House of Representatives) vote can serve as a barometer of a state's present political temperament. The advantages of a figure based on congressional voting are as follows: (1) Congressional races are likely to be somewhat more competitive than races for most statewide offices; hence they should more closely resemble the competition for governor than would lesser state offices.[6] (2) The voting for congressional seats would be more likely to reflect national (or statewide) trends—not only detecting them but also indicating their relative strength. It would thus at least indirectly control for "extraneous" forces influencing the vote for governor. (3) Unlike data on state races, the congressional data are readily available.

Finally, to ascertain the present standing—and not merely the change in standing—of a governor vis-à-vis his party's candidates in House races, we can compare the two pluralities. A compared margin of victory will measure whether or not the governor ran ahead or behind his party's congressional candidates. Zero on this scale would not necessarily correspond to absolute uniformity in the partisan division of the vote for the two offices, but it would indicate indentical pluralities.

For present purposes a "gubernatorial incumbent" may be defined as the person holding the office of governor, provided that he has served at least one year. Those, therefore, succeeding to the office may, at times, be treated as incumbents.[7] There are many reasons for proceeding in this manner. Among the most significant is the fact that the nomination itself would be expected to indicate some fairly high level of political strength. It is noteworthy that about 40 per cent of those persons succeeding to the office did not, for one reason or another, receive the nomination of their party in the subsequent election.

Some successors will be considered incumbents because those benefits which traditionally accrue to an incumbent would also, even if in a lesser

[5] *American State Politics* (New York: Alfred A. Knopf, 1956), p. 205. Additionally, see the statement by Jewell, "State Decision-Making: The Governor Revisited," in Wildavsky and Polshy, p. 564: "When demands are made on government, they are made on the governor."

[6] This is probably true notwithstanding the contention that most of the seats in Congress are safe for one party or the other.

[7] Incumbency in most instances was ascertained from *The Governors of the States 1900–1966* (Chicago: Council of State Governments, 1966). The latter factor in the definition is negligible, comprising less than 5 per cent of all the elections with incumbents. If a successor's party affiliation differed from that of his predecessor—a not too uncommon situation in the earlier years—he was not considered an incumbent.

TABLE 1 *Governors Seeking Re-Election, by Period*

Period	Number of elections held	Elections with incumbents Number	Percent
I (1900–09)	76	35	46.1
II (1910–19)	77	44	57.1
III (1920–29)	77	37	48.1
IV (1930–39)	75	44	58.7
V (1940–49)	72	49	68.1
VI (1950–59)	68	44	64.7
VII (1960–69)	59	43	72.9

degree, be available to an incumbent's successor if he had served a long enough time. We would expect, for example, that a large amount of publicity would have surrounded his activities—something which most challengers could not be expected to have received over such an extended period of time. Of recognition, Stokes and Miller maintain: "In the main, recognition carries a positive valence; to be perceived at all is to be perceived favorably." [8]

Nineteen states with at least moderately competitive gubernatorial elections in both the pre- and post-Depression years,[9] and in which a governor could constitutionally succeed himself at least once, constitute the universe for this analysis.[10] These states, representing all regions with the single exception of the South, have held a total of 505 gubernatorial elections over the last 70 years. For analytical purposes the data[11] were examined in seven periods, each covering a decade of the 20th century. Ten

[8] Donald E. Stokes and Warren E. Miller, "Party Government and the Saliency of Congress," in Angus Campbell, Philip E. Converse, Warren E. Miller, and Donald E. Stokes, *Elections and the Political Order* (New York: John Wiley & Sons, Inc., 1966), p. 205. The statement was specifically made in regard to congressional candidates but probably has general applicability for most offices below President and Vice President.

[9] This does not mean of course that there would have been no utility in examining non-competitive states. What is crucial for a study of this type, however, is the place where the actual decision is made. In some states—especially, but not exclusively, the South—the crucial point for decision has been the primary. In these states the primary has been the election—the latter being, for all practical purposes, merely a ratification of a previous decision.

[10] All of the following remarks are confined to these states. States were first ranked according to the average margin of victory for governors from 1900–1928 and 1929–1969. This was then combined with a won-lost criterion to determine competitiveness. The status of each state (excluding Alaska and Hawaii) is given in the Appendix.

[11] Electoral data were made available through the Inter-University Consortium for Political Research. From 1900–1969 there have been a total of 1246 gubernatorial elections.

TABLE 2 *Partisan Affiliation of Governors Seeking Re-Election, by Period*

Period	Number of elections with incumbents		Percent of incumbents	
	Democratic	Republican	Democratic	Republican
I (1900–09)	9	26	25.7	74.3
II (1910–19)	21	23	47.7	52.3
III (1920–29)	18	19	48.6	51.4
IV (1930–39)	32	12	72.7	27.3
V (1940–49)	24	25	49.0	51.0
VI (1950–59)	20	24	45.4	54.6
VII (1960–69)	21	22	48.8	51.2

year intervals have a dual advantage: they are usually long enough to provide a large enough number of cases from which to generalize, and they are short enough to discern trends. As a check, three other intervals (seven, fourteen, and twenty-three years) were also examined, none of which altered the general findings.

II

At the outset, two things are immediately noticeable. In the first place, the number of gubernatorial elections (Table 1) has steadily decreased over the last 50 years. The decline can be attributed to an increase in the number of states adopting four-year terms of office. Whereas in 1920 more than half of the 19 states had two year terms for governor, by 1968 less than a quarter of them had such short terms. The steep drop in the number of elections in Period VII is the result of state constitutional revisions in the 1950's and early 1960's.

Secondly, the percentage of elections with incumbents has correspondingly increased—despite the fact that three of the states have now made changes which limit their governors to only two consecutive terms. Slightly less than half of the races had incumbents in them in the first decade of this century, while in the sixties nearly three-fourths did. Incumbents, as Table 2 makes clear, have been evenly divided between the two parties in five of the seven periods, including the final three. Only in the religiously Republican years of Period I and the equally dominant Democratic years of Period IV do the party balances differ significantly. And even these two periods are strikingly similar in one respect: the controlling party at the national level fields three-fourths of the incumbents—no doubt due, in great part, to high rates of defeat for candidates of the other party in the earlier years of both decades.

TABLE 3 *Three Measures of Vulnerability of Incumbent Governors, by Period*

Period		Defeated		Negative			
				Change in plurality		Critical change	
		%	(N)	%	(N)	%	(N)
I	(1900–09)	28.6	(35)[a]	69.0	(29)	57.1	(14)
II	(1910–19)	45.5	(44)	68.2	(44)	60.6	(33)
III	(1920–29)	29.7	(37)	67.6	(37)	51.4	(35)
IV	(1930–39)	25.0	(44)	59.1	(44)	67.4	(43)
V	(1940–49)	34.7	(49)	65.3	(49)	49.0	(49)
VI	(1950–59)	36.4	(44)	68.2	(44)	61.4	(44)
VII	(1960–69)	34.9	(43)	62.8	(43)	48.8	(43)

[a] Numbers in parentheses refer to the bases upon which percentages are calculated.

Turning from the preliminaries to the various indicators of vulnerability, we find that they lead to remarkably similar conclusions. There is no difference in the rate of defeat (Table 3) for the last three decades; in each, the proportion defeated hovers around one-third. Neither the per-

FIGURE 1 *Comparison of measures of vulnerability by period. (Data from Table 3.)*

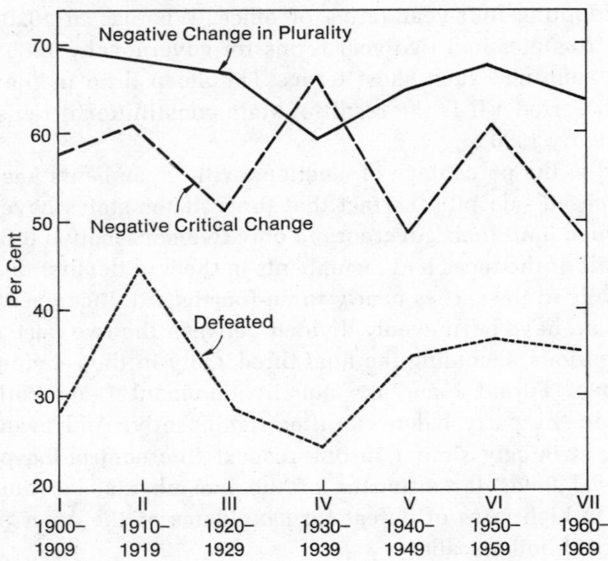

TABLE 4 *Incumbent Governors and House Races: Mean Scores on Comparative Measures, by Period*

Period	A. Critical change	B. Difference in critical change for winners and losers	C. Compared margin of victory
I (1900–09)	0.29	2.17	−2.22
II (1910–19)	−3.46	5.64	−0.12
III (1920–29)	−0.71	2.03	−1.00
IV (1930–39)	−5.28	1.64	−2.72
V (1940–49)	−0.41	7.59	2.07
VI (1950–59)	−3.40	7.02	1.27
VII (1960–69)	−0.48	12.83	9.02

centage nor the number defeated has changed. For five of the seven periods the defeat rate falls within a 10 percent range—between 28 and 38 per cent. Periods II and IV, by contrast, are at the polar positions: from 1910–1919, 45 per cent of all incumbents were defeated, but from 1930–1939 only 25 per cent lost.

The percentage of incumbents with a negative change in their plurality is uniformly higher than the percentage defeated. Between 60 and 70 per cent of all incumbents do less well in their bids for re-election (Table 3), and the coefficient of variation for this second measure is even smaller than that for the percentage defeated. In fact, the changes in the percentages in the second set of figures in Table 3 closely parallel similar shifts in the percentage defeated (Figure 1). In Period IV, that with the lowest rate of defeat, the percentage of governors with a decreased plurality was also the lowest. Nevertheless, only two-fifths of the incumbents could improve upon their previous pluralities. Somewhat surprisingly, perhaps, governors in Period VII fared nearly as well.

The critical change complements the other indicators. With a major exception in Period IV, when most incumbent Democratic governors did not benefit as greatly by the Roosevelt candidacy and program as did Democratic House nominees, the critical change figures tend to oscillate in much the same way as the previous two measures. Comparing the percentages with a negative critical change lends no credence at all to the thesis of increased vulnerability. Quite the contrary. They show that governors, as compared to House candidates of the same party, are running better now than ever before. For only the second time in seven decades, less than half of the governors had a negative critical change. Additional evidence is provided by the accompanying figures in Section A of Table 4. To facilitate comparisons, a mass of data has been telescoped into Figure 1.

The compared margin of victory conveys the same impression. Section

C of Table 4 demonstrates, as did the last column of percentages in Table 3, that the position of governors is improving rather than deteriorating. Especially in Period VII is the improvement manifest: incumbent governors are today, on the average, running 9 per cent ahead of the statewide House vote for their party. Through the 1950's a very different pattern prevailed.

The above characteristics suggest the conclusion that governors, perceived in perspective, are no more vulnerable today than they have been in previous years. What we are witnessing, it appears, and what has caught the eye of political scientists, is increasing visibility, not vulnerability.

Despite the fact that governors do not seem to have become *more vulnerable,* it would nevertheless be interesting to ascertain what factors, if any, are related to *vulnerability itself.* Although vulnerability has not varied, there still could be merit in explanations which relate vulnerability to diverse demographic characteristics, disparities in economic wealth, or differences in the level of governmental activity and the nature of public services provided. To test for such a relationship, the 43 elections with incumbents in the 1960's were selected for study. Data for each of these elections were collected for seven variables: urbanization, industrialization, crime, unemployment, tax burden, total expenditure effort, and educational expenditure effort.[12]

An attempt was also made to explain vulnerability in terms of intrastate changes on the above variables. For example, crime rates per 100,000 inhabitants, while greater in highly urbanized states, are increasing rapidly in some less urbanized, western states.[13] Thus, the rate of change was used as the independent variable rather than the base figures. Rates of change were calculated over two-year periods (e.g., the change from 1960–1962) since they coincide with the terms of office in some of the states.

[12] There were no significant differences in the analysis when per capita expenditure and revenue data were substituted for the burden and effort variables. Ideally, the nature of public services provided rather than merely the level of expenditures should have been examined. The former, however, are not easily assessable. The expenditure and revenue data examined here are for both state and local governments since the extent to which services have been centralized at the state level or supported by state grants is not uniform. Ira Sharkansky in assessing the relationship between spending and services has proceeded in a similar manner "because of technical problems which preclude the assessment of services supported by *state agencies, per se. . . .*" He found that "the levels of state and local government spending do not exert pervasive influence upon the nature of public services." *Spending in the American States* (Chicago: Rand McNally & Company, 1968), Chapter 7. Others though (cited by Sharkansky) have claimed that governmental expenditures reflect the "scope and character" or the "alpha and omega" of public services.

[13] The crime data are significant in at least one respect. The mean rate of increase in crime under Democratic incumbents seeking re-election (21 elections) was only 10.6 per cent, while that for Republicans (22 elections) was 24.9 per cent. Cf. Thomas R. Dye, *Politics, Economics, and the Public* (Chicago: Rand McNally & Company, 1966), pp. 233–234.

TABLE 5 *Coefficients of Simple Correlation Between Economic, Demographic, and Vulnerability Measures*[a]

Variable[b]		Base values		Rate of change	
		Change in plurality	Critical change	Change in plurality	Critical change
1. Urbanization	(+)	.06	.03	—.06	—.03
2. Industrialization	(+)	.11	.05	—.16	—.09
3. Crime	(+)	.02	.10	.02	—.02
4. Unemployment	(+)	.13	.06	—.01	—.04
5. Tax Burden[c]	(+)	—.09	0.0	.02	.09
6. Expenditure Effort	(—)	—.04	—.01	—.03	.17
7. Educational Effort	(—)	—.12	—.12	.03	.29

[a] The individual vulnerability scores were multiplied by — 1 in order that high positive scores would be more vulnerable than low negative scores.

[b] The proposed relationships between independent variables, nos. 1–7, and the two measures of vulnerability are shown in parentheses.

[c] Burden and effort are defined in terms of taxes or expenditures per $1000 of personal income.

Table 5 emphasizes the point that there is no linear relationship between any of the independent variables and vulnerability. Most of the simple correlations are close to zero and none is statistically significant at the .05 level. Although the correlation with the variable of percentage change in educational expenditure effort approaches statistical significance, it is not in the expected direction. In short, changes within states in crime, unemployment, taxes, expenditures, and so on, are—like the prevailing levels themselves—not crucial determinants of vulnerability.[14]

III

Since "the American states operate, not as independent and autonomous political entities, but as units of the nation," it would be valuable to determine the manner in which nationwide trends and presidential elections affect gubernatorial races. Although federal theory "presuppose[s] a political capacity congruent with the constitutional competence of each federated unit," [15] the states obviously do not operate in a political vacuum. The affairs of states and the outcomes of state elections might be inundated by the prevailing presidential politics. With certain major exceptions there is, concluded Key,

[14] A more comprehensive examination of nearly 90 elections from 1950–1969, employing some of the same variables, led to the same conclusion.

[15] Key, *American State Politics*, pp. 18–19.

TABLE 6 *Incumbent Governors Running in Presidential Years*

Period	Elections (#) Total	Elections (#) Pres. yrs.	% Pres. yrs. of total	Incumbents (#) Total	Incumbents (#) Pres. yrs.	% Pres. yrs. of Total
I	76	41	53.9	35	13	37.1
II	77	30	39.0	44	18	40.9
III	77	49	63.6	37	22	59.5
IV	75	33	44.0	44	18	40.9
V	72	44	61.1	49	29	59.2
VI	68	26	38.2	44	18	40.9
VII	59	31	52.5	43	21	48.8

> a striking interlocking of state and national voting. . . . When a region shifts its political preferences from Democratic to Republican, the presidential result, the elections to the House of Representatives, and the choices of governors tend to move in the same direction. Republicans replace Democrats, or vice versa, in about the same proportions. While both state and national voting may, in these great swings, be responsive to common causes, to some extent voting on state and local offices represents a more or less automatic extension of strong preferences or dislikes in national politics. The pervasive effect of national politics becomes patent when inconspicuous state and local candidates, hidden away far down the ballot, ride into—or are ousted from—office with the movement of the national pendulum.[16]

Regarding the influence of presidential elections on gubernatorial races, it is interesting to note that some states have attempted, in Key's words, to shield state politics from the blasts of national conflict by scheduling gubernatorial elections in the off-years. There has thus been a secular decline in the number of gubernatorial elections held in presidential years. Of those states switching from two-year to four-year terms for governor in the fifties and sixties, none have made them concurrent with the presidential election. The changes through the century are summarized in Table 6. In the 1960's, for only the second time when there were three presidential elections in a decade, more than half of all gubernatorial elections with incumbents were held in the two off-years. About 60 per cent of the elections were held in the presidential years in the two comparable periods (III and V).[17]

[16] *Politics, Parties, and Pressure Groups* (5th ed.; New York: Thomas Y. Crowell Company, 1964), pp. 304–305.

[17] Period I, which also had three presidential elections, is not strictly comparable because two states then held annual elections.

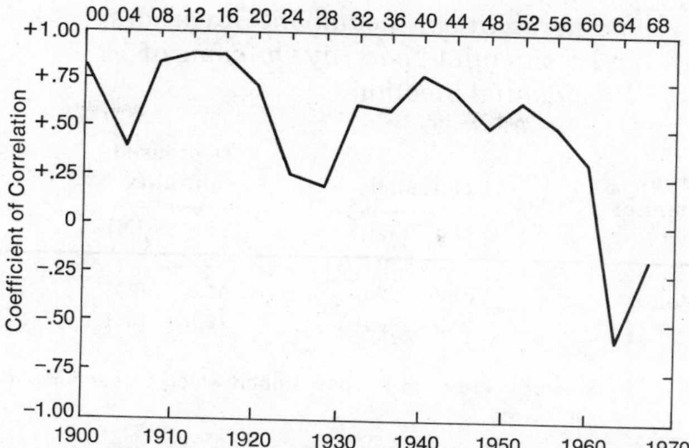

FIGURE 2 Declining relationship between percentage of total vote Democratic for governor and percentage of total vote Democratic for president.

While the sharp decrease of gubernatorial elections in presidential years makes an historical evaluation of the relationship of presidential and gubernatorial voting more difficult, Figure 2 is nevertheless revealing.[18] Attenuated correlation coefficients in presidential years suggest a dissociation of presidential and gubernatorial voting. The close articulation of presidential and gubernatorial voting, evident especially in Periods I and

[18] Correlations may have been higher had percentages of the two-party vote been examined. To increase the number of elections, and to embellish with more credibility, the simple correlations (based again on the total vote) for the examined states can be compared to those for all non-Southern states. The trend is basically unchanged, as the following table indicates:

Presidential and Gubernatorial Voting

Year	Simple correlations	
	Examined states	All non-Southern states
1944	.72	.77
1948	.54	.73
1952	.67	.77
1956	.56	.13
1960	.35	.46
1964	−.53	−.23
1968	−.133	−.09

* Excludes elections in North Dakota (1944) and Utah (1956) because of exceedingly strong showings by third-party candidates.

TABLE 7 *Vulnerability of Incumbent Governors in Presidential Years, by Outcome of Presidential Election*

Governor's presidential party	Defeated		Decreased plurality		Negative-critical change	
	%	(N)[a]	%	(N)	%	(N)
Won	19.7	(76)	51.4	(74)	63.0	(73)
Lost	42.9	(63)	73.8	(61)	44.8	(58)

[a] Numbers in parentheses refer to the bases upon which percentages are calculated.

II, has apparently given way to a greater seperability of national and state politics.[19]

One way of discussing the problem of national or statewide trends is to calculate the differences in the critical change for winning and losing incumbents. As the figure diverges from zero, the salience of factors common to both governor and House races decreases. If, in other words, the critical changes for winners and losers were the same, then the changes in winning margins for gubernatorial candidates would be equal to those of their party's House candidates. This could easily be the result of a national movement toward one party; on the other hand, it is possible that the effects are peculiar to a single state. At any rate, it would be impossible to argue that characteristics inherent in the governor's office are responsible for fluctuations in both gubernatorial and House voting. Section B of Table 4 shows, not unexpectedly, that trends were most important in Periods IV and II, precisely the decades in which presidential winners won by the largest pluralities. By contrast, trends were least prominent in Period VII, the decade with two of the closest presidential elections in history.

Characteristically, members of the party winning the White House have done better than members of the defeated presidential party, and, further, suffer a loss in the ensuing off-year election. As is evident from Table 7, incumbents of the losing presidential party are twice as likely to be

19 The relationship between gubernatorial and presidential voting has probably always been weaker than that between House and presidential voting. While only about 25 per cent of the incumbent Democrats in 1932 and 1936 had a smaller plurality, almost 75 per cent had a negative critical change. Democratic incumbent governors ran behind their party's nominees for the House by an average of over 3 per cent. Republican incumbent governors ran over 5 per cent ahead of their party's House nominees. For a discussion of presidential and congressional voting see, in addition to the sources cited in note 29, Milton C. Cummings, Jr., *Congressmen and the Electorate* (New York: The Free Press, 1966), Chapter 7.

TABLE 8 *Vulnerability of Income Governors in Off-Years, by Presidential Party*

Party	Defeated		Decreased plurality		Negative-critical change	
	%	(N)[a]	%	(N)	%	(N)
In	42.0	(100)	77.6	(98)	57.5	(80)z
Out	26.3	(57)	54.4	(57)	61.7	(47)

[a] Numbers in parentheses refer to the bases upon which percentages are calculated.

defeated in presidential years; and whereas only half of the incumbents of the presidential party had decreased pluralities, three-fourths of the incumbents of the party losing the Presidency suffered such declines. But in the off-years the roles are reversed (Table 8).[20] This pattern repeats itself in virtually every period (Tables 9 and 10). With only two exceptions in presidential years (Periods III and VII), the percentage of incumbents of the defeated presidential party with a negative change in their plurality has exceeded that for the winning presidential party. In the off-years members of the party previously losing the Presidency consistently run stronger than incumbents of the President's party.

In most instances the above alternating advantage is probably a function of differentials in voter participation. Upsurges in turnout, as both Key and Campbell have found, are accompanied by an exceptionally high rate of increase in the vote for one party with little or no change in the vote for the other.[21] The electorate responds differently to the stimuli of different elections. Surge and decline is thus a cyclical process—one in which the peripheral voters, drawn into the active voting universe by the stimulation of some specific short-term election situation, recede from it upon the

[20] In determining the relationship between presidential outcome and gubernatorial voting, the only two measures of importance are the number defeated and the number with a negative change in their plurality. The critical change, with functions as a trend controlling measure, would be expected to negate any relationship. In the off-years, for example, the Φ relating previous success of presidential party to negative change in plurality dims perceptibly—increasing from −.24 to .04—when critical change is substituted; similarly, Yule Q goes from −.34 to .09. The limitations of Φ and its comparisons to Q are discussed in John H. Mueller and Karl F. Schuessler, *Statistical Reasoning in Sociology* (Boston: Houghton Mifflin Company, 1961), pp. 252–258.

[21] *Politics, Parties and Pressure Groups*, pp. 590–591; and Angus Campbell, "Surge and Decline: A Study of Electoral Change," *Public Opinion Quarterly*, XXIV (Fall, 1960), 397–418.

TABLE 9 *Defeat Rates of Incumbent Governors in Presidential and Off-Years, by Period and National Success of the Governor's Presidential Party*

	Governor's presidential party							
	Won				Lost			
	Presidential years		Off years		Presidential years		Off years	
Period	%	(N)	%	(N)	%	(N)	%	(N)
I	33.3	(9)[a]	17.6	(17)	50.0	(4)	40.0	(5)
II	42.9	(7)	50.0	(14)	45.0	(11)	41.7	(12)
III	16.7	(12)	28.6	(7)	40.0	(10)	37.5	(8)
IV	0.0	(15)	42.9	(21)	33.3	(3)	20.0	(5)
V	27.3	(11)	38.5	(13)	44.4	(18)	14.3	(7)
VI	0.0	(10)	62.5	(16)	50.0	(8)	20.0	(10)
VII	33.3	(12)	50.0	(12)	33.3	(9)	20.0	(10)

[a] Numbers in parentheses refer to the bases upon which percentages are calculated. In this table and Table 10 the number of elections in most cells is so small that the percentages should be regarded as no more than suggestive.

TABLE 10 *Incumbent Governors with a Decreased Plurality in Presidential and Off-Years, by Period and National Success of the Governor's Presidential Party*

	Governor's presidential party							
	Won				Lost			
	Presidential years		Off years		Presidential years		Off years	
Period	%	(N)	%	(N)	%	(N)	%	(N)
I	71.4	(7)[a]	66.7	(15)	100.0	(2)	60.0	(5)
II	57.1	(7)	71.4	(14)	81.8	(11)	58.3	(12)
III	66.7	(12)	85.7	(7)	60.0	(10)	62.5	(8)
IV	26.7	(15)	76.2	(21)	100.0	(3)	60.0	(5)
V	45.5	(11)	76.9	(13)	83.3	(18)	28.6	(7)
VI	40.0	(10)	93.8	(16)	75.0	(8)	50.0	(10)
VII	66.7	(12)	75.0	(12)	44.0	(9)	60.0	(10)

[a] Numbers in parentheses refer to the bases upon which percentages are calculated.

TABLE 11 *Articulation of Presidential and Gubernatorial Voting*

% of state vote[a] for governor's presidential party	Defeated		Decreased plurality	
	%	(N)[b]	%	(N)
Under 45	58.1	(31)[c]	76.7	(30)[d]
45–49.9	46.2	(26)	80.0	(25)
50–54.9	16.0	(25)	54.2	(24)
55–59.9	11.5	(27)	44.0	(25)
60 or More	16.1	(31)	51.6	(31)[e]

[a] Two-party vote.

[b] Numbers in parentheses refer to the bases upon which percentages are calculated.

[c] Seven of the 13 deviant elections in this cell occurred in Periods III and VI.

[d] Five of the 7 deviant elections in this cell were also in Periods III and VI.

[e] Seven of the 15 deviant elections in this cell occurred in Period III.

removal of the stimulus.[22] "As long as there is no significant shift in the distribution of standing party attachments within the electorate," Campbell wrote, "the decline in turnout will almost certainly be associated with a decline in the proportion of the vote received by the presidential party." [23]

The success of incumbents would also be expected to depend on the magnitude of the presidential victory in the governor's state. To some extent this is the case, although the relationship is certainly not as clear-cut as might have been anticipated. State political shifts, as Table 11 suggests, may lag—perhaps considerably—behind shifts in presidential party preference. Approximately 40 per cent of the incumbents whose party's nominee for the Presidency polled less than 45 per cent of the two-party vote actually won; however, only 25 per cent of them had improved winning margins. At the other extreme, about 15 per cent of the incumbents were defeated when their party's presidential nominee polled at least 60 per cent of the two-party vote, and fully half had smaller pluralities. For the most part, the deviant elections occurred in Periods III and VI—two periods in which voter preference for Republicans at the presidential level

[22] Peripheral voters form what Campbell calls "a rather inert reservoir of voters, available for service under conditions of high stimulation but not highly motivated by an intrinsic interest in politics." Campbell, "Surge and Decline," p. 409.

[23] Campbell, "Surge and Decline," p. 417.

TABLE 12 *Indicators of Vulnerability in Landslide and Non-Landslide Presidential Years, by Outcome of Presidential Election*

Governor's presidential party	Landslide				Non-landslide			
	Defeated		Decreased plurality		Defeated		Decreased plurality	
	%	(N)	%	(N)	%	(N)	%	(N)
Won	7.1	(42)[a]	38.1	(42)	35.3	(34)	68.8	(22)
Lost	40.0	(20)	70.0	(20)	44.2	(43)	75.6	(31)

[a] Numbers in parentheses refer to the bases upon which percentages are calculated.

did not extend to the state level. Throughout the 1920's the national Democratic Party was in disarray, and in the 1950's Republicans could not entirely capitalize on Eisenhower's popularity.

When presidential years are separated into two types—landslide and non-landslide—the differences in party success are more distinct. Landslide years may be defined as those in which the presidential winner polls over 55 per cent of the total national vote. Incumbents of the winning presidential party in landslide years run far ahead of incumbents of the defeated presidential party (Table 12)[24] Surprisingly though, for incumbents of the losing presidential party the type of presidential election is not important: their rate of defeat and their percentage with a smaller plurality are the same in both landslide and non-landslide years. Moreover, in non-landslide years the party differences are not large. Marked differences in Table 7, therefore, must be attributed almost solely to landslide years. On both

[24] The differences between the results in landslide and non-landslide years are even more sharply delineated when Key's definition of a landslide is employed. He limits landslides to votes of lack of confidence which clearly express "a widespread unhappiness with past performance." In these elections, "the party in power, in comparison with the preceding election, loses voting strength in most counties of the nation. Though the data are lacking, the odds are that the decline in strength also permeates most social and economic classes." *Politics, Parties and Pressure Groups*, p. 522. Three presidential elections—1920, 1932, and 1952—are classified as landslides. No incumbent of the party winning the White House in these years was defeated and only about 10 per cent had a smaller winning margin. Conversely, more than half of the incumbents of the party losing the Presidency were defeated, and virtually all had a negative change in their plurality. Frank Lausche (D-Ohio) ran a somewhat stronger race in 1952 than he had in 1950, even though General Eisenhower swept the state. The electorate appears to have acted consistently though since Lausche's Republican opponent was widely considered the more liberal of the two candidates, a kind of Republican New Dealer.

measures of vulnerability, the Φ expressing the relationship between the success of a governor's presidential party and the results of governors' races in non-landslide years is very close to zero. The fact that both presidential elections in Periods IV and VI were landslides accounts for the strength of incumbent governors of the winning presidential party in these decades (Tables 9 and 10). Just as significantly, it would seem to explain the relative weakness of presidential party incumbents in the 1960's.

IV

Some of the findings which emerge from this study are at variance with apparently widely held suppositions. In the first place, it was shown that governors, historically viewed, have not become more vulnerable. Briefly, gubernatorial visibility—not vulnerability—has increased. There has been, particularly in the past three decades, no detrimental change in the status of governors seeking re-election. In fact, today they are running farther ahead of their party's congressional nominees than ever before. The contention, therefore, that vulnerability has increased cannot be advanced to explain the weakened position of governors in contending for presidential nominations. Recent Senatorial accession to the Presidency is the result of other factors.

Secondly, economic and demographic differences between states are not related to vulnerability. Changes within states on these characteristics are likewise not decisive determinants of vulnerability. Urbanization, crime, unemployment, expenditures, and taxes exhibit no discernible agreement with gubernatorial vulnerability. No pattern of vulnerability was found.

And finally, the impact of presidential elections on governor's races is dependent, in general, upon the type of presidential election, and, probably more directly, upon the state vote for a governor's presidential party nominees. Incumbents of the party winning the White House do significantly better than incumbents of the defeated presidential party only in landslide presidential years. In other presidential years, the success of a governor's presidential party is not the controlling factor. States are now making an effort to isolate their politics from national political conflict; fewer are scheduling governor's elections in presidential years. In those states still holding gubernatorial elections in presidential years, however, there is strong evidence that the previous close articulation of presidential and gubernatorial voting has, to some extent, deteriorated. Keen competition in presidential elections in the 1960's, and continuing constitutional revisions by states, have recently reduced the influence which presidential candidates have been able to exert on state races.

Appendix

State	Examined	Not competitive 1900–28	Not competitive 1929–69	No consecutive re-election permitted at some time since 1900
Alabama		X	X	X
Arizona	X			
Arkansas		X	X	
California		X	X	
Colorado	X			
Connecticut	X			
Delaware	X			
Florida		X	X	X
Georgia		X	X	X
Idaho	X			
Illinois	X			
Indiana				X
Iowa		X		
Kansas		X		
Kentucky				X
Louisiana		X	X	X
Maine		X	X	
Maryland	X			
Massachusetts	X			
Michigan		X		
Minnesota		X		
Mississippi		X	X	X
Missouri			X	X
Montana	X	X		
Nebraska	X			
Nevada	X			
New Hampshire	X			
New Jersey				X
New Mexico	X			
New York	X			
North Carolina		X	X	X
North Dakota		X		
Ohio	X			
Oklahoma			X	X
Oregon			X	
Pennsylvania		X		X
Rhode Island	X			
South Carolina		X	X	X
South Dakota		X	X	
Tennessee		X	X	X
Texas		X	X	
Utah	X			
Vermont		X	X	
Virginia		X	X	X
Washington	X			
West Virginia				X
Wisconsin		X		
Wyoming	X			

Thomas R. Dye

Executive Power and Public Policy in the United States

Although a great deal of attention has begun to be paid to the President's role in the policy-making process, little had been done until recently to explore and expose gubernatorial involvement in policy implementation. As Thad Beyle and J. Oliver Williams observe, "There are . . . numerous case studies of particular governors facing particular problems at particular times and of certain governors' tenure in office; but few generalizations on the governors' relationship to policy implementation" exist. In their reader they offered Dye's study as an attempt "to provide an analytical base from which more general statements can be made" in the future. [Thad Beyle and J. Oliver Williams, *The American Governor in Behavioral Perspective* (New York: Harper & Row, 1972), p. 217.]

This research explores the linkage between some major structural characteristics of state government and the content of public policies in the states. Specifically, the focus is upon the policy consequences of (1) the organizational structure of state executives, and (2) the formal powers of governors. What are the policy consequences of a fragmented state executive with many separately elected officials and independent boards, in contrast to a more streamlined executive organization? Does it make any difference in educational outcomes whether the chief educational officer in the state is elected, appointed by an independent board, or appointed by the governor? Are welfare benefits noticeably more liberal in states with an appointed welfare director in contrast to an independent welfare board?

Reprinted from *Western Political Quarterly*, Vol. 22, No. 4 (December 1969), 926–939, by Thomas R. Dye. Reprinted by permission of the University of Utah, Copyright holder.

Does it make any difference whether the highway department is headed by an appointee of the governor or an independent board? What are the policy consequences of providing the governor with strong budgetary, appointive, and veto powers? Are there any significant differences in the public policies of states with strong and weak governors? Or are public policies primarily a function of the economic environment of a state—its wealth, industrialization, urbanization, and educational level?

In assessing the impact of structural variables on policies in the fifty states, we will inquire: (1) whether states with fragmented executive structures and weak governors pursue significantly different policies from states with streamlined executive structures and strong governors, and (2) whether any policy differences which are observed can be traced to these structural variables rather than other environmental factors. If the policies of states with fragmented executive structures and weak governors are noticeably different from the policies of states with streamlined executive structures and strong governors, and these policy differences can be attributed to structural rather than environmental variables, then we can infer that the structure of state government has a significant impact on state policies. However, if the policy choices of states with different structural characteristics and strong and weak governors do not differ significantly, or if differences which do occur are the product of environmental conditions rather than structural variables, then we must infer that the structure of state government is not an important determinant of public policies in the states.

Measures of public policy were selected from four of the most important areas of state activity—education, health and welfare, taxation, and highways. Education is the largest category of state spending, followed by health and welfare, and highways. The tax burden and revenue structure of the states was assumed to be an important policy area. Most of the policy variables combine state and local activities; this means we view local governments as integral parts of state political systems. Policy outcomes which depend in part upon decisions made at the local level are treated as attributes of state political systems. For example, the expenditure variables are based on *total* state and local expenditures, rather than just expenditures made by state government. To ignore local expenditures in the comparative analysis of state policy would be to overlook great variations among the states in their reliance upon state versus local levels of government for the provision of public services. The degree to which a state relies upon local governments for the provisions of services or financial support is viewed here as a policy outcome of the state political system. The divisions of state-local responsibility in education, health, welfare, highways, and tax collection are considered as separate policy variables.

Most of the policy variables are *levels or amounts* of public service, and it is possible that results obtained with distributive or regulatory policies would be different. However, the rural-urban distribution of state highway funds and the percentage of highway revenues diverted to non-highway purposes are two of the selected variables, and the relative reliance placed on state sales and income taxation are also considered. All of these variables would seem to involve distributive decisions.

A total of twenty-five policy variables were selected for analysis:[1]

Education

Public school expenditures per pupil in average daily attendance, 1960–61
Average annual salary per members of instructional staff, 1961–62
Pupil-teacher ratio: enrollment per member of instructional staff, 1961–62
Drop-out rate: high school grads in 1963 as per cent of ninth graders in 1959
Per cent of selective service examinees disqualified for failing mental test, 1962
Average size of school district in pupils, 1961–62
State participation: school revenues from state as per cent of total school revenue

Health and Welfare

Average weekly payment per recipient, Unemployment Compensation, 1961
Average monthly payment per family, Aid to Dependent Children, 1961
Average monthly payment, General Assistance, 1961
Per capita state and local expenditures for health and hospitals, 1961
Per capita state and local expenditures for welfare, 1961
State participation: per cent state expenditures of total expenditures for welfare, 1961
State participation: per cent state expenditures of total expenditures for health and hospitals, 1961
Recipients of Aid to Dependent Children per 10,000 population, 1961
Recipients of Unemployment Compensation per 10,000 population, 1961

Taxation

Total state and local tax revenues per capita, 1961
Total tax revenues as a per cent of personal income, 1961

[1] Actually, all operations were performed on a total of over 100 policy measures. The measures listed, and the analysis presented in this article concern only key, representative policy measures.

State revenues as a per cent of total state and local revenues, 1961
Income tax revenues as a per cent of total tax revenues, 1961
Sales tax revenues as a per cent of total tax revenues, 1961

Highways

Per capita state and local expenditures for highways, 1961
State participation: per cent state expenditures of total expenditures for highways, 1961
Per cent of highway-user revenues diverted to nonhighway purposes, 1959
Discrimination against urban areas in state highways expenditures, 1957–59

Previous research has shown that many of these policy variables are related to environmental variables, particularly those reflecting levels of economic development.[2] Urbanization, industrialization, wealth, and adult education levels have been shown to be key environmental variables influencing a wide variety of state policy outcomes in education, health and welfare, highways, and taxation. The simple coefficients for the relationships between these economic development variables and twenty-five policy outcomes are shown in Table 1.

These economic-development, public-policy relationships present some problems in assessing the impact of structural characteristics of state governments and state policy outcomes. This means that in any assessment of the *independent* effect of structural variables on public policy, we must endeavor to sort out the intervening effects of economic development. In order to isolate the effects of structural variables, it is necessary to control for these latter variables. This required that partial correlation coefficients be computed which would show the relationships between structural variables and public policy outcomes, while controlling for the effect of urbanization, industrialization, wealth, and education. If relationships between structural variables and state policies which appear in simple correlation coefficients disappear when economic development variables are controlled, then we must infer that there is no independent relationship between governmental structure and public policy among the fifty states. On the other hand, if correlation coefficients between structural variables and state policies remain

[2] See Richard E. Dawson and James A. Robinson, "Inter-party Competition, Economic Variables and Welfare Policies in the American States," *Journal of Politics*, Vol. 25 (May 1963), pp. 265–289; Richard I. Hofferbert, "The Relation Between Public Policy and Some Structural and Environmental Variables in the American States," *American Political Science Review*, Vol. 60 (March 1966), pp. 73–82; Thomas R. Dye, *Politics, Economics, and the Public: Policy Outcomes in the American States* (Chicago: Rand McNally, 1966).

TABLE 1 *Economic Development and State Policy Outcomes*

	Income	Industrial-ization	Education	Urban-ization
EDUCATION				
Per pupil expenditures	.83*	.36*	.59*	.51*
State % educational expenditures	.88*	.64*	.57*	.69*
Average teachers' salaries	−.18	.26	−.37*	
Size of school district	−.43*	.19	−.50*	−.13
Teacher-pupil ratio	.54*	−.09	.60*	.40*
Dropout rate	−.46*	.13	−.70*	−.05
Mental failures	.80*	.30*	.67*	.55*
HEALTH AND WELFARE				
Unemployment benefits	.74*	.26	.55*	.51*
ADC benefits	.76*	.39*	.43*	.58*
General asst. benefits	−.30	.16	−.42*	−.15
ADC recipients	.58*	.69*	.23	.39*
Unemployment recipients	−.01	.07	.08	.19
Per capita welfare expenditure	.56*	.39*	.42*	.45*
Per capita health expenditure	−.35*	−.15	−.17	−.11
State % welfare expenditure	−.08	−.07	−.15	−.30*
State % health expenditure	−.16	−.52*	.16	−.15
TAXATION				
Per capita tax revenues	.76*	.23	.74*	.59*
Taxes relative to income	−.34*	−.08	−.24	−.28
State % taxes	−.15	.02	−.19	.03
Sales taxes	−.10	−.01	−.22	−.10
Income taxes	.02	−.51*	.36*	
HIGHWAYS				
Per capita highway expenditure	−.15	.05	−.04	−.29*
State % highway expenditure	.07	.29	−.06	.42*
Highway fund diversions	−.24	−.15	−.16	−.11
Rural-urban distribution	.33*	.21	.20	.29

Source: U.S. Bureau of the Census, *Census of Population 1960* PCI-IC (Washington, D.C.: U.S. Government Printing Office, 1961).

Note: Figures are simple correlation coefficients: an asterisk indicates a significant relationship. Economic development measures in all tables are: median family income; one minus the per cent of work force in agriculture, forestry and fishing; median school year completed by the population 25 and over; per cent of population living in urban areas.

significant, even after controlling for the effects of these environmental variables, then we may more readily infer that structural variables have an independent effect on state policy.

"Fragmentation" of State Executives

The organizational structure of American state governments appears to reflect colonial thinking about "fear of the executive." Among the fifty states one finds many constitutional restrictions on a governor's term of office, his ability to succeed himself and his control over appointments and removals; the executive branch of many of the state governments is composed of a variety of separate boards and commissions, and there are long overlapping terms for the members of the boards and commissions. Jacksonian ideas about popular democracy led many states to elect rather than appoint a variety of executive officers.

Fortunately, for the sake of comparative analysis, the "fragmentation" of executive authority is not experienced uniformly by all the fifty states. There are wide variations from state to state in the number of elected state officers, and the number of executive agencies which are headed by elected officials, appointees, or independent boards and commissions. The Council of State Governments reports in 1965 that 2 states (Alaska and New Jersey) elected only their governor and lieutenant-governor, while Michigan elected 31 executive officers, commissioners, and board members; Texas, 33; and Nevada, 42.[3] The Council also reports that 2 states (Alaska and New Jersey again) had only 2 executive departments headed by elected officials, while Mississippi and South Carolina had a total of 13 executive departments headed by elected officials. Turning to specific agencies: 14 states had elected Public Utility Commissions while all other states handled this responsibility through appointed officials. In 6 states the education department was headed by an appointed official, in 23 states it was headed by an independent board, and in 21 states by a separately elected official. The health departments of 26 states are headed by an appointed official, but in 24 states they are headed by an independent board. The welfare departments of 29 states are headed by an appointed official, but in 21 states they are run by independent boards. One state (Mississippi), has an elected highway commissioner, while the highway departments of 26 states are headed by an appointed official and 23 states by a highway board. In short, there is sufficient variation among the states in the extent of executive "fragmentation" to permit systematic comparative analysis of the environmental correlates and policy consequences of such fragmentation.

In general, the fragmentation of executive authority in the American states is inversely related to measures of economic development. (See Table 2.) On the whole, wealthy, urban, industrial states have less "fragmented" executive structures than poor, rural, agricultural states. Perhaps the complexities of governing an urban industrial state require more streamlined

[3] Council of State Governments, *Book of the States, 1964–1965* (Chicago: Council of State Governments, 1965).

TABLE 2 *Economic Development and the Fragmentation of State Executives*

		Average of States on Measures of			
		Income	Industrial-ization	Education	Urban-ization
NUMBER OF ELECTED OFFICIALS					
Less than 7	(*N* = 15)	$5,833	92.8%	10.7 yrs	63.8%
8–14	(*N* = 17)	4,989	89.7	10.5	59.4
15–21	(*N* = 18)	5,295	89.3	10.7	62.3
NUMBER OF AGENCIES WITH ELECTED HEADS					
Less than 6	(*N* = 16)	5,836	93.6	10.7	68.6
6–18	(*N* = 16)	5,520	89.9	11.0	64.0
Over 18	(*N* = 18)	4,763	87.0	10.2	56.5
PUBLIC UTILITY COMMISSION					
Appointed	(*N* = 36)	5,660	92.3	10.5	63.7
Elected	(*N* = 14)	4,562	84.4	10.2	56.5
EDUCATION AGENCY					
Appointed	(*N* = 6)	5,912	94.9	10.6	65.4
Board	(*N* = 23)	5,603	90.8	10.9	66.0
Elected	(*N* = 21)	4,918	83.5	9.8	55.8
HEALTH AGENCY					
Appointed	(*N* = 24)	5,638	92.8	11.4	66.0
Board	(*N* = 26)	5,085	88.5	10.7	57.2
WELFARE					
Appointed	(*N* = 29)	5,419	89.8	10.6	65.7
Board	(*N* = 21)	5,247	89.9	10.7	61.3
HIGHWAYS					
Appointed	(*N* = 26)	5,380	92.0	10.3	63.6
Board	(*N* = 23)	5,299	89.3	11.0	62.0
Elected	(*N* = 1)	2,884	98.6	8.9	37.7

Source: Data on executive organization from Council of State Governments, *Book of the States 1964–65* (Chicago: Council of State Governments, 1965).

executive structure, while rural agricultural states can continue in their apparent preference for Jacksonian democracy. There is a tendency for more agricultural states to elect more state officials, to elect more agency heads, to have an elected rather than an appointed public utility commission, to have an elected chief educational officer, and to have independent boards rather than appointed heads of their health, welfare and highway departments.

These relationships between economic development variables and structural characteristics are important to keep in mind when exploring the effect of these structural variables on public policy. The problem will be to sort out the effects of economic variables on policy outcomes from the effects of structural variables. For example, it may turn out that states which appoint their chief education official spend more for education than states which elect their top educational officer. But since we know that states with appointed educational heads tend to be wealthier than states with elected educational heads, it may be that wealth rather than the method of selecting their chief educational officer is the real determinant of educational expenditures. To identify the independent effect of a fragmented executive, it will be necessary to control for the effect of environmental variables.

Executive "Fragmentation" and Public Policy

There is very little evidence to support the notion that executive fragmentation itself affects the content of public policy in the states. While states with fragmented executive structures pursue somewhat different policies than states with more streamlined executive branches, most of these policy differences are attributable to the impact of economic development rather than the structure of state executives. For example, Table 3 shows that there is some tendency for states which elect many agency heads to spend less money per pupil for education, to pay lower teachers' salaries, to provide lower welfare benefits, to have fewer unemployment recipients, and to pay a larger share of welfare costs with state rather than local funds. However, these relationships appear to be a product of the intervening effects of economic development. That is, states with fragmented executives tend to be poorer, rural, and agricultural, and it is these environmental variables rather than executive fragmentation itself which accounts for policy differences. The relationships between fragmentation and public policy which appear in simple correlations in Table 3 disappear when the effects of economic development are controlled. The partial coefficients show no significant relationships between fragmentation and public policy while controlling for urbanization, industrialization, wealth, and adult education. (In contrast, partial coefficients for the relationships between economic development variables and public policy remain significant after controlling for executive fragmentation; these coefficients are not shown here.)

Table 4 examines the specific policy differences between states having elected officials, appointed officials, or independent boards heading education, health, welfare, and highway departments. In educational policy,

TABLE 3 *Executive Fragmentation and Public Policy Outcomes*

	Number of elected state agency heads				
	Averages on policy measures			Simple correlation coefficient*	Partial correlation coefficient†
	Less than 6 ($N=16$)	6–8 ($N=16$)	More than 8 ($N=18$)		
EDUCATION					
Per pupil exp.	442	306	360	−.43*	−.12
State % educ. exp.	42.2	30.3	47.7	.20	.08
Average teachers' salaries	5703	5459	4963	−.41*	−.08
Size of school district	3851	1767	3066	−.02	.16
Teacher-pupil ratio	23.8	23.7	24.5	.19	.07
Dropout rate	72.6	75.1	69.3	−.22	.08
Mental failures	14.8	12.0	19.4	.27	.14
HEALTH AND WELFARE					
Unemployment benefits	33	32	29	−.34*	.19
ADC benefits	134	129	151	−.38*	−.03
General asst. benefits	61	54	43	−.38*	−.02
ADC recipients	190	154	200	.11	.07
Unemployment recipients	378	365	294	−.45*	−.11
Per capita welfare exp.	21	28	26	.27	.23
Per capita health exp.	22	21	18	−.24	.01
State % welfare exp.	84	85	96	.37*	.29
State % health exp.	69	60	64	−.17	−.03
TAXATION					
Per capita tax revenue	205	212	186	−.22	−.16
Taxes relative to income	9.0	9.7	9.9	.36*	.24
State % taxes	62	55	68	.27	.13
Sales taxes	17	12	7	.22	.29
Income taxes	17	23	28	−.03	.01
HIGHWAYS					
Per capita highway exp.	61	63	64	.06	.09
State % highway exp.	79	83	84	.17	.26
Highway fund diversions	6.6	3.5	5.8	.00	−.04
Rural-urban distribution	189	170	207	.27	.12

* Simple correlation coefficients between policy measures and number of elected agency heads; an asterisk indicates a significant relationship.

† Partial coefficients show the relationship between policy measures and number of elected agency heads, while controlling for urbanization, industrialization, income, and education.

TABLE 4 *The Method of Selecting Agency Heads and Public Policy Outcomes*

	Chief education officer				
	Averages on policy measures			Simple correlation coefficient*	Partial correlation coefficient†
	Appointed (N = 6)	Board (N = 23)	Elected (N = 21)		
EDUCATION					
Per pupil exp.	440	410	379	—.22	.05
State % educ. exp.	41.1	38.2	42.8	.06	—.03
Average teachers' salaries	5903	5467	5083	—.30*	.11
Size of school district	3397	2774	2901	.03	.02
Teacher-pupil ratio	24.6	23.7	24.2	.00	—.05
Dropout rate	71.4	73.3	71.0	.05	.13
Mental failures	18.3	12.9	17.6	.06	—.08

	Head of health department			
	Averages on policy measures		Simple correlation coefficient*	Partial correlation coefficient†
	Appointed (N = 26)	Board (N = 24)		
HEALTH				
Per capita exp. health	21	19	—.15	—.03
State % health exp.	67	59	—.19	—.28

* Simple coefficients were computed with structural variables assigned weights as follows: 1—Appointed, 2—Board, 3—Elected, that is, in the direction of independence from the governor. An asterisk indicates a significant relationship.

states with elected educational heads have somewhat lower pupil expenditures, and lower teachers' salaries than states with appointed educational directors or independent boards. But there are no other systematic differences between states with separate methods of selecting their chief educational officer. And it is probable that even these differences in pupil expenditures and teachers' salaries are a product of economic development. While regression analysis is somewhat less satisfactory with these dichotomous and trichotomous variables, nonetheless, the behavior of the simple and partial coefficients suggests that environmental variables and not the structural variables are more influential in determining policy outcomes.

An examination of contrasting health and welfare policy outcomes in states with appointed heads and states with independent boards suggests

	Head of welfare department			
	Averages on policy measures		Simple correlation coefficient*	Partial correlation coefficient†
	Appointed (N = 30)	Board (N = 20		
WELFARE				
Unemployment benefits	31	30	−.10	−.25
ADC benefits	127	118	−.20	−.24
General asst. benefits	56	47	−.20	−.20
ADC recipients	190	170	.05	−.10
Unemployment recipients	378	325	−.21	−.21
Per capita exp. welfare	24	26	.06	−.05
State % welfare exp.			.15	.01

	Head of highway department				
	Averages on policy measures			Simple correlation coefficient*	Partial correlation coefficient†
	Appointed (N = 26)	Board (N = 23)	Elected (N = 1)		
HIGHWAY					
Per capita highway exp.	52	70	58	.28	21
State % highway exp.	80	85	76	.21	.13
Highway fund diversions	7.0	3.7	0.1	.20	−.24
Rural-urban distribution	17.2	18.4	27.4	.11	.02

† Partial coefficients show the relationship between structural variables and policy outcomes, while controlling for urbanization, industrialization, income, and education.

that the latter are more conservative in health and welfare benefits, in spending for health and welfare, and in numbers of recipients. However, these differences are not great, and here again it is probable that these differences are a product of the fact that wealthy, urban, industrial states are more likely to have appointed heads and more likely to pursue liberal welfare policies. There are no significant simple or partial correlation coefficients between methods of selecting health and welfare department heads and health and welfare policies.

While independent boards are associated with *lower* health and welfare expenditures, just the opposite is true with highway expenditures. States with independent highway boards (and Mississippi with an elected highway director) spend *more* per capita for highways, assume more direct state responsibility for highway finance, and permit fewer diversions of highway funds. There are no discernable differences between states with appointed directors and states with independent boards in the rural-urban distribution of highway funds. Here again the association between independent highway boards and increased highway spending is probably a product of the fact that rural agricultural states spend more for highways and show a structural preference for independent boards.

While we cannot say that these structural variations have *no* impact on policy outcomes, they certainly do not appear to have as much impact as the economic development variables.

The Formal Powers of Governors

Commentators on state politics typically speak of "strong" and "weak" governors. And certainly the power of governors in state politics seems to vary among the fifty states and even to vary from one administration to another in the same state. Yet it is very difficult systematically to describe variations among the states in gubernatorial influence, owing to our inability to find a suitable method of measuring and comparing political influence. Unfortunately, the theory and measurement of influence is not sufficiently advanced in our discipline to permit rigorous comparative analysis of executive influence. Probably the best that can be done in comparing executive power in the states is to focus on the formal powers of governors.

Joseph M. Schlesinger has compiled an index of the formal powers of governors in the fifty states.[4] This index considers the governor's tenure and ability to succeed himself, his appointive powers over executive agency heads, his responsibilities for budget preparation, and his power to veto bills passed by the legislature. The Schlesinger scale of values for a governor's "Tenure Potential" is as follows:

Four-year term, no restraint on reelection	5
Four-year term, one reelection permitted	4
Four-year term, unable to succeed himself	3
Two-year term, no restraint on reelection	2
Two-year term, one reelection permitted	1

The scale of values for appointive powers considers principal functions:

The governor appoints alone	5
Governor must obtain approval of one house	4
Governor must obtain approval of both houses	3
Appointment by board of which governor is member	2

[4] Joseph M. Schlesinger, "The Politics of the Executive," in Herbert Jacob and Kenneth Vines (Eds.), *Politics in the American States* (Boston: Little, Brown, 1965).

Appointment by board or individual other than governor	1
Popularly elected	0

The governor's budgetary powers are scaled as follows:

Governor has responsibility for preparing the budget and shares it only with persons appointed directly by him	5
Governor has responsibility but shares it with civil servant or appointee of someone other than himself	4
Governor shares power with committee selected by himself, but from a restricted list (Indiana is the only case)	3
Governor shares authority with another official whom he does not appoint, the elected state auditor	2
Governor prepares budget only as a member of a group, usually other elected executives and legislators	1

The measures of veto power rely upon a four-point scale derived by F. W. Prescott.[5] Only in North Carolina is the governor given no veto powers; but in others, the veto may be restricted by limitations on the length of time that a governor may consider a bill after it is passed by the legislature, by permitting a simple majority to override the veto, or by requiring that a vetoed bill reappear at the next legislative session. The veto power may be strengthened by the item veto, by greater time periods for the governor's consideration, and by the size of the majority needed to override a veto.

In addition to these evaluations of separate aspects of the governor's formal powers, it is possible to combine the four measures into a general index of the governor's formal powers. This combined index ranges from a low of 7 in Mississippi, South Carolina, Texas, and North Dakota, to a high of 18 in New Jersey and Illinois and 19 in New York. This does not necessarily mean, as Schlesinger points out, that within the context of their own states, the governors of Mississippi and North Dakota do not have as much influence as the governors of New York and Illinois. It means only that the governors of New York and Illinois need more *formal* powers to control the large complex bureaucracies in those states. Within their own borders, the governors of Mississippi and North Dakota are still central figures in their states' political system. It may be that patronage jobs, contracts, and petty favors provide governors of rural agricultural states with relatively more influence than the governors of urban, industrial states. Patronage and pork are probably less important in urban industrial states where governors need formal controls .

Schlesinger has already identified the environmental correlates of the formal strength of governors. He notes that there is a clear relationship

[5] F. W. Prescott, "The Executive Veto in the American States," *Western Political Quarterly*, Vol. 3 (1950), pp. 98–112; also cited by Schlesinger, op. cit.

TABLE 5 *Economic Development and the Formal Powers of Governors*

	Income	Industrial-ization	Education	Urban-ization
GOVERNOR'S				
Budget powers	.33*	.21	.20	.30*
Appointive powers	.39*	.27	.12	.24
Tenure potential	.49*	.36*	.39*	.30*
Veto powers	.34*	.10	.30*	.32*
Total power index	.60*	.38*	.37*	.44*

Note: Figures are simple correlation coefficients: an asterisk indicates a significant relationship.

between the size of the states and formal executive power: Texas is the only populous state where the governor's formal strength is low, while the nation's largest states—California, New York, Pennsylvania, Illinois, and New Jersey—all rank near the top in governor's powers. He also observes that formal governors' powers are related to economic development. As wealth, urbanization and industrialization increase, so also does the complexity of state administration and the need for formal executive control. Table 5 confirms Schlesinger's observations about economic development and governors' power. Again it is important that we keep in mind the relationships between these environmental variables and the powers of governors, since environmental variables are also related to policy outcomes. This means that in order to sort out the impact of governors' formal powers on public policy, it will be necessary to control for the effect of these environmental variables.

Governors' Powers and Public Policy

There is little evidence that a governor's formal powers significantly affect policy outcomes in the fifty states. While "strong" and "weak" governor states pursue somewhat different policies in education, health, welfare, highways and taxation, these differences are largely attributable to the impact of economic development rather than to the governor's power. Table 6 indicates that "strong" governor states spend more per pupil for education, pay higher teachers' salaries, have lower drop-out rates, pay higher welfare benefits, spend more per capita for health, collect more taxes, and rely more on local governments for revenues and services, than "weak" governor states. However, these relationships are clearly a product of the intervening effect of economic development; that is, a product of the fact that strong governor states are wealthy, urban, and industrial while weak governor states are not. The partial coefficients in Table 6 show no significant relationships between the governor's powers and public policy, while controlling for urbanization, industrialization, income, and adult education. In other words, the relationships between the governor's powers and public policy "wash out" when economic development is controlled. (The only exception is the relationship between the governor's tenure power and avoidance of income taxation; interestingly, the coefficient suggests that short-term governors are more likely to get state income taxes passed than governors who can succeed themselves.) If these operations are reversed and one examines partial coefficients for the relationships between economic development variables and public policy (not shown here), one finds that controlling for the governor's powers does *not* wash out the effect of economic development variables. This lends additional evidence that economic development is more influential than the governor's powers in determining public policy.

Assessing Executive Influence: Macro- and Microanalysis

Comparative analysis of policy outcomes in the fifty states suggests that economic development variables are more influential than the organizational structure of state government or the formal powers of governors in determining a wide variety of important policy outcomes. On the whole, states with fragmented executive structures do not pursue notably different policies than states with streamlined executive structures; most of the policy differences which do occur turn out to be a product of socioeconomic differences among the states rather than a direct product of structural variables. Likewise, there are few systematic policy differences between states with "strong" and "weak" governors, when these terms are employed to describe formal governor's powers. Most of the policy differences which do occur are largely a product of the fact that the strong governor states are wealthy, urban, and industrial, while the weak governor states are poor, rural, and agricultural. Of course, it is conceivable that structural variables or governor's powers could have a more observable impact on some policy outcomes which were not investigated. Yet public expenditures for education, health, welfare, and highways, the liberality of welfare benefits, teachers' salaries and the quality of education, the tax burden and revenue structure, the rural-urban distribution of highway funds, and the degree of reliance upon state versus local governments in the provision of public service—all appear at face value to be important policy outcomes in state politics. Yet the organization of state government and the formal powers of governors seem to have little impact on these outcomes.

How do these findings compare with what we know about the effect of structural features and governers' powers on political processes *within*

TABLE 6 *Public Policy and the Formal Powers of Governors*

	Governor's formal powers									
	Budget		Appointive		Tenure		Veto		Total index	
Public policy outcomes	Sim.	Par.	Sim.	Par.	Sim.	Par.	Sim.	Par.	Sim.	Par.
EDUCATION										
Per pupil expenditures	.28	.23	.36*	.24	.27	.19	.38*	.26	.49*	-.04
State % educ. exp.	-.24	-.09	-.08	-.07	.15	-.03	.01	-.03	-.08	.05
Average teachers' salaries	.23	.13	.40*	.17	.39*	.13	.28	.15	.50*	.19
Size of school district	-.10	-.10	.07	-.08	.18	-.04	-.13	-.09	.01	.04
Teacher-pupil ratio	-.11	-.17	-.05	-.16	.04	-.13	-.23	-.18	-.12	.20
Dropout rate	.22	.10	.19	.10	.13	.07	.25	.08	.30*	-.04
Mental failures	-.25	-.08	-.11	-.06	.01	.01	-.10	-.02	-.18	.07
HEALTH AND WELFARE										
Unemployment benefits	.29	.08	.29*	.07	.44*	.09	.35*	.08	.52*	.10
ADC benefits	.35	.15	.32*	.13	.26	.12	.26	.11	.46*	.02
General asst's benefits	.37	-.06	.38*	-.07	.26	-.10	.32*	-.07	.53*	.10
ADC recipients	-.25	-.02	-.02	.01	-.01	.02	-.14	.01	-.16	-.01
Unemployment recipients	.24	.12	.26	.09	.37*	.12	-.03	.06	.34*	-.02
Per capita welfare exp.	.18	.10	-.27	.05	.04	.09	.35*	.13	.07	.11
Per capita health exp.	.30*	-.09	.15	-.12	.41*	-.08	.17	-.12	.41*	.11
State % welfare exp.	-.24	.19	-.29*	.19	.01	.23	-.01	.21	-.24	-.04
State % health exp.	-.10	.12	-.03	.13	-.17	.10	.02	.16	-.12	-.08

TAXATION										
Per capita tax revenues	.28	.04	.13	.03	.37*	.05	.36*	.05	.42*	–.05
Taxes relative to income	–.10	.07	–.27	.02	–.11	.07	.11	.05	–.17	–.08
State % taxes	–.40*	–.03	–.32*	–.01	–.12	.01	.01	.04	–.36*	–.21
Sales taxes	.00	–.20	.04	–.20	.08	–.17	–.27	–.25	–.03	.05
Income taxes	.05	–.29	.01	–.29	–.28	–.33*	.08	–.26	–.08	–.05
HIGHWAYS										
Per capita highway exp.	.00	.01	–.17	–.02	–.10	–.02	.00	–.01	–.12	–.12
State % highway exp.	–.22	.05	.01	.08	.10	.09	–.32	.03	–.16	–.05
Highway fund diversions	–.09	.01	–.08	.01	.06	.03	.05	.02	–.03	–.17
Rural-urban distribution	–.03	.05	.08	.07	.08	.05	–.11	.04	–.04	.13

Note: Figures are simple and partial correlations coefficients; partial coefficients control for the effects of urbanization, industrialization, income, and education; an asterisk indicates a significant relationship.

states? If these structural variables are relatively unimportant in determining policy outcomes, are they important in determining political relationships *within* states?

Deil Wright has reported that agency heads tend to prefer direct gubernatorial control of their agencies, in contrast to control by an independent commission or by the legislature.[6] Wright asked 933 agency heads in all fifty states a series of questions about governor versus legislative influence in executive administration. These agency heads felt that the governor was more sympathetic to the goals of their agency and less likely to reduce their budgets than was the legislature. The implication of Wright's survey is that an increase in gubernatorial control over state administration would increase public service levels, assuming that the perceptions of agency heads about benevolent governors is accurate.

Ira Sharkansky provides more direct evidence that the governor's formal powers affect budgetary allocations within states.[7] Sharkansky examined the relationships between the budget requests of 592 agencies in nineteen states, the governors' recommendations regarding these requests, and legislative appropriations vis-à-vis agency requests and governors' recommendations. He was able to identify states where the governor's recommendations were closely adhered to by the legislature, and to distinguish them from states where the governor's recommendations were somewhat less influential. It turned out that the governor was more influential in agency-governor-legislative interaction in those states where he had long tenure and strong veto powers. Sharkansky concluded:

> The veto and tenure powers of the Governor help to strengthen his position with both agencies and the legislature. Because of formal perogatives, the governor appears to be in a more secure position when he reduces agency requests and makes recommendations to the legislature; the governors that have these powers are more likely to be severe in cutting agency requests and they are more likely to be successful in their recommendations to the legislature. In contrast, the presence of numerous separately elected executives appears to benefit agencies at the Governor's expense. In the states where there are many elected officials, agencies are more likely to get their acquisitive requests approved by the legislature and the governor's recommendation is most likely to be altered in the legislature.

These findings about the relative influence of "strong" and "weak" governors *within* their respective states are not inconsistent with our find-

[6] Deil Wright "Executive Leadership in State Administration," *Midwest Journal of Political Science*, Vol. 11 (February 1967), pp. 1–26.

[7] Ira Sharkansky, "Agency Requests Gubernatorial Support and Budget Success in State Legislatures," *American Political Science Review*, Vol. 62 (December 1968), pp. 1220–1231.

ings that throughout the fifty states the public policies of "strong" and "weak" governor states cannot be systematically distinguished. We contend only that economic development levels in the fifty states are more influential determinants of policy outcomes than structural variables. However, within any particular state with a given level of economic development, the role of the governor in policy formations is still vitally affected by the formal powers at his disposal.

Deil S. Wright

Executive Leadership in State Administration

Governors are not the only state executive officers with influence on the policy process. State constitutions generally provide for a plural executive, the governor sharing part of the executive role with several other officers elected by the people to serve simultaneous terms with him. In practice, many of these officers develop constituency support independent of that of the governor and so are not automatically allies of his in office, even if they are of the same party. In addition to these administrators, of course, there are always others appointed by and responsible to the governor.

Needless to say, this three-way breakup of executive leadership in state government has a profound effect not only on the governor's power in state administration but on the administrative process as well. The relationship between the governor and state administrators is perhaps the most important factor in the successful operation of the policy process at the state level.

Wright tackled that relationship head on in the reading that follows and comes to some interesting conclusions. The passage of time since the study was conducted has not appreciably altered the situation it describes.

The issue of executive leadership in state and local government has been the fulcrum of debate among academicians and the focus of power struggles among public officials for most of the 20th century. From the

From the *Midwest Journal of Political Science*, Vol. 11, No. 1 (February 1967), pp. 1–26. Some descriptive and bibliographical footnotes have been omitted for considerations of space and textual format.

distant days of Seth Low and Frank Lowden to latest state or local reorganization study commission the theme has remained essentially the same—concentrate power in the chief executive and hold him responsible! The standard solution to this "problem" has been the prescription of more power for the executive, although there have been noted and articulate dissents from this prognosis. Herbert Kaufman has termed "executive leadership" one of the three doctrines permeating the history of public administration in the United States.[1] The other two doctrines, representativeness and neutral competence, Kaufman posits as preceding and overlaying the executive leadership doctrine. He also argues that the last-mentioned doctrine had been in sharp conflict with neutral competence in recent years and is currently dominant, at least among political scientists.

In addition to Kaufman's analysis there is a much larger body of literature on state government that describes the primacy of the governor in state politics and administration. Writing in the late 1930's, Leslie Lipson argued that the govenor's role had evolved "from figurehead to leader."[2] A decade ago Coleman Ransone completed a broad-ranging interview-based study of American governors that both updated Lipson's analysis and elaborated more broadly the governor's role in state political systems.[3] More recently the position of the governor has been appraised in short critical discussions. Malcolm Jewell expresses cautious optimism about the present and future abilities of the governor to marshal the resources and manage the political complexities.[4] Another observer, Joseph Schlesinger, is not as optimistic. He contends that the position of the governor, as well as the entire apparatus of state government, is one of "uncertainty" and "indeterminacy." These conditions, he suggests, can be traced to the "intermediary and ambiguous role of the state in the American political system."[5]

The preceding references are illustrative of the few critical and systematic efforts analyzing the governor's role in state government. They are valuable and insightful within their defined limits. We still lack, however, a deeper grasp of the relationship between the chief executive and the

[1] Herbert Kaufman, "Emerging Conflicts in the Doctrines of Public Administration," *American Political Science Review,* Vol. 50, No. 4 (December, 1956), pp. 1057–1073; and *Politics and Policies in State and Local Governments* (Englewood Cliffs, New Jersey: Prentice–Hall, 1963), pp. 35–44.

[2] Leslie Lipson, *The American Governor: From Figurehead to Leader* (Chicago: University of Chicago Press, 1939), 282 pp.

[3] Coleman B. Ransone, Jr., *The Office of Governor in the United States* (University of Alabama Press, 1956), 417 pp.

[4] Malcolm Jewell, "State Decision-Making: The Governor Revisited," paper presented at the 1963 annual meeting of the American Political Science Association, New York City, September 4–7, 1963.

[5] Joseph A. Schlesinger, "The Politics of the Executive," in Herbert Jacob and Kenneth Vines (eds.), *Politics in the American States: A Comparative Analysis* (Boston: Little, Brown, 1965), p. 208.

administrative process at the state level. One approach to this relationship is from the governor's standpoint; it is best implemented by interviewing governors, as Ransone did in his study. An alternative approach to studying this relationship is to survey top state administrators. This latter approach, employing a mailed questionnaire, was the one adopted to secure data reported and interpreted in this article. A brief discussion of the methodological aspects of the study appear as an appendix. Two additional comments are required here: (1) These data on the attitudes of 933 department and agency heads from all 50 states constitute a large and representative cross-section of top-echelon administrators at the state level, and (2) this discussion of executive leadership and state administration is only one of several major dimensions encompassed by the research.

Political Relationships and Administration

It is axiomatic that public administration proceeds within a political setting. This is particularly true at the state level. Here the governor and the legislature are the formal institutions of political control. To assess the respective roles and relationships of these two political actors to the administrative process we asked questions designed to measure the attitudes of state administrators toward these authoritative institutions. One question asked the agency head to judge which of these political actors, the governor or the legislature, exercised the greater control over the affairs of his department or agency. Money is an important means to the accomplishment of agency goals. A second question therefore inquired about the administrator's views on who had the greater tendency to cut agency budget requests, the legislature or the governor. We sought an additional and more generalized measure of the administrator's evaluation of gubernatorial versus legislative support of agency goals. Here we simply asked whether the governor or the legislature was more sympathetic to the aims and purposes of the administrator's agency. These three questions were intended to demark the perceptions of political controls by the state administrators.

The summary of marginal responses to these three questions is provided in Table 1. The data relevant to generalized control and budget reduction reveal the lesser role of the governor in comparison with the legislature vis-à-vis state administration. Thirty-two per cent of the agency heads felt that the governor exercised greater control; 25 per cent thought that the governor tended to be more restrictive than the legislature on budget requests. The respective percentages responding in terms of greater legislative control and legislative budget reduction were 44 and 60 per cent.

The primacy of the legislature in controlling administration at the state level has many ramifications and raises several questions. Since legislatures in most states meet only biennially, it is perhaps surprising to note the degree to which their non-continuous impact reverberates through the ad-

TABLE 1 *Attitudes of American State Executives on Political Relationships**

	Percentages** ($N = 933$)
Who Exercises Greater Control Over Your Agency's Affairs?	
Governor	32
Each About the Same	22
Legislature	44
Other and N.A.	2
	100
Who Has The Greater Tendency To Reduce Budget Requests?	
Governor	25
Legislature	60
Other and N.A.	15
	100
Who Is More Sympathetic To The Goals Of Your Agency?	
Governor	55
Each About the Same	14
Legislature	20
Other and N.A.	11
	100
What Type Of Control Do You Prefer?	
Governor	42
Independent Commission	28
Legislature	24
Other and N.A.	5
	100

* For the source of data and the survey instrument containing the precise wording of the questions see: Deil S. Wright and Richard L. McAnaw, "American State Administrators: Study Code and Marginal Tabulations for the State Administrative Officials Questionnaire," (Iowa City, Iowa: Department of Political Science and Institute of Public Affairs, January, 1965), Mimeographed, 40 pp.

** Tabled percentages throughout this article may not add to 100 because of rounding.

ministrative establishment. One might expect the continuity of the governorship contrasted with the discontinuous convening of the legislature to produce a more significant role for the state's chief executive than that accorded him in these findings.

It may be, however, that our notion of the discontinuous role of state legislatures with respect to the administrative process is a mistaken one. Legislative interim committees of a research or investigative nature, plus the very real possibility of continuous legislative oversight by one or a few important legislators, may be occurring to such an extent that our results accurately reflect continuous rather than discontinuous legislative control of state administration. Numerous observers have emphasized that individual congressmen and congressional committees are wont to tell administrators what to do in specific instances. The same pervasive legislative interest in administration is evidently present in several, if not most states as well as the national level.[6]

It is also possible that these results may reflect a particular response set on the part of state administrators. A substantial proportion (more than one fourth) of the responding administrators had legal training. This gives a strong law-oriented cast to our group of state executives. This law-oriented focus may have prompted many of our respondents to interpret the question of control largely in legal terms rather than in political or policy terms. Under such conditions the legislature, as law-giver, would most likely occupy a position of primacy.

The preceding qualification is negated to some extent by responses to the budget reduction question. Finances are central to program levels and policy directions and are less likely to be viewed in terms of law-oriented controls or anticipated negative reactions. In this sphere the legislature appears to exercise an even larger restrictive and containment role over state administration than on the dimension of generalized control.

Advocates of gubernatorial executive leadership will not be overjoyed by the results reported here. Since no trend data exist on gubernatorial versus legislative control we cannot document the effects of reorganizations designed to strengthen the position of the governor over state administration. We cannot, for example, confirm nor contradict Lipson's judgment of trends "from figurehead to leadership." But our findings a quarter-century after Lipson's thesis was advanced are inconsistent with his contention so far as the governor's present-day role as *administrative* chief. The governor apparently is not viewed as the primary power-wielder over state administrators.

We have attempted to delineate the perceptions of actual control over administration in state government. Perceptions of actual control may be usefully distinguished from other relational conditions and circumstances. Some of these other circumstances are:

1. perceptions concerning a positive orientation toward agency goals by governor and legislature in contradistinction to the negative implications of control and budget reduction;

[6] It was interesting to note that on a regional basis more administrators from the midwest reported greater legislative control than administrators in other regions, i.e., 53 per cent contrasted with approximately 40 per cent in the three other regions. The limited number of respondents from any one state (ranging from seven to twenty-seven) makes individual state-by-state comparisons and conclusions hazardous at best.

TABLE 2 *Control Over Agency Affairs by Sympathy for Agency Goals, American State Executives*

Agency goals greater sympathy for	Greater control over agency affairs: Governor	Each about the same	Legislature
	(percentages; number of cases in parentheses)		
Governor	81	52	52
Each About the Same	11	29	13
Legislature	8	19	35
Total	100 (276)	100 (183)	100 (359)

2. preferred alternative conditions of control in contrast to the existing perceptions of control; and
3. objective, researcher-defined conditions of actual control contrasted with the subjective, administrator-perceived conditions of control.

Each of these circumstances deserves discussion and comment.

A measure of the political basis for positive orientations toward agency goals was obtained by asking the state executives: "Who do you feel is the more sympathetic to the aims and purposes of your agency or department? ( ) Governor ( ) Legislature." The tabulation of responses to this question also appears in Table 1. State administrators find the chief institutional basis of support for their program goals in the office of the governor. Over half of the executives believe that the governor is more sympathetic to their agency's goals; only one-fifth report that the legislature is more inclined than the governor to share their agency's aims and purposes. This finding documents the widespread and impressionistically held belief that the governor is the primary institutional means through which new or expanded state programs are advanced, advocated, and accepted. The data underscore the policy leadership role of the governor and reveal the specialized significance of the governor's position with respect to the administrative establishment. This leadership role persists despite the prior finding that from a control standpoint the governor's influence is exceeded by that of the legislature.

What is the relationship between perceptions of control and views concerning positive support? Do administrators who perceive the governor as the primary control agent over their operations also find him more supportive than the legislature of their agency's goals? What are the goal support views of administrators who felt they were under the primary control of the legislature? The tabulation presented in Table 2 reveals a strong association between the support and control variables.

Those under gubernatorial control obtain their chief support from that source. Of those under legislative domination, however, a majority obtain primary support from the governor. A similar patterns exists among administrators in the "each about the same" category. It seems evident that the administrators in these two majority categories are those who experience most acutely the vice-grip in which our traditional separation of powers locks most top-level administrators. To borrow a phrase from voting studies, these are the "cross-pressured" administrators.

Perceptions of actual control, we suggested, could be distinguished from conditions of control preferred or desired by state agency chiefs. Under what control conditions or under whose primary influence would state executives prefer to operate? We tapped this attitude dimension by means of the following question: "If your state's governmental structure were to be reorganized and you were able to choose who should exercise the greater control over your agency, which of the following would you choose? ( ) Governor; ( ) Legislature; ( ) Independent Commission."

We had a special reason for posing the problem in this particular manner. Our preceding questions were presented in terms of legislative versus governor influence. In probing preferred control conditions we felt it necessay to offer the respondents a third alternative, independence of either primary legislative or primary gubernatorial control. We were cognizant of the strong centrifugal forces present in government agencies generally and at the state level in particular. We therefore included the alternative "Independent Commission" as one of the three institutional sources of control over the state administrator and as an indicator of the pressures for independence at the state level. In more general terms this option gave the respondent an opportunity to "take administration out of politics." Indeed, this motive force behind the neutral competence school was, as Kaufman has indicated, chiefly responsible for the proliferation of independent boards and commissions.[7]

The marginal responses to the preferred control question are indicated in Table 1. The most preferred condition for state executives is under the primary control of the governor. While 42 per cent of the executives selected this alternative, equally significant results are: (1) that less than a majority of the state administrators opted for gubernatorial control, and (2) that more than one fourth (28 per cent) preferred to function under the primary control of an independent commission. We have no standard for judging the requisite or appropriate degree of independence, if any, at the state level. But a figure in excess of one-fourth of all state agency heads favoring independence clearly identifies the extent to which there are strong centrifugal pressures fractionalizing state administration.

The sources of pressures for independence are many and varied. Interest groups, professional associations, popular election, and special meth-

[7] Kaufman, "Emerging Conflicts . . . ," p. 1060.

TABLE 3 *Perceived and Preferred Political Relationships of American State Executives*

Preferred type of control	Governor	About Equal	Legislature
	(percentages; number of cases in parentheses)		
	Greater control over agency affairs		
Governor	77	42	22
Independent Commission	20	40	31
Legislature	3	18	47
Total	100 (294)	100 (188)	100 (394)
	Greater sympathy for agency goals		
Governor	58	45	14
Independent Commission	28	30	31
Legislature	14	25	55
Total	100 (503)	100 (115)	100 (179)
	Greater tendency to reduce budget requests		
Governor	53		42
Independent Commission	27		29
Legislature	20		29
Total	100 (226)		100 (540)

ods of financing particular programs are only a few sources. We were not able to probe these and other sources of possible pressures toward independence within the limited confines of our questionnaire. It is important, however, to examine the relationships between preferred control and the other relational measures of perceived actual control sympathy for agency goals, and budget reduction tendencies. The relationships between these variables are presented in Table 3.

Comparisons of the percentages across the rows for the governor and for the legislature categories in the cross-tabulations reveal exceptionally powerful associations between the first two "independent" variables and the "dependent" variable of preferred control. Only 3 per cent of those presently under the primary control of the governor would prefer a shift to primary control by the legislature and 20 per cent desire a change to dominance by an independent commission. The relationship is considerably attentuated in the case of the budget reduction—preferred control relationship.

Interesting and substantial defections occur among those administrators presently under the dominant influence or finding greatest goal sympathy from the legislature. About half (47 per cent) of those under legislative control prefer to remain there; 22 per cent indicate a desired shift to gubernatorial control while an even larger proportion, 31 per cent, desire a shift to independent commission control. A similar pattern exists among administrators believing that the legislature affords greater support for agency goals. On the matter of budget reduction the shift away from the legislature is even more pronounced with only 29 per cent preferring to remain under legislative control.

These data disclose powerful preferences for a shift away from legislative control at the state level. More importantly, however, these preferences for altered control do not accrue chiefly to the benefit of the governor. Rather, they are in the direction of independence from both gubernatorial and legislative control. In recognition of the governor's position as nominal head of state administration, we should acknowledge the clear majorities preferring to remain under the governor's primary control among those who find themselves currently under his primary control and among those who find him most sympathetic to their agency goals. Additionally, the governor is first choice for preferred control (1) among the administrators who perceive the governor and legislature about equal in terms of actual control and sympathy for agency goals, and (2) administrators who find either the legislature or the governor more inclined to reduce their budget requests. In this latter instance it seems clear that the state administrator is left with almost no alternative but to opt for gubernatorial control in hopes of making the best of a bad set of circumstances.

Further indication of the holding power of the governor among state administrators is disclosed by the data in Table 3. The pertinent figures are the respective percentages in the upper-left and lower-right cells of each of the three cross tabulations: 77, 58, and 53; 47, 55, and 29. These percentages constitute the proportions appearing respectively in the governor-governor and legislature-legislature cells of the three tabulations. Two points merit comment. First, the variable most influential in orienting the administrators' attitudes in the direction of preferred control by the governor is the variable of actual control. Second, it is somewhat surprising to find approximate consistency and similarity among all but the first and last percentages roughly in the neighborhood of 50 per cent. This suggests, interestingly enough, that the retention of state administrators' allegiance (options on preferred control) is about 50–50 proposition, with two exceptions. The first exception, the holding-power of actual control by the governor, has been mentioned. The second exception, the 29 per cent of those finding the legislature most restrictive on budget matters but preferring legislative control, might be called the losing power of state legislature. In other words, only this proportion of the state administrators are not disaffected or alienated from preferring legislative control by the fact that the legislature is more disposed than the governor to reduce their budget requests.

The findings outlined above suggests several provisional observations worthy of further reflection and subsequent investigation.

1. The challenges to the governor's primary as chief executive are several and are potent insofar as state administrator's preferences are accurate measures of the challenges.
2. The lack of integration within the administrative establishment at the state level is clearly evident. Indeed, it is perhaps a misnomer to speak of *an* administrative establishment. There appear to be deep cleavages within state administration along the relational dimensions of perceived political control, fiscal control, goal congruence, and preferred types of control.
3. There are strong pressures bending administrator's preferences in the direction of independence from either primary gubernatorial or primary legislative control. The exact sources of these pressures remain undetermined but their containment undoubtedly constitutes one of the major problems of state government today.

We might sum our findings to this point by indicating that Schlesinger's hypothesis about the "indeterminacy" of state government appears to be amply confirmed as far as state administration is concerned. This indeterminacy is perhaps best characterized in the author's words as "The unclear function of state administration, its varied character, and its relative freedom [and apparent desire] from public reckoning . . ."[8]

Formal Structure and Administration

Do the state administrator's perceptions of control correspond closely with the degree of formal influence exerted by the governor on state administration? For objective indicators of the formal influence of the governor we have utilized two measures. One is the appointive powers of the governor; the other is an overall index of the formal power position of the governor developed by Joseph Schlesinger.[9] The former variable is based on the method of appointment indicated by the state administrator in his response to our questionnaire. Schlesinger's index is based on four components of the governor's position—tenure potential and appointment, budgetary, and veto powers. Schlesinger allocated a range of points for each of these four power dimensions and derived an index of governor's powers ranging from 19 (in New York) down to 7 (in Mississippi, North Dakota, South Carolina, and Texas). This rank-order index is used to relate the per-

[8] Schlesinger, op. cit., p. 208.

[9] Schlesinger, op. cit., pp. 217–229.

TABLE 4 *Index of Formal Powers of State Governors* and Perceived and Preferred Political Relationships of American State Executives*

	Formal powers of the governor			
	Strong	Moderate	Weak	Very Weak
	(percentages; number of cases in parentheses)			
GREATER CONTROL OVER AGENCY AFFAIRS				
Governor	37	41	25	21
Each About the Same	28	21	23	16
Legislature	35	38	52	63
Total	100 (261)	100 (194)	100 (232)	100 (184)
GREATER TENDENCY TO REDUCE BUDGET REQUESTS				
Governor	37	34	19	22
Legislature	63	66	81	78
Total	100 (227)	100 (164)	100 (211)	100 (157)
SYMPATHY FOR AGENCY GOALS				
Governor	64	65	66	50
Each About the Same	17	12	15	19
Legislature	19	24	19	31
Total	100 (227)	100 (178)	100 (219)	100 (163)
PREFERRED TYPE OF CONTROL				
Governor	49	49	41	29
Commission	37	29	33	32
Legislature	23	22	26	39
Total	100 (252)	100 (190)	100 (220)	100 (182)

* Source of index: Joseph A. Schlesinger, "The Politics of the Executive," in Herbert Jacob and Kenneth Vines (eds), *Politics in the American States* (Boston: 1965), pp. 217–229.

ceptions of control by state administrators to the governor's formal power position. In other words, we are testing the association between objective and subjective measures of control. (See Table 4.)

Are the formal powers of the governor positively associated with administrator's perceptions of gubernatorial control? The answer is a qualified yes. In states where governors have stronger formal powers administrators acknowledge somewhat greater control by governors than in states where governors are weaker. The respective percentages are 37 and 41 compared with 25 and 21. The complement to this relationship is evident from the row percentages for legislative control. As one moves from the "strong" to the "very weak" categories the proportion of administrators reporting primary legislative control rises from 35 per cent to 63 per cent. These results tend to confirm the long-held contention of reformers and reorganizers that formal powers and prerogatives of a governor *do* make a significant difference so far as administrator-perceived (actual) control is concerned.

Our interpretation of the percentages should recognize the comparative, rather than the absolute nature of the inferences. This qualification is important. Examination of the percentages for executives in states where "strong" governors hold sway reveals that the competition for control over state administrators is approximately a stand-off; 37 per cent of the administrators report primary control by the governor, 35 per cent report control by the legislature, and 28 per cent indicate that control is equally divided. Here is further empirical confirmation of dispersed influence and powerful cross-pressures within administration at the state level. In this instance, however, our data disclose the presence and potency of these patterns in a political context where governors are the most powerful in a formal sense.

If these findings withstand challenge in their own right and are further confirmed by other research we may conclude that the net effect of structural reform and reorganization at the state level has *not* been to elevate the governor as *the* master of administrative management. Rather, the effects of strengthening the governor, based on the data from states where governors are stronger, has been to give him about an even chance in competing with the legislature for influence over the courses of action taken by state administrators. In a backhanded way this finding might be construed as a basis for advancing reorganization proposals that would strengthen the weaker governors. One frequent argument against such reorganization efforts is the cry of dictatorship, the charge that a more powerful governor will monopolize state government and state administration. Our findings show that even in states where governors are the strongest they are far from having dictatorial, monopoly, or predominant control in the eyes of top state administrators.

The associations between the formal powers of the governor and administrators' views on other political relations run generally in the expected directions. (See Table 4.) The relationships are less pronounced than in the instance of perceived control. Perhaps the most notable feature is the subordinated role of the "very weak" governors regarding preferred type of control. Only 29 per cent of the department heads in states with weak governors would prefer to be under the primary control of the governor in a reorganized setting. Lack of gubernatorial power evidently breeds disaffection and/or contempt for the weak governor.

The power of appointment is a much coveted prerogative in any system of government. Its significance stems largely from the presumed element of control attaching to the appointing privilege. Is there a close association between the method of appointment of state agency heads and their perceptions of control by the governor and legislature? We should recognize, however, that 14 per cent (126) of the 933 agency heads fall outside the appointment category, that is, they were popularly elected. These officials were, as one would expect, mainly secretaries of state, treasurers, auditors, and attorneys general. These elected officials directly reflect the doctrine of representativeness in public administration as that concept has been elaborated by Herbert Kaufman.[10]

Among the 807 non-elected administrators, appointment methods were varied and widely distributed. The percentages appointed by the various methods were:

Governor only	16%
Governor with Senate or Council consent	29
Board or Commission with Governor's consent	11
Board or Commission without Governor's consent	19
Department head	17
Other and N.A.	8
	100%

The above figures underscore the limited and extensively shared role of the governor in the appointment of top state administrators. Only one-sixth are appointed by the governor acting alone.

What of the association between appointment method and the several relational dimensions discussed earlier? If the gubernatorial power of appointment were extended more widely throughout state administration would there likely be a change in the perceptions and preferences of state administrators? Our data, presented in Table 5, permit us to make observations only on a cross-sectional basis. The "appointment" categories have been arranged in approximate descending order of the governor's involvement in the appointment process, from appointment by the governor only to popular election of the administrative official.[11]

There is a marked and consistent relationship between the manner in which a state administrator obtains his position and his perceptions of governor versus legislative control. The association is strong and positive between the degree of gubernatorial participation in appointment and per-

[10] Kaufman, "Emerging Conflicts . . . ," pp. 1058–59.

[11] Administrators appointed by department heads are omitted from this discussion since we were unable to ascertain the precise role of the governor in their appointment. The reason for the appearance of this type of appointment method-department head—in a survey of top state "agency heads" is the inconsistent administrative organizational pattern among the states. For example, in some states mental health is a separate department in its own right but in many others it is organizationally located with a state health department and the mental health director is appointed by the health department head.

TABLE 5 *Appointment Method and Perceived and Preferred Political Relationships of American State Executives*

	Appointment method									
	Governor alone		Governor with advice & consent		Board with governor's consent		Board without governor's consent		Popularly elected	
	(percentages; number of cases in parentheses)									
GREATER CONTROL OVER AGENCY AFFAIRS										
Governor	57		41		28		15		9	
Each About the Same	18		26		30		30		11	
Legislature	25		33		42		55		80	
	100	(131)	100	(230)	100	(89)	100	(149)	100	(124)
GREATER TENDENCY TO REDUCE BUDGET REQUESTS										
Governor	35		29		37		24		17	
Legislature	65		71		63		76		83	
	100	(115)	100	(204)	100	(78)	100	(123)	100	(111)
SYMPATHY FOR AGENCY GOALS										
Governor	80		70		66		58		33	
Each About the Same	16		18		16		18		15	
Legislature	4		12		18		24		51	
	100	(123)	100	(213)	100	(80)	100	(135)	100	(105)
PREFERRED TYPE OF CONTROL										
Governor	68		67		31		27		18	
Commission	20		17		47		53		18	
Legislature	13		16		22		20		65	
	100	(126)	100	(227)	100	(87)	100	(144)	100	(114)

ceived gubernatorial control. The more the governor is involved, the more he is perceived as having control; the less he is involved, the less he is perceived as having control. The extreme is reached with popular election. Only 9 per cent of the elected administrators view the governor as having more control than the legislature over their agency's affairs. Proponents of the short ballot and of strengthening the appointive powers of the governor were "right" from the standpoint of their objectives and proposed reforms. The method of appointment does make a significant difference regarding executive leadership. In contrast to fiscal reforms, however, broadening the personnel (appointment) powers of the governor has been far more difficult to accomplish. The above findings reveal this limited progress and also emphasize the significance of the personnel dimension for executive leadership at the state level.

A scanning of the percentages for the budget reduction and agency goal support variables tends to confirm the preceding observations. The positive associations between appointment method and gubernatorial influence on these two variables exist but are much less sharp and consistent, especially if elected officials are not considered. Varying appointment methods produce some differences in administrators' perceptions of the governor vis-à-vis the legislature on budget reduction and goal sympathy. But the variations, while substantial, are not as pronounced as in the case of the control dimension.

Large differences do appear, however, when preferred control is tabulated by appointment method. These differences can be observed in the final set of percentages in Table 5. Preference for gubernatorial control is, as expected, most divergent between the administrators who are popularly elected and those who are appointed by the governor alone or by him with senatorial consent. But a wide difference also exists between administrators in these latter two categories and those who are appointed by a board or commission (with or without the governor's consent). Less than one-third of the board-appointed administrators would prefer gubernatorial control whereas two-thirds of those appointed in some manner by the governor prefer gubernatorial control. The most popular option among the board-appointed agency heads is for primary control by an independent commission. Approximately half elect this alternative.

In broad terms these data can be meaningfully interpreted in the context of Kaufman's conflicting doctrines in public administration. Popular election at the state level enshrines the doctrine of "representativeness" for the most part in constitutional prescriptions. It is interesting to note how closely aligned and oriented these elected administrators are to the legislative body. The second sense in which Kaufman used representativeness—legislative supremacy over administration—is pointedly in evidence among these elected administrators. From the standpoint of executive leadership and popular election one is reminded of Max Weber's observation that if officials are elected instead of appointed discipline and control will be greatly weakened.[12]

Kaufman's doctrine of neutral competence is represented structurally by the appointive process involving boards and commissions. This institutionalized method of "taking administration out of politics" has notable consequences for the perceptions (and presumably conduct) of state administrators. Its most outstanding result is an undercutting of executive

[12] Max Weber, *The Theory of Social and Economic Organization,* translated by M. Henderson and T. Parsons (Glencoe, Illinois: The Free Press, 1947), p. 335.

TABLE 6 *Attitudes of American State Executives on Expansion of State and Own Agency's Services and Expenditures*

Attitude toward degree of expansion	Overall expansion of state services and expenditures	Expansion of own agency services and expenditures
	(percentages; number of cases in parentheses)	
No Expansion	30	24
Expand 0–5 Per Cent	7	8
Expand 5–10 Per Cent	19	16
Expand 10–15 Per Cent	16	16
Expand 15 Plus Per Cent	18	31
Other and N.A.	10	6
Total	100 (933)	100 (933)

leadership and a strong preference to maintain this special organizational status. About one half of those administrators appointed by a board or commission prefer primary control over their agency's affairs by this institutional arrangement. The close proximity of the percentage distributions for board-appointed administrators appointed with and without gubernatorial consent suggests a further observation. The institutional protection and insulation of a board or commission effectively prevents the governor from gaining the administrator's loyalties (preferred control) although gubernatorial consent to a board appointment does appear to make some difference in perceived actual control, i.e., 28 compared with 15 per cent.

Public Policy, Political Relationships, and Administration

Today the persistent policy issues in public administration at all levels of government are between the pressures for program expansion versus the inertia toward the status quo. It therefore seemed desirable to probe the attitudes of state department heads toward the expansion of some programs and services. This was accomplished by using two questions, one set in the context of overall expansion of state services, the other in the context of expanding the administrator's own agency's services and programs. If an administrator favored some expansion, that is, he answered yes to the lead question, a follow-up probe inquired about the preferred extent or degree of expansion. Alternatives ranged from "0-5 per cent" expansion to "more than 15 per cent" expansion. Table 6 presents a tabulation of the responses to the two questions and probes.

State executives are evidently disposed to respond in favor of enlarging their own programs and those of state government generally. Such

TABLE 7 *Attitude on Expansion of Own Agency's Services and Expenditures and Perceived and Preferred Political Relationships of American State Executives*

	Attitudes on expansion of own services						
	No expansion	0–5%	5–10%	10–15%	15+%	Total	Number of cases
GREATER CONTROL OVER AGENCY AFFAIRS							
			(percentages)				
Governor	25	8	16	19	33	100	276
Each About the Same	24	7	19	19	30	100	193
Legislature	26	8	17	14	35	100	387
GREATER TENDENCY TO REDUCE BUDGET REQUESTS							
Governor	22	9	15	15	38	100	222
Legislature	25	7	17	18	33	100	529
SYMPATHY FOR AGENCY GOALS							
Governor	20	9	19	18	34	100	488
Each About the Same	28	7	10	16	39	100	121
Legislature	30	8	15	16	31	100	172
PREFERRED TYPE OF CONTROL							
Governor	22	9	18	18	32	100	369
Commission	19	8	13	20	41	100	250
Legislature	36	7	19	13	26	100	210

views do not approach unanimity, however, since rather significant proportions (24 and 30 per cent respectively) do not favor any expansion of their own or their state's program.[13]

[13] A comparison of *desired expansions* by state executives with *actual* expansions of agency expenditures at the federal level is possible. Of the state executives who responded yes to the expansion question about two-thirds favored expansion of their own programs and expenditures by 10 per cent or more. At the federal level nearly one half of the 444 cases examined by Aaron Wildavsky (37 domestic agencies over a 12 year span) showed appropriation increases of more than 10 per cent in a single year. See, Aaron Wildavsky, *The Politics of the Budgeting Process* (Boston: 1964), p. 14. The legitimacy of such an inter-level comparison between desired and actual expenditure increases is open to challenge. It is justified on the similarity in the 1952–63 average annual percentage increases in state general expenditures and Federal non-military budgeted expenditures. These average annual increases are 8.02 and 9.43 per cent respectively. Derivation of the percentages is based on data from: U.S. Bureau of Census, *Census of Government: 1962,* Vol. VI, No. 4, *Historical Statistics on Government Finances and Employment* (Washington: 1964), and *Governmental Finances in 1963*, G-GF63-No. 2, November 1964.

What relationship exists between the program expansion preferences of administrators and their perceptions of control by the governor and legislature? The initial set of percentages in Table 7 provides the basis for observing that there is no apparent association. Nearly equal proportions of these under gubernatorial and legislative control are inclined against any expansion; a like situation is present in the categories favoring each of the varying degrees of program expansion. In other words, there is no concentration of sentiment for program expansion within a grouping of state executives that view themselves under the primary control of either the legislature or the governor.

There is no consequential variation in program expansion attitudes according to whether the governor or legislature is more disposed to reduce budget requests. Administrator's preferences for expanding their programs are not biased along lines of economy-minded governors or legislatures.

When we shift our focus from the dimension of actual control and examine executives' judgments concerning general goal support we observe the presence of a slight relationship between expansionist preferences and a perception of the governor as more sympathetic to agency goals. The relationship is not strong nor statistically significant and the lack of a clear and consistent association tends to confirm our prior observation concerning the extensiveness of pressures for expansion. The policy pressures for expanding expenditures and services at the state level are evidently so great, as witnessed by the majority favoring expansion, that expansion is a permeating and preponderant goal throughout state administration. The extensiveness and apparent intensiveness of expansion preferences override the previously-documented cleavages in control over administration between the governor and legislature.

Parenthetically, we might also mention the results of further data analyses that have a bearing on interpreting the expansionist attitudes of state administrators. We tabulated these attitudes by four socioeconomic characteristics of the respective states in which the administrators held their position. The characteristics were: urbanism, labor-force engaged in manufacturing, labor force in white collar occupations, and per capita income. In none of the cross tabulations was there any consistent or significant association between these macro-system socioeconomic characteristics and the micro-measured data of administrator attitudes. If any slight consistency could be discerned it was that administrators from the least urban, lowest income, and lowest manufacturing white collar states were a little more in favor of expansion than were administrators from states located at the other end of the spectrum on these variables. Aspirations for increased services are at least equal if not slightly more concentrated in the so-called "have-not" states. These attitudes may reflect a realistic assessment and a genuine commitment among administrators to meet the need for public services in these economically disadvantaged states.[14]

When policy attitudes are tabulated by preference for type of control in a reorganized state government a clear and statistically significant relationship is evident. The nature of this relationship is interesting and revealing. Administrators who prefer legislative control are more in favor of no expansion and less in favor of increases greater than 15 per cent. The agency chiefs most in favor of increases exceeding 15 per cent and least in favor of no expansion were the executives who preferred to operate under commission control—independent of either primary legislative or primary gubernatorial control! This finding solidifies the conclusion advanced and partially confirmed in the preceding section regarding the strong centrifugal tendencies toward independence at the state level. In this particular instance we see the tendency demonstrated in terms of those desiring organizational independence (a degree of isolation or insulation from control by the governor and legislature) and preferring service and expenditure increases. This additional finding poses not only the problem of centrifugal tendencies but also the issue of the political responsibility of the administrators most disposed to expand their programs. Can and should such independence . . . be tolerated at the state level where power is more fragmented than in the federal government?

An alternative interpretation might be placed on the relationship between preferred control and agency expansion. Instead of viewing the relationship as a drive for independence among "expansionist" state administrators the association could reflect the lack of past political support from either the governor or legislature. The absence of such support, especially under board or commission organizational arrangements, could be both the cause and effect of the observed relationship. Little policy support from the governor or legislature produces conditions prompting administrators to be more desirous of substantial program expansions. The same limited policy support may have alienated administrators from the governor and legislature, pushing them in the direction of more reliance on and confidence in their own resources for policy support, e.g., from clientele groups, professional associations, and other organized interest groups.

Concluding Observations

In this article we have briefly explored a few of the dimensions of executive leadership over state administration. A repetition of our findings is less necessary than an elaboration of their possible implications. These

14 The very slight relationship noted here may be the result of several uncontrolled and unknown factors, including the *lower* response rate from administrators in the low-income southern states. Response rates were generally in the 40–50 per cent range in the south; elsewhere they ranged from 70 to 90

implications raise several questions that may be conveniently classified under two headings.

1. What are the implications of these findings for chief executives and "executive leadership" reformers? These one-point-in-time results constitute a benchmark regarding the progress made to date in bringing state administration under the aegis of the governor. The results also constitute a challenge to those concerned about executive policy coordination at the state level. The structural insulation of portions of state government under boards and commissions has produced demonstrably "independent" attitudes among state administrators. These inclinations toward independence pose a major challenge, some might say a threat, to the firmly held tenet of a politically responsible bureaucracy. Are not administrative officials revealing a substantial degree of political irresponsibility when one-third opt for a measure of independence from executive *and* legislative control over administration? And is there not a greater threat presented when the "independence-oriented" administrators are also those most inclined toward expansion of their programs?

We need to be cautious in our response. Political responsibility is obviously a complex concept, one that undoubtedly has several dimensions, both attitudinal and behavioral. Our attitudinal probings deal only with preferred types of institutional control. It would be unwise and premature to judge harshly administrators' responsibility strictly in structural-institutional terms. Indeed, commitments to program accomplishment, clientele groups, administrative due process, and impartiality are other elements worthy of inclusion in the broad concept of political responsibility. Norton Long, for example, has argued that the bureaucracy itself is a more representative institution, both in democratic ethos and socio-economic composition, than our legislative bodies.[15] His concept of representation is in sharp contrast to the representativeness doctrine elaborated by Kaufman. The latter has defined representation in structural terms, i.e., direct popular election of administrative officials and/or legislative supremacy over the administrative establishment. Long's concept of representation includes the normative orientations of the administrator as well as their socio-economic and demographic personal characteristics.

Whatever the reform emphasis or focus in structural terms, it seems necessary to recognize additional elements in judging where and how to alter formal organizational arrangements. Neither structural symmetry nor

---

per cent. Among the southern administrators who did respond, however, 40 per cent favored expansion in their own agency's expenditures of "more than 15 per cent." This percentage is higher than in any other region where the figures were 31, 33, and 28 per cent for the northwest, midwest, and west respectively.

[15] Norton Long, "Bureaucracy and Constitutionalism," *American Political Science Review*, Vol. 46, No. 3 (September, 1952), pp. 808–818.

reasoned simplicity can be or should be the only consideration guiding governmental reforms.

2. The problem of reform-related structural arrangements is closely associated with a second broad area in which our findings have some significant implications. It has been said that in any struggle for power, power gravitates toward the participant who can use it the best. This axiom can be imposed on our findings and interpreted in an intergovernmental context. What do our results suggest regarding the role of the states vis-à-vis local and national governments?

Recent commentators have contended that the states are now or soon will become mere administrative districts of the national government, dispensing funds but effecting little if any policy influence. Our findings do not bear directly on this point but in an indirect way we can make some pertinent observations. One main theme persistent through our survey findings (which go beyond the data presented here) is the strong pluralism and wide diversity present in state administration. Pluralism and diversity are present in the social backgrounds, personal characteristics, career patterns, and attitudes of the state officials. These features are important factors operating against strong, effective state action, especially when it involves matters and relationships with other levels of government. If we grant a substantial degree of truth to the statement that power distributions in administration directly reflect power patterns at large, then York Willbern's analysis of political forces at the state level is accurate. Willbern contends that non-governmental constellations of power are much stronger at the state level than at the national or local levels and further, that "liberty" (by which he means pluralism or shared power) has tended to predominate as an important value in state government.[16]

Where do our results leave state government in this intergovernmental context? The results are not very favorable, at least from the administrative standpoint. There is the already-documented desire to substantially expand state services. Additionally, a majority of state administrators are prepared to accept activity and financing by any and all levels of government in various program areas. In very broad but somewhat oversimplified terms, we can say that the program orientations of state administrators appear to outweigh their commitments to state government as a unit of government. This tendency in administrative attitudes and loyalties has been given different terms: "functionalism," "vertical functional autocracies," and "programmatic values" are three examples. In the latter instance, programmatic values were posited in opposition to "expediency" or unit-of-government values. More recently, this phenomenon of administrator attitudes has been

[16] York Willbern, "The State as Components in an Areal Division of Powers," in Arthur Maass (ed.), *Area and Power: A Theory of Local Government* (Glencoe, Ill.: The Free Press, 1959), pp. 70–88.

examined at the federal level with regard to federal grant-in-aid programs. The conclusions reported there tend to mirror the results we have uncovered at the state level. When it comes to a choice between program considerations and intra- or intergovernmental coordination, administrators are not strongly inclined toward the latter choices. The long range consequences of these administrative tendencies at the state level are too imponderable for speculation. In the short run, however, unless these centrifugal forces are at least contained, if not rolled back, we are likely to see a further diminution of the general politico-administrative significance of state government.

James S. Lee

Toward an Understanding of State Legislative Decision-Making

Even in this volume the editors have fallen into the current American habit of putting executive power first in discussing governmental decision making. Perhaps it is because group behavior remains more difficult for analysis and understanding than than individual behavior. It is probably also because it is easier to focus attention on the few executives than on the many legislators. Even so, the legislative role in making public policy is obviously crucial in a representative democracy like the United States. It is even more crucial at the state level, where tradition combines with constitutional emphasis to keep legislatures central in the decision-making process. In this original piece, James Lee helps us understand how legislatures make the choices they do on public policy questions.

Introduction

As is true of many areas of political studies, research in the field of legislative behavior has been characterized by (1) the accumulation of an often bewildering multitude of disparate empirical findings and (2) comparatively few attempts to incorporate these results into more generally applicable theories. With respect to the subject of this essay, contemporary research on legislative decision-making (particularly that employing roll-call analysis) has attempted to explain policy choices by means of a wide variety of independent variables, including, among other things, party membership, demographic and political characteristics of constituencies, electoral competition, and individual characteristics of legislators. Because of their relevance to decision-making, there has also been a pronounced

This article was written especially for this volume.

interest in such social features of legislative bodies as communication and informal influence patterns.

Given this abundance of material, my main purpose in this essay is simply to discuss some of the varieties of this kind of research, particularly as it relates to state legislative decision-making, and to suggest a framework, synthesized from a number of these hypotheses and ideas, within which the policy outcomes (or aggregate decisions) produced by state legislative bodies might be better understood. The focus of analysis is specifically upon the determinants of choices made by individuals within the social and political contexts of such institutions rather than upon the economic or demographic correlates of aggregate policy decisions. Owing to the wide variety of state legislative environments in America, it should be noted that the choice of hypotheses included in this review has been based primarily upon an interest in theoretical parsimony. With certain important exceptions, only those studies which could apply to state legislative decision-making generally will be discussed.

Because of this diversity in American legislative institutions, the essay begins with a general discussion of the normal context and nature of choice in state legislative environments. Second, I review those hypotheses that relate decisions in a legislative context (in many cases, roll-call votes) to those variables deemed to have the greatest explanatory power; namely (1) the attitudes of individual legislators, (2) interest group activity, (3) party or factional affiliation and loyalty, and (4) constituency characteristics.

However, given what I believe to be the normal context of legislative decision-making, many of these variables are often demonstrably incapable of adequately explaining decisions in many circumstances. In other words, in numerous situations where the legislator is required to make some choice, the decision premises provided by such attitudes or sources of information are either irrelevant to him or may conflict to the point where he must search for additional premises upon which to base his decision. Where this is the case, I suggest that the legislator will search for decision cues from among his colleagues in the Assembly whom he perceives either as friends or as especially knowledgeable about the substance of legislation or the rules of the legislative game.[1] This aspect of legislative behavior

[1] The primary rationale for this stems from work done by Donald R. Matthews and James A. Stimson. See their two papers, "The Decision-Making Approach to the Study of Legislative Behavior: The Example of the U.S. House of Representatives," presented at the Annual Meeting of the American Political Science Association, New York, 1969; and "Decision Making by U.S. Representatives: A Preliminary Model," presented at the Conference on Political Decision Making, University of Kentucky, Lexington, Kentucky, 1968. Also, Cherryholmes and Shapiro use decision cues in the "communication" phase of a simulation model. Cleo H. Cherryholmes and Michael J. Shapiro, *Representatives and Roll Calls* (New York: Bobbs-Merrill, 1969), chap. 4. See

is discussed in a subsequent section of the essay. The concluding passages are concerned with combining these analytical perspectives into what hopefully will be a general and readily comprehensible model of state legislative decision-making.

The Context and Nature of Legislative Decision-Making

The environment in which state legislators make decisions is often muddled and complex. To begin with, members of state legislatures are normally called upon to cast numerous roll-call votes each session. And as one delves beneath the surface of public decision-making and notes the many decisions made in committee, office work, and caucuses, it becomes readily apparent that each legislator must make an enormous number of decisions. Moreover, while some of these decisions are substantively rather closely related, it is clear that the subject matter of most are incredibly diverse. Legislators are required to decide on topics ranging from small personal damage claims to costly welfare programs, from conservation to school needs to automobile insurance and back again.

In addition, as Matthews and Stimson have noted, apart from the number and scope of such decisions,

> most legislative proposals are complex, specific actions in specific cases in an attempt to cover every contingency. They attempt "fine tuning" around an already existing body of legislation that is itself specific and technical, containing amidst the many threes of precise legislative prescriptions the unclear and often inconsistent outlines of a forest of policy.[2]

Naturally enough, as the number, scope, and complexity of problems proliferates, the information required (and available) for making policy decisions increases as well, while the time available for consideration of problems—already diminished by a blossoming constituent case load and extrainstitutional activity—falls off sharply. What this means in practice is that the number of policy areas in which any single legislator is qualified to decide, by virtue of expertise and specialization, has been reduced.

Legislative decisions are also complicated by the legislator's awareness of his political vulnerability, of his need to make a good showing both to his constituents and colleagues. At the very least, he wants to avoid the

---

also, James S. Lee and William Mishler, "A Diacronic Analysis of Three Dimensions of Congressional Decision-Making: A Model of Freshmen Cue-Taking and Socialization in the Eighty-Nineth and Ninetieth Congresses," Duke University, 1971 (unpublished master's thesis).

[2] Donald R. Matthews and James A. Stimson, "The Decision-Making Approach to the Study of Legislative Behavior: The Example of the U.S. House of Representatives," op. cit., p. 9.

kinds of blunders that might diminish his chances for reelection. Moreover, typically he is interested in advancing his career,[3] in identifying himself with a collectively powerful group so as to maximize his political efficacy, and in earning the approval of those who are in a position to give him choice committee assignments, publicity, and assistance in realizing his policy proposals. He may feel the necessity to conform, to avoid alienating various powerful groups and leaders. He assumes, however, that success in the aforementioned areas will be determined in large part by the numerous, varied, and complex decisions that he must make in the legislative arena.

Even if one were to ignore the consequences of state legislative decision-making upon state and national environments, it is clear that the stakes of those decisions are very high for the legislator, whereas his ability to decide is severely and profoundly limited by the number, scope, and complexity of issues as well as by limitations on time, resources, and information. How, then, does he decide? To begin with, his mode of decision-making is essentially that of rationality. At its most unsophisticated level, a decision can simply be a patterned response to familiar stimuli. In the case of the legislator, choices in the past will theoretically determine and condition choices in the future. At the other extreme, an unfamiliar stimulus will evoke problem-solving activity directed toward finding performance activities with which to complete the response. It is this "search" phenomenon that is perhaps most characteristic of state legislative decision-making. The difficulty of arriving at a psychologically acceptable decision depends upon the criterion set. According to March and Simon, "finding the optimal alternative is a radically different problem from finding a satisfactory alternative." An alternative is optimal if "there exists a set of criteria that permits all alternatives to be compared and if the alternative in question is preferred, by these criteria, to all other alternatives." An alternative is satisfactory if "there exists a set of criteria that describes minimally satisfactory alternatives and if the alternatives in question meet or exceed all these criteria." [4] Since, in any given legislative decision-making situation, an optimal set of criteria is often impossible to obtain, the legislator can only be concerned with discovering and selecting satisfactory alternatives. Legislators, in Simon's phrase, will "satisfice" rather than "optimize." They will try to attain their goals, whatever they might be, by

[3] A majority of state legislators interviewed by Wahlke and his associates said they expected to seek reelection; a large percentage indicated that they aspired to another office (usually Congress, state Senate, or state judicial office). For a full discussion of their legislative careers, see John C. Wahlke, Heinz Eulau, William Buchanan, and Leroy C. Ferguson, *The Legislative System: Explorations in Legislative Behavior* (New York: Wiley, 1962), chaps. 4–6.

[4] James G. March and Herbert A. Simon, *Organizations* (New York: Wiley, 1959), pp. 139–140.

striving for the ideal of rationality in their choices without ever achieving it; by being satisfied with gaining certain minimal as opposed to maximal criteria in their calculations for goal attainment.

How, then, does the legislator simplify and limit his model of reality, his definition of the situation? On what basis does he establish a minimally satisfying set of decision criteria?

Initial Premises of Decision: The Impact of Attitude

I began this essay by noting a number of variables which previous research had suggested to be most powerful in explaining legislative decisions at an aggregate level. When dealing with particular individuals, however, it is unreasonable to assume that such influences are of equal importance to everyone. On the contrary, the decision criteria upon which an individual bases a decision will vary in their relative importance according to the legislator's perception of their relevance to him. For example, party sponsorship or position on a piece of legislation is relevant to the legislator's decision on that issue to the degree that party loyalty is important to him. At one extreme would be the legislator who is totally dependent on, and loyal to, his party, as in the case of most members of parliamentary systems; at the other extreme would be the maverick or "outsider" who bases his decisions upon such criteria as the ideological character of the legislation or constituent's demands. In the former instance, party affiliation provides a useful simplifying strategy for decision and renders his voting behavior, on any issue that the party voices its position on, completely predictable. In the latter case, party affiliation does not serve as a simplifying strategy and is a theoretically useless predictor of legislative decision.

As Wahlke and others put it, "The public policy decisions of legislatures cannot realistically be visualized as simple mathematical resultants of a given number of 'pressures,' each of measurable direction and strength, impinging on passively reacting legislators." [5] The legislator, rather than functioning as a vacuous throughput mechanism, brings to the legislative arena certain roles, ideologies, prejudices, and ambitions which color and influence his perceptions of any possible set of decisional criteria. He cannot be considered, therefore,

> equivalent to the steel ball in a pinball game, bumping passively from post to post down an inclined plane. He is a human being, involved in a variety of relationships

[5] John C. Wahlke, William Buchanan, Heinz Eulau, and Leroy C. Ferguson, "American State Legislators' Role Orientations Toward Pressure Groups," *Journal of Politics*, **22** (1960), 204. Similar views are expressed by Peter Odegard, "A Group Basis of Politics: A New Name for an Ancient Myth," *Western Political Quarterly*, **2** (1958), 689–712.

> with other human beings. In his role as legislator his accessibility to various groups is affected by the whole series of relationships that define him as a person.[6]

It is important to note that many of these attitudes constitute distinct identifiable role sets—defined here as "patterns of behavior associated with a given position or status in the expectations and orientations of people." [7] With respect to the legislative environment, Wahlke and his colleagues explain the concept of role in this way: "Membership in the legislature constitutes a *status* or *position* in society. This means that people in the society *expect* certain behaviors by incumbents of that position. Legislators have similar expectations toward each other, and they all have expectations with respect to other classes of actors they encounter in doing their legislative business." [8] The important point here, of course, is that the aforementioned attitudes of legislators are not entirely idiosyncratic to particular individuals but rather are often combined to produce role sets common to many legislators. In fact, the development and perpetuation of such roles is one important way to define the ongoing institutionalization of American legislative bodies.

The varieties of possible roles and attitudes adopted by state legislators are, of course, quite numerous; no attempt will be made here to summarize the large amount of research that has been devoted to their identification and analysis. However, of principal importance[9] would be role orientations toward area represented (i.e., does the legislator represent his own district, some region of the state, the state as a whole, etc.?),

[6] David B. Truman, *The Governmental Process* (New York: Knopf, 1957), pp. 332–333. This point is also argued persuasively in Lewis A. Froman, Jr., *Congressmen and Their Constituencies* (Chicago: Rand McNally, 1963), chap. 8; and Corinne Silverman, "The Legislator's View of the Legislative Process," *Public Opinion Quarterly,* **18** (1954), 180–190.

[7] Wahlke, Buchanan, Eulau, and Ferguson, "American State Legislator's Role Orientations Toward Pressure Groups," op. cit., p. 205. The concept of role is used extensively in a variety of disciplines, often with rather inconsistent connotations. For a critical review of much of this work, see Neal Gross, Ward S. Mason, and Alexander W. McEachern, *Explorations in Role Analysis: Studies of the School Superintendency Role* (New York: Wiley, 1966). Good studies which employ role theory in the analyses of legislative politics include: Allan Kornberg, *Canadian Legislative Behavior* (New York: Holt, Rinehart and Winston, 1967), Roger Davidson, *The Role of the Congressman* (New York: Pegasus, 1969), chap. 5, and the various works by Wahlke and his colleagues cited previously.

[8] Wahlke, Buchanan, Eulau, and Ferguson, "American State Legislators' Role Orientations Toward Pressure Groups," op. cit., p. 205. This view is encapsulated in Kornberg's definition of role as, "a set of expectations held for a position by its incumbent and by the incumbents of related positions." See Allan Kornberg, op. cit., p. 8.

[9] The following discussion is based upon a summary of role types described by Malcolm Jewell and Samuel Patterson in *The Legislative Process in the United States* (New York: Random House, 1966), pp. 385–386.

interest groups, political parties, and bureaucracy (i.e., orientations toward the governor or toward the administrative apparatus). Also of interest are role orientations relating to (1) representational style (i.e., does he base his decisions on the wishes of his constituents, his own principles, or some combination of the two?); (2) his own purpose in the legislative institution (e.g., as a compromiser of various interests and points of view, as an innovator, or an advocate of popular demands); (3) the structure of the legislature (including the roles associated with expertise, friendship, or various levels of the legislative hierarchy such as party leader, committee chairman, committee member, or freshman member); and (4) ideology. Bell has suggested, moreover, that it would be useful to employ certain personality typologies—such as Riesman's distinction between inner- and other-directed individuals[10]—as a shorthand means of accounting for more idiosyncratic variations in the psychological sets of legislators.[11]

While the possibilities are numerous, it seems clear that most such attitudinal characteristics are likely to screen or distort the impact of other influences on the legislator—influences which normally emanate from sources "external" to the state legislative environment. It is to a discussion of these that we now turn.

The Effect of Party Membership

On the whole, party appears to be the single most important influence on the decisions made by legislators. The evidence for this conclusion stems mainly from a variety of roll-call analyses of voting in Congress and in two-party state legislatures. Most of these studies have come to the general conclusion that, while voting patterns on some roll calls might exhibit the influence of other factors, voting normally follows party lines (in varying degrees).

Obviously, where a single party dominates (controlling most if not all of the legislative seats) party is not apt to be an important influence, since there is very little incentive to maintain voting cohesion. In geographic terms, party appears to be most influential in the two-party states of the Northeast and Midwest, such as New York, Pennsylvania, New Jersey, Ohio, Indiana, or Illinois. Party is a significant, though somewhat less important, factor in state legislative voting in most of the western and border states, such as California, Oregon, Arizona, Kentucky, West Virginia, and

[10] David Riesman, with Nathan Glazer and Reuel Denny, *The Lonely Crowd: A Study of the Changing American Character* (Garden City, N.Y.: Doubleday-Anchor, 1956).

[11] Roderick Bell, "Notes for a Theory of Legislative Behavior: The Conceptual Scheme," in Herbert Hirsch and M. Donald Hancock, eds., *Comparative Legislative Systems* (New York: Free Press, 1971).

Missouri. In general terms, the influence of party in two-party state legislatures varies according to the characteristics of the state and the nature of its parties' politics (for example, the state's level of urbanization and industrialization, ideological or issue cohesiveness of the parties, strength of local party organizations, and the socio-economic and urban-rural polarization of constituencies).

For example, Malcolm Jewell, in an analysis of voting in state legislatures, found relatively high levels of party voting in six of the eight states studied. But he noted also that, although Republicans were no more cohesive than Democrats on issues where a majority of the parties opposed one another, party voting was more characteristic of large urban industrialized states.[12] Greenstein and Jackson, in a reanalysis of Crane's data on roll-call voting in the Wisconsin Assembly, concluded that there was a close correspondence between those votes which exhibit party differences and the votes that the Assemblymen perceived as party issues.[13] In Massachusetts, MacRae suggested that party loyalty in voting was not unidimensional, but rather was composed of loyalty to the organization and ideological affinity.[14] In general, party leaders tended to exhibit higher loyalty than did the regular members. In addition, Lockard[15] and Souraf[16] have noted that party influence varies according to the strength of local party organizations.

At the other end of the spectrum, there are numerous states whose legislatures are dominated by a single party. The Democrats, for example, still maintain huge majorities in the legislatures of the South all the way from Texas to South Carolina. Republican domination is less common but still occurs in some rural states of the Midwest and Northeast, such as Kansas, Vermont, and New Hampshire.

In these states, obviously, other factors must be considered to account for variations in the decisions reached by legislators. But although these other influences–for example, lobby activity or constituency interests–could be expected to take on greater saliency in such situations, they rarely

[12] Malcolm E. Jewell, "Party Voting in American State Legislatures," *American Political Science Review,* **49** (1955), 773–779. See also Hugh L. LeBlanc, "Voting in State Senates: Party and Constituency Influences," in Herbert Hirsch and M. Donald Hancock, eds., *Comparative Legislative Systems,* op. cit., pp. 373–391.

[13] Fred Greenstein and Alton F. Jackson, "A Second Look at the Validity of Roll Call Analysis," *Midwest Journal of Political Science,* **7** (1963), 156–166.

[14] Duncan MacRae, Jr., "Roll-Call Votes and Leadership," *Public Opinion Quarterly,* **20** (1956), 543–558.

[15] Duane Lockard, *New England State Politics* (Princeton, N.J.: Princeton University Press, 1959), pp. 156–159, 298.

[16] Frank J. Sorauf, *Party and Representation* (New York: Atherton Press, 1962). See also, Thomas Flinn, "Party Responsibility in the States: Some Causal Factors," *American Political Science Review,* **58** (1964), 60–71.

become as important as the party is in two-party legislatures. Instead, decision premises come to be provided by factional groupings within the dominant party, groupings that are normally shifting and impermanent.

The evidence to date suggests that factions are based upon a variety of circumstances, including such things as ideological differences within a party, opposition and support for a particular governor or his program, differences on particular issues or organizational matters, and regional or urban-rural differences. As a consequence, such contextual variations must be taken into account in determining the impact of party or faction on decisions made within any particular legislative institution.

The Effect of Interest Group Activity

"What would politics in America be like without lobbies and lobbyists?" This "silly and fanciful" question of Heinz Eulau's appeared in a review[17] of Milbrath's *The Washington Lobbyists*[18] in 1964, at a time when information on lobbying came primarily from three sources: journalists, Congressional investigations, and political scientists. These works, "descriptive rather than systematically explanatory or theoretical, and focused on institutions or organizations rather than on individual actors," [19] commonly take the form of case studies at a number of levels of analysis. But, as Zeigler observed, "most case studies of 'interest groups in action' *begin* with the assumption that the group model is correct:" [20] most "commit the *faux pas* of taking for granted whatever is to be discovered and tested." [21]

Earlier theoretical attention to interest group politics, beginning with Bentley's work and culminating with Truman's,[22] had largely taken interest group impact as given. However, more recent work has tended to question those earlier assumptions and has gone on to indicate that policy outcomes

[17] Heinz Eulau, "Lobbyists: The Wasted Profession," *Public Opinion Quarterly*, **28** (Spring 1964), 27–38.

[18] Lester W. Milbrath, *The Washington Lobbyists* (Chicago: Rand McNally, 1963).

[19] Eulau, op. cit., p. 28.

[20] Harmon Zeigler, "The Effects of Lobbying: A Comparative Assessment," *Western Political Quarterly*, **22** (March 1969), 122.

[21] Eulau, op. cit., p. 29.

[22] See Arthur F. Bentley, *The Process of Government* (Chicago: University of Chicago Press, 1908); Peter H. Odegard, *Pressure Politics: The Story of the Anti-salon League* (Boulder: University of Colorado Press, 1968); E. Pendleton Herring, *Group Representation Before Congress* (Baltimore: Johns Hopkins University Press, 1929) and *The Politics of Democracy* (New York: Rinehart, 1940); Harwood L. Childs, *Labor and Capital in National Politics* (Columbia: Ohio State University Press, 1930); E. E. Schattschneider, *Politics, Pressures and the Tariff* (New York: Prentice-Hall, 1935); David E. Truman, *The Governmental Process* (New York: Knopf, 1951).

would not have been especially different if lobbyists had been eliminated from the decision-making process. Matthews,[23] Zeigler,[24] Milbrath,[25] Bauer, Pool, and Dexter[26] all concluded that the effects of interest group activity on governmental decision-making and policy was minimal or at least greatly exaggerated. Wahlke and others suggested that interest group strength varied considerably from state to state.[27]

The real thrust of Eulau's critique of group theory was directed at the virtual absence of empirically verifiable generalizations about the "impact of lobbying on governmental decisions." [28] In his own work, he is quite properly interested in approaching this problem by developing complete descriptions of the role-sets of decision-makers (including their own attitudes and those of their colleagues toward interest groups). However, the linkage is never established between such role-sets and the overt behavior of legislators. The effect of interest groups upon roll-call decisions, for example, is still very much an open question.

One important exception to this is the recent work by Zeigler and Baer on lobbying at the state legislative level. Among other things, they asked both legislators and lobbyists in four states the extent of interest group effectiveness, ranging from whether a lobbyist had induced legislators to question a previously held opinion to outright conversion from one position to another. Although the findings vary from state to state and between legislators and lobbyists (who generally rated themselves as more influential than did the legislators), the author's data strongly suggest that both groups believe that the extent of influence is much greater than earlier studies would indicate.[29]

In addition, Patterson found that pressure groups determined voting

[23] Donald R. Matthews, *U.S. Senators and Their World* (Chapel Hill: University of North Carolina Press, 1960), pp. 195–196.

[24] Harmon Zeigler, *Interest Groups in American Society* (Englewood Cliffs: Prentice-Hall, 1964), and *The Politics of Small Business* (Washington, D.C.: The Public Affairs Press, 1961).

[25] Milbrath, op. cit., and "Lobbying as a Communication Process," *Public Opinion Quarterly,* **24** (1960), 32–53.

[26] Raymond A. Bauer, Ithiel de Sola Pool, and Lewis A. Dexter, *American Business and Public Policy* (New York: Atherton Press, 1963).

[27] Wahlke, Eulau, Buchanan, and Ferguson, *The Legislative System*, op. cit., pp. 311–342.

[28] Eulau, op. cit., p. 35.

[29] Harmon Zeigler and Michael Baer, *Lobbying: Interaction and Influence in American State Legislatures* (Belmont, Calif.: Wadsworth Publishing Company, 1969), pp. 155 ff. Further evidence for this finding can be found in Dayton D. McKean, "Elections and Political Parties," and "Patterns of Politics," in James W. Fesler, ed., *The 50 States and Their Local Governments* (New York: Knopf, 1967; and Duane Lockard, *The Politics of State and Local Government* (New York: Macmillan, 1963), pp. 155–160.

patterns on a number of issues in Oklahoma,[30] while Crane suggested that legislators were influenced most by powerful groups in their own constituencies.[31] Interest group effect also tends to vary inversely with party competitiveness.[32]

Zeigler and van Dalen also note that the effect of interest groups varied inversely with the cohesion of the parties in the legislature, the state's wealth, and levels of urbanization and industrialization. Thus, in states that rank low on such indices, such as Maine, Alabama, Montana, or New Mexico, pressure groups are apt to be especially influential. Relatedly, among states with strong lobby systems, Zeigler and van Dalen draw distinctions among several patterns of interest group activity:

1. Where strength is achieved through an alliance of dominant interest groups—for example, the alliance of timber, electric power, and manufacturing interests in Maine.
2. Where strength is in the form of a single dominant group—for example, the Anaconda (*sic*) Company in Montana.
3. Where there is a conflict between two dominant groups —as between union and management in the automotive industry in Michigan.
4. Where there is a wide variety of powerful and successful interest groups—as in California.[33]

We seem to have come full circle. The paucity and inconsistency of the evidence on interest group influence make it difficult to reach theoretically meaningful conclusions. However, in seeking the determinants of legislative choice, there does seem to be enough recent evidence to suggest that interest group activity should be at least investigated in studies of decision-making in any particular state legislature.

The Effect of Constituency

When confronted with the necessity to choose, one of the more frequently suggested ways in which the legislator simplifies his set of decision criteria is simply to vote according to the best interests of his constituency.

30 See Samuel C. Patterson, Dimensions of Voting Behavior in a One-Party State Legislature," *Public Opinion Quarterly*, **26** (1962), 185–200, and "The Role of the Lobbyist: The Case of Oklahoma," *Journal of Politics*, **25** (1963), 72–92.

31 Wilder Crane, Jr., "A Test of Effectiveness of Interest-Group Pressures on Legislators," *Southwest Social Science Quarterly*, **41** (1960), 335–340.

32 See, for example, Robert I. Golembiewski, "A Taxonomic Approach to State Political Party Strength," *Western Political Quarterly*, **11** (1958), 500–501, or Lockard, *New England State Politics*, op. cit., pp. 332–334.

33 Harmon Zeigler and Hendrick van Dalen, "Interest Groups in the States," in Herbert Jacob and Kenneth N. Vines, eds., *Politics in the American States: A Comparative Analysis* (Boston: Little, Brown, 1971), pp. 122–160.

After all, the popular perception of representative democracy embodies, in part, the view that legislators act upon the instructions of their constituents. In situations where advice from constituents is forthcoming, this strategy not only provides a means of "satisficing" but helps the legislator to get reelected as well.

While such views have long been expressed, it has only been within the last two decades that political scientists have been concerned with empirically analyzing the actual linkages between constituency characteristics (and attitudes) and the behavior of legislators. The literature in this problem area is, of course, enormous, and no attempt will be made to review it here. Much of this work, however, has concluded that constituency factors do have considerable impact on legislative decision-making.[34]

Apart from such general agreement, however, scholars have attempted to explain this relationship in a number of ways. Some, such as Jones, Boynton, Patterson, and Hedlund, have preferred to emphasize the impact of "policy" or "attentitive" constituents.[35] Others, such as Miller and Stokes, Cnudde and McCrone, Dexter, and Wahlke and his associates, have focused on the legislators' perceptions of, and attitudes toward, constituency views.[36]

Additional studies have revealed that constituency factors account for variance in roll-call voting when party has been controlled for.[37] It has also

[34] See, for example, Julius Turner, *Party and Constituency: Pressures on Congress* (Baltimore: Johns Hopkins University Press, 1951); Duncan MacRae, Jr., "The Relation Between Roll Call Votes and Constituencies in the Massachusetts House of Representatives," *American Political Science Review,* **46** (1952), 1046–1055; V. O. Key, Jr., *Public Opinion and American Democracy* (New York: Knopf, 1961), pp. 482–486; Lewis A. Dexter, "The Representative and His District," *Human Organization,* **16** (1957), 2–13; H. Ingram, "The Impact of Constituency on the Process of Legislation," *Western Political Quarterly,* **22** (1969), 265–279; and LeBlanc, "Voting in State Senates: Party and Constituency Influences," op. cit.

[35] Charles O. Jones, "Representation in Congress: The Case of the House Agriculture Committee," *American Political Science Review,* **55** (1961), 358–367; and G. R. Boynton, Samuel C. Patterson, and Ronald D. Hedlund, "The Missing Links in Legislative Politics: Attentive Constituents," *Journal of Politics,* **31** (1969), 700–721.

[36] See Warren E. Miller and Donald Stokes, "Constituency Influence in Congress," *American Political Science Review,* **57** (1963), 46–56; Charles F. Cnudde and Donald J. McCrone, "The Linkage Between Constituency Attitudes and Congressional Voting Behavior: A Causal Model," *American Political Science Review,* **60** (1966), 66–72; Dexter, "The Representative and His District," op. cit.; and Wahlke, Eulau, Buchanan and Ferguson, *The Legislative System,* op. cit., chap. 12.

[37] See Matthews, *U.S. Senators and Their World,* op. cit., pp. 230 ff; MacRae, "The Relations Between Roll-Call Votes and Constituencies in the Massachusetts House of Representatives," op. cit.; Malcolm G. Parsons, "Quasi-Partisan Conflict in a One-Party Legislative System: The Florida Senate, 1947–1961," *American Political Science Review,* **56** (1962), 605–14; and Patterson, "Dimensions of Voting in a One-Party State Legislature," op. cit.

been suggested that constituency influence varies with district size (an inverse relationship),[38] district composition,[39] and issue.[40] Regarding the relationship between constituency influence and inter-party competition of the district, the evidence is highly inconsistent. A number of works indicate that legislators elected by close margins tend to be more sensitive to constituency influences at the roll-call stage,[41] while others suggest the opposite relationship.[42]

The Impact of Governors

Another important influence on legislative decision-making is the governor and the administrative apparatus of the state. While there is very little statistical evidence to support this conclusion, it seems clear that most governors and many bureaucrats command sufficient political resources to have an impact on the behavior of individuals in state legislatures.

Governors, after all, usually have considerable influence on legislative programs, proposals, and executive budgets. Most are empowered to veto legislation and to call special sessions of the legislature. They also function as party leaders, public opinion leaders and manipulators, and dispensers of patronage. Such influence, of course, varies from state to state according to constitutional and informal limitations of the chief executive's prerogatives, his tenure in office, whether his own party also controls the legislature, and whether he and a legislative majority represent similar constituencies.[43] For example, where governors have high levels of tenure potential, budget, veto, and appointive powers, such as in New York,

38 Thomas R. Dye, "A Comparison of Constituency Influences in the Upper and Lower Chambers of a State Legislature," *Western Political Quarterly*, **14** (1961), 473–480.

39 MacRae, "The Relation Between Roll Call Votes and Constituencies in the Massachusetts House of Representatives," op. cit.; Froman, *Congressmen and Their Constituencies*, op. cit.; and Sorauf, *Party and Representation*, op. cit.

40 See Miller and Stokes, "Constituency Influence in Congress," op. cit.

41 Samuel D. Patterson, "The Role of the Deviant in the State Legislative System: The Wisconsin Assembly," *Western Political Quarterly*, **14** (1961), 460–472; Dye, "A Comparison of Constituency Influences in the Upper and Lower Chambers of a State Legislature," op. cit.; and MacRae, "The Relation Between Roll Call Votes and Constituencies in the Massachusetts House of Representatives," op. cit.

42 Samuel P. Huntington, "A Revised Theory of American Party Politics," *American Political Science Review*, **44** (1950), 669–677. Froman found very little relationship at all. See his *Congressmen and Their Constituencies*, op. cit., chap. 9.

43 For a useful index of such powers, see Joseph A. Schlesinger, "The Politics of the Executive," in Herbert Jacob and Kenneth N. Vines, eds., *Politics in the American States*, op. cit.

Good discussions of these variations can be found in Wilder Crane, Jr., and Meredith W. Watts, Jr., *State Legislative Systems* (Englewood Cliffs, N.J.: Prentice-Hall, 1968), pp. 99 ff. and Malcolm E. Jewell and Samuel C. Patterson,

Illinois, and California, we would expect such individuals to be an especially potent source of decision criteria for the legislators of those states. Conversely, where the powers of governors are more severely circumscribed, as in Texas, North Carolina, or West Virginia, other influences are apt to be more germane to any explanation of the behavior of those in legislative institutions.

In any case, it seems reasonable to assume that in their attempts to reach sufficiently rational decisions most state legislators will consider the policy positions and attitudes of their governor. In states where the chief executive is especially strong, not to do so could be extremely foolhardy.

Cue-Taking in Legislative Decision

I began this discussion by describing a context of legislative decision characterized by high stakes, low information, and complexity. Assuming that this assessment is reasonably accurate, it is possible to conclude that the external and attitudinal variables already discussed are often an insufficient basis upon which to make a psychologically satisfying or optimally rational decision. This appears to be the case because of two frequently occuring sets of circumstances: (1) when the decision premises provided by such variables conflict with one another to a large degree; and (2) when the decision premises provided by these variables are unclear or irrelevant to the legislator.

With regard to the first of these situations, cross-pressure theories of political decision-making suggest that the predisposition to choose at any given point in time is a function of the number of identifiable, salient, convergent decision premises available to the legislator.[44] In other words, choice is possible when factors relevant to a decision are available and tend to reinforce one another. A simple example would be the case where a piece of legislation has a perceptible ideological content (to which the legislator is sympathetic) and is sponsored by the legislator's own party (assuming the legislator is not a maverick). If these were the only two salient premises, then an affirmative vote on the bill is a relatively easy decision. But what happens if these two premises are in conflict or if other salient conflicting factors—say, opposition by constituents or powerful lobbies—are introduced? The legislator then experiences cross pressure;

The Legislative Process in the United States (New York: Random House, 1966), chap. 13.

[44] See, for example, Ithiel de Sola Pool, Robert P. Abelson, and Samuel Popkin, *Candidates, Issues, and Strategies* (Cambridge, Mass.: M.I.T. Press, 1964), pp. 12–14 and 73–77; Angus Campbell, Phillip E. Converse, Warren E. Miller, and Donald E. Stokes, *The American Voter* (New York: Wiley, 1960), pp. 81–82; and Paul F. Lazarsfeld, Bernard Barelson, and Hazel Gaudet, *The People's Choice* (New York: Columbia University Press, 1948), pp. 64 ff.

his choice becomes more problematic, and he must search for additional premises to resolve his dilemma.

In the second set of circumstances, the premises provided may be (a) irrelevant, or (b) unclear. In the former case, for example, party position is, by definition, unimportant to the decisions made by mavericks; lobby pressure is less relevant to the "resistor" than it is to the "facilitator."[45]

In the latter circumstance, decision premises emanating from our various "external" sources may be muddled or not forthcoming. For example, I noted that an important simplifying strategy of decision for legislators is to "vote their district." Depending on the representational role of the legislator, such premises may or may not be relevant. Assuming that they are, however, a coherent sense of constituency desires may not be available. In the first place, legislators do not hear from their constituents on most issues. Moreover, even if they do receive such information, it is often contradictory. Also, given the political and social heterogeneity of many districts, the claim that legislators somehow develop a "feel" for their constituents' opinions[46] seems rather unwarranted.

Similar objections can be raised with regard to other decision premises. Ideology may be a useful premise to decide on an unequivocal piece of social welfare policy; it is less clear what the ideological content is of decisions involving the location of dam sites. Similarly, party or factional position may not be articulated on many issues or, when it is, may be inconsistent (e.g., disagreements between party leadership and local party spokesmen). Likewise, the attitudes expressed by lobby groups are often in conflict, particularly on significant, highly visible issues where the legislator is especially concerned to make the "right" choice.

Hence, the state legislator is often asked to make high risk decisions in a complex environment on the basis of decision premises which may be in conflict, irrelevant, and/or unclear. In such situations, how does the legislator approximate rationality in his voting behavior?

The Strategy of Cue-Taking

In these circumstances, it has been suggested that the decision-maker normally will search for additional premises, or "cues," from others in his immediate institutional environment: his colleagues in the legislature.[47] In

[45] These terms refer to legislators who are either hostile or friendly toward group activity. See the typology developed in Wahlke, Buchanan, Eulau, and Ferguson, "American State Legislators' Role Orientations Toward Pressure Groups," op. cit.

[46] See, for instance, Froman, *Congressmen and their Constituencies,* op. cit., pp. 9–10.

[47] The most persuasive evidence for this comes from the previously cited work by Donald Matthews and James Stimson. See also Cherryholmes and Shapiro, *Representatives and Roll Calls,* op. cit., p. 117.

other words, the legislator will simplify his conception of certain decision-making situations with which he is confronted by emulating the decisions of those whom he perceives as trustworthy or cognizant of the political, substantive, and procedural content and consequences of such decisions. Specifically, this means that he will take decision cues from (a) those whom he believes are expert in any given area of substantive policy or procedure; (b) friends in the legislature; (c) those whom he perceives as being in a position to improve his chances of goal attainment in exchange for his conformity to their decisions (e.g., party leaders or committee chairmen); and (d) those whom he believes are cognizant of the political consequences of any given decision (e.g., members with similar constituencies). It would appear, then, that the availability of such information sources enables the legislator to obtain rapidly the additional premises required for a satisfactorily rational choice—that is, a decision that is more nearly rational than could be otherwise reached in the circumstances described above.

This strategy of legislative decision-making suggests, however, that some legislators act as "lightning rods" in their reception of decision premises. That is to say, some members will receive premises for decision disproportionate to the numbers garnered by their colleagues. For example, at the national level, Kovenock notes that "policy specialists outside the Congressional system 'wholesale' communications to parallel specialists within the legislature; these men in turn 'retail' it to others in the House." [48] It is reasonable to expect that this familiar two-step process of communication, typical of the polity and society as a whole,[49] should also be characteristic of state legislatures as well.

Technical expertise, political "savvy," and assistance in goal achievement are normally available from outside the institution of the state legislature. But, as Matthews and Stimson point out, the legislative expert "is also a professional politician, and thus can be assumed to have weighed political factors in reaching his decision. Members value such political judgment highly, and no one is in as good a position to make such judgments as another member." [50] This factor is especially important when one considers

[48] David Kovenock, "Influence in the U.S. House of Representatives: Some Preliminary Statistical 'Snapshots,' " paper presented at the American Political Science Association Meeting, Chicago, September 1967, p. 26. Also see his "Communications and Influence in Congressional Decision-Making: Employing the Communication Audit Technique in a U.S. House of Representatives Subcommittee," paper presented to the American Political Science Association Meeting, Chicago, September 1964.

[49] See Elihu Katz, "The Two-Step Flow of Communication: An Up-to-Date Report on a Hypothesis," *Public Opinion Quarterly* (1957), 61–78; and Lazarsfeld, Berelson, and Gaudet, *The People's Choice,* op. cit., chap. 16.

[50] Matthews and Stimson, "The Decision-Making Approach to the Study of Legislative Behavior: The Example of the U.S. House of Representatives," op. cit., p. 16.

that there is usually more than one expert on any given subject, so that cues can be solicited from those with similar or identical views, interests, or goals.

It is also the case that legislators are in virtual day-to-day, face-to-face contact with one another. Because of it, they are in a position to assess the political costs and benefits and technical worth of the cues they receive from their colleagues. Past experience is a strong indicator of reliability. If decision cues were to be solicited from outside sources, much time might be consumed in evaluating the source itself as well as the advice it supplied. Moreover, the intra-institutional cue-giver must almost necessarily be trustworthy. As Matthews and Stimson note,

> at the first sign of unreliability the member's influence is likely to be permanently impaired. Members *do* trust their colleagues, and it is partly the result of the continuing sanctions they have over them. One [legislator] comments: "I go to a person on the committee who I trust, and whose views are more or less synonomous with mine. . . . That's my best source of information, since they have to live with me. As a colleague, I am able to hold them accountable better than anybody else." The withholding of trust is a powerful sanction. . . . The actors in the game understand that deception on one occasion will likely lead to a position of legislative isolation in the future, where others' advice is no longer given and theirs is no longer sought.[51]

For all of these reasons, then, cue-taking does appear to provide a useful strategy for decision in certain circumstances. But as the student approaches the study of the behavior of state legislatures or a particular institution, how is he to know who the cue sources are? The problem of identifying such individuals obviously is going to vary according to the characteristics of the legislature or legislatures that the researcher is interested in. As a general strategy, however, one might follow the example of Wahlke and his associates by asking the legislators themselves to identify their major intra-institutional sources of decision premises. While the Wahlke group did not seek to assess the relative impact of these individuals on the decisions made by state legislators, they did ask the legislators interviewed to name those in the institution whom they considered to be (1) close personal friends; (2) especially knowledgeable of the legislative "rules of the game"; and (3) particularly expert in various areas of substantive policy.[52] As a supplement to (or in lieu of) this kind of data, important cue sources might be identified by their formal and informal positions within the legislature. For reasons already discussed, one could

[51] Ibid., pp. 16–17.

[52] See the Wahlke et al. interview schedule and relevant data analysis in *The Legislative System,* op. cit., pp. 492–504 and chaps. 9–10.

expect that individuals in leadership positions would be apt to function as relatively powerful (and sought after) sources of decision cues. Such possibilities might include legislative party leaders and whips, committee chairmen, speakers, or spokesmen for informal groupings based upon regional interests (as in California), ideological affinity (e.g., the Liberal and Conservative caucuses in the Minnesota legislature), urban-rural differences (as in Florida), and so on.

Because of the comparatively small amount of research that has been done on this aspect of legislative decision-making, the statements and suggestions I have made on this topic should be regarded as extremely tentative. However, given the legislators' motives and opportunity to obtain trustworthy information as well as the little supportive evidence we do have, it seems possible that the investigation of cue-taking among state legislators can provide us with additional insights or explanations of the policies they produce. At the very least, it appears likely that cue analysis can strengthen our explanations of legislative decisions where the premises provided by sources external to the institution are inconsistent, unclear, or inconsequential.

Summary and Conclusions

This essay has been concerned with exploring the varieties of research that have approached the study of state legislative behavior from the perspective of the decisions made by individuals within such institutions. Because of its relevance to the understanding of state legislative decision-making, I began by describing the context in which such choices are made —a context which imposes severe limits on optimally rational decisions. Subsequently, I discussed those factors that were believed to have the greatest impact on the decisions made by state legislators. These included:

I. "External" stimuli. Derived largely from previous roll-call analyses, this section focused upon the impact on decision of actors and influences normally outside the institutional boundaries of the legislative arena. These included the effects of party affiliation, constituency interests, executive inputs, and lobby group activity.

II. Psychological sets. Of principal importance were the personal predispositions, attitudes, and roles of the individual legislator, including such things as ideological preferences, attitudes toward constituents and party, orientation toward interest group activity, personality type, and the behavior patterns and expectations associated with various levels of the legislative hierarchy. Such variables were included, not only because of their independent effects upon decision-making, but also because they serve to screen and distort the effects of external determinants.

III. Intra-Institutional Communication. The operative assumption was that the effects of the aforementioned variables may be replaced or aug-

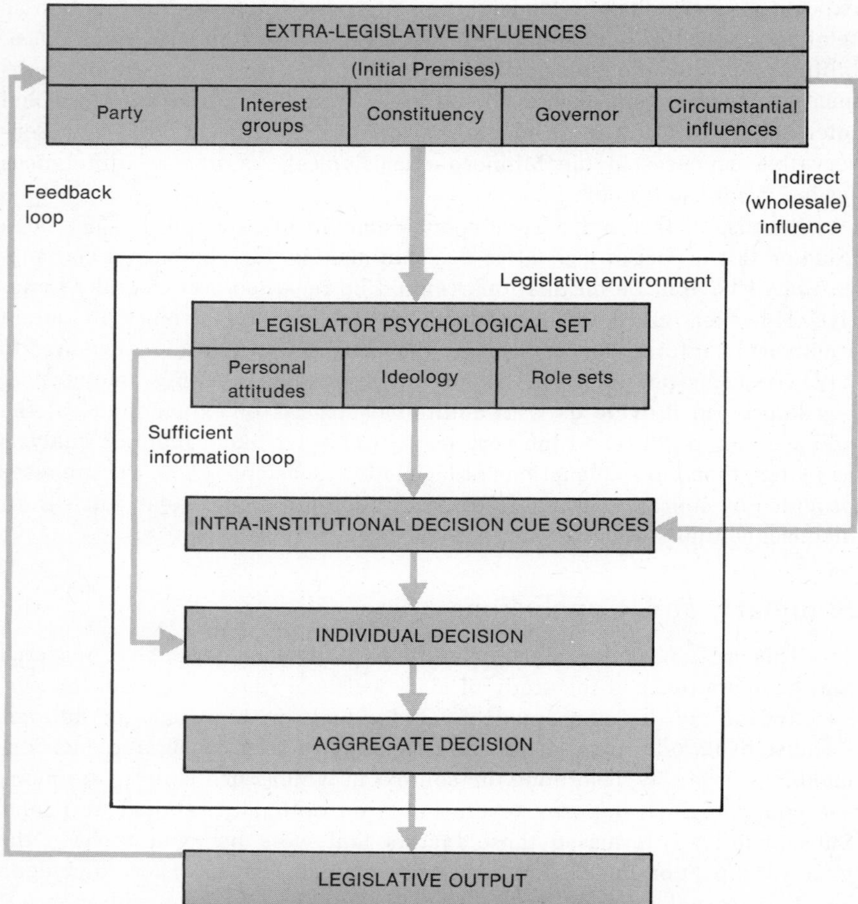

FIGURE 1 A framework for the study of state legislative decision-making. This chart is, in large measure, a modified version of John C. Wahlke's "framework" for the analysis of legislative processes, in John C. Wahlke, Heinz Eulau, William Buchanan, and Leroy C. Ferguson, The Legislative System: Explorations in Legislative Behavior. *New York: John Wiley & Sons, Inc., 1962, p. 18.*

mented by the decision premises or "cues" provided by others within the legislative environment. These premises were said to stem not only from formal communication networks (e.g., the cues available from party leaders, committee chairmen, etc.) but also from informal friendship and influence linkages within the institution.

The theoretical notions presented in this essay have been depicted schematically in Figure 1. In this framework, the particular legislative environment is suspended in the larger political arena comprised of the many individuals, groups, and institutions that make demands upon and provide support for the legislature through a process of interaction (i.e., standard feedback mechanisms).

Within the legislature, the principal participant is the individual legislator who, when confronted with the necessity to choose, synthesizes, where available, the external influences upon him as he perceives them through the prism of his psychological set. In situations where such influences are clearly defined, meaningful to him, and mutually reinforcing, the legislator is able to reach a satisfactorily rational decision immediately. Hence, the "sufficient information" loop.

In situations where the decision premises provided by external sources are irrelevant, unclear, or in conflict, the legislator seeks additional premises from his colleagues. His decision is made then on the basis of the cues solicited or provided by those whom he regards as expert, politically useful, and friendly—individuals who often function as retailers of decision premises received from external sources. This sequence is repeated for each individual legislator; the decisions ultimately reached by each become the aggregate output of the institution.

In conclusion, then, it should be noted that such a framework does not constitute a theory of state legislative decision-making. The development of such a theory would require, among other things, careful measurement of the variables I have chosen to include as well as the specification of the relative importance of each in determining the choices made by state legislators. It is clear, too, that a satisfactory theory would probably include a number of other concepts which, through ignorance or choice, have been excluded from consideration here. In any event, it is hoped that the information provided will enable the student to better understand the behavior of legislative bodies in America; optimally, through greater appreciation of the subject matter, it is hoped that some might be encouraged to continue the complex and arduous task of theory construction.

The Citizens Conference on State Legislatures

Evaluation of State Legislatures

In the foreword to *The Sometime Governments,* John W. Gardner notes that "This study breaks through long-standing but contrasting barriers of disinterest and timidity that have deterred political science scholars and public administrators alike from analyzing the capability and vitality of one of the key parts of American Government." The selection reproduced here shows the bases on which the 50 legislatures were judged and the ranking that resulted from applying those criteria to the legislatures.

In 1941, a young Oregon state legislator—and later United States Senator—named Richard Neuberger wrote about the difference between his original expectations and his actual experience in the statehouse:

> I arrived at our new marble Capitol to spend most of my time considering momentous issues—social security, taxes, conservation, civil liberties. Instead we have devoted long hours to the discussion of the regulations for labelling eggs. We have argued about the alignment of irrigation ditches, the speed of motorboats on mountain lakes, the salaries of justices of the peace, and whether or not barbers and beauty parlor attendants should be high school graduates. For two days we wrangled about a bill specifying the proper scales for weighing logs and lumber.

"None of these questions," he concluded, "concerns large numbers of people. Yet each question concerns a few people vitally." [1]

[1] Quoted in Charles Adrian, *Governing Our Fifty States and Their Communities* (New York: McGraw-Hill, 1967), p. 322.

Reprinted from *The Sometime Governments: A Critical Study of the 50 American Legislatures* (New York: Bantam, 1971), Chapters 3 and 4, pp. 37–54; by permission of The Citizens Conference on State Legislatures, Kansas City, MO.

Thirty years later, that remains an accurate description of what all state legislatures do almost all of the time. It is not that the "alignment of irrigation ditches" or "the salaries of justices of the peace" are frivolous matters. They are not and they have an impact upon the lives of people beyond those immediately affected. But they must not occupy most of a legislature's time or absorb so much of its energies. All too often they comprise the *only* subjects a state legislature is capable of handling.

Instead of operating as an independent or even important policy-making body, the state legislature too often serves merely as a funnel or screen for outside initiatives. It responds to the initiatives of various organized interest groups—such as barbers or beauticians—and it reacts to the initiatives of the governor. It does not itself have the resources to make policy and relies, as a result, on the only resources available to it. Take, for example, the Pennsylvania Legislature. Most of its members have no professional staff to help dig out facts, or do preliminary analysis, on the multitude of bills legislators must consider. As a result, one observer has said, "lobbyists . . . are often the main source of research for legislators. The best lobbyists have reputations for providing fast, accurate information, presenting their point of view in factual terms." [2]

The problem is not simply that the legislature lacks its own sources of information; rather the problem is that, when you put that deficiency together with the lack of time, money, staff, and other resources, you come up with an institution that is not equipped to act as an effective agent of the people, or as a branch of government equal in power and responsibility with the executive. The one branch of government which most closely reflects, in all its diversity, the people of a state is least able to act on their behalf.

The role of the legislature—in relation to the executive—is too often limited to passing upon the governor's proposals on the basis of information supplied by the governor, by an executive agency, or by some lobbyist. "To think of the governor principally as the chief executive," observes one authority, "is to ignore his development, in most states, into the chief legislator." [3] It is the governor who prepares and proposes the budget. It is the governor, or a lobbyist, who initiates most of the important legislation passed by the legislature. When the governor has put forward his proposals, the legislature is unable to subject them to critical, constructive analysis. When these proposals are approved, when the policies and programs they authorize are already in operation, the legislature cannot effectively evaluate their performance. The legislature, in short, cannot do its job.

There are those who deny that a legislature should be able to operate

[2] Bernard McCormick, "The House of Ill Repute," *Philadelphia Magazine* (November 1969).

[3] Karl A. Bosworth, in James Fesler, ed., *The Fifty States and Their Local Governments* (New York: Knopf, 1967), p. 88.

as an equal branch of government—who believe it should serve as a decidedly junior partner, "revising what the governor submits, exercising in effect a veto power over his program, studying in depth specific matters and upon occasion initiating ideas, but not too frequently."[4] Most legislatures are not even capable of effectively "revising what the governor submits," much less "initiating ideas." Moreover, to say that the function of legislatures must be essentially negative, that their job is not to act but to react, is to turn back the pages of history to the predemocratic days of feudal Europe when the first "legislatures," the king's vassals, could present petitions or formal protests against his agents—and to the later days in England when representatives of the influential classes won the right to give or withhold consent to any unusual expenditures or risky undertakings proposed by the king.

In a modern democratic society, however, the legislature must be something more than simply a yea- or nay-sayer to the executive. Rather, the legislature and the executive should be genuinely equal branches of government; each should have whatever powers it needs to share fully in the making of public policy. The governor, for example, should have full control over his administration—he should not have to contend with elected heads of executive agencies. The legislature, on the other hand, should be fully capable of developing sound proposals of its own, of analyzing and revising the governor's proposals and of assessing programs and policies already under way.

The state legislature should, in fact, function as an independent, continuous, creative, democratic policy-making body. It is the one branch of government that most closely represents the people in all their plurality; to the extent that the legislature is powerless, so are the people.

Ideally, every state legislature should be able to:

—innovate in the development of public policy;
—exercise continuing oversight over state administrative agencies and their programs;
—undertake comprehensive long-range planning for the state's economic and social development;
—evaluate and review its own performance; and
—identify and provide for future needs before they become critical.

There is, of course, a yawning gap between the real and the ideal. And state legislatures are not always capable of fulfilling even their two most elemental functions: adequately representing their constituents, and intelligently deliberating and deciding upon the legislative proposals that come before them.

[4] John H. Chafee, former governor of Rhode Island, Speech to American Assembly, New York, N.Y., April 29, 1966.

The Bare Necessities

Somewhere between the real and the ideal, between what state legislatures actually are and what they ultimately ought to be, there is a middle ground. It is upon that middle ground that we have constructed the conceptual framework for the Legislative Evaluation Study. At a minimum, every citizen should expect his legislature to be *functional, accountable, informed, independent,* and *representative* (FAIIR). Every legislature should, at the very least, exhibit these five qualities or characteristics; to the extent that it does not, it is not fulfilling the essential requirements of a legislature in a modern democratic society. These five characteristics are the bare necessities of legislative capability.

The five categories do not cover everything that a legislature ought to be: someone might argue, for example, that a legislature should be *creative,* or *responsive,* and that the FAIIR system does not directly touch upon either of these categories. But to determine how creative or responsive a legislature is would require going beyond the structural aspects of a legislature to an evaluation of legislation that it actually passes—and that is beyond the bounds of this study. In terms of legislative structure, the five characteristics of the FAIIR system do include everything that a citizen might reasonably expect his legislature to be.

The FAIIR System

At the start of the Legislature Evaluation Study, the Citizens Conference set out to find out—in detail—how well each of the 50 state legislatures performs in nine basic fields:

STAFFING: The leaders, the members of the legislature, and the legislative service agencies should have the competent professional and clerical staff they need to do their job.

COMPENSATION: Legislators should be paid salaries that reflect the heavy demands and high importance of their job, and should be reimbursed for actual and necessary expenses.

TIME: Legislatures should be able to meet as long and often as the needs and problems of the state require. They should not be subject to arbitrary and outmoded restrictions on length, frequency, or flexibility of sessions.

COMMITTEE STRUCTURE: The number of committees should be manageable, and the number of committee assignments per member should be reasonable. The announcements of meetings, agendas, the meetings themselves, and the records of discussion should be available to the public.

FACILITIES: The leaders, the members of the legislature, and the legislative service agencies should have adequate office space. There should also be adequate facilities for committee meetings, public hearings, caucus activities, and press coverage.

LEADERSHIP: The method of electing leaders, the length of terms, the powers of the presiding officers, and the powers of minority leaders should contribute to an orderly flow of business and a fair and effective distribution of power and authority.

RULES AND PROCEDURES: Bills should be prepared, introduced, printed, and handled in committee and on the floor in a way that ensures their fair and effective consideration. All legislators should have a reasonable opportunity to participate in the process. The process itself should not be so complex and convoluted that the public cannot understand it; and legislators and the public should have ready access to information about that process.

SIZE: Each house should be small enough in size so that it is manageable and so that all members can fully participate in its workings.

ETHICS: There should be effective provisions for dealing with conflicts of interest and for regulating lobbyists.

There is no inherent value, for example, in large legislative structure and organization. They form the basis of the 68-page questionnaire which the Citizens Conference used to gather detailed information on the workings of the 50 state legislatures. But while the nine criteria are excellent instruments for seeking out and organizing information, to use them as an evaluative instrument would result merely in mechanical rankings, lifeless listings of legislatures, that would have little immediate relevance to their functions in the real world. Better professional staff, better facilities, better pay, streamlined committee structures, more time—these are not ends in themselves, but means. They enable a legislature to achieve various objectives.

There is no inherent value, for example, in large legislative staffs as such. A staff is important and useful to the extent that it heightens the ability of a legislature to learn, retain, analyze, and evaluate large volumes of complicated information. An informed legislature is an end in itself. As a matter of principle, nobody would prefer an ignorant to an informed legislature.

Similarly, adequate office space and well designed and equipped committee rooms mean something only to the degree that they enable legislators and staff to do their work better and to the degree that they open up the legislative process to citizens and interest groups who want to lobby for their views and talk to an individual legislator. It is hard for a constituent to talk to a legislator whom he cannot find because the legislator has no office. It is impossible for the public to show support for a bill under consideration by a committee which meets in a room with no chairs for members of the public to sit on. Facilities, then, are important because they enable a legislature to function better and to be more accountable.

The FAIIR system was developed in order to relate the nine criteria—and the information we gathered on the basis of them—more closely and compellingly to characteristics everyone can understand and accept as essential, *in* themselves, to a state legislature. That system serves as a gauge of how well legislatures actually perform and as a guide to legislative reform.

The five characteristics of the FAIIR system are themselves composed of various criteria (see the outline below). These, in turn, are based on specific items in the questionnaires that were filled out for each legislature. Take, for example, the independence category: one of the five major criteria for the evaluation of a legislature's independence is its degree of freedom from domination by the executive branch. The criterion is composed of a number of subcriteria, one of which concerns veto relationships. The subcriterion refers directly to several specific questions contained in the questionnaire concerning the veto powers and practices of the governor and those of a legislature for overriding his veto. As an evaluative apparatus, therefore, the FAIIR system directly reflects the factual information obtained through the questionnaires. It is a way of organizing that information to show how close a legislature comes to achieving its basic objectives as an institution.

The five characteristics of the FAIIR system are not mutually exclusive; they are in varying degrees overlapping and even interdependent. A legislature cannot really be *independent* unless it is both well *informed* and able to draw upon its own sources of information. A legislature cannot really be *accountable* if it is not *representative,* or if the public is not informed or does not understand what it does and why. As a result of these interrelationships, some of the same data, the same facts, may contribute to more than one of these major characteristics. A sufficient supply of well-designed and well-equipped committee rooms, for example, makes it easier to schedule public hearings on various issues, and thus helps a legislature become better *informed.* The same facilities also help make a legislature more *accountable* by encouraging public hearings and by enabling the public to attend or take part in them. Yet data on these facilities—and any other data used more than once—are not necessarily given the same weight in each category because they do not necessarily have the same significance in each. An ample number of well-designed hearing rooms is more important as a factor that enables a legislature to become better informed than as a factor that makes it more accountable.

Indeed, the last and most sensitive step in the study was to decide how important each question (each criterion and subcriterion) was in rating a legislature in relation to each of the five major objectives. This required not only weighing but deciding whether to count something as a strength or a weakness. Each of these decisions was tested and checked. For their views on specific evaluations, a panel of more than two thousand individuals was polled. This panel consisted of individuals connected with the legislative process, including legislative leaders, legislators, political scientists, journalists, broadcasters, civic leaders, labor representatives, and corporate executives. The views of this expert panel were carefully considered before making the final decisions—for which, of course, the Citizens Conference on State Legislatures is fully responsible.

Categories, Criteria, and Subcriteria of Questionnaire

I. Functionality
  A. Time and Its Utilization
    1. Restrictions on the Frequency, Length, and Agendas of Sessions, and Interim Periods
    2. Techniques for the Management of Time Resources
    3. Uses of Presession Time
  B. General Purpose Staff
    4. Personal Aides and Assistants to Leaders and Members
  C. Facilities
    5. Chambers
    6. Leaders' Offices
    7. Committee Facilities
    8. Facilities for Service Agencies
    9. Members' Offices
  D. Structural Characteristics Related to Manageability
    10. Size of Houses
    11. Standing Committee Structure
  E. Organization and Procedures to Expedite Flow of Work
    12. Organization and Sponsorship of Bills
    13. Joint Committee Usage
    14. Treatment of Committee Reports
    15. Antilimbo Provisions
    16. Emergency Procedures
    17. Bill Carry-over
  F. Provisions for Management and Coordination
    18. Continuity and Powers of Leadership
    19. Interhouse Coordination
  G. Order and Dignity of Office
    20. Order and Decorum

II. Accountability
 A. Comprehensibility in Principle
  1. Districting
  2. Selection of Leaders
  3. General Complexity
  4. Explicit Rules and Procedures
  5. Antilimbo Provisions
  6. Planning, Scheduling, Coordination, and Budgeting
 B. Adequacy of Information and Public Access to It (Comprehensibility in Practice)
  7. Public Access to Legislative Activities
  8. Records of Voting and Deliberation
  9. Character and Quality of Bill Documents
  10. Conditions of Access by Press and Media
  11. Information on Legislators' Interests
  12. Information on Lobbyists
 C. Internal Accountability
  13. Diffusion and Constraints on Leadership
  14. Treatment of Minority

III. Informedness
 A. Enough Time
  1. Session Time
  2. Presession Activities
 B. Standing Committees (as Information-Processing and -Applying Units)
  3. Number of Committees
  4. Testimony
  5. Facilities
 C. Interim Activities
  6. Interim Activities
  7. Structure and Staffing
  8. Reporting and Records
 D. Form and Character of Bills
  9. Bill Status and History
  10. Bill Content and Summaries
  11. Quantity and Distribution
  12. Timeliness and Quality
 E. Professional Staff Resources
  13. General Research Coverage
  14. Legal
 F. Fiscal Review Capabilities
  15. Fiscal Responsibility
  16. Staff Support for Fiscal Analysis and Review
  17. Fiscal Notes

IV. Independence
 A. Legislative Autonomy Regarding Legislative Procedures
  1. Frequency and Duration of Sessions
  2. Expenditure Control and Compensation-Reimbursement Powers
  3. Reapportionment

- B. Legislative Independence of Executive Branch
    - 4. Access to Information and Analysis
    - 5. Veto Relationships
    - 6. Lieutenant-Governor Problem
    - 7. Budget Powers
    - 8. Miscellaneous
- C. Capability for Effective Oversight of Executive Operations
    - 9. Oversight Capabilities
    - 10. Audit Capability
- D. Interest Groups
    - 11. Lobbyists
- E. Conflicts and Dilution of Interest
    - 12. Dilution of Interest

V. Representativeness
- A. Identification of Members and Constituents
    - 1. Identification
- B. Diversity
    - 2. Qualifications
    - 3. Compensation
    - 4. Voting Requirements
- C. Member Effectiveness
    - 5. Size and Complexity of Legislative Body
    - 6. Diffusion and Constraints on Leadership
    - 7. Access to Resources
    - 8. Treatment of Minority
    - 9. Known Rules
    - 10. Bill Reading

Table 1 shows the results of the first roll call ever taken of how the 50 state legislatures measure up to minimum standards of legislative capability. The overall rankings arrived at in the Legislative Evaluation Study come from a consolidation of factors that have been considered under five major category groupings: *functional, accountable, informed, independent* and *representative.* Table 2 shows the rank order by state overall and on these five FAIIR criteria.

Reading the Rankings

The overall ranking and the rankings in each of the five categories are general in nature. They tell us that one legislature is "better" or "worse" than another, but not how much better or worse. The differences between adjoining states—say between the 10th- and 11th-ranked, and the 25th- and 26th-ranked—are sometimes very small. The best way to read the rankings, then, is in terms of groups: states ranked 6th through 9th are clearly "better" than those ranked 36th through 40th. Taken in groups, the rankings do show the stronger and weaker legislatures across the country as well as the strong and weak points of each legislature.

TABLE 1 *Rank Order of the 50 State Legislatures*

Overall rank	State	Overall rank	State	Overall rank	State
1	California	18	Idaho	35	Missouri
2	New York	19	Washington	36	Rhode Island
3	Illinois	20	Maryland	37	Vermont
4	Florida	21	Pennsylvania	38	Texas
5	Wisconsin	22	North Dakota	39	New Hampshire
6	Iowa	23	Kansas	40	Indiana
7	Hawaii	24	Connecticut	41	Montana
8	Michigan	25	West Virginia	42	Mississippi
9	Nebraska	26	Tennessee	43	Arizona
10	Minnesota	27	Oregon	44	South Carolina
11	New Mexico	28	Colorado	45	Georgia
12	Alaska	29	Massachusetts	46	Arkansas
13	Nevada	30	Maine	47	North Carolina
14	Oklahoma	31	Kentucky	48	Delaware
15	Utah	32	New Jersey	49	Wyoming
16	Ohio	33	Louisiana	50	Alabama
17	South Dakota	34	Virginia		

It must also be emphasized that these rankings do not tell you of the sometimes dramatic changes that have taken place, and are taking place, in a number of state legislatures. Indiana, for example, ranks 40th. But it has, in fact, done a good deal to strengthen itself over the past few years. Had the rankings been made four or five years ago, Indiana probably would have been farther down the line. Florida, Iowa, and New York, which are among the top ten legislatures, have made rapid progress in recent years. Connecticut ranks 24th, yet it has recently made important and extensive improvements in its structures and procedures which are only beginning to make themselves felt. The rankings, in short, are like a "stop-action" photograph: they show only where states stand at a particular point in time—midyear 1970—not where they are going or how far they have come.

On the overall rankings, the differences between states are *net* differences—the *net* results of a host of detailed differences, themselves reflecting various weights and averages. The differences between adjoining states may, therefore, be extremely slight; they may hinge, for example, on the fact that one state has fewer committees than another, or on the fact that one state has a more extensive program of interim activities.

The graph [see Figure 1] illustrates the relative "distances" between states on the overall ranking. It shows, for example, that there is considerable difference between California and Alabama, or even between California and New York, but relatively little between North Dakota and Maine, even though these latter states are eight rank positions apart.

TABLE 2 *Overall Ranking and FAIIR Criteria*

Overall rank	State	Functional	Accountable	Informed	Independent	Representative
1	Calif.	1	3	2	3	2
2	N.Y.	4	13	1	8	1
3	Ill.	17	4	6	2	13
4	Fla.	5	8	4	1	30
5	Wis.	7	21	3	4	10
6	Iowa	6	6	5	11	25
7	Haw.	2	11	20	7	16
8	Mich.	15	22	9	12	3
9	Nebr.	35	1	16	30	18
10	Minn.	27	7	13	23	12
11	N.M.	3	16	28	39	4
12	Alaska	8	29	12	6	40
13	Nev.	13	10	19	14	32
14	Okla.	9	27	24	22	8
15	Utah.	38	5	8	29	24
16	Ohio	18	24	7	40	9
17	SD.	23	12	15	16	37
18	Ida.	20	9	29	27	21
19	Wash	12	17	25	19	39
20	Md.	16	31	10	15	45
21	Pa.	37	23	23	5	36
22	N.D.	22	18	17	37	31
23	Kan.	31	15	14	32	34
24	Conn.	39	26	26	25	6

Because each of the five FAIIR categories is of equal importance—each is an essential aspect of legislative capability—no weights or similar devices were applied in arriving at the *overall* ranking. At the same time, this ranking was meant to reflect as fully as possible the variations between legislatures *within* each of the five categories. Rather, therefore, than simply add up the rank positions of each state in each of the five categories, the actual scores of each state in each category were summed.

In Table 2, the variously ranked states can be "profiled" across the FAIIR system to see how they ranked within each category. Thus, 1st-ranked California is 1st in being functional, 3d in being accountable, 2d in being informed, 3d in being independent, and 2d in being representative. The lowest-ranked state, Alabama, also shows a consistency across the FAIIR system, ranking among the last ten states in each category.

There are also some unbalanced profiles. Missouri, the 35th-ranked state, ranks 36th in being functional, 30th in being accountable, 40th in

Overall rank	State	Functional	Accountable	Informed	Independent	Repre-sentative
25	W. Va.	10	32	37	24	15
26	Tenn.	30	44	11	9	26
27	Ore.	28	14	35	35	19
28	Colo.	21	25	21	28	27
29	Mass.	32	35	22	21	23
30	Maine	29	34	32	18	22
31	Ky.	49	2	48	44	7
32	N.J.	14	42	18	31	35
33	La.	47	39	33	13	14
34	Va.	25	19	27	26	48
35	Mo.	36	30	40	49	5
36	R.I.	33	46	30	41	11
37	Vt.	19	20	34	42	47
38	Tex.	45	36	43	45	17
39	N.H.	34	33	42	36	43
40	Ind.	44	38	41	43	20
41	Mont.	26	28	31	46	49
42	Miss.	46	43	45	20	28
43	Ariz.	11	47	38	17	50
44	S.C.	50	45	39	10	46
45	Ga.	40	49	36	33	38
46	Ark.	41	40	46	34	33
47	N.C.	24	37	44	47	44
48	Del.	43	48	47	38	29
49	Wyo.	42	41	50	48	42
50	Ala.	48	50	49	50	41

being informed, 49th—second-to-last—in being independent, and a very high 5th in being representative. An even more erratic example is Kentucky which goes across the FAIIR system with two very high rankings—2d in being accountable and 7th in being representative—and three very low—49th in being functional, 48th in being informed, and 44th in being independent.

The overall ranking does not reflect any distinction between states which rank at roughly the same levels across the five categories and states which rank very high in one and very low in another and in the middle in a third. The evaluation is based in favor of balance across the five criteria on the assumption that the negative impact of a very poor capability in one or more categories—all five of which are equally important—more than offsets a very high capability in one or more. The fact, for example, that a

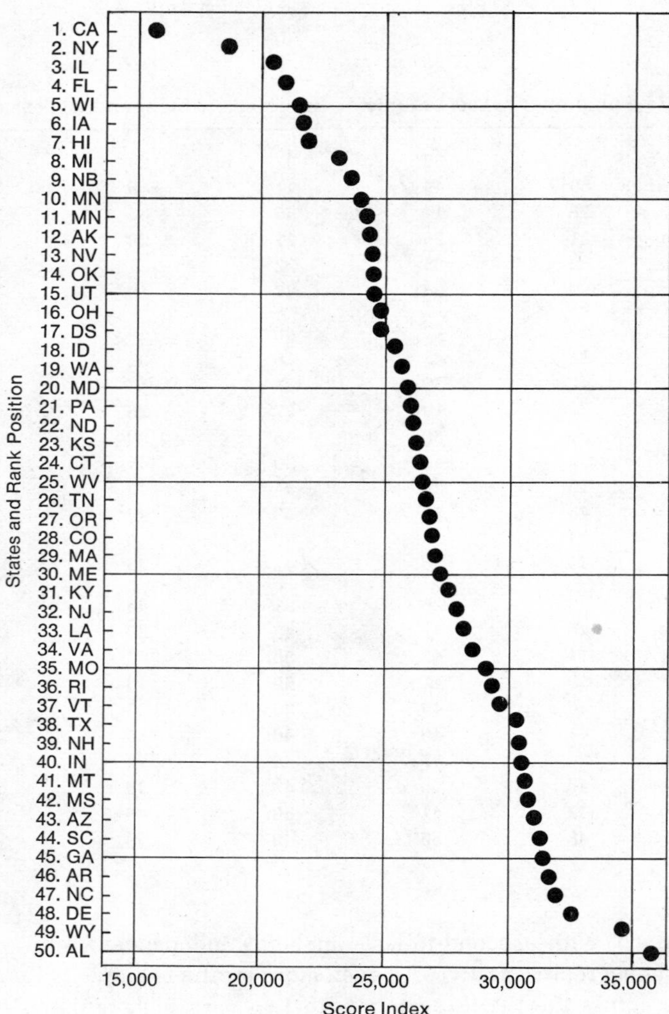

FIGURE 1 Final distribution of states on the weighted index scale.

given legislature functions very badly more than cancels out the fact that it is also highly representative or moderately independent.

Finally, the rankings—both overall and in each category—show where states stand in relation to minimum rather than ideal standards of legislative capability. The state that ranks first according to the minimum standards would rank much lower when tested against an imaginary "ideal" legislature. There is no "perfect" state. Even the best needs improvement. . . .

From Rankings to Reform

The general rankings [here given] are designed to serve as instructive rather than invidious comparisons. They highlight the stronger and weaker legislatures across the nation, and the stronger and weaker features of each legislature. But their aim is not to single out one legislature for praise and another for blame; it is to spur them all on to reform.

No state that ranks first in a category has a "perfect" score in that category. No state in the union, in other words, has a legislature that lives up to minimum standards of competence in any of these five categories, let alone in all of them.

Robert S. Erikson

The Partisan Impact of State Legislative Reapportionment

Central to the makeup of the environment in which policy decisions are made is the way seats are apportioned on the one hand and party composition on the other. Reapportionment was a major event in the 1960s; Erikson analyzes the impact of reapportionment on state legislatures and finds that for the most part it has helped the Democratic party gain seats at the expense of the Republican party.

In 1962, in the landmark *Baker vs. Carr* decision, the Supreme Court made its first ruling that a state legislature had to be apportioned on a "one man–one vote" basis. Since then, most state legislatures have been reapportioned on a far more equitable basis than had been found in the past. The political consequences of this rapid decline in malapportionment, however, have not been so clear. Efforts by political scientists to uncover the political effects of malapportionment have centered on the relationship between malapportionment and policy output. . . . These studies have generally reported only negligible correlations between a state's level of malapportionment and its policy decisions. These findings are generally reported with some caution, with proper note taken of the possibility that extraneous variables that cannot easily be controlled may conceivably be obscuring an actual malapportionment impact. Often it has been suggested that the appropriate means of detecting any true malapportionment impact that cannot be located by correlation analysis is a before-after design in which post-reapportionment policy outcomes are compared to those deter-

Reprinted from the *Midwest Journal of Political Science,* Vol. 11, No. 1 (February 1967), pp. 1–26, by permission of the Wayne State University Press and the author. Some descriptive and bibliographical footnotes have been omitted for considerations of space and textual format.

mined prior to reapportionment. Adequate empirical investigations of this type have not been forthcoming, however, presumably because of the difficult task of sorting any post-reapportionment policy changes that are found into those attributable to reapportionment and those attributable to other environmental changes.

The present study applies an indirect test for a policy impact of malapportionment by examining the impact of reapportionment in the 1960's on the partisan distribution of seats in the northern state legislatures. Because malapportionment generally discriminated against urban areas, the party with the most urban electoral base would be the one most hurt by malapportionment and with the most to gain by redistricting. In most northern states it is the Democratic party that has its greatest strength in the urban areas. Therefore it is expected that reapportionment generally produced an increase in Democratic legislative strength.[1] Since party affiliation is usually the major source of cleavage in roll call voting, with "progressive" or "liberal" legislation supported more frequently by Democrats than by Republicans[2] it follows that any evidence of a Democratic legislative gain due to reapportionment would also be evidence that reapportionment has caused state policy output to move in a somewhat more "liberal" direction.

Several years ago, V. O. Key investigated the relationship between the party controlling the governorship and party control of the legislature, and found that it was more likely for a northern governor's party to control the legislature when the governor was a Republican than when he was a Democrat.[3] Since this pattern was found to hold even when the governor's margin of victory is held constant and when the analysis is limited to cases in which the governor and entire legislature were elected the same year, malapportionment may have been responsible. But, as Key himself noted, this interpretation should be made with some caution, since a general upsurge in Democratic strength during Key's period of analysis may have had greater momentum in gubernatorial elections than in legislative contests and thus, in itself, made it easier for the Democratic party to win governorships than legislative majorities. Even so, Key's findings are at least suggestive of partisan discrimination in legislative malapportionment.

[1] Still another reason for expecting reapportionment to help the Democratic party is that any Republican gerrymander that had developed would be corrected by reapportionment plans imposed by courts or, as often was the case following the 1964 election, by a Democratic controlled legislature.

[2] Party affiliation has consistently been found to be the major source of cleavage in two-party state legislatures and one that remains when constituency characteristics are held constant.

[3] V. O. Key, Jr., *American State Politics* (New York: Alfred A. Knopf, 1956), pp. 57–73. Key's period of analysis is 1930 through 1950. Key's findings have been replicated for the period 1952 through 1962 by Malcolm E. Jewell in *The State Legislature: Politics and Practice* (New York: Random House, 1962), pp. 9–17.

Method

In the present study, the relationship between election results and the partisan seat division both before and after reapportionment is examined for thirty-eight northern state legislative chambers. Since the statewide partisan vote divisions in elections for the state legislature are often unavailable, the measurement of election results that is employed here is the statewide vote for the U.S. House of Representatives.[4] The thirty-eight chambers were selected for analysis because their entire membership is elected in each even numbered year—congruent with congressional elections. All thirty-eight chambers were reapportioned between 1962 and 1968.[5] For each chamber a regression equation was computed with the form:

[4] There are several reasons why the statewide congressional vote is preferable to the gubernatorial vote as an indicator of election results. For one thing, gubernatorial elections are often held at four-year intervals rather than the two-year intervals of congressional elections. Secondly, gubernatorial elections are often influenced by short-term electoral forces generated by relatively salient gubernatorial candidates and issues, thus making gubernatorial election results a poor indicator of voting at the legislative level. Fluctuating short-term forces are less of a problem with congressional elections, especially in large states where idiosyncratic factors influencing the vote in individual congressional contests would tend to cancel each other out across districts. An additional consideration is that there may be a tendency for the state's minority party to have greater electoral strength in the statewide contest for governor than in the district level contests for the U.S. House and state legislature.

For the calculation of the statewide congressional vote divisions, the results for districts with uncontested elections are estimated from the vote divisions in surrounding election years in which there had been a two-party contest. For such corrections, estimates of the numbers of Republican voters and Democratic voters there would have been if the election were contested are made by adjusting the results in the contested elections for the swings of the turnout and two-party vote division. Failure to make this minor correction would exaggerate the statewide strength of parties with unopposed congressional candidacies.

[5] The "North" is defined so as to exclude from analysis the former Confederate states and the Border states of Kentucky, Maryland, Missouri, Oklahoma, and West Virginia. The South and Border states—in which reapportionment may have generally hurt the Democratic party because of its traditional strength in rural areas—are excluded because of considerable uncertainty about the correspondence between the vote for state legislature and the vote for Congress and because of the unpredictability of the policy impact of any partisan effect of reapportionment in these states.

The only northern states that are not represented in the sample of chambers are Alaska and Hawaii (because of the recency of their statehood), Minnesota and Nebraska (because of their non-partisan legislative elections), New Jersey (because of its practice of holding legislative elections in odd-numbered years), and Oregon (where the lower House has not been reapportioned since *Baker vs. Carr*).

Since the election of the entire membership at two-year intervals is found more frequently for lower chambers than for upper chambers of state legislatures, the preponderance of the thirty-eight legislative chambers in the sample are lower houses.

$$S = a + b_1V + b_2R$$

where S is the Democratic percentage of the seats held by a major party, V is the Democratic percentage of the two-party congressional vote, and R is a dummy variable coded as 0 if the election is pre-reapportionment and as 1 if the election is post-reapportionment.[6] Results in the nine elections between 1952 and 1968 provide the data points on which the thirty-eight equations are based.

The regression coefficients for the reapportionment variable provide estimates of the partisan impact of reapportionment in the thirty-eight chambers when statewide election results are controlled. That is, the b_2 values are estimates of the reapportionment-produced changes in the percentage of seats that the Democrats get for a given vote division. The regression equations also provide estimates of the "fairness" of the states' apportionment systems both before and after reapportionment. Of course, the standard of fairness cannot be the requirement of equality between a party's vote proportion and its seat proportion, since with "winner take all" elections the majority party is expected to win a greater proportion of seats than votes. However, one reasonable standard of fairness is that the party with the majority of votes should also be the party with the majority of seats. By this standard, when the votes are split 50–50 between the two parties, the seats should also be evenly divided. Both the pre-reapportionment and post-reapportionment seat divisions that would occur when there is an even partisan split in the vote can be estimated from the regression equations. The estimated pre-reapportionment seat division when the votes are evenly divided is the chamber's predicted party composition when the congressional vote is 50 per cent Democratic and the reapportionment variable has a value of zero: i.e., $S = a + b_1 (50)$. The estimated post-reapportionment seat division when the votes are evenly divided is the chamber's predicted party composition when the congressional vote is 50 per cent Democratic and the reapportionment variable has a value of unity: i.e., $S = a + b_1 (50) + b_2$. The deviations of these values from the ideal 50–50 seat division serve as indicators of partisan imbalance.[7]

[6] The date of the first post-reapportionment election is defined as the first election year, beginning with 1964, in which there had been some redistricting since the previous election. Sources: *Representation and Apportionment* (Washington: Congressional Quarterly, 1966), pp. 68–69; "Suburbs Will be Biggest Gainers After 1970 Census," *Congressional Quarterly,* XXVII (November 21, 1969), 2342.

[7] The data sources for congressional election results are various editions of: U.S. Bureau of Census, *Statistical Abstract of the United States* (Washington, D.C.: U.S. Government Printing Office); and Richard M. Scammon, ed., *America Votes* (Washington: Government Affairs Institute). The data sources for legislative party composition are *Statistical Abstracts* and Council of State Governments, *The Book of the States, 1954–55,* Vol. 10 (Chicago: Council of State Governments, 1954).

TABLE 1 *Reapportionment and Party Strengths in Selected State Legislatures*

		Estimated Dem. seat percentage given vote division of 50% Dem.					
State	Chamber	First post-reapp't election	Pre-reapp't	Post reapp't	Change	Regression of Dem. seat % on Dem. vote %	R
Ariz.	H	1966	64.4	55.9	− 8.5	1.75	.914
Ariz.	S	1966	88.4	50.4	−38.0	0.83	.967
Calif.	H	1966	46.4	63.0	+16.6	3.25	.708
Colo.	H	1966	46.2	40.3	− 5.9	1.19	.915
Conn.	H*	1966	33.8	55.9	+22.1	2.14	.973
Conn.	S*	1966	55.5	54.1	− 1.3	3.59	.958
Dela.	H	1964	60.7	60.6	− 0.1	3.77	.942
Idaho	H	1966	46.6	61.5	+14.9	1.83	.798
Idaho	S	1966	48.3	51.0	+ 2.7	1.39	.658
Ill.	H*	1966	48.2	48.8	+ 0.6	0.80	.906
Ind.	H	1966	54.8	52.8	− 2.0	6.23	.959
Iowa	H	1966	49.8	42.8	− 7.0	3.80	.928
Kans.	H	1966	43.1	62.2	+19.1	2.09	.828

Note: The estimated Democratic percentages of the seats given a fifty-fifty vote division in the *congressional* vote are based on regression equations predicting the seat distribution from the vote division and whether or not the particular election is post-reapportionment, with election results from each election year between 1952 and 1968 as the units of analysis. The intercepts of the equations can be calculated by subtracting 50 times the regression coefficient for the vote distribution from the estimated pre-reapportionment Democratic percentage of seats given a fifty-fifty vote division. For example, the regression equation for the Arizona House is

$$S = -23.1 + 1.75V - 8.5R$$

where the symbols S, V, and R have the meaning indicated in the text.

* For Connecticut and Illinois, the 1964 election results are not included, since the Connecticut legislative election scheduled for 1964 was postponed and the Illinois House was elected on an at-large basis in 1964.

Results

Table 1 presents the results of this analysis for each of the thirty-eight chambers. The results for any one chamber should be interpreted with considerable caution, since the correspondence of the statewide congressional vote to the statewide legislative vote may vary from state to state or from year to year within the same state. Despite this limitation, the estimates tend to be consistent with expectations gleaned from the literature.

State	Chamber	First post-reapp't election	Estimated Dem. seat percentage given vote division of 50% Dem. Pre-reapp't	Post reapp't	Change	Regression of Dem. seat % on Dem. vote %	R
Maine	H	1964	32.9	35.6	+ 2.7	1.00	.975
Maine	S	1968	30.5	28.5	— 2.0	2.30	.942
Mass.	H	1964	47.2	55.5	+ 8.3	1.50	.941
Mich.	H	1964	44.3	53.8	+ 9.6	1.85	.944
Mich.	S	1964	31.3	49.7	+18.4	1.44	.985
Mont.	H	1966	48.0	49.2	+ 1.2	1.40	.815
Nev.	H	1966	64.6	44.8	—19.8	0.21	.941
N.H.	H	1966	40.8	47.8	+ 6.9	0.76	.854
N.H.	S	1966	46.5	61.5	+15.1	1.04	.856
N.M.	H	1966	54.7	62.3	+ 7.6	3.39	.856
N.Y.	H	1966	42.2	47.6	+ 5.4	1.57	.925
N.Y.	S	1966	42.2	41.1	— 1.1	1.47	.929
N.D.	H	1966	48.6	46.7	— 1.9	2.49	.945
Ohio	H	1966	47.0	58.3	+11.3	2.62	.803
Pa.	H	1966	49.1	52.4	+ 3.3	1.42	.819
R.I.	H	1966	58.7	61.9	+ 3.2	0.92	.859
R.I.	S	1966	37.2	55.6	+18.4	1.29	.988
S.D.	H	1966	40.2	38.7	— 1.7	1.77	.893
S.D.	S	1966	52.4	49.3	— 3.1	2.67	.924
Utah	H	1966	54.5	50.5	— 4.0	2.00	.888
Vt.	H	1966	31.1	53.0	+21.9	1.13	.880
Vt.	S	1966	35.2	43.7	+ 8.5	1.08	.693
Wash.	H	1966	60.7	42.7	—18.0	0.88	.742
Wisc.	H	1964	45.9	52.8	+ 6.9	1.80	.934
Wyo.	H	1964	51.4	50.6	— 0.8	1.88	.754
Mean			48.0	50.9	+ 2.9	1.91	.882
Median			47.1	50.8	+ 2.8	1.76	.915

For example, the commonly assumed pre-reapportionment Republican bias in the Connecticut House and Democratic bias in the Connecticut Senate are found, as are the notorious prereapportionment Republican bias of the Michigan legislature and Democratic bias of the Arizona legislature.

It is, of course, the general tendencies found in Table 1 that are of greatest interest. In general, the findings do support the notion that reapportionment helped to correct a Republican imbalance. For example, it is estimated that given an even partisan vote balance, the Republicans would have had a majority of seats in 68 per cent of the chambers prior to reapportionment but in only 42 per cent of the chambers after reapportionment. In 58 per cent of the chambers, the estimated direction of the partisan impact of reapportionment was an increase in Democratic rather than Republican legislative strength. In 82 per cent of the chambers, the estimated partisan direction of the reapportionment impact was in favor of the party that appears to have had the pre-reapportionment disadvantage.

Despite this reasonable fit with expectations, the overall impact of reapportionment on party strength appears to be slight. Although the *mean* seat division given an electoral balance is an equitable 50.9 per cent Democrat following reapportionment, it had already been a not altogether unreasonable 48.0 per cent Democratic prior to reapportionment. Thus, on the average, reapportionment appeared to help the Democratic party gain only an additional 2.9 per cent of the seats.[8] But, although the net partisan impact of reapportionment may have been slight in the North, the states in which reapportionment appeared to help the Democrats and the states in in which reapportionment appeared to help the Republicans fall in a noticeable geographic pattern. As Table 2 shows, east of the Mississipi River there was an unmistakable tendency for reapportionment to help the Democrats (the average Democratic gain was 7.4 per cent of the seats), while west of the Mississippi River there was an apparent slight tendency for reapportionment to help the Republican party (an average Democratic loss of 2.9 per cent of the seats). As will be shown below, this geographic pattern is a function of state-to-state differences in the relationship between the partisan cleavage and the urban-rural cleavage.

If our measures of the partisan impact of malapportionment are valid, they should be correlated with certain other variables in the direction that

[8] Since upper houses had generally been more poorly apportioned than lower houses, the underrepresentation of upper houses in the sample of chambers may be biasing the estimate of the net Democratic gain from reapportionment downward. However, in seven of the ten states in which an estimate of the reapportionment impact is made for both houses, it is the lower house where the Democrats are estimated to have gained most from reapportionment. An entirely different factor that may be thought of as adding a downward bias to the estimate of Democratic gain is that reapportionment appears to have helped the Democratic party most in the most heavily populated states. If the reapportionment impact in each chamber is weighted in proportion to the state's population, the average partisan impact of reapportionment is a Democratic gain of 5.4 per cent of the seats, or almost double the unweighted estimate of the Democratic gain.

TABLE 2 *Region and the Partisan Impact of Malapportionment*

	West of Mississippi River	East of Mississippi River
% with Republican Imbalance, Pre-Reapportionment	53	81
% with Republican Imbalance, Post-Reapportionment	47	38
% with Democratic Seat Gain Due to Reapportionment	35	76
Mean Democratic % of Seats Given Vote Balance, Pre-Reapportionment	53.5	43.6
Mean Democratic % of Seats Given Vote Balance, Post-Reapportionment	50.6	50.9
Mean Democratic Seat Gain Due to Reapportionment	−2.9	+7.4
	(N = 17)	(N = 21)

existing theory would suggest. For example, the estimated partisan impact of malapportionment should be greatest for the chambers that had been the most malapportioned. Also, our indicators should register the greatest pre-reapportionment Republican advantage and greatest Democratic gain following reapportionment in those states in which the Democratic electoral strength had been most clustered in the urban part of the state. The following section reports the fit of the data to these expectations.

Table 3 shows how three standard indices of malapportionment are correlated with the estimated partisan imbalance of the state legislature (both pre-reapportionment and post-reapportionment) and the estimated change in party legislative strength attributable to reapportionment.[9] Both

[9] The three indices of malapportionment are the Dauer-Kelsay index, the David-Eisenberg index, and Schubert and Press' inverse coefficient of variation (ICV). The Dauer-Kelsay index is the theoretical minimum percentage of the state's population that can elect a majority of the house. See Manning J. Dauer and Robert G. Kelsay, "Unrepresentative States," *National Municipal Review*, XLIV (December, 1955), 571–575. Scores on this index were given for the apportionment at the time of the 1962 election. Source: *Representation and Apportionment, op. cit.* The David-Eisenberg index is a measure of the value of the vote in elections for the particular chamber in the most urban counties of the state. See Paul T. David and Ralph Eisenberg, *Devaluation of the Urban and Suburban Vote* (Charlottsville, Virgina: University of Virginia Press, 1961). The ICV index of Schubert and Press is a measure of the ratio of the standard deviation of district population to the mean district population. See Glendon Schubert and Charles Press, "Measuring Malapportionment," *American Political Science Review* LVIII (June, 1964), 302–327; and the corrections published December, 1964, pp. 966–970. The three malapportionment indices are correlated quite highly with each other for the thirty-eight chambers studied here. The Dauer-Kelsay and Schubert-Press indices are correlated at .84; their correlations with the David-Eisenberg index are .65 and .67 respectively.

TABLE 3 *Malapportionment, Partisan Imbalance, and the Partisan Impact of Reapportionment*

Index of malapportionment	Partisan Imbalance*		Partisan change (non-directional)
	Pre-reapp't	Post-reapp't	
David-Eisenberg	+.30	−.11	+.30
Dauer-Kelsay	+.40	−.16	+.49
Schubert-Press ICV	+.34	−.20	+.56

* Cell entries are correlation coefficients. The original malapportionment indices have been inverted so that high scores indicate malapportionment and low scores indicate equitable apportionment.

partisan imbalance and partisan change are measured non-directionally. That is, partisan imbalance is measured as the deviation of the seat division from 50–50 when the vote division is 50–50, while partisan change is measured as the absolute magnitude of the reapportionment regression coefficient, disregarding whether the sign is positive or negative. As can be seen, all three malapportionment indices are correlated positively, at a minimum of + .30 with pre-reapportionment partisan imbalance and with the amount of change in party strength following reapportionment. Thus, as expected, the greater the malapportionment, the greater the partisan imbalance, and the more the partisan seat distribution is affected by reapportionment. Also, as expected, the three measures of malapportionment prior to redistricting are correlated only minimally (and negatively at that) with post-reapportionment partisan imbalance.

The next task is to see whether it is the state's most urban party that tends to be the party most disadvantaged by the initial partisan imbalance and the party that benefitted from reapportionment. To do this, we first need a measure of the within-state relationship between urbanism and relative party strength. A simple index of this sort, labelled the "Democratic–urban alignment" index, was constructed by the formula

$$(DUA) = D_u - D_r$$

where D_u is the Democratic percentage of the gubernatorial two-party vote in what is approximately the most urban "half" of the state and D_r is the Democratic percentage of the gubernatorial party vote in what is approximately the most rural "half" of the state. The more positive the *DUA* score, the more it is the state's Democratic party that has its greatest strength in urban areas; the more negative the *DUA* score, the more it is the state's Republican party that has its greatest strength in urban areas. When possible, scores on this index were based on the gubernatorial election of 1966. If there was no gubernatorial election in 1966, the 1964 results were substituted. For each state, the more urban "half" was determined by including in this category the most populous metropolitan areas and non-metropolitan counties, in descending order of population, until at least 45 per cent of the state's population was included.[10] *DUA* scores for each of the 28 states included in this analysis are found in the Appendix. Nineteen of the twenty-eight states have *DUA* scores in the positive direction, indicating that it is the Democratic party that has the more urban electoral base. The remaining nine states have negative scores, signifying that the Republican party has the more urban base. As expected, the pattern of *DUA* scores roughly follows the East-West geographic continuum, with positive scores found for eleven of the fourteen states east of the Mississippi but only eight of the fourteen states west of the Mississippi.[11]

The *DUA* index can also be refined to reflect the degree to which the most urban "half" of the state had been underrepresented in the particular chamber prior to reapportionment. This new index, which will be called the index of "Democratic underrepresentation," was constructed by the formula

$$(DPU) = D_{actual} - (L_u D_u + L_r D_r)$$

where D_{actual} is the actual statewide Democratic percentage of the two-party gubernatorial vote; L_u and L_r are the proportions of the chamber's legislators who represented the most urban and rural "halves," respectively, prior to reapportionment; and D_u and D_r are the Democratic percentages of the vote in the most urban and rural "halves." Thus the *DPU* index is simply the deviation of the actual vote from what it would be if the election results in the most urban and most rural "halves" of the state were weighted on the basis of their pre-reapportionment levels of repre-

[10] For the six New England States, metropolitan economic areas are substituted for standard metropolitan statistical areas since New England SMSA's do not necessarily correspond to county boundaries. SMSA boundaries are those of January 1, 1967. Where SMSA boundaries cross state lines, it is the total SMSA population that is the criteria for including the portion in the particular state in the most urban "half." No non-SMSA county was included in the most urban "half" if it did not contain at least one municipality of 10,000 or more population.

[11] The relative lack of an urban bias to Democratic strength in the West appears to be due to both a Democratic tradition in many rural sections of western states and a tendency for the larger cities in the West to be more Republican than their eastern counterparts.

TABLE 4 *Democratic-Urbanism Alignment, Democratic Underrepresentation, Republican Imbalance, and Democratic Post-Reapportionment Gain*

	Republican imbalance*		Democratic
	Pre-reapp't	Post-reapp't	gain
Democratic-Urbanism Alignment	+.58	+.06	+.50
Democratic Party Underrepresentation	+.67	+.10	+.54

* Cell entries are correlation coefficients.

sentation. *DPU* scores for the thirty-eight chambers are found in the Appendix.[12]

Table 4 presents the correlations between both the *DUA* and *DPU* indices and the measures of the partisan effect of reapportionment. Here, the measures of effect are given a partisan direction, so that the three indicators are the estimated pre- and post-reapportionment levels of Republican imbalance (the Republican proportion of seats given a vote balance) and the estimated Democratic seat gain due to reapportionment. As expected, the index of "Democratic—urban alignment" is correlated quite positively with pre-reapportionment Republican imbalance (+ .58) and the Democratic seat gain (+ .50). The index of "Democratic Party underrepresentation" is even more strongly correlated with initial levels of Republican imbalance (+ .67) and with the Democratic seat gain (+ .54).[13]

[12] The proportions of the seats held by representatives of the most urban and rural "halves" were calculated from the data in David and Eisenberg, Vol. II. *DPU* scores were in the expected positive direction in 66 per cent of the thirty-eight cases, indicating a pre-*Baker* underrepresentation of the most Democratic "half" of the state. The *DPU* scores and *DUA* scores are highly correlated at .78. Although the *DPU* scores do not depart much from the ideal zero point, they would probably have much larger magnitudes if votes were assigned weights in proportion to the value of the vote in their particular district rather than the overall value of the vote in their particular urban or rural "half" of the state.

[13] These relationships are also apparent when the variables are dichotomized. For example, 77 per cent of the chambers in states with positive *DUA* scores had a pre-*Baker* partisan imbalance that was in the Republican direction, compared to only 50 per cent of those with negative *DUA* scores. The comparable figures for a post-*Baker* Democratic gain are 65 per cent and 42 per cent. Similarly, 76 per cent of the chambers with positive *DPU* scores but only 54 per cent of those with negative *DPU* scores had a pre-apportionment Republican imbalance. Sixty-eight per cent of the chambers with positive *DPU* scores but only 38 per cent of the chambers with negative *DPU* scores had post-reapportionment Democratic gains.

(Consistent with the expectation that urban areas are no longer underrepresented, neither index is strongly correlated with the estimated *post*-reapportionment Republican imbalance.) Thus, the more a state's Democratic party has dis-proportionate strength in the urban areas (a high *DUA* score) and the more the areas of Democratic strength had been underrepresented (a high *DPU* score), the more the Democratic party had been hurt by malapportionment and the more it gained from redistricting.[14]

Conclusion

This paper has shown that reapportionment has tended to restore the party composition of state legislatures to a more equitable representation of election results. In most instances—but certainly not all—the Democratic party was the beneficiary of this shift. For our sample of thirty-eight northern state legislative chambers, the average partisan impact of reapportionment appears to be an increase in Democratic legislative strength of about 2.9 per cent of the legislative seats. Although the average Democratic gain from reapportionment is not large, the states where reapportionment has produced the greatest apparent gains for the Democratic party tend to be the most densely populated and most industrialized states, in which the policy differences between the two parties are probably greatest. This suggests that in several states reapportionment may have resulted in the movement of policy onto a somewhat more liberal course than otherwise would have been the case. There are, of course, additional reasons for suspecting an influence of reapportionment on policy. For one thing, as reapportionment tends to restore a party balance to the legislature, the frequency of divided party government should become significantly reduced, so that the incidence of partisan deadlock to policy-making may be on the wane. Also, apart from an impact via a partisan change, the decrease in representation may be moving the ideological center of gravity of each party's legislative membership in a somewhat more liberal direc-

[14] A subsidiary hypothesis that received faint support from the data is that the party that does the redistricting benefits from the post-reapportionment partisan imbalance. Six of the seven chambers that were reapportioned by Democratic legislatures with a Democratic governor in power had an apparent post-reapportionment Democratic imbalance, while half of the eight chambers that were reapportioned by Republican legislatures with Republican governors in power had a post-reapportionment Democratic imbalance and half had a Republican imbalance. (The remaining twenty-three chambers were reapportioned by either a court, a bipartisan commission, or by the legislature under conditions of divided party control of the legislature and governorship.)

tion.[15] Thus, while the impact of reapportionment may not have been as revolutionary as was once believed, there is obviously sufficient reason to believe that some impact is there.

Appendix

State	Chamber	Index of Democratic-urban alignment	Index of Democratic Party underrepresentation
Arizona	House	−11.2	−1.1
Arizona	Senate	−11.2	−4.7
California	House	6.3	−0.4
Colorado	House	−8.3	−1.4
Connecticut	House	4.5	0.8
Connecticut	Senate	4.5	−0.1
Delaware	House	−0.5	−0.1
Idaho	House	−2.7	−0.5
Idaho	Senate	−2.7	−0.9
Illinois	House	0.2	0.0
Indiana	House	1.4	0.3
Iowa	House	9.7	2.2
Kansas	House	5.4	1.3
Maine	House	7.1	0.3
Maine	Senate	7.1	0.6
Massachusetts	House	−1.7	0.0
Michigan	House	12.2	0.5
Michigan	Senate	12.2	1.5
Montana	House	5.4	0.5
Nevada	House	0.2	0.1
New Hampshire	Senate	7.6	0.3
New Hampshire	House	7.6	0.3
New Mexico	House	−10.8	−2.3
New York	House	0.4	0.0
New York	Senate	0.4	0.0
North Dakota	House	2.2	0.3
Ohio	House	−2.1	−1.0
Pennsylvania	House	9.8	0.6
Rhode Island	House	6.9	0.1
Rhode Island	Senate	6.9	1.5
South Dakota	House	−0.6	−0.0
South Dakota	Senate	−0.6	−0.0
Utah	House	2.3	0.4
Vermont	House	5.8	1.2
Vermont	Senate	5.8	0.8
Washington	House	−2.9	−0.2
Wisconsin	House	5.8	0.3
Wyoming	House	7.5	0.9

[15] The overwhelming tendency for the state's most urbanized counties to have been underrepresented is conclusively shown in David and Eisenberg, *op. cit.* In all but two of the thirty-eight chambers analyzed in the present study, the proportion of legislators from the most urban "half" was less than the most urban "half's" proportion of the state's population.

Henry Robert Glick

Policy-Making and State Supreme Courts: The Judiciary as an Interest Group

It has not been too long since courts were "discovered" as participants in the policy-making process. The fiction that courts exercised only judgment, not will, as they matched legislation against constitutions and actions against both in the cases before them prevailed for many years. Thanks to the work of such scholars as C. Herman Pritchett and Glendon Schubert, the important role of national courts as policy makers has been explored and explicated. Recently attention has been given to state courts in the policy arena.

In this reading, Glick considers state supreme courts as interest groups which seek access to other political decision makers in order to urge the adoption of policies which they cannot implement themselves. In this way, he concludes, "the courts can be viewed as attempting to increase their influence in state policy-making beyond the limitations imposed by the formal structure of the judiciary."

The most frequent and visible sources of judicial policy are decisions in court cases in which judges create new solutions to problems and conflicts presented to them. Sometimes important policies are established in a single case or policy may develop gradually in a series of cases dealing with similar situations. This form of policy-making frequently occurs without much direct interaction between courts, legislatures, and executive agencies. Though the implementation of court policies may depend on the

Reprinted from Henry Robert Glick, *Law and Society Review*, **5**:271–288 (November 1970), official publication of the Law and Society Association. Reprinted by permission of the publisher and the author. Some descriptive and bibliographical footnotes have been omitted for considerations of space and textual format.

cooperation of other officials, the initiation and early shaping of a particular policy may be done almost exclusively by the courts.

There are other policy-making situations, however, in which courts do interact in important ways with other political agencies. One which has received the greatest amount of attention in judicial politics research concerns the reactions of other political actors to decisions of the United States Supreme Court and the tactics adopted by various groups to restrict or enhance the power of the Court. Much research, for example, has described the negative reactions which members of Congress have had to court decisions affecting a variety of highly salient and controversial political issues. Legislative debate, strategy, and specific proposals intended to limit the Court's jurisdiction and legislation designed to reverse Court decisions have been described.

This aspect of judicial-legislative interactions in policy-making probably has received much emphasis because the interactions involve intense political conflict and concern highly controversial governmental policies which are generally important to many groups. However, another form of interaction which is important in judicial policy-making but which has received little attention is the effort by judges to influence governmental policy outside the regular channels of judicial decision-making. A familiar limitation imposed on the courts, of course, is the requirement that judges must wait until an appropriate case is brought before them before they make decisions which establish judicial policies. However, if relevant cases do not come before the court, or if judges are restricted in their decisions by existing statutes or jurisdiction, they may still attempt to affect governmental policy by influencing the decisions of legislative or executive officials. This may be intended to achieve several objectives: (1) to establish a policy which cannot be implemented by the courts due to limitations on the scope of judicial power (for example, the court's inability to appropriate money), (2) to alter existing statutes to increase flexibility which judges will have in making decisions in the future, and (3) to pass new laws which enhance the breadth of the courts' current decisions. In attempting to influence the decisions of other officials, courts can be viewed as interest groups which, like private organizations or other governmental agencies, seek favorable policies which they cannot implement themselves.

Most information about the ways in which judges seek to influence legislative and executive policy in order to achieve their own policy goals is found in research on the United States Supreme Court. The most systematic discussion is Walter Murphy's . . . description of the techniques which judges use to limit the effects of various political checks on their own policy-making power. Specifically, to influence members of Congress, a judge's strategy may include:

1. presenting judicial views in court opinions which hopefully will be seen and considered by the legislators;

2. interpreting current statutes so restrictively that they become essentially ineffective with the intent of forcing Congress to revise the law;
3. presenting policy preferences in dicta;
4. using informal personal contacts between judges and legislators for the exchange of views; and
5. lobbying in a systematic and well-organized fashion in order to influence the votes of Congressmen on bills important to the court.[1]

Parallel political interests may motivate the President to support the court and judges may attempt to persuade him or other executive officials and advisors to adopt certain policies or programs.

Another way in which the United States Supreme Court influences Congressional policy is through the Judicial Conference of the United States. The Judicial Conference, headed by the Chief Justice and including the chief judges and certain other members of the federal courts, meets once each year to discuss policy matters relevant to the federal judiciary. It also makes recommendations to Congress concerning needed legislation or expresses its views toward pending legislative policy. . . . A portion of the Conference's recommendations concern primarily routine administrative matters such as the appointment of court clerks and court reporters, fees charged by the courts, the assignment of judges, and court expenses. Other recommendations, however, have concerned important changes in existing statutes in areas such as bankruptcy and the special treatment of youthful criminals in the federal courts. The Conference also was active in securing legislation making picketing of a federal court illegal, and at one time it opposed the creation of a new administrative court which would have been added to the federal court system.

Recent research on the role of state supreme court judges also shows that state courts may seek positive legislative action in order to maximize their own influence in state policy-making. This may be accomplished in several ways. Courts may discuss policy alternatives in written opinions and indicate their own preferences with the expectation that state legislatures will adopt certain programs. If this is ineffective, however, a copy of the opinion may be sent directly to legislative leaders. Certain state courts may go even further in influencing policy. The New Jersey Supreme Court, for example, has established a system of regular interactions with legislative leaders in order to discuss the court's various policy proposals. Recently it made important recommendations in a variety of policy areas which included arrests, mortgages, law practice, unemployment and workmen's compensation, public employees, voting, paroles, contracts, and zoning. The court also submitted a list of twenty items to the state assembly

[1] Walter F. Murphy, *Elements of Judicial Strategy* (Chicago: University of Chicago Press, 1964), pp. 123–155.

which included its own recommendations concerning the administration of the state court system. While several of these administrative proposals appeared to be routine, others such as one to increase the salaries of certain officials and another designed to change the jurisdiction of several local courts are potentially important politically. Members of the legislature and the chief justice also agreed that the administrative director of the courts would provide the legislature with all future supreme court opinions which contained recommendations for legislative action. . . .

To investigate this feature of court involvement in state policy-making more completely, a mail survey was conducted of all fifty state supreme court chief justices, leaders of state senates and houses, and presidents of state bar associations. Requests for information also were directed to all court administrative officers and state judicial councils.

The rate of response to the mail questionnaire varied considerably: questionnaires were returned from 42 of the chief justices (84%, a high return for a mail questionnaire), 20 state senators (40%) and 26 house leaders and 26 bar association presidents (52%). The higher response rate from the chief justices probably reflects the greater salience which the focus of the research had for them. State legislative leaders probably view contacts between legislatures and courts as only a small aspect of legislative behavior and, therefore, they probably were less interested in the research. In addition, eight legislators and ten bar association presidents said they would not return their questionnaires because they first contacted the state supreme court before deciding whether or not to respond. When they learned that the chief justice was cooperating with the research, they chose to defer to his response. Most of them believed that his answers would be more accurate and include information with which they were not familiar.

The smaller number of responses from three of the four groups places some restrictions on the analysis which can be conducted. First, intrastate comparisons cannot be made because there were few states in which all questionnaires were returned. In addition, some useful information probably was lost because fewer legislators and bar association presidents returned questionnaires. This also makes it difficult to make comparisons among groups of respondents.

The judges' responses constitute the most important and most complete set of data. The questions did not deal with *attitudes* toward supreme court-legislative interactions in policy-making, which would require an adequate representation of all relevant views, but focused entirely on gathering factual information about court efforts to influence policy. The judges' questionnaires indicate that they are more knowledgeable about these interactions, for they frequently provided highly detailed descriptions of their relations with other political actors.

TABLE 1 *Percentage of Supreme Courts Using Channels of Communication Between Courts and Other Institutions*

(judges' responses, n = 41)

Court opinions	69.0%[a]
Conferences with legislators	59.5
Conferences with governor, staff or other executive officials	21.4
Judicial Council makes recommendations to governor and/or legislature	21.4
Legislative hearings; formal reports to legislature	16.7
Advisory opinions	9.5
Court opinions sent to legislature	9.5
Allied interest groups make demands	2.4

[a] Percentages will not total 100 because some judges mentioned more than one channel of communication.

Channels of Communication

It is clear that state supreme courts do attempt to influence policy in ways outside the regular channels of judicial decision-making. All but one chief justice and all but three of each of the other groups of respondents agreed that state supreme courts make recommendations to the legislature concerning state law. A few officials raised questions about the propriety of making recommendations, believing this violated the principle of the separation of powers, but this formal doctrine contributes little to an accurate description of interactions which actually occur among these governmental institutions. The separation of powers argument may have been raised in this context, however, because interactions between courts, legislatures, and other agencies often are informal and occur on an irregular basis. Unlike the power of judicial review, which also establishes a direct policy-making link between courts and other officials, informal interactions between courts and other agencies are not very visible and have no legal traditions or philosophies to legitimize them. Since they are not well-established in the formal legal system, they may appear improper and a violation of the scope of judicial power.

There is a variety of ways in which supreme courts convey their policy proposals to other officials (Table 1). Usually the proposals are directed to the state legislature, which has the most direct power to alter existing statutes and pass new laws. However, as Table 1 shows, about one-fourth of the chief justices stated that they also met with the governor, members of his staff or other officials in the executive branch in order to contribute policy proposals which might become part of the governor's legislative program.

The most frequent way in which supreme courts make policy proposals is through comments in written opinions. In this way the judges may suggest the need for legislative action in a particular area dealt with in a case. Occasionally, as Table 1 shows, supreme courts send copies of the opinions to legislative leaders, but this evidently occurs only in a few courts. It is possible that members of the legislature, especially those who are lawyers, will notice the recommendations contained in court opinions, but this is not the most efficient form of communication. Unless the opinions are followed with other contacts, it seems likely that recommendations found in court opinions easily could be forgotten or overlooked. However, two judges added that in their states all court opinions are read by a legislative council or revisor of statutes in order to check for court recommendations. Nevertheless, we should add that only five state courts rely on opinions as their sole channel of communication.[2]

The remaining state supreme courts utilize a variety of additional techniques to make policy proposals, but the most widely used is the personal conference between judges and legislators. The frequency and character of these meetings vary. Most judges indicated that meetings occur generally from one to four times a year, but in three states the judges said that they meet with legislators ten or more times annually. The meetings may be highly informal and take place generally between judges and legislators who are friends; other formal meetings, however, are specially arranged between judges and leaders of legislative committees in order to discuss various problems. The state courts also use other methods of communication, but there seem to be no clear patterns in the sets of communication channels chosen by the judges. For example, courts which use personal conferences with legislators also have contacts with executive officials to the same extent as those courts which do not use legislative meetings. Similarly, the presence of a judicial council which makes recommendations does not necessarily preclude the court from maintaining its own contacts with other officials.

It would seem that the presence of certain channels of communication between supreme courts and legislatures may depend upon differences in the political backgrounds of state officials and the characteristics of state institutions. For example, Murphy suggests that personal contacts between justices of the United States Supreme Court and members of Congress may occur more frequently and easily when the judges themselves are former

[2] In order to protect respondents' anonymity, the names of individual states will not be given when the data involved is drawn from questionnaire responses. It is possible to say, however, that the five states which use court opinions as their only channel of communication are found in all sections of the country; no regional concentration exists.

senators.[3] Personal friendships, political debts, and past political influence all may help a justice obtain congressional action which favors his policy goals. In order to test this and other hypotheses for the state courts, background information for each of the state supreme court judges and additional information relating to state courts and legislatures was obtained.

We found, first of all, that the effect of judges' legislative experience on court-legislative interactions is mixed. There is no relationship between the proportion of judges on a particular court who have been state legislators and the probability that their court will use informal meetings with state legislators to transmit their policy proposals. However, a slight relationship was found to exist between the legislative experience of *chief justices* and the existence of court contacts with legislatures ($Q = .33$).[4] This indicates that chief justices, who act as the major spokesmen for the courts in making policy suggestions, are somewhat more likely to meet with legislators if they themselves have been members of the legislature than if they have not had experience in the other branch of government.

Additional variables also were examined concerning the existence of court contacts with state legislatures. It was hypothesized that differences in recruitment systems might explain some variation: specifically, that judges elected to the court by the legislature or recruited in partisan elections would be more likely to be linked to legislative and/or state party politics and, therefore, might have closer ties to legislatures. No significant differences among the states emerged, however.

In addition, the effect of party dominance on state courts and state legislatures was examined. It was anticipated that courts and legislatures which were controlled by the same political party would be more likely to have contacts than those courts and legislatures dominated by opposite parties. Again, no differences emerged. Recruitment systems and links to political parties have been shown to be important in judicial recruitment and various features of decision-making, but they apparently do not operate in the establishment of links between courts and legislatures in state policy-making.

One final hypothesis concerning structural variations among state legislatures was investigated. We hypothesized that courts would be more likely to initiate contacts with the state legislatures if either the senate or the house or both have a judiciary committee established to deal specifically with problems relating to the courts. This organizational feature of state legislatures would seem to facilitate initiation and maintenance of interactions between the two institutions. A slight relationship does exist between these two variables ($Q = .34$).

[3] Murphy, *Elements of Judicial Strategy*, p. 132.

[4] Q is a measure of association used in relating nominal scales in a 2 x 2 table.

TABLE 2 *Percentage of State Supreme Courts Which Make Policy Proposals in Selected Areas*

(judge's responses, n = 41)

State judiciary[a]	59.5%[b]
Criminal law and procedure	16.7
Counsel to indigents	11.9
Workmen's compensation	7.1
Property and mortgages	7.1
Taxation	7.1
Governmental liability	4.8
Governmental regulation of business	4.8
Other	16.7

[a] This is a broad category which includes matters directly affecting the courts: court administration, organization, judicial salaries, regulation of law practice and court procedure.

[b] Percentages will not total 100 because some judges mentioned more than one type of recommendation.

The Scope of Judicial Policy Recommendations

Like other interest groups, the courts most frequently make recommendations which involve the benefits and well-being of the judiciary, concerning things such as court administration, organization, judicial salaries, regulation of law practice, and court procedure (Table 2). However, the supreme courts propose policies in other areas as well. Highest on the list are criminal law and procedure and counsel to indigents, but other recommendations affecting various economic relationships are also made.

It is important to add that only five of the courts limit themselves to offering recommendations which they made originally in court opinions. All of the remaining chief justices stated that court proposals may deal with issues and problems which have not been the subject of litigation. This does not mean that judges make proposals involving matters which do not relate to the courts; however, court recommendations may have important implications for other governmental policies, other political institutions, and the goals of other groups. As stated before, under these circumstances, the separation of powers becomes a very fuzzy and generally irrelevant concept.

Although the political implications of judicial policy proposals are most apparent when the courts deal with issues such as economic relations or criminal law and procedure, court proposals calling for changes in the judicial system may also affect other interests. Some of these proposals are routine and rarely involve political controversy, but it is incorrect to assume that all of them are unimportant. For example, one chief justice reported that the state supreme court recently was consulted by the legislature concerning whether a new court, an administrative agency, or the existing court structure should be used to deal with a new problem involving conflicts over the ownership of certain property. At another time, the judges had been asked their views on eliminating certain procedures in settling workmen's compensation claims in order to make judicial operations more efficient.

These and similar actions involving the creation of new judgeships or the consolidation of certain courts are likely to be extremely important to various groups, such as political parties concerned with the availability of patronage positions, the incumbents of court positions who want to retain their jobs, and lawyers and judges who are accustomed to working under the existing judicial system. In addition, many proposed changes in court rules may seem innocuous, but if, for example, they should call for limiting the political participation permitted lower court officials, the rules affect local political party organizations, in which judges and others may be active, and the ability of lower court personnel to campaign for reelection. It also is useful to add that several judges suggested in their responses that modest changes in statutes which deal with matters such as workmen's compensation or taxation sometimes are easier to implement than proposed changes in court procedures and salaries which may require fundamental changes in judicial institutions.

As stated earlier, the courts make proposals concerning other matters as well which also have the potential to affect groups interested in certain policy areas. An example of the courts' potential impact on important public policy may be found in a recent New Jersey case (State v. Rush, 1966) concerning public compensation for lawyers assigned to defend indigents. Current state law provided for payment only in murder cases, and a lawyer brought a suit against the state to contest this limitation. The supreme court decided that it could not decree that lawyers be paid in all cases in which they represented the poor, but in its opinion it referred the matter to the legislature. Moreover, the supreme court clearly indicated the policy alternatives it believed were available to the state and the kinds of research which the legislature needed to do to determine the best policy. The court explicitly discussed the fees lawyers should receive, the procedures used to select attorneys for the poor, and whether the program should be combined with a public defender system. In terms of impact on public policy, the case can be viewed from several perspectives. First, it was a matter which directly affected the operation of the courts and the relationship between lawyers and court bureaucracies. Second, the court's suggested policy innovations would have required additional public expenditures, to be determined by the legislature. Finally, the case raised the important question of the right of the poor to have free legal counsel in criminal cases and the adequacy of unpaid counsel. These concerns involve political issues relating to constitutional rights which are highly salient to many different political groups.

It is difficult to determine precisely how forcefully the courts press for the adoption of their policy recommendations. The five courts which rely exclusively on written opinions to express their views would not appear to be very active in making demands; however, other state courts which have established personal contacts with legislators and executive personnel would seem to have a greater opportunity to see that their proposals are implemented. One chief justice stated, for example, that in proposals which call for alterations in court structures or procedures, the supreme court frequently drafts the necessary legislation itself and forwards it to the governor and to legislative leaders. This strongly suggests that this court in particular is confident of its ability to persuade others to accept its views. Other chief justices, who said that battles sometimes occur between the court and the legislature, provide further evidence that certain courts are prepared and willing to press hard for their demands.

Other Participants in Policy-Making

Supreme courts, legislatures and governors are not the only participants concerned with policy affecting the judiciary. In some instances, supreme courts cooperate with and rely on others in making demands; at other times, however, differences may occur between the supreme court and other groups, indicating the existence of group conflict in policy-making.

State trial courts sometimes act as competing interest groups in the policy-making process. Several states have court rules which require lower-court judges to send their own policy recommendations to the supreme court which, in turn, will direct them to the legislature or the governor. This process does not always work smoothly, however, for few state supreme courts exercise very tight control over the lower courts. Although about one-third of the state supreme courts have formal rule-making powers which enable them to control court rules and procedures . . . this does not prevent lower-court judges from having their own policy goals and using their own political resources to have them implemented. One chief justice indicated, for example, that there are instances in which trial court judges contact legislators and make suggestions on their own concerning changes in statutes and court organization. The supreme court may, at the same time, make its own recommendations. This sometimes results in having conflicting proposals before the legislature. Since the supreme court has the primary responsibility for the operation of the entire state court system, the presence of opposing recommendations causes confusion, dilutes the supreme court's influence, and delays the adoption of its own recommendations.

State judicial councils also make policy proposals. These organizations, which usually are closely linked to the supreme court, study the operation of the state judiciary, court rules and procedures, and other related matters in order to make recommendations concerning necessary changes in judicial structure. About one-half of the states have judicial councils composed entirely of judges and headed usually by the chief justice. Some states have councils consisting of judges and legislators, and still other councils include judges, legislators, and various other state officials. . . . The composition of the state judicial council does not correlate, however, with the manner in which judges choose to transmit their policy proposals. A supreme court whose state has a judicial council composed only of judges is just as likely to have contacts with legislative leaders as a court in a state where the judicial council includes judges as well as legislators.

One explanation for the lack of relationship between the type of judicial council in the states and channels of communication used by the courts is that the activity of state judicial councils varies greatly. In an effort to learn more about the functions of these organizations, I requested each council to send me the most recent available report of their activities and policy recommendations. I received reports from only twenty-six councils. (Three states do not have judicial councils, eleven did not issue reports, and ten were inactive.) Although the absence of reports or council statements indicating inactivity do not mean by themselves that the organizations perform no functions, it strongly suggests that they play little or no active role in judicial policy-making.

Most of the 26 functioning councils do appear to take part in policy-making, and they have made a variety of recommendations (Table 3). Most of their attention was directed to problems relating to the organization and functioning of the state judicial system, but a fairly large number of judicial councils also made recommendations in the fields of criminal law and public defender programs. However, 6 of the 26 judicial councils made no recommendations. It also is important to note that judicial councils frequently make numerous recommendations in a particular policy area, and many also write the proposed legislation themselves. This would seem to indicate that many councils do not simply perform a passive role in presenting general ideas for policy changes, but that they take the initiative in proposing recommendations that they have planned and outlined in proposed legislation.[5]

[5] One exception is the Judicial Council of Massachusetts which makes recommendations only on pending legislation which has been sent to the council by the legislature.

TABLE 3 *Recommendations of State Judicial Councils*[a]

State judiciary[b] (states, n = 18)		Criminal law (states, n = 11)		Public defender counsel to indigents (states, n = 8)		Wills, trusts, estates (states, n = 3)		Property, mortgages (states, n = 4)		Other (states, n = 2)		None (states, n = 6)
State	Number of proposals	State	Number of proposals	State	Number of proposals	State	Number of proposals	State	Number of proposals	State	Number of proposals	State
Alaska	2	Calif.	1[c]	Alaska	1	Conn.	3[c]	Conn.	2[c]	Mass.	6[e]	Ark.
Calif.	3[c]	Conn.	10[c]	Conn.	1	Mass.	4	Mass.	3	Wash.	1[f]	Ill.
Conn.	7[c]	Kan.	1[c,d]	Minn.	1	Wash.	1[c]	N.H.	3[c]			Ky.
Fla.	3[c]	Mass.	9	N.H.	1[c]			Wash.	1	Total	7	Mo.
La.	1	Minn.	1[c]	Ore.	1	Total	8					N.J.
Mass.	9	N.H.	4[c]	R.I.	1			Total	9			Tex.
Minn.	2	N.C.	8[c]	Vt.	1							
N.H.	4[c]	Penn.	1[d]	Wis.	1							
N.Y.	3	Va.	1									
N.C.	5[c]	Wash.	2[c]	Total	8							
Ohio	4	Wis.	1									
Ore.	3											
Penn.	1	Total	39									
R.I.	4											
Vt.	5											
Va.	4											
Wash.	12[c]											
Wis.	6											
Total	78											

[a] The data is derived from the latest judicial council report available in each state. Reports include those from 1966 to 1969.
[b] This category includes court administration, organization, judicial salaries, regulation of law practice and court procedure.
[c] The judicial council drafted the legislation for its policy proposals.
[d] This proposal includes a detailed plan for an entirely revised criminal code.
[e] Recommendations in the areas of liability law, zoning and regulation of cable television.
[f] Recommendation concerning the conduct of elections.

Some of the proposals put forth by the councils request very specific, technical changes in court rules and procedures. Most of these probably do not cause much controversy and are adopted without difficulty. However, like some of the proposals made by the state supreme courts, other judicial council proposals suggest extensive changes in court structures and other areas of law. Judging from the scope of their recommendations, 16 of the 26 judicial councils could be viewed as being very active in making policy proposals.[6] For example, the Kansas and Pennsylvania judicial councils recently proposed important changes in the entire state criminal code, and other judicial councils have suggested changes in the imposition of the death penalty for certain types of crimes. In the general area of court organization, several councils have called for the addition of new judges, changes in the procedures for selecting jurors, creation of new courts, consolidation of various lower courts, and even changes in the method of judicial selection. As indicated before, these kinds of proposals have implications not only for the operation of the courts, but also for the goals and interests of other political groups.

It is not possible to determine from the reports precisely how effective the judicial councils have been in having their proposals adopted. Furthermore, research on the amount of legislation which has been revised or new laws which have been passed in each state in response to demands of the judicial council could not be undertaken by this study. Several reports do suggest, however, that proposals calling for new judges, changes in court organization and procedure, or changes in the method of judicial recruitment—all of which are important in political terms—meet with some opposition from both the legislature and certain state judges. A case in point can be found in the 1968 report of the judicial council of Connecticut. Of all the proposals contained in the report, two-thirds were repeated from an earlier report, indicating that they had not been adopted as requested. A similar situation occurred in New York where, in 1968, the judicial council recommended the addition of 125 new judges. In making its request, the council summarized the history of the legislature's poor response to the needs of the courts: from 1961 to 1967 the requests for new judges were met by only very small additions to the courts, and the largest number ever allocated by the legislature still was at least one-third below the number requested. In 1966 and 1967, no judges were added even though approximately 100 were requested in each of the two years.

Opposition to proposed changes offered by the judicial council also

[6] The system for placing judicial councils into more and less active categories distinguishes between councils which make recommendations for only minor changes in existing statutes, rules of procedure, or court organization (less active in policy-making) and those councils which recommend fundamental and frequently major revisions in statutory law and court organization (more active in policy-making).

may come from various state judges. In 1966, for example, the Pennsylvania judicial council debated the merits of three different plans of judicial selection and other court reforms. Some judges spoke in favor of changing the selection system from partisan election to a nonpartisan plan, and they also favored certain alterations in the structure of various courts. Others defended the current system, however, because it had always worked well in the past and because they did not believe the proposed changes would remedy any existing defects.

In addition to judicial councils and state trial courts, bar associations may participate in the policy-making process. The involvement of the bar is fairly widespread, for all but seven of the chief justices indicated that their court seeks the aid of the bar in pressing for legislative action. However, the frequency of cooperation between supreme courts and bar associations varies widely. Of those judges who noted bar involvement in policy-making, only 13.3% of the judges said that the court "almost always" looks to the bar for help; 30% said the aid of the bar was sought "often"; and 56.7% of the judges indicated that the bar was asked to participate "only occasionally."

It is clear that most supreme courts do not rely routinely on the bar for help in working for policy changes. These findings are interesting in view of relationships which might be expected to exist between bar associations and the courts. Lawyers and judges are closely linked in the judiciary, and it would seem that both groups have much to gain through mutual cooperation and support. This is useful in personal relationships in certain courts and contributes to the formation of informal rules of the game which make each court system function more smoothly. . . . We might expect, then, that supreme courts and bar associations would cooperate closely.

This does not always occur, however, and it may be that cooperation operates differently at various levels of the judicial system. Certain lawyers and trial court judges probably have interests in common concerning the functioning of their own particular court. These may conflict, however, with the goals of state supreme courts which may ignore the special problems of some courts or seek to change informal procedures and traditions which exist in various counties or districts. Under these conditions, lawyers and judges throughout the state may oppose certain supreme court proposals. Several responses to the questionnaires suggest that such conflict between supreme courts and bar associations sometimes does exist. In addition, the bar may be internally divided and unable to cooperate with the supreme court in lobbying for legislative action.

It is important to add that when the bar is requested to help in influencing legislative policy, it becomes involved almost exclusively in the area of court organization, administration, and law practice. In a few states, the bar has participated in requesting legislative action in other areas such as counsel to indigents and tax policy, but this is very insignificant in comparison with its role in influencing legislation which directly concerns the courts and the legal profession.

This nearly exclusive involvement of the bar in such issues very likely reflects, in part, the perceptions of judges who consider the expertise of the bar applicable primarily to this policy area. It also may reflect the issues which lawyers consider most important to them. Individual attorneys may be concerned with other policies, but as an organization the bar probably is concerned most often with policies directly affecting the courts and the legal profession.

The Success of Judicial Policy Recommendations

All but a few justices and senate and house leaders agreed that state legislatures do adopt some of the recommendations of state supreme courts. It is difficult, however, to assess the levels of success which courts achieve because many of the respondents were unwilling or unable to estimate the percentage and types of court recommendations which were adopted. Nevertheless, some conclusions can be drawn. First, the success achieved by the state supreme courts varies. Of the judges who rated their success, forty per cent indicated that the legislature adopts fifty per cent or less of the court's recommendations; twenty per cent of the judges said the legislature implements between one-half and three-fourths of its recommendations and the remaining forty per cent of the judges said the legislature enacts between seventy-five and one hundred per cent of the court's proposals. The senate and house leaders generally believed the courts were more successful than this, but since so few of them indicated a percentage level of court success, these findings are inconclusive.

As shown in Table 2, state supreme courts make policy recommendations most frequently in the "state judiciary" policy area. Compared with the number of courts making proposals in the other areas, this category clearly was the most important one. Achievements made by the courts also follow this pattern. Of those officials responding to the questions dealing with the adoption of judicial policy recommendations, chief justices and senate and house leaders all agreed that the "state judiciary" category was the one in which the courts were most successful. In contrast, only a few listed successes in other policy areas.

From one point of view, these findings are not surprising since the courts concentrate most of their energies on making proposals in areas which most directly concern the courts. If more officials had responded to the questions, we would still expect reports of court success to follow this pattern. While the order of success is as anticipated, it is striking that so few recommendations made in other policy areas seem to be adopted. This suggests that court recommendations are received more favorably by state legislatures when they are confined to matters which primarily, and perhaps exclusively, affect the courts. Frequently the successful proposals also appear to be uncontroversial and have little impact on other groups. Most judges, for example, reported that proposals concerning court budgets, salaries, and facilities received the most favorable action.

While these kinds of proposals seem to constitute the bulk of successful court recommendations, some state supreme courts have been able to achieve their policy objectives in other more important areas. In particular, several judges reported success in having additional personnel allocated to the courts and were influential in the revision of the criminal code, court procedure, creation of a juvenile court, mental health legislation, provision of counsel to indigents, and other specific statutory clarifications. However, while they sometimes are adopted, these kinds of proposals probably are implemented infrequently, because they vitally affect other interest groups and because they require state expenditures not contained in routine appropriations. Thus these proposals may become the subject of heated political conflict and state supreme courts are more likely to lose some of the battles which take place.

SUGGESTED READINGS

Policy Making and State Government

The following entries are designed to acquaint the reader with a broader spectrum of scholarly research than can be compiled in one reader. There are only a few comments necessary in regard to these readings. First, the greatest amount of research has been undertaken in regard to the study of legislatures—a fact emphasized by the comparative study presented in this volume. We are listing studies in this section which also cover reapportionment, roles of legislators, parties, etc. in addition to standard works. Second, studies of the governor are more prevalent than studies of the executive branch as a whole or its relations with other branches of government. Third, there is a paucity of information in regard to both state and local organs of the judicial branch. Perhaps this selective bibliography will provide the basis for exploratory research which can eventually fill some of the major gaps in our understanding of the machinations of state governments.

THE EXECUTIVE BRANCH

For a general discussion of the future roles of governors, the reader should consult a symposium of articles, "The American Governor in the 1970's," Coleman B. Ransone, Jr., ed., *Public Administration Review,* **30** (January–February, 1970), 1–43. Decision-making at the gubernatorial level is examined by Malcolm Jewell, "State Decision-Making: The Governor Revisited," in Aaron Wildavsky and Nelson Polsby, eds., *American Governmental Institutions* (Chicago: Rand-McNally, 1968). An excellent analysis of the role of the executive branch as a whole is found in Ira Sharkansky, "State Administrators in the Political Process," in Herbert Jacob and Kenneth Vines, eds., *Politics in the American States, Second Edition* (Boston: Little, Brown, 1971), pp. 238–271. Finally, for an excellent and rare analysis of the governor and his legislative party, consult Sarah P. McCally, "The Governor and His Legislative Party," *American Political Science Review,* 60 (December, 1966), 923–942.

OTHER READINGS OF INTEREST

Beyle, Thad L., and J. Oliver Williams, eds. *The American Governor in Behavioral Perspective.* New York: Harper and Row, 1972.

Block, Earl. "Southern Governors and Political Change: Campaign Stances on Racial Segregation and Economic Development, 1950–1969," *The Journal of Politics*, 33 (August, 1971), 703–734.

Kallenbach, Joseph. *The American Chief Executive: The Presidency and the Governorship.* New York: Harper and Row, 1966.

Olsen, Raymond T. "The American Governor: Executive Management for System Change," *State Government,* **44** (Winter, 1971), 26–31.

Ransone, Coleman B., Jr. "Political Leadership in the Governor's Office," *The Journal of Politics,* **26** (February 1964), 197–220.

Rise, John C. *Executives in the American Political System.* Belmont, Calif.: Dickenson Publishing Co., 1969.

Schlesinger, Joseph A. "The Politics of the Executive," in Herbert Jacob and Kenneth N. Vines, eds. *Politics in the American States, Second Edition.* Boston: Little, Brown, 1971, 210–237.

ADMINISTRATION

Council of State Governments. *Cabinets in State Government.* Chicago: Council of State Governments, 1969.

Dittenhofer, Mortimer A. "The Growing Role of the Auditor in Managing State Government," *State Government,* **43** (Spring 1970), 119–123.

Eley, Lynn W. *The Executive Reorganization Plan: A Survey of State Experience.* Berkeley: Institute of Governmental Studies, University of California, 1967.

Friedman, Robert, Bernard H. Klein, and John H. Roman. "Administrative Agencies and the Publics They Serve," *Public Administration Review,* **26** (September 1966), 192–204.

Schick, Allen. "Control Patterns in State Budget Execution," *Public Administration Review,* **24** (June 1964), 97–106.

Sharkansky, Ira, and Augustus B. Turnbull. "Budget-Making in Georgia and Wisconsin: A Test of a Model," *Midwest Journal of Political Science,* **13** (November 1969), 631–645.

Simmons, Robert. "American State Executive Systems: An Heuristic Model," *Western Political Quarterly,* **28** (March 1965), 19–26.

THE LEGISLATIVE BRANCH

The research on state legislatures is so vast, especially in comparison to research on the other areas of state government, as to preclude any statements as to the most interesting writings. Therefore, we simply list a rather lengthy, yet far from exhaustive, set of readings in this area of research.

Baker, Gordon E. *The Reapportionment Revolution: Representation, Political Power, and the Supreme Court.* New York: Random House, 1967.

Barber, James David. *The Lawmakers: Recruitment and Adaptation to Legislative Life.* New Haven: Yale University Press, 1965.

Barber, James David. "Leadership Strategies for Legislative Party Cohesion," *Journal of Politics,* **28** (May 1966), 347–367.

Blair, George. *American Legislatures: Structure and Process.* New York: Harper & Row, 1967.

Boynton, G. R., Samuel C. Patterson, and Ronald D. Hedlund. "The Missing Links in Legislative Politics: Attentive Constituents," *Journal of Politics,* **31** (August 1969), 700–721.

Bushnell, Eleanore, ed. *Impact of Reapportionment on the Thirteen Western States.* Salt Lake City: University of Utah Press, 1970.

Cnudde, Charles, and Donald J. McCrone. "Party Competitors and Welfare Policies in the American States," *American Political Science Review,* **63** (September 1969), 858–866.

Council of State Governments. *American State Legislatures: Their Structures and Procedures.* Chicago: Council of State Governments, 1971.

Council of State Governments. *Permanent Legislative Service Agencies.* Lexington, Kentucky: Council of State Governments, 1971.

Crane, Wilder, and Meredith Watts. *State Legislative Systems.* Englewood Cliffs, N.J.: Prentice-Hall, 1968.

Dixon, Robert G., Jr. *Democratic Representation: Reapportionment in Law and Politics.* New York: Oxford University Press, 1968.

Dye, Thomas R. "Malapportionment and Public Policy in the States," *The Journal of Politics,* **27** (August 1965), 586–601.

Dye, Thomas R. "State Legislative Politics," in Herbert Jacob and Kenneth N. Vines, eds. *Politics in the American States,* Second Edition. Boston: Little, Brown, 1971, 163–209.

Edsall, P. W. "State Legislatures and Legislative Representation," *The Journal of Politics,* **30** (May 1968), 277–289.

Gazell, James A. "One-Man, One-Vote: Its Long Germination," *Western Political Quarterly,* **23** (September 1970), 445–462.

Goldwin, Robert A., ed. *Representation and Misrepresentation: Legislative Reapportionment in Theory and Practice.* Chicago: Rand McNally, 1968.

Goodman, Jay, Wayne R. Swanson, and Elmer E. Cornwell, Jr. "Political Recruitment in Four Selection Systems," *Western Political Quarterly,* **23** (March 1970), 92–103.

Grumm, John G. "The Effects of Legislative Structure on Legislative Performance," in Richard Hofferbert and Ira Sharkansky, eds., *State and Urban Politics.* Boston: Little, Brown, 1971, 298–322.

Hahn, Harlan D. "Leadership in a One-Party Legislative Body," *The Journal of Politics,* **32** (February 1970), 140–155.

Hardin, C. M. "Issues in Legislative Reapportionment," *Review of Politics,* **27** (April 1965), 147–172.

Heard, Alexander. "Reform: Limits and Opportunities," in Alexander Heard, ed., *State Legislatures in American Politics.* Englewood Cliffs, N.J.: Prentice-Hall, 1966, 154–162.

Herzberg, Donald G., and Jesse M. Unruh, eds. *Essays in the State Legislative Process.* New York: Holt, Rinehart and Winston, 1971.

Hofstetter, C. Richard. "Malapportionment and Roll-Call Voting in Indiana, 1923–1968: A Computer Simulation," *The Journal of Politics,* **33** (February 1971), 92–111.

Jewell, Malcolm. *The State Legislature.* Rev. ed., New York: Random House, 1969.

Jewell, Malcolm, and Samuel C. Patterson. *The Legislative Process in the United States.* New York: Random House, 1966.

Jewell, Malcolm. *Legislative Representation in the Contemporary South.* Durham, N.C.: Duke University Press, 1967.

Keefe, William J. "The Functions and Powers of the State Legislature," in

Alexander Heard, ed., *State Legislatures in American Politics.* Englewood Cliffs, N.J.: Prentice-Hall, 1966, 37–69.

Keefe, William J., and Morris S. Ogul. *American Legislative Process: Congress and the States, Third Edition.* Englewood Cliffs, N.J.: Prentice-Hall, 1972.

LeBlanc, Hugh. "Voting in State Senates: Party and Constituency Influences," *Midwest Journal of Political Science,* **13** (February 1969), 33–57.

Lockard, Duane. "The State Legislator," in Alexander Heard, ed., *State Legislatures in American Politics.* Englewood Cliffs, N.J.: Prentice-Hall, 1966, 98–125.

Moore, David W. "Legislative Effectiveness and Majority Party Size: A Test in the Indiana House," *The Journal of Politics,* **31** (November 1969), 1063–1079.

Polsby, Nelson, ed. *Reapportionment in the 1970s.* Berkeley: University of California Press, 1971.

Ruchelman, Leonard. *Political Careers: Recruitment Through the Legislature.* Cranbury, N.J.: Fairleigh Dickinson University Press, 1970.

Sowle, John W. "Future Political Ambitions and the Behavior of Incumbent State Legislators," *Midwest Journal of Political Science,* **12** (August 1969), 439–454.

Werner, Emmy E. "Women in State Legislatures," *Western Political Quarterly,* **21** (March 1968), 50–58.

THE JUDICIAL BRANCH

The area of state and local judiciary is largely unexplored. A major work on the political aspect of a local judicial system is Kenneth M. Dolbeare's *Trial Courts in Urban Politics* (New York: Wiley, 1967). Henry Robert Glick has done comparative work with state supreme courts resulting in *Supreme Courts in State Politics* (New York: Basic Books, 1971). Glick and Kenneth N. Vines have also published "Law Making in the State Judiciary," *Polity,* **2** (Winter 1969), in which they discuss the role orientations of supreme court judges of four states. Somewhat dated but still a good general introduction to the judicial process is the chapter by Herbert Jacob and Kenneth N. Vines, "The Role of the Judiciary in American State Politics," in Glendon Schubert, ed., *Judicial Decisionmaking* (New York: Free Press, 1963).

OTHER READINGS OF INTEREST

Adamany, David W. "Party Variable in Judge's Voting: Conceptual Notes and a Case Study," *American Political Science Review,* **63** (March 1969), 57–63.

Cook, B. B. *The Judicial Process in California.* Belmont, Calif.: Dickenson Publishing Company, 1967.

Council of State Governments. *State Court Systems.* Lexington, Ky.: Council of State Governments, 1962.

Dimond, A. J. *The Superior Court of Massachusetts: Its Origin and Development.* Boston: Little, Brown, 1960.

Fair, Daryl R. "State Intermediate Appellate Courts: An Introduction," *Western Political Quarterly,* **24** (September 1971), 415–424.

Feeley, Malcolm M. "Another Look at the Party Variable in Judicial Decision-Making: An Analysis of the Michigan Supreme Court," *Polity,* **4** (Autumn 1971), 91–104.

Glick, Henry Robert. "Policy-Making and State Supreme Courts," *Law and Society Review,* **5** (November 1970), 271–292.

Jacob, Herbert. "The Effect of Institutional Differences in the Recruitment Process: The Case of State Judges," *Journal of Public Law,* **13** (June 1964), 104–119.

Jacob, Herbert. *Justice in America.* Boston: Little, Brown, 1972.

Nagel, Stuart. "Political Party Affiliation and Judges' Decisions," *American Political Science Review,* **55** (December 1961), 843–850.

Saye, A. B. "Revolution by Judicial Action in Georgia," *Western Political Quarterly,* **17** (March 1964), 10–14.

Sickels, Robert J. "The Illusion of Judicial Consensus: Zoning Decisions in Maryland's Court of Appeals," *American Political Science Review,* **59** (March 1965), 100–104.

Vines, Kenneth N. "Southern State Supreme Courts and Race Relations," *Western Political Quarterly,* **18** (March 1965), 5–18.

Vines, Kenneth N., and Herbert Jacob. "State Courts," in Herbert Jacob and Kenneth N. Vines, eds., *Politics in the American States, Second Edition.* Boston: Little, Brown, 1971.

Vines, Kenneth N., and Herbert Jacob. *Studies in Judicial Politics.* New Orleans: Tulane University Studies in Political Science, 1963.

Part III

Policy Making at the Urban Level

Perhaps the first comment most observers would make about policy making at the Urban level is that it has been a failure. At least, there is general agreement (except for Edward Banfield in his *The Unheavenly City)* that the quality of urban life is deteriorating, and blame for that deterioration has been laid partly to the ineffective way the policy process has dealt with the manifold problems in urban areas. For a while it could be argued that malapportionment kept state legislatures and the Congress from recognizing urban problems, but *Baker* v. *Carr* in 1962 began to remove the basis of that argument. And the very complexity of urban problems themselves seems to excuse the failure of the policy process to deal with them adequately.

But in part the urban "crisis" is a crisis of the policy-making process itself. We still do not know very much about that process, at any level of government, and as varied and involved as the process is at the urban level, it defies quick understanding. Some progress has been made in exploring it, as the readings that follow demonstrate.

Edward C. Banfield

Introduction to The Unheavenly City Revisited

> ... the clock is ticking, time is moving ..., we must ask ourselves every night when we go home, are we doing all that we should do in our nation's capital, in all the other big cities of the country.
>
> —President Johnson, after the Watts Riot, August 1965

> A few years ago we constantly heard that urban America was on the brink of collapse. It was one minute to midnight, we were told. ... Today, America is no longer coming apart. ... The hour of crisis is passed.
>
> —President Nixon, March 1973

The reason for juxtaposing the quotations above is not to suggest that whereas a few years ago the cities were in great peril now all is well with them. Rather it is to call attention both to the simplistic nature of all such sweeping judgments and to the fact that one's perception of urban America is a function of time and place and also, if one is a politician, of whatever winds are blowing. A few blocks' walk through the heart of any large city was enough in 1965—and is enough in 1973—to show much that was (and is) in crying need of improvement. That a society so technologically advanced and prosperous has many hundreds of blocks ranging from dreary to dismal is disturbing at least and when one takes into account that by the end of the century the urban population will be at least 20 per cent larger than in 1970, with six out of every ten persons living in a metropolitan area of more than a million, the prospect may appear alarming.

There is, however, another side to the matter. The plain fact is that the

---

From Edward C. Banfield, *The Unheavenly City Revisited*, Chapter 1.

overwhelming majority of city dwellers live more comfortably and conveniently than ever before. They have more and better housing, more and better schools, more and better transportation, and so on. By any conceivable measure of material welfare the present generation of urban Americans is, on the whole, better off than any other large group of people has ever been anywhere. What is more, there is every reason to expect that the general level of comfort and convenience will continue to rise at an even more rapid rate through the foreseeable future.

It is true that many people do not share, or do not share fully, this general prosperity, some because they are the victims of racial prejudice and others for other reasons that are equally beyond their control. If the chorus of complaint about the city arose mainly from these disadvantaged people or on behalf of them, it would be entirely understandable, especially if their numbers were increasing and their plight were getting worse. But the fact is that until very recently most of the talk about the urban crisis has had to do with the comfort, convenience, and business advantage of the well-off white majority and not with the more serious problems of the poor, the Negro, and others who stand outside the charmed circle. And the fact also is that the number of those standing outside the circle is decreasing, as is the relative disadvantage that they suffer. There is still much poverty and much racial discrimination. But there is less of both than ever before.

The question arises, therefore, not of whether we are faced with an urban crisis, but rather, *in what sense* we are faced with one. Whose interest and what interests are involved? How deeply? What should be done? Given the political and other realities of the situation, what *can* be done?

The first need is to clear away some semantic confusions. Consider the statement, so frequently used to alarm luncheon groups, that more than 70 per cent of the population now lives in urban places and that this number may increase to nearly 90 per cent in the next two decades if present trends continue. Such figures give the impression of standing room only in the city, but what exactly do they mean?

When we are told that the population of the United States is rapidly becoming overwhelmingly urban, we probably suppose this to mean that most people are coming to live in the big cities. This is true in one sense but false in another. It is true that most people live closer physically and psychologically to a big city than ever before; rural occupations and a rural style of life are no longer widespread. On the other hand, the percentage of the population living in cities of 250,000 or more (there are only fifty-six of them) is about the same now as it was in 1920. In Census terminology an "urban place" is any settlement having a population of 2,500 or more; obviously places of 2,500 are not what we have in mind when we use words like "urban" and "city"[1] It is somewhat misleading to say that the country is becoming more urban, when what is meant is that more people are living in places like White River Junction, Vermont (pop. 6,311), and fewer in places like Boston, Massachusetts (pop. 641,000). But it is not *altogether* misleading, for most of the small urban places are now close enough (in terms of time and other costs of travel) to large cities to be part of a metropolitan complex. White River Junction, for example, is now very much influenced by Boston. The average population density in all "urban areas," however, has been decreasing: from 5,408 per square mile in 1950 to 3,752 in 1960, to 3,376 in 1970.

A great many so-called urban problems are really conditions that we either cannot eliminate or do not want to incur the disadvantages of eliminating. Consider the "problem of congestion." The presence of a great many people in one place is a cause of inconvenience, to say the least. But the advantages of having so many people in one place far outweigh these inconveniences, and we cannot possibly have the advantages without the disadvantages. To "eliminate congestion" in the city must mean eliminating the city's reason for being. Congestion in the city is a "problem" only in the sense that congestion in Times Square on New Year's Eve is one; in fact, of course, people come to the city, just as they do to Times Square, precisely *because* it is congested. If it were not congested, it would not be worth coming to.

Strictly speaking, a problem exists only as we should want something different from what we do want or as by better management we could get a larger total of what we want. If we think it a good thing that many people have the satisfaction of driving their cars in and out of the city, and if we see no way of arranging the situation to get them in and out more conveniently that does not entail more than offsetting disadvantages for them or others, then we ought not to speak of a "traffic congestion problem." By the same token, urban sprawl is a "problem," as opposed to a "condition," only if (1) fewer people should have the satisfaction of living in the low-density

[1] The 1970 Census defined as "urban" places, unincorporated as well as incorporated, with 2,500 inhabitants or more (excluding persons living in rural portions of extended cities) as well as other territory within Urbanized Areas. An "Urbanized Area" comprises at least one city of 50,000 inhabitants (the "central city") plus contiguous, closely settled areas ("urban fringe"). A "Standard Metropolitan Statistical Area (SMSA)" is a county or group of contiguous counties (except in New England) containing a city (or "twin" cities) of at least 50,000 population; contiguous counties are included in an SMSA if they are essentially metropolitan in character and are socially and economically integrated with the central city. That part of the United States lying outside of any SMSA is "nonmetropolitan." All of these definitions were somewhat different in 1960 and also in 1950.

See Daniel J. Elazar, "Are We a Nation of Cities?," *The Public Interest*, 4 (Summer 1966), pp. 42–44.

fringe of the city, or (2) we might, by better planning, build homes in the fringe without destroying so much landscape and without incurring costs (for example, higher per-unit construction costs) or forgoing benefits (for example, a larger number of low-income families who can have the satisfaction of living in the low-density area) of greater value than the saving in landscape.

Few problems, in this strict sense, are anywhere near as big as they seem. The amount of urban sprawl that could be eliminated simply by better planning—that is, without the sacrifice of other ends that are also wanted, such as giving the satisfaction of owning a house and yard to many low-income people—is probably trivial as compared to the total urban sprawl (that is, to the "problem" defined simple-mindedly as "a condition that is unpleasant").

Many so-called urban problems (crime is a conspicuous exception) are more characteristic of rural and small-town places than of cities. Housing is generally worse in rural areas, for example, and so are schools. "Low verbal ability," Sloan R. Wayland of Columbia Teachers College has written, "is described as though it could only happen in an urban slum." Actually, he points out, all but a very small fraction of mankind has always been "culturally deprived," and the task of formal education has always been to attack such conditions.[2]

Most of the "problems" that are generally supposed to constitute "the urban crisis" could not conceivably lead to disaster. They are—some of them—important in the sense that a bad cold is important, but they are not critical in the sense that a cancer is critical. They have to do with comfort, convenience, amenity, and business advantage, all of which are important, but they do not affect either the essential welfare of individuals or what may be called the good health of the society.

Consider, for example, an item that often appears near the top of the list of complaints about the city—the journey to work. It takes the average commuter between 21 and 34 minutes to get to work (the difference in the average time depending upon the population of the metropolitan area).[3] It would, of course, be very nice if the journey to work were much shorter. No one can suppose, however, that the essential welfare of many people would be much affected even if it were fifteen minutes longer. Certainly its

[2] Sloan R. Wayland, "Old Problems, New Faces, and New Standards," in A. Harry Passow, ed., *Education in Depressed Areas* (New York: Columbia University Teachers College, 1963), p. 66.

[3] Irving Hoch, "Urban Scale and Environmental Quality," in *Population, Resources, and the Environment,* vol. III of task force reports of Commission on Population Growth and the American Future, Ronald G. Ridker, ed. (Washington, D.C., Government Printing Office, 1972), p. 243. The figures are for 1966.

being longer or shorter would not make the difference between a good society and a bad.

Another matter causing widespread alarm is the decline of the central business district, by which is meant the loss of patronage to downtown department stores, theatres, restaurants, museums, and so on, which has resulted from the movement of many well-off people to suburbs. Clearly, the movement of good customers from one place to another involves inconvenience and business loss to many people, especially to the owners of real estate that is no longer in so great demand. These losses, however, are essentially no different from those that occur from other causes—say, a shift of consumers' tastes that suddenly renders a once-valuable patent valueless. Moreover, though some lose by the change, others gain by it: the overall gain of wealth by building in the suburbs may more than offset the loss of it caused by letting the downtown deteriorate.

There are those who claim that cultural and intellectual activity flourishes only in big cities and that therefore the decline of the downtown business districts and the replacement of cities by suburbs threaten the very survival of civilization. This claim is farfetched, to say the very least, if it means that we cannot have good music and good theater (not to mention philosophy, literature, and science) unless customers do their shopping in the downtown districts of Oakland, St. Louis, Nashville, Boston, and so on, rather than in the suburbs around them. Public efforts to preserve the downtown districts of these and other cities may perhaps be worth what they cost—although, so far as cultural and intellectual activities are concerned, there is no reason to assume that public efforts would not bring at least as much return if directed to metropolitan areas as wholes. The return, however, will be in the comfort, convenience, and business advantage of the relatively well-off and not in anyone's essential welfare.

The same can be said about efforts to "beautify" the cities. That for the most part the cities are dreary and depressing if not offensively ugly may be granted: the desirability of improving their appearance, even if only a little, cannot be questioned. It is very doubtful, however, that people are dehumanized (to use a favorite word of those who complain about the cities) by the ugliness of the city or that they would be in any sense humanized by its being made beautiful. (If they were humanized, they would doubtless build beautiful cities, but that is an entirely different matter. One has only to read Machiavelli's Florentine Histories to see that living in a beautiful city is not in itself enough to bring out the best in one. So far as their humanity is concerned, the people of, say, Jersey City compare very favorably to the Florentines of the era of that city's greatest glory.) At worst, the American city's ugliness–or, more, its lack of splendor or charm –occasions loss of visual pleasure. This loss is an important one (it is surely much larger than most people realize), but it cannot lead to any kind of disaster either for the individual or for the society.

Air pollution comes closer than any of these problems to threatening essential welfare, as opposed to comfort, convenience, amenity, and business advantage. Some people die early because of it and many more suffer various degrees of bad health; there is also some possibility (no one knows how much) that a meteorological coincidence (an "air inversion") over a large city might suddenly kill thousands or even tens of thousands. Important as it is, however, the air pollution problem is rather minor as compared to other threats to health and welfare not generally regarded as "crises."[4] Moreover, steps are being taken to clear the air. The Clean Air Act Amendment of 1970 is expected to reduce pollution from auto emissions (by far the most serious source) to half of what they were in 1967 (the base year) by 1980 and to a quarter by 1985.[5]

Many of the "problems" that are supposed to constitute the "crisis" could be quickly and easily solved, or much alleviated, by the application of well-known measures that lie right at hand. In some instances, the money cost of these measures would be very small. For example, the rush-hour traffic problem in the central cities (which, incidentally, is almost the whole of the traffic problem in these cities) could be much reduced and in some cases eliminated entirely just by staggering working hours in the largest offices and factories. Manhattan presents the hardest case of all, but even there, an elaborate study showed, rush-hour crowding could be reduced by 25 per cent, enough to make the strap-hanger reasonably comfortable.[6] Another quick and easy way of improving urban transportation in most cities would be to eliminate a mass of archaic regulations on the granting of public transit and taxi franchises. At present, the cities are in effect going out of their way to place obstacles in the paths of those who might offer the public better transportation.[7] Metropolitan transportation could also easily be improved in those areas—there are a number of them—where extensive expressway networks link the downtown with outlying cities and towns. In these areas, according to the Harvard economist John F. Kain, "all that is currently needed to create extensive metropolitan rapid

[4] According to the U.S. Public Health Service, the most polluted air is nowhere near as dangerous as inhaled cigarette smoke. It is of interest also that the mortality rate from emphysema is higher in rural parts of New York than in metropolitan ones (*New York Times*, October 30, 1970) and that the state with the highest death rate from respiratory disease is Vermont (*New York Times*, December 20, 1972).

[5] For data see U.S. Environmental Protection Agency, *Air Quality Data*, an annual, *Air Pollution Measurements of the National Air Sampling Network, 1957–1961*, and *The Fourth Annual Report of the Council on Environmental Quality*, U.S. Government Printing Office, September 1973, pp. 265–275.

[6] This was the finding of a six-year study directed by Lawrence B. Cohen of the Department of Industrial Engineering of Columbia University and reported in the *New York Times*, December 16, 1965.

[7] J. R. Meyer, J. F. Kain, and M. Wohl, *The Urban Transportation Problem* (Cambridge, Mass.: Harvard University Press, 1965), p. 359.

transit systems . . . is a limited outlay for instrumentation, some modification of ramp arrangement and design, and most importantly *a policy decision to keep congestion at very low levels during peak hours and to provide priority access for public transit vehicles.*" [8]

The "price" of solving, or alleviating, some much-talked-about city problems, it would appear from this, may be largely political. Keeping congestion at low levels at peak hours would necessitate placing big toll charges on roads at the very times when most people want to use them; some would regard this as grossly unfair (as indeed in a way it would be) and so the probabilities are that if any official had the authority to make the decision (none does, which is part of the problem) he would not raise tolls at rush hours for fear of being voted out of office.

If the transportation problem is basically political, so is the revenue problem. A great part of the wealth of our country is in the cities. When a mayor says that his city is on the verge of bankruptcy, he means that when the time comes to run for reelection he wants to be able to claim credit for straightening out a mess that was left him by his predecessor. What he means when he says that his city *must* have state or federal aid to finance some improvements is (1) the taxpayers of the city (or some important group of them) would rather go without the improvement than pay for it themselves; or (2) although they would pay for it themselves if they had to, they would much prefer to have some other taxpayer pay for it. Rarely if ever does a mayor who makes such a statement mean (1) that for the city to pay for the improvement would necessarily force some taxpayers into poverty; or (2) that the city could not raise the money even if it were willing to force some of its taxpayers into poverty. In short, the "revenue crisis" mainly reflects the fact that people hate to pay taxes and that they think that by crying poverty they can shift some of the bill to someone else.[9]

To some extent, also, the revenue problem of the cities arises from the

[8] John Kain, "How to Improve Urban Transportation at Practically No Cost," *Public Policy,* 20 (Summer 1972):352. Italics are in the original.

[9] Arnold J. Meltsner titles his contribution to a collection of essays "Local Revenue: A Political Problem." He explains: "Officials are sometimes reluctant to raise taxes because they believe that taxes have reached a political limit. How do you know, Mr. Mayor, that the property tax has reached a political limit? Answer: I do not know; I just feel it. A political limit is a fuzzy constraint, perhaps fictitious, that local officials worry about, but have difficulty predicting. Even social scientists cannot tell when a political limit is about to be reached." In John P. Crecine, ed., *Financing the Metropolis,* Urban Affairs Annual Reviews, vol. 4 (Beverly Hills, Calif.: Sage Publications, 1970), p. 108.

In 1973 a survey of 30 cities with "serious financial problems" "failed to locate any cities in which conditions were such that timely action by local, or in a few cases, State officials could not avert or promptly relieve a financial emergency." Advisory Commission on Intergovernmental Relations, *City Financial Emergencies: The Intergovernmental Dimensions,* (Washington, D.C.: U.S. Government Printing Office, July 1973), p. 4.

way jurisdictional boundaries are drawn or, more precisely, from what are considered to be inequities resulting from the movement of taxable wealth from one side of a boundary line to another. When many large taxpayers move to the suburbs, the central city must tax those who remain at a higher rate if it is to maintain the same level of services. The "problem" in this case is not that the taxpayers who remain are absolutely unable to pay the increased taxes; rather, it is that they do not want to pay them and that they consider it unfair that they should have to pay more simply because other people have moved away. The simple and costless solution (in all but a political sense) would be to charge nonresidents for services that they receive from the city or, failing that, to redraw boundary lines so that everyone in the metropolitan area would be taxed on the same basis. As the historian Kenneth T. Jackson points out, those central cities that are declining in numbers of residents and in wealth are doing so because their state legislatures will not permit them to enlarge their boundaries by annexations; even before the Civil War many large cities would have been surrounded by suburbs—and therefore suffering from the same revenue problem—if they had not been permitted to annex freely.[10]

That we have not yet been willing to pay the price of solving, or alleviating, such "problems" even when the price is a very small one suggests that they are not really critical. Indeed, one might say that, by definition, a critical problem is one that people *are* willing to pay a considerable price to have solved.

With regard to these problems for which solutions are at hand, we will know that a real crisis impends when we see the solutions actually being applied. The solution, that is, will be applied when—and only when—the inconvenience or other disadvantage of allowing the problem to continue unabated is judged to have become greater than that of taking the necessary measures to abate it. In other words, a bad-but-not-quite-critical problem is one that it would almost-but-not-quite pay us to do something about.

If some real disaster impends in the city, it is not because parking spaces are hard to find, because architecture is bad, because department store sales are declining, or even because taxes are rising. If there is a genuine crisis, it has to do with the essential welfare of individuals or with the good health of the society, not merely with comfort, convenience, amenity, and business advantage, important as these are. It is not necessary here to try to define "essential welfare" rigorously: it is enough to say that whatever may cause people to die before their time, to suffer

[10] Kenneth T. Jackson, "Metropolitan Government versus Suburban Autonomy," in Kenneth T. Jackson and Stanley K. Schultz, eds., *Cities in American History* (New York: Alfred A. Knopf, 1972), pp. 446 and 456.

serious impairment of their health or of their powers, to waste their lives, to be deeply unhappy or happy in a way that is less than human affects their essential welfare. It is harder to indicate in a sentence or two what is meant by the "good health" of the society. The ability of the society to maintain itself as a going concern is certainly a primary consideration; so is its free and democratic character. In the last analysis, however, the quality of a society must be judged by its tendency to produce desirable human types; the healthy society, then, is one that not only stays alive but also moves in the direction of giving greater scope and expression to what is distinctively human. In general, of course, what serves the essential welfare of individuals also promotes the good health of the society; there are occasions, however, when the two goals conflict. In such cases, the essential welfare of individuals must be sacrificed for the good health of the society. This happens on a very large scale when there is a war, but it may happen at other times as well. The conditions about which we should be most concerned, therefore, are those that affect, or may affect, the good health of the society. If there is an urban crisis in any ultimate sense, it must be constituted of these conditions.

It is a good deal easier to say what matters are not serious (that is, do not affect either the essential welfare of individuals or the good health of the society) than it is to say what ones are. It is clear, however, that crime, poverty, ignorance, and racial (and other) injustices are among the most important of the general conditions affecting the essential welfare of individuals. It is plausible, too, to suppose that these conditions have a very direct bearing upon the good health of the society, although in this connection other factors that are much harder to guess about—for example, the nature and strength of the consensual bonds that hold the society together—may be much more important. To begin with, anyway, it seems reasonable to look in these general directions for what may be called the serious problems of the cities.

It is clear at the outset that serious problems directly affect only a rather small minority of the whole urban population. In the relatively new residential suburbs and in the better residential neighborhoods in the outlying parts of the central cities and in the older, larger, suburbs, the overwhelming majority of people are safely above the poverty line, have at least a high school education, and do not suffer from racial discrimination. For something like two-thirds of all city dwellers, the urban problems that touch them directly have to do with comfort, convenience, amenity, and business advantage. In the terminology used here, such problems are "important" but not "serious." In many cases, they cannot even fairly be called important; a considerable part of the urban population—those who reside in the "nicer" suburbs—lives under material conditions that will be hard to improve upon.

The serious problems are to be found in all large cities and in most small ones. But they affect only parts of these cities—mainly the inner parts of the larger ones—and only a small proportion of the whole urban population. Crime is a partial exception, but in Chicago (so the Violence Commission was told) a person who lives in the inner city faces a yearly risk of 1 in 77 of being assaulted whereas for those who live in the better areas of the city the risk is only 1 in 2,000 and for those who live in the rich suburbs only 1 in 10,000.[11] Apart from those in the inner districts, which comprise about 10 to 20 per cent of the city's total area, there are few serious urban problems. If what really matters is the essential welfare of individuals and the good health of the society, as opposed to comfort, convenience, amenity, and business advantage, then the problem is less an "urban" one than an "inner-(big)-city" one.

Although the poor and the black (and in some cities other minority groups also) are concentrated in the inner city and although the districts in which they live include many blocks of unrelieved squalor, it should not be supposed that the "poverty areas" of the inner cities are uniformly black, poor, or squalid. This can be seen from the findings of a special survey made in 1970 and 1971 by the Census of what it defined as the "low-income areas" of fifty-one of the largest cities.[12] A brief listing of some of these findings should dispel any notion that an inner-city "poverty area" is occupied only by the "disinherited."

[11] *Final Report of the National Commission on the Causes and Prevention of Violence* (Washington, D.C.: U.S. Government Printing Office, 1969), footnote p. 29.

[12] U.S. Bureau of the Census, *Census of Population: 1970, Employment Profiles of Selected Low-Income Areas,* Final Report PHC(3)-1, United States Summary —Urban Areas (January 1972). The low-income areas were defined by the Census Bureau in the middle 1960's for the use of OEO and Model Cities agencies. The following (equally weighted) criteria were used: family income below $3,000, children in broken homes, persons with low educational attainments, males in unskilled jobs, and substandard housing. Census tracts in the lowest quartile were defined as "low income." In 1970 the boundaries so established were reexamined by the Census in consultation with local planning and other officials; in most instances areas were enlarged somewhat.

A Census report (distributed after the text of this book was in type) provides data for the low-income areas of the 50 largest cities using figures from the decennial census (a 15 per cent sample) and defining a low-income area to consist of all census tracts in which 20 per cent or more of all persons were below the poverty line in 1969. On this basis, there were 10,555,918 persons in the poverty areas, 60 per cent of whom were Negro. The median family income was $6,099; 27 per cent of the families were below the poverty line and 22 per cent had incomes at least three times greater than the poverty standard. About one-third of the families in the low-income areas paid rents of less than 20 per cent of their income; however, of the renters whose incomes were below the poverty line, more than half paid more than half of their incomes in rent. Census tracts with a poverty rate of 40 per cent or more had 2,017,513 persons, nearly three-fourths of whom were Negro. U.S. Bureau of the Census, Census of Population: 1970 Subject Reports, Final Report (PC(2)-9B, Low-Income Areas in Large Cities.

Of the almost nine million persons aged sixteen or over who were counted, half were black and 35 per cent non-Spanish white.

More than three-fourths reported incomes *above* the poverty level.

The median income of a male-headed family was $7,782 (the comparable figure for the United States population as a whole was $10,480).

Among such families, 25 per cent of the white and 20 per cent of the Negro reported incomes above $12,000.

Of the nearly two million persons below the poverty level, whites and blacks were distributed in about the same proportion as in the whole "poverty area" population. (Spanish families were considerably overrepresented among the poor in the nineteen cities where they were numerous enough to be surveyed separately.)

The median income of male-headed white families was $425 more than that of black and the median income of black $849 more than Spanish.

In twenty-one of the fifty-one cities, however, the blacks in poverty areas had higher median family incomes than whites and in twelve more cities the difference (in favor of the whites) was trivial—less than 5 per cent.

The median years of schooling for persons twenty-five years of age or older was almost identical—10 and a small fraction—for whites and blacks, males and females; for persons twenty-five to thirty-four it was also almost identical and surprisingly high: twelve and a small fraction.

Although a large share of the income of many families went for housing, the reverse was also true: 40 per cent of white and 25 per cent of Negro (male-headed) families paid less than 10 per cent of their income for housing. Ninety per cent of the white and 80 per cent of the black (male-headed) families had housing that was not overcrowded—that is, there was at least one room per person.

Of the nearly 9 million persons aged 16 or over, 478,000 (9.6 per cent of those in the labor force) were unemployed. Less than half of these had been laid off; most had either quit or were just entering the labor force. Only 82,000 had been unemployed for as long as six months. Most were teenagers or unattached men and women in their early twenties, and many of these were students who wanted part-time or summer jobs.

The unemployment rate among male Negro family heads was 5.3 per cent; among male white (non-Spanish) family heads it was 4.5 per cent.

About 10 per cent of those *not* in the labor force said that they intended looking for a job (most non-participants were housewives, of course). Ask why they did not look, "inability to find work" was given as a reason by 8,000 males and 24,000 females. Of these, 25 per cent were aged 16-21. Asked what would be their minimum acceptable wage, the median figure given by black males in this age group was $83 weekly; whites expected one dollar more. Both black and white men who were heads of families expected $108.

Within or overlapping, some "poverty areas" are huge enclaves—a few have populations of several hundred thousand—that are almost entirely Negro or, in some cities, Puerto Rican or Mexican-American.[13] These enclaves—they are often called ghettoes, but as will be explained in Chapter Four this usage is extremely ambiguous—constitute a problem that is both serious and unique to the large cities. The problem arises because the enclaves are psychologically—and in some degree physically—cut off from the rest of the city. Whatever may be the effect of this on the welfare of the individual—and it may possibly be trivial—it is clear that the existence of a large enclave of persons who perceive themselves, and are perceived by others, as having a separate identity, not sharing, or not sharing fully, the attachment that others feel to the "city," constitutes a potential hazard not only to present peace and order but—what is more important—to the well-being of the society over the long run. Problems of individual welfare may be no greater by virtue of the fact that people live together in huge enclaves rather than in relative isolation on farms and in small towns, although about this one cannot be sure (such problems *appear* greater when people live in enclaves, of course, but this is because they are too conspicuous to be ignored). The problem that they may present to the good health of the society, however, is very different in kind and vastly greater in importance solely by virtue of their living in huge enclaves. Unlike those who live on farms and in small towns, disaffected people who are massed together may develop a collective consciousness and sense of identity. From some standpoints it may be highly desirable that they do so: feeling the strength of their numbers may give them confidence and encourage them to act politically and in other ways that will help them. On the other hand, the effect of numbers may be to support attitudes and institutions that will hamper progress. There is no doubt, however, that such enclaves represent a threat to peace and order, one made greater by the high proportion of young people in them. As the Commission on Population Growth and the American Future recently remarked,

> The decade 1960 to 1970 saw a doubling of the numbers of young black men and women aged 15 to 24 in the metropolitan areas of every part of the nation except the south. This increase, twice that for comparable white youth, was the result of higher black fertility to begin with, participation in the post-World War II baby boom, and continued migration away from southern rural poverty. The result has been more and more young black people ill-equipped to cope with the demands of urban

[13] In *Dark Ghetto,* Kenneth B. Clark presents 1960 Census data showing that eight cities—New York, Los Angeles, Baltimore, Washington, Cleveland, St. Louis, New Orleans, and Chicago—contain a total of sixteen areas, all of at least 15,000 population and five of more than 100,000, that are exclusively (more than 94 per cent) Negro (New York: Harper & Row, 1965), table, p. 25.

> life, more likely to wind up unemployed or in dead-end, low-paying jobs, and caught in the vicious wheel of poverty, welfare, degradation, and crime.
>
> The facts we have cited describe a crisis for our society. They add up to a demographic recipe for more turmoil in our cities, more bitterness among our "have-nots," and greater divisiveness among all of our peoples.[14]

The political danger in the presence of great concentrations of people who feel little attachment to the society has long been regarded by some as *the* serious problem of the cities—the one problem that might eventuate in disaster for the society. "The dark ghettoes," Dr. Clark has written, "now represent a nuclear stockpile which can annihilate the very foundations of America."[15] These words bring to mind the apprehensions that were expressed by some of the Founding Fathers and that Tocqueville set forth in a famous passage of *Democracy in America:*

> The United States has no metropolis, but it already contains several very large cities. Philadelphia reckoned 161,000 inhabitants, and New York 202,000, in the year 1830. The lower ranks which inhabit these cities constitute a rabble even more formidable than the populace of European towns. They consist of freed blacks, in the first place, who are condemned by the laws and by public opinion to a hereditary state of misery and degradation. They also contain a multitude of Europeans who have been driven to the shores of the New World by their misfortunes or their misconduct; and they bring to the United States all our greatest vices, without any of those interests which counteract their baneful influence. As inhabitants of a country where they have no civil rights, they are ready to turn all the passions which agitate the community to their own advantage, thus, within the last few months, serious riots have broken out in Philadelphia and New York. Disturbances of this kind are unknown in the rest of the country, which is not alarmed by them, because the population of the cities has hitherto exercised neither power nor influence over the rural districts.
>
> Nevertheless, I look upon the size of certain American cities, and especially on the nature of their population, as a real danger which threatens the future security of the democratic republics of the New World; and I venture to predict that they will perish from this

[14] Commission on Population Growth and the American Future, *Population and the American Future* (Washington, D.C.: U.S. Government Printing Office, 1972), p. 74.

[15] Kenneth B. Clark, "The Wonder Is There Have Been So Few Riots," *New York Times Magazine,* September 5, 1965, p. 10.

> circumstance, unless the government succeeds in creating an armed force which, while it remains under the control of the majority of the nation, will be independent of the town population and able to repress its excesses.[16]

Strange as it may seem, the mammoth government programs to aid the cities are directed mainly toward the problems of comfort, convenience, amenity, and business advantage. Insofar as they have an effect on the serious problems, it is, on the whole, to aggravate them. . .

Two programs account for a very large part of federal government expenditure for the improvement of the cities (as opposed to the maintenance of more or less routine functions). Neither is intended to deal with the serious problems. Both make them worse.

The improvement of urban transportation is one program. The federal contribution for urban highway construction and improvement which as long ago as 1960 was more than $1 billion a year, has since doubled. The main effect of urban expressways, for which most of the money is spent, is to enable suburbanites to move about the metropolitan area more conveniently, to open up some areas for business and residential expansion, and to bring a few more customers from the suburbs downtown to shop. These are worthy objects when considered by themselves; in context, however, their justification is doubtful, for their principal effect is to encourage—in effect to subsidize—further movement of industry, commerce, and relatively well-off residents (mostly white) from the inner city. This, of course, makes matters worse for the poor by reducing the number of jobs for them and by making neighborhoods, schools, and other community facilities still more segregated. These injuries are only partially offset by enabling a certain number of the inner-city poor to commute to jobs in the suburbs.

The huge expenditure being made for improvement of mass transit—$1 billion in fiscal 1974—may be justifiable for the contribution that it will make to comfort, convenience, and business advantage. It will not, however, make any contribution to the solution of the serious problems of the city. Even if every city had a subway as fancy as Moscow's, all these problems would remain.

The second great federal urban program concerns housing and renewal. Since the creation in 1934 of the Federal Housing Authority (FHA), the government has subsidized home building on a vast scale by insuring mortgages that are written on easy terms and, in the case of the Veterans Administration (VA), by guaranteeing mortgages. Most of the mortgages have been for the purchase of *new* homes. (This was partly because FHA wanted gilt-edged collateral behind the mortgages that it insured, but it

[16] Alexis de Tocqueville, *Democracy in America,* trans. by Henry Reeve (New York: Alfred A. Knopf, 1945), **1:** 289–290.

was also because it shared the American predilection for newness.) It was cheaper to build on vacant land, but there was little such land left in the central cities and in their larger, older suburbs; therefore, most of the new homes were built in new suburbs. These were almost always zoned so as to exclude the relatively few Negroes and other "undesirables" who could afford to build new houses and until late 1962 (when a presidential order barred discrimination in federally aided housing) FHA acted on its own to encourage all-white developments by instructing its appraisers to make low ratings of properties in neighborhoods occupied by what its Underwriting Manual termed "inharmonious racial or nationality groups" and by recommending a model racial restrictive covenant.[17] In effect, then, the FHA and VA programs have subsidized the movement of the white middle class out of the central cities and older suburbs while at the same time penalizing investment in the rehabilitation of the run-down neighborhoods of these older cities. The poor—especially the Negro poor—have not received any direct benefit from these programs. (They have, however, received a very substantial unintended and indirect benefits, as will be explained later, because the departure of the white middle class has made more housing available to them.) After the appointment of Robert C. Weaver as head of the Housing and Home Finance Agency, FHA changed its regulations to encourage the rehabilitation of existing houses and neighborhoods. Very few such loans have been made, however.

Urban renewal has also turned out to be mainly for the advantage of the well-off—indeed, of the rich—and to do the poor more harm than good. The purpose of the federal housing program was declared by Congress to be "the realization as soon as feasible of the goal of a decent home and a suitable living environment for every American family." In practice, however, the principal objectives of the renewal program have been to attract the middle class back into the central city (as well as to slow its exodus out of the city) and to stabilize and restore the central business districts.[18] Unfortunately, these objectives can be served only at the expense of the poor. Hundreds of thousands of low-income people, most of them Negroes or Puerto Ricans, have been forced out of low-cost housing, by no means all of it substandard, in order to make way for luxury apartments, office buildings, hotels, civic centers, industrial parks, and the like. Insofar as renewal has involved the "conservation" of "rehabilitation" of residential areas, its effect has been to keep the poorest of the poor out of these

[17] George Grier, "Washington," *City Magazine* (February 1971), p. 47, quoted by Bennett Harrison, *Education, Training and the Urban Ghetto* (Baltimore: The Johns Hopkins University Press, 1972), p. 167.

[18] Cf. Robert C. Weaver, "Class, Race and Urban Renewal," *Land Economics,* **36** (August 1960): 235–251. On urban renewal in general, see James Q. Wilson, ed., *Urban Renewal: The Record and the Controversy* (Cambridge, Mass.: M.I.T. Press, 1966).

neighborhoods—that is, to keep them in the highest-density slums. "At a cost of more than three billion dollars," sociologist Scott Greer wrote in 1965, "the Urban Renewal Agency (URA) has succeeded in materially reducing the supply of low-cost housing in American cities." [19]

The injury to the poor inflicted by renewal has not been offset by benefits to them in the form of public housing (that is, housing owned by public bodies and rented by them to families deemed eligible on income and other grounds). With the important exception of New York and the less important ones of some Southern cities, such housing is not a significant part of the total supply. Moreover, the poorest of the poor are usually, for one reason or another, ineligible for public housing.

Another housing program that has subsidized the relatively well-off and hastened their movement out of the central city is seldom thought of as a housing program at all. It consists of benefits to homeowners under the federal income tax laws. *The President's Fourth Annual Report on National Housing Goals,* issued in 1972, estimated that by allowing homeowners to deduct mortgage interest and property taxes from their gross incomes federal revenues had been reduced by $4.7 billion the previous year.[20] The subsidies, the report said, "are worth relatively more to higher income homeowners." Renters were not benefited at all except as owners might pass some of their tax savings on to them. To dramatize the inequity of these arrangements, a tax authority testifying before a Senate subcommittee imagined what it would sound like if a housing program having the same effects were to be proposed to Congress:

> We have a program to assist people who own homes. . . . If there is a married couple with more than $200,000 of income, why for each $100 of mortgage that they have, HUD will pay that couple $70. On the other hand, if there is a married couple with an income of $10,000, then under this HUD program we will pay that married couple

[19] Scott Greer, *Urban Renewal and American Cities* (Indianapolis: Bobbs-Merrill, 1965), p. 3.

As William G. Grigsby has pointed out, the "flight to the suburbs," which most renewal projects in central cities have been intended to stop or reverse, may be a good thing from the standpoint of the society as a whole even if undesirable from that of the central city. "It is not understood that . . . exodus from the city has produced a much higher standard of housing than could otherwise have been attained, and that the market forces that produced this shift should, therefore, be stimulated." *Housing Markets and Public Policy* (Philadelphia: University of Pennsylvania Press, 1963), p. 333.

[20] *The President's Fourth Annual Report on National Housing Goals,* 92d Congress, 2d Session, House Document No. 92–319, June 29, 1972. The report includes a table (p. 48) showing the revenue cost for 1971 by gross income class.

This and another form of concealed subsidy (the noninclusion of imputed net rent in gross income reported for tax purposes) are discussed by Henry J. Aaron, *Shelter and Subsidies: Who Benefits from Federal Housing Policies?* (Washington, D.C.: The Brookings Institution, 1972), ch. 4.

> only $19 on their $100 mortgage interest bill. And, of course, if they are too poor to pay an income tax then we are not going to pay them anything.[21]

Obviously these various government programs work at cross-purposes, one undoing (or *trying* to undo) what another does (or *tries* to do). The expressway and (with minor exceptions) the housing programs in effect pay the middle-class person to leave the central city for the suburbs. At the same time the urban renewal and mass transit programs pay him to stay in the central city or to move back to it. ". . . [F]ederal housing programs over the years," the presidential report cited above acknowledges, "have contributed to rapid suburbanization and unplanned urban sprawl, to growing residential separation of the races, and to the concentration of the poor and minorities in decaying central cities." [22] In the opinion of the economist Richard Muth, expressways ("the major contributor to urban decentralization in the postwar period") and federal aids to home ownership may have caused the land area of cities to be as much as 17 per cent larger than it would otherwise be and the central city's share of the urbanized area population to be 3 to 7 per cent smaller.[23]

In at least one respect, however, these government programs are consistent: they aim at problems of comfort, convenience, amenity, and business advantage, not at ones involving the essential welfare of individuals or the good health of the society. Indeed, on the contrary, they all sacrifice these latter, more important interests for the sake of the former, less important ones. In this the urban programs are no different from a great many other government programs. Price production programs in agriculture, Theodore Schultz has remarked, take up almost all the time of the Department of Agriculture, the agricultural committees of Congress, and the farm organizations, and exhaust the influence of farm people. But these programs, he says, "do not improve the schooling of farm children, they do not reduce the inequalities in personal distribution of wealth and income, they do not remove the causes of poverty in agriculture, nor do they alleviate it.

[21] Stanley S. Surrey, Professor of Law, Harvard University, in U.S. Congress, Senate, Subcommittee on Priorities and Economy in Government of the Joint Economic Committee, *Hearings, The Economics of Federal Subsidy Programs*, 92d Congress, 1st Session, January 13, 14, and 17, 1972, p. 45.

[22] *The President's Fourth Annual Report*, p. 32. The report goes on to add: "While housing programs have contributed to these problems and in many cases intensified them, it is important to emphasize that they did not *cause* them. The causes stem from the complex interaction of population migration, community attitudes and prejudices, consumer preferences, local governmental fragmentation, and the impact of other federal programs such as urban renewal and the highway programs."

[23] Richard Muth, "The Urban Economy and Public Problems," in John P. Crecine, ed., *Financing the Metropolis*, p. 454. See also Muth's book, *Cities and Housing, The Spatial Pattern of Urban Residential Land Use* (Chicago: University of Chicago Press, 1969), pp. 319–322.

On the contrary, they worsen the personal distribution of income within agriculture." [24]

It is widely supposed that the serious problems of the cities are unprecedented both in kind and in magnitude. Between 1950 and 1960 there occurred the greatest population increase in the nation's history. At the same time, a considerable part of the white middle class moved to the newer suburbs, and its place in the central cities and older suburbs was taken by Negroes (and in New York by Puerto Ricans as well). These and other events—especially the civil rights revolution—are widely supposed to have changed completely the character of "the urban problem."

If the present situation is indeed radically different from previous ones, then we have nothing to go on in judging what is likely to happen next. At the very least, we face a crisis of uncertainty.

In a real sense, of course, *every* situation is unique. Even in making statistical probability judgments, one must decide on more or less subjective grounds whether it is reasonable to treat certain events as if they were the "same." The National Safety Council, for example, must decide whether cars, highways, and drivers this year are enough like those of past years to justify predicting future experience from past. From a logical standpoint, it is no more possible to decide this question in a purely objective way than it is to decide, for example, whether the composition of the urban population is now so different from what it was that nothing can be inferred from the past about the future. Karl and Alma Taeuber are both right and wrong when they write that we do not know enough about immigrant and Negro assimilation patterns to be able to compare the two and that "such evidence as we could compile indicates that it is more likely to be misleading than instructive to make such comparisons." [25] They are certainly right in saying that one can only guess whether the pattern of Negro assimilation will resemble that of the immigrant. But they are wrong to imply that we can avoid making guesses and still compare things that are not known to be alike in all respects except one. (What, after all, would be the point of comparing immigrant and Negro assimilation patterns if we knew that the only difference between the two was, say, skin color?) They are also wrong in suggesting that the evidence indicates anything about what is likely to be instructive. If there were enough evidence to indicate that, there would be enough to indicate what is likely to happen; indeed, a judgment as to what is likely to be instructive is inseparable from one as to what is likely to happen. Strictly speaking, the Taeubers' statement expresses *their* guess as to what the evidence indicates.

[24] Theodore W. Schultz, *Economic Crises in World Agriculture* (Ann Arbor: University of Michigan Press, 1965), p. 94.

[25] Karl E. and Alma F. Taeuber, "The Negro as an Immigrant Group: Recent Trends in Racial and Ethnic Segregation in Chicago," *American Journal of Sociology,* **69** (January 1964): 382.

The facts by no means compel one to take the view that the serious problems of the cities are unprecedented either in kind or in magnitude. That the population of metropolitan areas increased during the 1960's by nearly 17 per cent to a record high of 139,374,000 persons need not hold much significance from the present standpoint: American cities have frequently grown at fantastic rates (consider the growth of Chicago from a prairie village of 4,470 in 1840 to a metropolis of more than a million in fifty years). In any case, the present population increase is leaving most cities less rather than more crowded. In the 1960's, 130 of the 292 central cities lost population, and the aggregate of their loss was 2.25 million persons; this was a greater decline than in the previous decade. Density of population in the central cities fell from 7,786 per square mile in 1950 to 4,463 in 1970; the comparable figures for suburban areas are 3,167 and 2,627.[26] Looking to the future, there is every reason to expect the trend toward "decongestion" to continue. But even if it were to reverse itself, there would be no obvious cause for concern. As Irving Hoch, a researcher for Resources for the Future has remarked, there has been much sound and fury about the presumed ill effects of city size and destiny on health and welfare but there is little hard evidence on the subject; moreover, such evidence as points in one direction can be countered by other evidence pointing in the opposite direction.[27]

The movement of farm and rural people (mostly Negroes and Puerto Ricans) to the large Northern cities was much smaller in the 1960's than in the previous decade and the outlook is for a continued decline both because natural increase was less during the 1960's and because rural areas appear to be retaining a higher proportion of their growth.[28] But even at its height the migration of Negroes and Puerto Ricans to the big cities was no more than about equal to immigration from Italy in its peak decade. (In New York, Chicago, and many other cities in 1910, two out of every three schoolchildren were the sons and daughters of immigrants.) When one takes into account the vastly greater size and wealth of the cities now as compared to half a century or more ago, it is obvious that by the only relevant measure—namely, the number of immigrants relative to the capacity of the cities to provide for them and to absorb them—the movement from the South and from Puerto Rico has been not large but small.

In many important respects the material conditions of life in the cities have long been improving. Incomes have increased steadily. In the 1960's, for example, white income rose by 69 per cent and black income by 100

[26] Executive Office of the President, Domestic Council, *Report on National Growth, 1972* (Washington, D.C.: U.S. Government Printing Office, 1972).

[27] Irving Hoch, "Income and City Size," *Urban Studies*, **9** (1972): 320.

[28] Peter A. Morrison, *The Impact and Significance of Rural-Urban Migration in the United States* (Santa Monica, Calif.: The Rand Corporation, #P-4752. March 1972), p. 2.

per cent. Despite this relative gain, the income of black families was still somewhat less than two-thirds that of whites. Housing is also better and consumption of it more than doubled in real per capita terms between 1950 and 1970. As Dean Dick Netzer has written,

> Not only has the housing improved, but also there have been huge investments in supporting public and institutional facilities—schools, roads, transit, hospitals, water supply and sewerage, airports, etc. In the twenty-year period, about $200 billion has been invested by state and local governments in new public facilities in metropolitan areas, almost as much as the total investment in new housing in these areas during the period. This hardly supports the charge that ours is a society of "public squalor amidst private opulence."[29]

At the turn of the century only one child in fifteen went beyond elementary school, now well over half finish high school. In this period blacks have increased the amount of their schooling faster than whites; in 1900 they averaged three years less than whites, but the present generation of pupils is expected to get almost as much, or—if comparison is made among pupils with about the same test scores—slightly more.[30] (In 1972, for the first time, the percentage of black and other minority-race high school graduates enrolling in college was the same as for whites). As these figures imply, racial discrimination has declined dramatically since the Second War. Studies made over a period of almost thirty years by the National Opinion Research Center reveal a trend "distinctly toward increasing approval of integration" with the highest pro-integration scores among the young and among residents of the largest metropolitan areas.[31]

The very movements that in some cities or parts of cities signalize, or constitute, an improvement in the situation tend, of course, to make matters worse in other places. For example, in Philadelphia the population of the districts designated "low income" by the Census dropped from more than

[29] Dick Netzer, *Economics and Urban Problems: Diagnosis and Prescriptions* (New York: Basic Books, 1970), p. 21.

[30] Christopher Jencks et al., *Inequality, A Reassessment of the Effect of Family and Schooling in America* (New York: Basic Books, 1972), pp. 141–142.

[31] Andrew M. Greeley and Paul B. Sheatsley, "Attitudes Toward Racial Integration," *Scientific American,* **225** (December 1971): 13 and 15.

Thomas F. Pettigrew has found that "white attitudes toward open housing have become increasingly more favorable over the past generation." See his paper on "Attitudes on Race and Housing: A Social-Psychological View," in Amos H. Hawley and Vincent P. Rock, eds., *Segregation in Residential Areas* (Washington, D.C.: National Academy of Sciences, 1973), pp. 21–84. See also Joel D. Aberbach and Jack L. Walker, *Race in the City* (Boston: Little, Brown and Company, 1973), which presents data on attitudes of blacks and whites in Detroit in surveys made in 1967 and 1971.

900,000 to nearly 800,000 in the 1960's. This happened partly because many families, black as well as white, became able to afford to move to better neighborhoods. The consequence of their moving out of the "low-income" areas, however, was to widen the income gap between those areas and the rest of the city. In other words, the poverty of the "low-income" areas has been intensified relative to other areas even though—conceivably—it may be that no one in any of them is poorer than before. (As a practical matter, there can be little doubt that the departure of the better-off families *does* entail disadvantages for those who remain.)

Surprising as it may seem, most American are reasonably well satisfied with their neighborhoods. A recent poll found that those who live in rural areas and in small towns are more likely to say that they are satisfied than those who live in cities, and, as one would expect, the well-off are more likely to be satisfied than the poor. But even among blacks (seven out of ten of whom are city dwellers) only 17 per cent say that they are dissatisfied with their neighborhoods.[32]

If the situation is improving, why, it may be asked, is there so much talk of an urban crisis? The answer is that the improvements in performance, great as they have been, have not kept pace with rising expectations. In other words, although things have been getting better absolutely, they have been getting worse *relative to what we think they should be*. And this is because, as people, we seem to act on the advice of the old jingle:

Good, better, best,
Never let it rest
Until your good is better
And your better best.

Consider the poverty problem, for example. Irving Kristol has pointed out that for nearly a century all studies, in all countries, have concluded that a third, a fourth, or a fifth of the nation in question is below the poverty line.[33] "Obviously," he remarks, "if one defines the poverty line as that which places one-fifth of the nation below it, then one-fifth of the nation will always be below the poverty line." The point is that even if everyone is better off there will be as much poverty as ever, provided that the line is redefined upward. Kristol notes that whereas in the depths of the Depression, F.D.R. found only one-third of the nation "ill-housed, ill-clad, ill-nourished," Leon Keyserling, a former head of the Council of Economic Advisers, in 1962 published a book called *Poverty and Deprivation in the U.S.—the Plight of Two-Fifths of a Nation*.

[32] William Watts and Lloyd A. Free, eds., *State of the Nation* (New York: Universal Books, 1973), p. 80.
[33] Irving Kristol, "The Lower Fifth," *The New Leader*, February 17, 1964, pp. 9–10.

Much the same thing has happened with respect to most urban problems. Police brutality, for example, would be a rather minor problem if we judged it by a fixed standard; it is a growing problem because we judge it by an ever more exacting standard. A generation ago the term meant hitting someone on the head with a nightstick. Now it often means something quite different:

> What the Negro community is presently complaining about when it cries "police brutality" is the more subtle attack on personal dignity that manifests itself in unexplainable questionings and searches, in hostile and insolent attitudes toward groups of young Negroes on the street, or in cars, and in the use of disrespectful and sometimes racist language. . . .[34]

Following Kristol, one can say that if the "police brutality line" is defined as that which places one-fifth of all police behavior below it, then one-fifth of all police behavior will always be brutal.

The school dropout problem is an even more striking example. At the turn of the century, when almost everyone was a dropout, the term and the "problem" did not exist. It was not until the 1960's, when for the first time a majority of boys and girls were graduating from high school and practically all had at least some high school training, that the "dropout problem" became acute. Then, although the dropout rate was still declining, various cities developed at least fifty-five separate programs to deal with the problem. Hundreds of articles on it were published in professional journals, the National Education Association established a special action project to deal with it, and the Commissioner of Education, the Secretary of Labor, and the President all made public statements on it.[35] Obviously, if one defines the "inadequate amount of schooling line" as that which places one-fifth of all boys and girls below it, then one-fifth of all boys and girls will always be receiving an inadequate amount of schooling.

Whatever our educational standards are today, Wayland writes, they will be higher tomorrow. He summarizes the received doctrine in these words.

> Start the child in school earlier; keep him in school more and more months of the year; retain all who start to school for twelve to fourteen years; expect him to learn more and more during this period, in wider and wider areas of human experience, under the guidance of a teacher, who has had more and more training, and who is assisted by more and more specialists, who provide an ever-expanding range of services, with access to more and

[34] Robert Blauner, "Whitewash Over Watts," *Trans-action* **3** (Mar.–Apr. 1966): 6.

[35] Burton A. Weisbrod, "Preventing High-School Drop-outs," in Robert Dorfman, ed., *Measuring Benefits of Government Investments* (Washington, D.C.: The Brookings Institution, 1965), p. 118.

more detailed personal records, based on more and more carefully validated tests.[36]

To a large extent, then, our urban problems are like the mechanical rabbit at the racetrack, which is set to keep just ahead of the dogs no matter how fast they may run. Our performance is better and better, but because we set our standards and expectations to keep ahead of performance, the problems are never any nearer to solution. Indeed, if standards and expectations rise *faster* than performance, the problems may get (relatively) worse as they get (absolutely) better.

Some may say that since almost everything about the city can stand improvement (to put it mildly), this mechanical rabbit effect is a good thing in that it spurs us on to make constant progress. No doubt this is true to some extent. On the other hand, there is danger that we may mistake failure to progress as fast as we would like for failure to progress at all and, in panic, rush into ill-considered measures that will only make matters worse. After all, an "urban crisis" that results largely from rising standards and expectations is not the sort of crisis that, unless something drastic is done, is bound to lead to disaster. To treat it as if it were might be a very serious mistake.

This danger is greatest in matters where our standards are unreasonably high. The effect of too-high standards cannot be to spur us on to reach the prescribed level of performance sooner than we otherwise would, when that level is impossible of attainment. At the same time, these standards may cause us to adopt measures that are wasteful and injurious and, in the long run, to conclude from the inevitable failure of these measures that there is something fundamentally wrong with our society.

To extend the range of present Department of Health, Education and Welfare services equitably—to all those similarly situated in need—would require an *additional* cost roughly equivalent to the *entire federal budget,* Elliot L. Richardson reported as he left the secretaryship of that department.[37] His point was that expectations, indeed claims authorized by Congress, far exceeded the capacity of the government to provide. "One can imagine," he said somberly, "a point of reckoning at which the magnitude of the ill-treated problems is fully perceived—along with a profound sense of failure. And one can only hope that the troubled reaction toward the institutions held accountable would be reasoned and responsible."

[36] Wayland, "Old Problems," p. 67.

[37] Elliot L. Richardson, *Responsibility and Responsiveness (II), A Report on the HEW Potential for the Seventies* (Washington, D.C.: U.S. Department of Health, Education, and Welfare, January 18, 1973).

Raymond E. Wolfinger

Why Political Machines Have Not Withered Away and Other Revisionist Thoughts

Over the years it has often been alleged that urban problems have been compounded by the hold of political machines on the policy-making process, and that reform in local government is necessary for effective problem solving. Indeed, by now it is generally accepted that machines are out and reform is in, and lately the urban machine has received so little attention that one might assume it is a thing of the past.

Wolfinger's study demonstrates not only that machines are still very much alive but that they are deeply involved in making urban policy. His findings require that the place of the machine in urban government be reevaluated.

Machine politics is always said to be on the point of disappearing, but nevertheless seems to endure. Scholarly analyses of machines usually explain why they have dwindled almost to the vanishing point. Since machine politics is still alive and well in many places, this conventional wisdom starts from a false premise. More important, it has several logical and definitional confusions that impede clear understanding of American local politics. This article shows that machine politics still flourishes, presents a clarified definition of "machine politics" as part of a typology of incentives

---

Reprinted from *The Journal of Politics*, **34**: 365–398 (May 1972) by permission of the publisher.

A more detailed description of machine politics in New Haven and discussion of other aspects of this general subject may be found in my *The Politics of Progress* (Englewood Cliffs, N.J.: Prentice-Hall, Inc., 1974).

for political participation, and argues that the familiar explanations both for the existence of machine politics and for its putative decline are inadequate.

The Persistence of Machine Politics

My first-hand experience with machine politics is limited to the city of New Haven.[1] Both parties there had what journalists like to call "old fashioned machines," of the type whose disappearance has been heralded for most of the twentieth century. Some people in New Haven were moved to participation in local election campaigns by such civic-minded concerns as public spirit, ideological enthusiasm, or a desire to influence governmental policy on a particular issue. For hundreds of the city's residents, however, politics was not a matter of issues or civic duty, but of bread and butter. There were (and are) a variety of material rewards for political activity. Service to the party or influential connections were prerequisites to appointment to hundreds of municipal jobs, and the placement of government contracts was often affected by political considerations. Thus the stimuli for political participation in local politics were, for most activists, wholly external.

A new administration taking over New Haven's city hall had at its immediate disposal about 75 politically-appointed policy-making positions, about 300 lower-level patronage jobs, and about the same number of appointments to boards and commissions. Summer employment provided around 150 additional patronage jobs. In the winter, snow removal required the immediate attention of hundreds of men and dozens of pieces of equipment.

A hundred or more jobs in field offices of the state government were filled with the advice of the party's local leaders. The City Court, appointed by the governor with the advice of the local dispensers of his patronage, had room for two or three dozen deserving people. The New Haven Probate Court had a considerable payroll, but its real political significance was the Judge of Probate's power to appoint appraisers and trustees of estates. Except in difficult cases, little technical knowledge was necessary for appraising, for which the fee was $1 per $1,000 of appraised worth.

A great deal of the city's business was done with men active in organization politics, particularly in such "political" businesses as printing, building, and playground supplies, construction, and insurance. Competitive bidding did not seriously increase the uncertainty of the outcome if the

[1] Data on New Haven are from an intensive study of that city's politics conducted primarily by Robert A. Dahl, William H. Flanigan, Nelson W. Polsby, and me. Our research is described most fully in Dahl's *Who Governs?* (New Haven: Yale University Press, 1961), pp. 330–340.

administration wanted a certain bidder to win.[2] As in many places, it was commonplace for city or party officials to "advise" a prime contractor about which local subcontractors, suppliers, and insurance agencies to patronize. Many government purchases were exempt from competitive bidding for one reason or another. The prices of some things, like insurance, are fixed. Thus the city's insurance business could be (and was) given to politically deserving agencies. Other kinds of services, particularly those supplied by professional men, are inherently unsuited to competitive bidding. Architects, for instance, are not chosen by cost. Indeed, some professional societies forbid price competition by their members.

The income that some party leaders received directly from the public treasury was dwarfed by trade from people who hoped to do business with the city or wanted friendly treatment at city hall, or in the courts, or at the state capitol, and thus sought to ingratiate themselves with party leaders. For example, a contractor hoping to build a school would be likely to buy his performance bonds from the bond and insurance agency headed by the Democratic National Committeeman. Similar considerations applied to "political" attorneys with part-time public jobs. Their real rewards came from clients who wanted to maximize their chances of favorable consideration in the courts or by public agencies.

Control of city and state government, then, provided either local party with a formidable array of resources that, by law, custom, and public acceptance, could be exploited for money and labor. Holders of the 75 policy-making jobs were assessed five per cent of their annual salaries in municipal election years and three per cent in other years. At the lower patronage levels, employees and board members gave from $25 to $100 and up. Politically-appointed employees were also expected to contribute their times during campaigns and were threatened with dismissal if they did not do enough electioneering.

Business and professional men who sold to the city, or who might want favors from it, were another important source of funds. Both sides in any public contractual relation usually assumed that a contribution would be forthcoming, but firms doing business with the city were often approached directly and bluntly. During one mayoralty campaign a party official asked a reluctant businessman, "Look, you son of a bitch, do you want a snow-removal contract or don't you?" In the 1957 mayoralty election the biggest individual contributor, who gave $1,500 to the ruling Democratic party, was a partner in the architectural firm that designed two new high schools. A

[2] The most important source of my information about New Haven politics was a year of participant-observation in city hall. Some years after my stay there Mayor Richard C. Lee denied that political considerations affected the placement of government contracts. That is not consistent with information we gathered during our study, or with the large campaign contributions made by these contractors.

contractor closely associated with a top-ranking Democratic politician gave $1,000. A partner in the firm that built the new high schools and an apartment house in a redevelopment project gave $900. Dozens of city, court, and party officials were listed as contributors of sums ranging from $250 to $1,000.[3]

In addition to jobs and politically influenced selection of contractors, the third sign of machine politics is "favors": for parents of school children, owners of houses with code violations, people wanting zoning changes, taxpayers wanting lower assessments, and so on. In these and numerous other categories of citizen relations with government, machine politicians were prepared to be obligingly flexible about the laws, but a *quid pro quo* was implicit in such requests.

Political spoils in New Haven came from several jurisdictions, chiefly the municipal government, the probate court, and the state government. The more numerous the sources of patronage, the lower the probability that all would be held by the same party, and hence the easier it was for both parties to maintain their organizations through hard times. When one party was triumphant everywhere in the state, as the Democrats were in the 1960s, there was considerable potential for intraparty disunity because the availability of more than one source of rewards or political for political activity made it difficult to establish wholly unified local party organizations. Inevitably state leaders would deal with one or more local figures in dispensing state patronage. This local representative need not be the same man who controlled probate or municipal patronage. Although the mayor had the power to give out city patronage, either directly or by telling his appointees what to do, he found it prudent to exercise this power in concert with those leaders who could control campaign organizations in New Haven through their access to state and probate patronage. In good measure because of the diverse sources of patronage, the loyalties of Democratic party workers went to different leaders. All this was true also of the Republican party. Thus neither local party organization was monolithic. The Republicans were badly split for much of the post-war generation. The Democrats maintained a working coalition, but not without a good deal of competition and constant vigilance on the part of the mayor and the two principal party leaders. Multiple sources of patronage are commonplace with machine politics and have important consequences, which will be explored in the next section.

A second typical feature of machine politics was that the elections most important to organization politicians were obscure primaries held on the ward level. Issue-oriented "amateurs" seldom could muster sufficient strength in these elections. The amateurs seemed to be interested chiefly in

[3] The Democratic report on campaign expenses and contributions was summarized in the *New Haven Journal-Courier*, December 4, 1957.

national and international affairs, and thus were most active and successful in presidential primaries and elections, where their policy concerns were salient. While the stakes in presidential contests may be global, they seldom include the topic of prime interest to machine politicians—control of patronage—and hence the regulars exert less than their maximum effort in them. Conveniently for both amateurs and regulars, the two sorts of elections are held at different times and usually in different years. When the amateurs' enthusiasm is at its peak, the professionals will be less interested; when the machine's spoils are at stake, the amateurs are less involved.

Participation in election campaigns is not the only form of political action. It is important to distinguish between electioneering and other types of political activity. In New Haven there was a major divergence between campaign and non-campaign activities. The likelihood that richer people would engage in non-campaign activity was far greater than the corresponding probability for campaigns.[4] This divergence reflected the probability that participation in a campaign is less autonomously motivated, for in New Haven the discipline of patronage compels campaign work. There are no such external inducements for most non-campaign political action. Indeed, because such activity usually consists of trying to exert pressure on public officials, it is likely to be viewed with apprehension or disfavor by those machine politicians who dispense patronage. A sense of political efficacy, education, a white-collar job, and higher income—all are thought to be associated with those personal qualities that lead people to try to influence the outcome of government decisions. In many parts of the country, these traits are also associated with electioneering. Some people participate in New Haven elections—particularly for national office—from such motives, but most activists, including party regulars, do not. The essentially involuntary character of much political participation in cities dominated by machine politics has received scant attention from students of participation, who customarily treat the phenomenon they study as the product of solely internal stimuli.

How typical is New Haven? Systematic trend data about the persistence of machine politics are scarce. Ideally, one would develop various measures of the incidence of machine politics and then compare these indicators, both over time and from city to city. One such index might be the proportion of city employees covered by civil-service regulations, a figure that is reported annually for all cities in *The Municipal Year Book*.[5]

[4] The tendency for the better-off to participate less in campaigns than in other arenas is discussed at length in Dahl, *Who Governs?* pp. 284–293. Dahl attributes it to the plebian dominance of the city's political parties, and says that the affluent can influence city officials through channels other than the parties. This assumes that political participation reflects primarily a desire to influence public policy, a proposition I consider insufficient for New Haven and cities like it.

[5] Published in Chicago by the International City Managers' Association.

As this source reveals, formal civil-service coverage is fairly widespread in cities of over 50,000 population. The states of Iowa, New York, and Ohio require their cities to use merit systems, and in Massachusetts local employees come under the jurisdiction of the state civil-service commission. In 1963, 51 per cent of cities in the other states had complete civil-service coverage for their employees, 6 per cent covered all but manual workers, 27 per cent covered only policemen and firemen, and 16 per cent (mostly in the South) did not have merit systems.[6] One might assume that in places where formal civil-service coverage is low, patronage is more abundant. The reverse probably is true also, but only in a very general way, for there are many cities where political realities or administrative loopholes weaken the effect of the regulations. Cities in New York, for example, can keep jobs from being covered by civil service by classifying them as "provisional," i.e., temporary, or "noncompetitive," which means that satisfactory tests cannot be devised. In Chicago all municipal workers except those in public utilities are "covered" by civil service, but as a matter of political reality, a great many city jobs can be used for patronage purposes with little difficulty.

Information on other kinds of patronage is also elusive. Two students of the subject in New York report that judicial patronage (receiverships, refereeships, and the like) is "almost impossible even to research," and for this reason "its value as political gifts is unquestionably priceless."[7] Because of the moral and legal delicacy of the subject, systematic and realistic data on machine politics are elusive, and thus comparisons are difficult. Nevertheless, some journalists and scholars have turned up useful information.

A *New York Times* survey of city and state government in New York concluded that "patronage has vastly expanded in the last several decades because of the tremendous growth of government, spiraling government spending, and the expansion of government's discretionary powers to regulate, control, and supervise private industry."[8] The same story reported that the annual payroll in city jobs exempt from civil-service regulations, which had been $10 million in the Wagner administration, soared to $32.8 million under Mayor Lindsay in poverty-program jobs alone. During the first three years of Mayor Lindsay's regime the number of "provisional" employees increased from 1,500 to 12,800. Under Mayor Wagner the City of New York also had 50,000 "noncompetitive" jobs; 24,000 more "noncom-

[6] Raymond E. Wolfinger and John Osgood Field, "Political Ethos and the Structure of City Government," *American Political Science Review,* **60** (June 1960), 314–315.

[7] Martin and Susan Tolchin, "How Judgeships Get Bought," *New York Magazine,* March 15, 1971, p. 34.

[8] *New York Times,* June 17, 1968, pp. 1, 30.

petitive" positions were added after Lindsay took office.[9] In the last year of the Wagner administration the city let $8 million in consulting contracts without competitive bidding. By 1969, the city's annual expenditure for outside consultants had risen to $75 million, with many indications that Lindsay was using these contracts as a form of patronage.[10] In addition to the jobs and contracts at his disposal, the Mayor of New York also can wield tremendous patronage power through his control of the municipal agencies that grant zoning variances. Lindsay has made good use of this power for political purposes.[11]

The patronage resources of the New York mayor's office are not much greater than those of the Manhattan Surrogate's Court, which does about $1 billion worth of estate work each year, appointing attorneys to administer estates. These appointments, which are often both undemanding and lucrative, generally are made on the basis of political considerations.[12] Other courts in New York City name referees, trustees, guardians, and receivers in a variety of situations. These appointments also are both rewarding and politically determined.[13] Trustees, in turn, decide where to bank the funds

[9] Martin and Susan Tolchin, "How Lindsay Learned the Patronage Lesson," *New York Magazine,* March 29, 1971, p. 48.

[10] Ibid., pp. 47–48.

[11] Ibid., pp. 43–46. Lindsay's expansion of patronage is in dramatic contrast to his image as a reformer, and to the widespread interpretation that his election was yet another sign of the decline of machine politics. Since the 19th century genuine and bogus reformers have been elected Mayor of New York over the opposition of various political organizations, to the accompaniment of public death rites for Tammany Hall and the less celebrated but more potent machines in the other boroughs. Yet just as regularly those mayors have been succeeded by organization politicians. Indeed, often the incumbent himself is recast in this role, so that his departure from city hall as well as his entry can be hailed as a symptom of the demise of the machine. Thus when Mayor Robert Wagner won renomination in 1961 by defeating the "organization candidate," this signalled "the machine's" decline. The same interpretation was offered four years later when Wagner, reading the portents as unfavorable to his reelection, withdrew and was succeeded by Lindsay. It appears that one of the reasons why we know Tammany is dead is that it has been killed so many times.

[12] *New York Times,* June 17, 1968, **30;** and Wallace S. Sayre and Herbert Kaufman, *Governing New York City* (New York: Russell Sage Foundation, 1960), pp. 540–541.

[13] Tolchin and Tolchin, "How Judgeships Get Bought," **33.** Presumably because of the very large amounts of money involved in numerous cases where judges appoint referees, trustees, guardians, etc., and the custom of making these appointments politically, judgeships of all sorts in New York are highly prized. Although most judges are elected rather than appointed, the parties effectively control the selection process. A man who wants to be a judge usually must have connections in one party or the other, and must also make a sizable payment to the appropriate party leader. Sayre and Kaufman estimated that a minimum payment for the lowest level court was $20,000 (542). Tolchin and Tolchin suggest that the payments usually are higher than this ("How Judgeships Get Bought," 29, 31).

for which they are responsible, and their power in this respect constitutes another form of patronage if decisions are made politically—as they seem to be.

Cities other than New Haven and New York have political systems in which patronage plays a crucial part. Mayor Richard Daley of Chicago is also chairman of the Cook County Democratic Committee. These two positions together give him control of about 35,000 patronage jobs.[14] It is reported that Daley personally scrutinizes each job application. Since there are 3,412 voting precincts in Chicago, the Democratic organization can deploy an average of ten workers to each precinct just on the basis of job patronage.

Over 8,000 state employees in Indiana owe their jobs to patronage and are assessed two per cent of their salaries for the coffers of the ruling party's state committee.[15] "Macing" public employees is not uncommon in some locales, including New Haven, but the Indiana method of issuing automobiles and drivers licenses and automobile titles is unique. These matters are handled by a franchise system, rather like service stations or Kentucky Fried Chicken outlets. Local "license branches" are "awarded to the county chairman of the Governor's party, or the persons they designate." [16] The branch pays the state party committee four cents for each license sold; otherwise, it retains all fees up to $10,000. Above that figure, half the take must be returned to the state Bureau of Motor Vehicles.

This brief survey shows that formidable patronage resources are available as rewards for political participation in various cities, and thus that New Haven's political practices are not an anachronistic freak. To put it another way, the dependent variable—machine politics—is still a common phenomenon. In the next section I will explore some of the definitional problems that have impeded clear understanding of machine politics, before turning directly to examination of the independent variables said to be associated with its rise and fall.

Machine Politics Defined

The terms "machine politics" and "political machine" are commonly used so as to confuse two quite different phenomena. "Machine politics" is the manipulation of certain *incentives* to partisan political participation: favoritism based on political criteria in personnel decisions, contracting,

[14] *Newsweek,* April 5, 1971, p. 82.

[15] Robert J. McNeil, *Democratic Campaign Financing in Indiana, 1964* (Bloomington, Ind., and Princeton, N.J.: Institute of Public Administration, Indiana University and Citizens' Research Foundation, 1966), pp. 15–16.

[16] Ibid., p. 19.

and administration of the laws. A "political machine" is an organization that practices machine politics, i.e., that attracts and directs its members primarily by means of these incentives. Unfortunately, the term "machine" is also used in a quite different and less useful sense to refer to the *centralization* of power in a party in a major political jurisdiction: a "machine" is a united and hierarchical party organization in a state, city, or county. Now there is no necessary relation between the two dimensions of incentives and centralization: machine politics (patronage incentives) need not produce centralized organization *at the city level or higher.*

The availability of patronage probably makes it easier to centralize influence in a cohesive party organization, since these resources can be distributed so as to discipline and reward the organization's workers. Quite often, however, all patronage is not controlled by the same people. There may be competing organizations or factions within each party in the same area, for where patronage is plentiful, it usually is available from more than one jurisdiction. In New Haven the municipal government had no monopoly on the spoils of government, which were also dispensed by the probate court and the state government. Thus the existence of a cohesive local organization in either party did not follow from the use of patronage to motivate party workers.

This distinction between machine politics and centralized local machines is far from academic, for the former is found many places where the latter is not. Chicago presently exhibits both machine politics and a very strong Democratic machine. Forty years ago it had the former but not the latter.[17] In Boston and New York there are the same kinds of incentives to political activity as in Chicago, but no cohesive citywide organizations. Instead, these cities have several contending party factions. In New York "the party" includes reform clubs with considerable influence as well as a variety of "regular" organizations. The frequently celebrated "decline" of Tammany Hall was not so much the subjugation of the regulars by the reformers, nor the disappearance of patronage and corruption (neither has happened yet), as the decentralization of the city's old-line Democratic organization. As Sayre and Kaufman describe the situation, "Party organizations in New York City are not monolithic in character. Each Assembly District is virtually an independent principality. . . . The parties are aggregations of segments rather than organic entities. They are decentralized and fragmented and undisciplined, but they achieve sufficient unity of purpose and action and leadership to identify them as organizations." [18]

[17] See, e.g., Donald S. Bradley and Mayer N. Zald, "From Commercial Elite to Political Administrator: The Recruitment of the Mayors of Chicago," in *The Structure of Community Power,* ed. by Michael Aiken and Paul E. Mott (New York: Random House, Inc., 1970), pp. 53–60.

[18] Sayre and Kaufman, *Governing New York City,* pp. 140, 141.

Multiple sources of patronage are one of the factors maintaining this organizational fragmentation. In the 1930s, when hostile organizations controlled city, state, and federal government, Tammany Hall was sustained by patronage from the Manhattan Surrogates' Court, which is thought to have about as much patronage as the Mayor of New York.[19]

While the distinction between *incentives* and *centralization* is useful for accurate description and definitional clarity, it also has important theoretical ramifications. Robert K. Merton's influential explanation of the persistence of machine politics (patronage) points to the presumed coordinating function of centralized political machines:

> The key structural function of the Boss is to organize, centralize and maintain in good working condition the "scattered fragments of power" which are at present dispersed through our political organization. By the centralized organization of political power, the Boss and his apparatus can satisfy the needs of diverse sub groups in a larger community which are not politically satisfied by legally devised and culturally approved social structures.[20]

Yet machine politics exists many places where, as in New York, the party "organization" is a congeries of competing factions.[21] In fact, cohesive organizations like Chicago's may be fairly uncommon, while pervasive favoritism and patronage—machine politics—are much less so. Hence Merton explained the persistence of the incentive system by referring to functions allegedly performed by an institution (a centralized, city-wide party organization) that may or may not be found where machine politics flourishes.

The rewards that create the incentives in machine politics are not only tangible but divisible, that is, they are "allocated by dividing the benefits piecemeal and allocating various pieces to specific individuals." [22] Moreover, they typically result from the routine operation of government, not from particular substantive policy outcomes. Any regime in a courthouse or city hall will hire roughly the same number of people, contract for roughly the same amounts of goods and services, and enforce (or fail to enforce) the same laws, irrespective of the differences in policies advocated

[19] Ibid., 541 n; Tolchin and Tolchin, "How Judgeships Get Bought," p. 32.

[20] Robert K. Merton, *Social Theory and Social Structure* (revised edition; Glencoe, Ill.: The Free Press, 1957), p. 73. This view of the "functions of the machine" has been expressed by a number of writers.

[21] For a description of a city with decentralized governmental institutions, fragmented party organizations, ample patronage, and major corruption, see John A. Gardiner, *The Politics of Corruption* (New York: Russell Sage Foundation, 1970).

[22] Dahl, *Who Governs?* p. 52.

	Routine	Substantive
Tangible	I. Patronage ——— Machine Politics	II. Favorable Policy ——— "Main Street"
Intangible	III. Sociability Intrinsic Enjoyment of Politics Loyalty to a Leader ——— Any Kind of Organization	IV. Ideology ——— "Amateur"

FIGURE 1 Incentives to political participation.

by one party or the other. The measures adopted by an activist, enterprising administration will generate a higher level of public employment and contracting than the output of a caretaker government. Yet the differences are not enough to change the generalization that the rewards of machine politics are essentially issue-free in that they will flow regardless of what policies are followed. This excepts, of course, reform of personnel and contracting practices.

One can thus distinguish two kinds of tangible incentives to political participation. The incentives that fuel machine politics are inevitable concomitants of government activity, available irrespective of the policies chosen by a particular regime. A second kind of tangible incentive results from a desire to influence the outcome of particular policy decisions. This second type includes those considerations that induce political participation by interest groups that do not want patronage, but do want the government to follow a particular line of action in a substantive policy area: lower tax rates, anti-discrimination legislation, minimum-wage laws, conservation of natural resources, and the like. A particularly pure example of a political organization animated by substantive incentives would be a taxpayers' group that acted as a political party—naming candidates, getting out the vote, etc.—in order to capture city hall for the purpose of enacting a policy of minimal expenditure. As an ideal type, such a group would not care *who* was hired or awarded contracts, so long as a policy of economy was followed.

Incentives to political activity can be classified along two dimensions: tangible/intangible and routine/substantive. The matrix in Figure 1 shows the possible combinations, and examples of organizations in which each incentive system predominates. These categories are ideal types, of course; in any city people will be drawn to party activity by each kind of incentive, and therefore few cities will display only one incentive system. But cities do vary enormously in the prevailing type of incentive system, which is determined by the resources available, the stakes of electoral outcomes, and the attitudes of the citizens. A kind of Gresham's Law also applies here: in cities with ample patronage resources, ideologically motivated people tend not to participate as actively in local elections, except perhaps in enclaves where they are numerous.

A word should be said about Category III, routine intangible incentives. This category includes several different motivations, all of which have in common certain negative characteristics: they do not involve material rewards for political action nor do they depend on the anticipation of preferred policy outcomes. Among these are "solidary" rewards for party work: personal gratification from membership in an organization or from social contact with other party workers. In principle, there is no reason why such pleasures could not be enjoyed by members of any sort of party organization. In practice, it may be that patronage-based organizations are more likely than other kinds to provide solidary rewards.

This has led some observers to suggest that at present machines are sustained as much by these nonmaterial returns as by monetary considerations.[23] It is more plausible, however, that the solidary gratifications are essentially a by-product of a material incentive system that produces more stable and frequent interactions than is the case with amateur politics. One would expect that these interactions would not be wholly instrumental in character, that they would have emotional and social dimensions, and that these would provide a framework of relations that could be satisfying to many of the participants. Since these politically-based social relations seldom exclude the "right kind of people," i.e., people who are not reformers, one might also expect that political clubhouses would offer social pleasures to people who were not at the patronage trough. Some of these people may work for the machine. It would, however, be a serious error to confuse this incidental *effect* with the tangible rewards that *cause* the machine to exist. Consider an analogy: many people get important emotional sustenance from the social relations at their jobs. These rewards, as "morale," may contribute to efficiency, easy recruitment, and low employee turnover. It does not appear useful, however, to argue that the firm exists because of the social benefits that may be a by-product of work.

Substantive policy issues are not normally among the incentives animating machine politics. They are irrelevant to this political style and more an irritant than anything else to its practitioners. One student of Chicago politics said that for the Democratic organization there, "Issues

[23] Edward C. Banfield and James Q. Wilson, *City Politics* (Cambridge: Harvard University Press and the MIT Press, 1963), p. 120.

are obstacles to be overcome, not opportunities to be sought."[24] Daniel Patrick Moynihan observed that in New York, "In the regular party, conferences on issues are regarded as women's work."[25] In California, on the other hand, conferences and resolutions about issues are meat and drink to the earnest middle-class activists who man both political parties. By the same token, local campaigns feature debate about issues in inverse ratio to the prevalence of machine politics, as James Q. Wilson noted: "In Chicago, issues in city elections are conspicuous by their rarity. In New York, they are somewhat more common. In Detroit and Los Angeles, candidates often must go to considerable lengths to *generate* issues in order to attract interest to their campaigns for public office."[26]

In New Haven, also, the party organizations did not play an important role in developing alternative courses of municipal governmental action. Indeed, since machine politicians drew their resources from the routine operations of government, they did not concern themselves with policy formulation. The party's two top leaders were seldom present at meetings where decisions about municipal policy were made, nor did they play an active part in those matters. On strictly party topics like nominations they formed, with Mayor Lee, a triumvirate. Appointments, contracts, and the like were negotiated among the three.[27] But substantive city affairs were another matter; here the organization leaders were neither interested nor consulted on the outlines of policy. They were not excluded against their will; they were largely indifferent. This does not seem to be an unusual situation. In New York, for example, Sayre and Kaufman report that "the most distinctive characteristic of the party leaders as participants in the city's political process is their relative neutrality toward the content of public policy."[28]

The concerns of machine politicians are not irrelevant to substantive policy formation, for while the politicians are neutral "toward the content of public policy," they are very interested indeed in the details of its execution; and in many policy areas the aggregate of their influence on all the details can be important. In Newark the politicians were not concerned about general policy in the city's urban renewal program, but they did scrutinize "with great care all actions of the staff involving hiring, classification, and compensation of [Newark Housing] Authority personnel, the appraisal and acquisition of properties, the awarding of contracts, the

24 James Q. Wilson, *Negro Politics* (Glencoe, Ill.: The Free Press, 1960), p. 117.

25 Daniel P. Moynihan, " 'Bosses' and 'Reformers': A Profile of the New York Democrats," *Commentary*, June 1961, p. 464.

26 Wilson, *Negro Politics*, p. 37 (emphasis in original).

27 Most appointments in urban renewal and related fields were made by Lee without accommodating the Democratic organization's interests.

28 Sayre and Kaufman, *Governing New York City*, p. 474.

maintenance of NHA-owned property, the selection of public housing tenants . . ." [29]

Sayre and Kaufman explain the considerations that lead to party interest in the execution of policy: "The interest of party leaders in public policy seems to vary directly with its possible effect upon their role in choosing officials. In fact, this perception of their relation to public policy impels party leaders to be most concerned with discrete aspects of policy and its application rather than its range and content." [30]

There are two interesting aspects of this tendency for machine politicians to be interested in the details of public policy rather than its basic outlines. One implication concerns Dahl's portrait of the ideal type politician, whom he called *"homo politicus."* In Dahl's view, "Political man . . . deliberately allocates a very sizable share of his resources to the process of gaining and maintaining control over the policies of government." [31] This may be an accurate characterization of many political leaders, but it is not suitable for machine politicians, who are relatively indifferent to public policy, do not consider issue appeals important or desirable elements of electoral strategies, and are primarily interested in control over the sources of patronage. Thus a political taxonomist could identify two subspecies of *homo politicus*. One of these fits Dahl's description and might be called *h. politicus substantus*. The other, the machine politician, is *h. politicus boodelus*. Forerunners of this classification can be found in the literature. In his autobiography, the late "Boss" Flynn, the famous Democratic leader in the Bronx, persistently distinguished between "Democrats," whom he admired, and "New Dealers," whom he scorned as impractical, rigid meddlers.[32]

A second implication of this tendency for machine politics to slight issues concerns theorizing and research on relations between the level of interparty competition and the character of public policy. The classic position on this topic, generally associated with the work of V. O. Key, was that policies beneficial to the lower classes were more likely with evenly matched parties, while one-party domination tended to benefit the rich.[33] Early quantitative research showed that competition and per-capita spending for various welfare measures were very weakly related at the state level, and thus seemed to disconfirm the old belief about the policy con-

[29] Harold Kaplan, *Urban Renewal Politics* (New York: Columbia University Press, 1963), pp. 47–48.

[30] Sayre and Kaufman, *Governing New York City*, p. 452.

[31] Dahl, *Who Governs?* p. 225.

[32] Edward J. Flynn, *You're the Boss* (New York: The Viking Press, 1947).

[33] See especially V. O. Key, Jr., *Southern Politics* (New York: Alfred A. Knopf, Inc., 1949), ch. 14.

sequences of party competition.[34] Both the original proposition and the subsequent research assumed that electoral competition would be "programmatic," i.e., based on alternative policy platforms. But where machine politicians regard issues as "women's work" and "obstacles to be overcome," campaign appeals are likely to include far less issue content. Thus a fair test of Key's proposition would separate "policy competition" from "patronage competition."[35]

Why Political Machines Have Not Withered Away

The conventional wisdom in American social science interprets machine politics as a product of the social needs and political techniques of a bygone era. Advocates of this position attempt to explain both the past existence of machines and their supposed current demise in terms of the functions that the machines performed.[36] In analyzing the functions—now supposedly obsolete—that machine politics served, it is useful to consider four questions:

1. Did political machines actually perform these functions in the past?
2. Do machines still perform them?
3. Has the need for the functions diminished?
4. Is machine politics found wherever these needs exist?

It is commonly argued that various historical trends have crucially diminished the natural constituencies of machines—people who provided votes or other political support in return for the machine's services. The essential machine constituency is thought to have been the poor in general and immigrants in particular. The decline of machine politics then is due to rising prosperity and education, which have reduced the number of people to whom the rewards of machine politics are attractive or necessary. These trends have also, as Thomas R. Dye puts it, spread "middle class values about honesty, efficiency, and good government, which inhibit party

[34] Research of this kind was published by economists as early as 1952, but the first such study that attracted much attention from political scientists was Richard E. Dawson and James A. Robinson, "Inter-Party Competition, Economic Variables and Welfare Policies in the American States," *Journal of Politics*, **25** (May 1963), 265–289. For a review and critique of the ensuing literature, more sophisticated measures, and different findings, see Brian R. Fry and Richard F. Winters, "The Politics of Redistribution," *American Political Science Review*, **64** (June 1970), 508–522.

[35] For one example of such a distinction, see John H. Fenton, *Midwest Politics* (New York: Holt, Rinehart and Winston, 1966).

[36] For a cautious, qualified synthesis of the orthodox position, see Fred I. Greenstein, "The Changing Pattern of Urban Party Politics," *The Annals*, **353** (May 1964), 2–13. Another presentation of the conventional wisdom, with fewer caveats, may be found in Thomas R. Dye, *Politics in States and Communities* (Englewood Cliffs, N.J.: Prentice-Hall, Inc., 1969), pp. 256–272.

organizations in purchases, contracts, and vote-buying, and other cruder forms of municipal corruption. The more successful machine [sic] today, like Daley's in Chicago, have had to reform themselves in order to maintain a good public image." [37]

One function that machines performed was furnishing needy people with food, clothing, and other *direct material assistance*—those legendary Christmas turkeys, buckets of coal, summer outings, and so on. There is no way of knowing just how much of this kind of help machines gave, but it seems to have been an important means of gleaning votes. From the time of the New Deal, government has assumed the burden of providing for the minimal physical needs of the poor, thus supposedly preempting a major source of the machine's appeal. The growth of the welfare state undeniably has limited politicians' opportunities to use charity as a means of incurring obligations that could be discharged by political support. Some political clubs still carry on the old traditions, however, including the distribution of free turkeys to needy families at Christmas time.[38]

Machines supposedly provided other tangible rewards, and the need for these has not been met by alternative institutions. The most obvious of these benefits is employment. The welfare state does not guarantee everyone a job and so the power to hire is still an important power resource. It has been argued, most ably by Frank J. Sorauf, that patronage jobs, mainly at the bottom of the pay scale, are not very attractive to most people.[39] But these positions are attractive to enough people to maintain an ample demand for them, and thus they still are a useful incentive.

A second major constituent service supplied by machine politics was *helping poor and unacculturated people deal with the bureaucratic demands of urban government.* Describing this function, some writers emphasized its affective dimension. Robert K. Merton put it this way: "the precinct captain is ever a friend in need. In our increasingly impersonal society, the machine, through its local agents, performs the important social *function of humanizing and personalizing all manner of assistance* to those in need." [40] In Dye's view, the machine "personalized government. With

[37] Dye, *Politics,* p. 276.

[38] Tolchin and Tolchin, " 'Honest Graft'—Playing the Patronage Game," *New York Magazine,* March 22, 1971, p. 42.

[39] See especially his "Patronage and Party," *Midwest Journal of Political Science,* **3** (May 1959), 115–126. In this and other articles Sorauf has argued not only that patronage is unattractive, but that it is inefficiently exploited by party leaders. His direct observations are limited to his study of the consequences of the 1954 Democratic gubernatorial victory for the highway maintenance crew in one rural county in Pennsylvania. Sorauf is more persuasive about the ineffectuality of Democratic leaders in Centre County than about the generalizability of his findings. He concludes, moreover, that "the parties need the strength of patronage, however minor and irregular it may be . . ." (ibid., p. 126).

[40] Merton, *Social Theory,* p. 74 (emphasis in original).

keen social intuition, the machine recognized the voter as a man, generally living in a neighborhood, who had specific personal problems and wants."[41] William F. Whyte saw a more cognitive element in politicians' services to the common man: "the uninitiated do not understand the complex organization of government and do not know how to find the channels through which they can obtain action."[42] Whyte's view of the relation between the citizen and his "friend in need" the precinct captain is a great deal less innocent than Merton's: "Everyone recognizes that when a politician does a favor for a constituent, the constituent becomes obligated to the politician."[43]

If machine politics were a response to "our increasingly impersonal society," it would seem to follow that continuing growth in the scope, complexity, and impersonality of institutional life would produce *greater* need for politicians to mediate between individuals and their government. The growth of the welfare state therefore has not diminished this need but increased it and presumably offers the machine politician new opportunities for helping citizens get what they want from the government. Describing the advent of New Deal social services in a poor Boston neighborhood, Whyte made it clear that the new welfare policies did not so much subvert machine politics as rearrange the channels of access while presenting some politicians with a new opportunity to accumulate obligations. Whyte quotes the wife of a state senator: "If you're qualified, you can get on [WPA] without going to a politician. But it will be four weeks before you get certified, and I can push things through so that you get on in a week. And I can see that you get a better job . . ."[44]

As far as local politicians are concerned, new public services may be new prizes that covetous or needy citizens can more easily obtain with political help. Writing a generation after Whyte, Harold Kaplan reported that in Newark "a public housing tenant, therefore, may find it easier to secure a public housing unit, prevent eviction from a project, secure a unit in a better project, or have NHA [Newark Housing Authority] reconsider his rent, if he has the right sponsor at City Hall."[45] There is no necessary connection, then, between expanded public services and a decline in the advantages of political help or in the number of people who want to use it. While the expansion and institutionalization of welfare may have ended "the party's monopoly of welfare services,"[46] they have vastly expanded

[41] Dye, *Politics*, p. 257.

[42] William F. Whyte, *Street Corner Society* (enlarged edition; Chicago: University of Chicago Press, 1955), p. 241.

[43] Ibid., p. 240.

[44] Ibid., p. 197.

[45] Kaplan, *Urban Renewal*, pp. 42–43.

[46] Dye, *Politics*, p. 271.

the need for information, guidance, and emotional support in relations between citizens and government officials, and thus there is no shortage of services that machines can provide the poor and unassimilated, who are still with us.[47]

There is no doubt that in the past 50 years income levels have risen and the flow of foreign immigrants has dwindled considerably. But there are plenty of poor people in the cities, the middle classes have been moving to the suburbs for the past two generations, and the European immigrants have been succeeded by blacks, Puerto Ricans, Mexicans, and poor rural whites.[48] Moreover, about two and a half million people came to this country as immigrants in the decade from 1950 to 1960. The argument that affluence and assimilation have choked machine politics at the roots, one familiar to scholars for decades, may now look a bit more threadbare. Yet the recent discovery of poverty and cultural deprivation has not had a major effect on thinking about trends in the viability of machine politics.

Along with the new interest in the urban poor has come a realization that existing institutions do not meet their needs. Among these inadequate institutions is the political machine, which, in the traditional view, should be expected to do for today's blacks, Chicanos, Puerto Ricans, and poor whites just what it is supposed to have done for yesterday's immigrants. But even in cities with flourishing machine politics there has been a tremendous development of all kinds of community action groups for advice, information exchange, and the representation of individual and neighborhood interests—precisely the functions that the machines are said to have performed. The gap between the disoriented poor and the public institutions serving them seems to be present equally in cities like Chicago, generally thought to be political anachronisms, and in places like Los Angeles that have never experienced machine politics. This leads to an important point: most American cities have had the social conditions that are said to give rise to machine politics, but many of these cities have not had machine politics for a generation or more.

This fact and the evident failure of existing machines to perform their functions cast doubt on the conventional ways of explaining both the functions of machines in their supposed heyday and the causes of their "decline." One conclusion is that the decline is real, but that the principal causes of the decline do not lie in affluence and assimilation. A second pos-

47 Some contemporary organizations do give advice and legal aid, mediate disputes, and serve as clearinghouses for information. See James Q. Wilson, *The Amateur Democrat* (Chicago: University of Chicago Press, 1962), p. 176; and Tolchin and Tolchin, " 'Honest Graft,' " p. 42.

48 As many writers are now beginning to realize, the acculturation and assimilation of the European immigrants is far from complete. See my "The Development and Persistence of Ethnic Voting," *American Political Science Review,* **59** (December 1965), 896–908; and *The Politics of Progress,* chap. 3.

sibility is that the machines persist, but have abandoned the beneficent functions they used to perform. A third is that they are still "humanizing and personalizing all manner of assistance to those in need," but cannot cope with a massive increase in the needs of their clienteles. And a fourth alternative is that the extent to which they ever performed these functions has been exaggerated.

It does seem that a whole generation of scholarship has been adversely affected by overreaction to the older judgmental style of describing machine politics. Until a decade or two ago most work on machines was moralistic and pejorative, dwelling on the seamy side of the subject and concerning itself largely with exposure and denunciation.[49] More contemporary social scientists have diverged from this tradition in two respects. One, apparently a reaction to the highly normative style of the old reformers, is a tendency to gloss over the very real evils they described. The other, addressed to the major problem of explaining the durability of machine politics, is the search for "functions": acculturating immigrants and giving them a channel of social mobility, providing a link between citizen and city hall, and co-ordinating formally fragmented government agencies. Some writers suggest that urban political organizations were a rudimentary form of the welfare state. While the tone of these later works has been realistic, some of them leaned toward idealizing their subject, perhaps in reaction to the earlier moralism or because functionalism has not been accompanied by an inclination to confront the sordid details. Thus the development of a more dispassionate social science has produced, on the descriptive level, a retreat from realism. The functionalists seem to have been somewhat over-credulous: "the precinct captain is ever a friend in need."

This innocence may explain the popularity in recent textbooks of a pious declaration by a celebrated and unsavory ward boss in Boston: " 'I think,' said Martin Lomasny [sic], 'that there's got to be in every ward somebody that any bloke can come to—no matter what he's done—and get help. Help, you understand; none of your law and your justice, but help.' "[50] The kind of "help" that could be expected is suggested by the remarks of another local leader in Boston that convey, I think, a more realistic sense of the priorities in machine politics:

> When people wanted help from the organization, they would come right up here to the office [of the political club]. Matt [the boss] would be in here every morning from nine to eleven, and if you couldn't see him then, you could

[49] For a description of trends in the study of city politics see Wallace S. Sayre and Nelson W. Polsby, "American Political Science and the Study of Urbanization," in *The Study of Urbanization,* ed. by Philip M. Hauser and Leo F. Schnore (New York: John Wiley & Sons, Inc., 1965), pp. 115–156.

[50] Originally quoted in *The Autobiography of Lincoln Steffens* (New York: Harcourt, Brace and Company, 1931), p. 618.

> find him in the ward almost any other time. If a man came in to ask Matt for a job, Matt would listen to him and then tell him he'd see what he could do; he should come back in a couple of days. That would give Matt time to get in touch with the precinct captain and find out all about the man. If he didn't vote in the last election, he was out. Matt wouldn't do anything for him—that is, unless he could show that he was so sick he couldn't get to the polls.[51]

"Helping" citizens deal with government is, in this context, usually thought to be a matter of advice about where to go, whom to see, and what to say. The poor undeniably need this service more than people whose schooling and experience equip them to cope with bureaucratic institutions and procedures. But in some local political cultures advice to citizens is often accompanied by pressure on officials. The machine politician's goal is to incur the maximum obligation from his constituents, and merely providing information is not as big a favor as helping bring about the desired outcome. Thus *"help" shades into "pull."*

Now there is no reason why the advantages of political influence appeal only to the poor. In places where the political culture supports expectations that official discretion will be exercised in accordance with political considerations, the constituency for machine politics extends across the socioeconomic spectrum. People whose interests are affected by governmental decisions can include those who want to sell to the government, as well as those whose economic or social activities may be subject to public regulation.

Favoritism animates machine politics, favoritism not just in filling pick-and-shovel jobs, but in a vast array of public decisions. The welfare state has little to do with the potential demand for favoritism, except to expand opportunities for its exercise. The New Deal did not abolish the contractor's natural desire to minimize the risks of competitive bidding, or the landlord's equally natural desire to avoid the burdens of the housing code. It is all very well to talk about "middle-class values of efficiency and honesty," but the thousands of lawyers whose political connections enable them to benefit from the billion-dollar-a-year case load of the Manhattan Surrogates' Court are surely not members of the working class.

While "help" in dealing with the government may be primarily appealing to people baffled by the complexities of modern society and too poor to hire lawyers, "pull" is useful in proportion to the size of one's dealings with government. Certain kinds of business and professional men are *more* likely to have interests requiring repeated and complicated relations with public agencies, and thus are potentially a *stronger* constituency for machine politics than the working classes. The conventional wisdom that the middle classes are hostile to machine politics rests on several types of

[51] Quoted in Whyte, *Street Corner Society*, p. 194.

evidence: (1) The undeniable fact that reform candidates almost always run better in well-to-do neighborhoods. (2) The equally undeniable fact that machine politics provides, in patronage and petty favors, a kind of reward for political participation that is not available in other incentive systems. (3) The less validated proposition that middle-class people think that governments should be run with impartial, impersonal honesty in accordance with abstract principles, while the working classes are more sympathetic to favoritism and particularistic criteria. These characterizations may be true in the aggregate for two diverse such categories as "the middle class" and "the working class" (although that has not yet been established), but even if these generalizations are true, they would still leave room for the existence of a sizable subcategory of the middle class who, in some political cultures, benefits from and endorses machine politics.

Textbook interpretations recognize these middle-class interests in machine politics, but generally relegate them to an hypothesized earlier stage in urban history. This was the era when America changed from a rural to an urban society, a shift that created a vast need in the new cities for municipal facilities and services: streetcars, electricity, paved streets, and so on. These needs were met by businessmen who corrupted officials wholesale in their eagerness to get franchises. Since the businessmen wanted action, they profited from political machines that could organize power to get things done by centralizing the formally fragmented agencies of government. Thus machine politics served the needs not just of poor immigrants, but also of the generation of businessmen who exploited the foundation of urban America. But after the first great rush of city building, the essential facilities and utilities had been supplied and business interest in local government declined. Machine politics no longer performed a coordinating function for the franchise seekers and hence lost an important constituency.

While this may be an accurate description of relations between business greed and governmental corruption in the Gilded Age, it has a number of deficiencies as an explanation of the rise and fall of machine politics. Three of these flaws have already been discussed in other contexts: (1) Like poverty, urban growth is not a bygone phenomenon, but continues to this day. (2) Machine politics does not occur wherever cities have experienced sudden and massive needs for municipal services. (3) This explanation confuses patronage and centralization of party organizations at the city level, two phenomena that may not be found together.

There are other difficulties with this line of thought. First, uncoordinated public agencies and jurisdictions continue to proliferate. If machine politics were a response to the formal decentralization of government, one would think that it, too, would increase, and that party organizations would grow stronger rather than weaker. It may be that one or more unstated intermediary conditions are preventing these latter trends from occurring;

if so, no writer has, to my knowledge, shown what this interactive relation is.

If it were true that "the key structural function of the Boss is to organize, centralize, and maintain in good working condition the 'scattered fragments of power'" typical of American local government, one would expect to find a positive relation between the prevalence of machine politics and municipal institutions that maximize fragmentation. "Strong-mayor" cities should be least ridden by patronage, and commission and council-manager cities should have the most. There is no systematic evidence available about these relations, but what data there are do not support the propositions. (They are also not supported by another piece of conventional wisdom, which associates city managers with reformism.) Machine politics seems to be far more common on the East Coast than in the West, but so are cities with elected mayors. Cities with mayors and cities with managers are equally likely to have merit systems for their employees, which could be considered an index of the weakness of machine politics.[52]

Finally, political centralization may not be conductive to the interests of businessmen who want prompt and affirmative action from local government. Whether centralized power is preferable depends on what the businessman wants. If he wants a license or franchise to sell goods or services, or to buy something belonging to the government, it may be in his interests to deal with an autonomous official or agency, not with a government-wide hierarchy. John A. Gardiner's study of the notoriously corrupt city of "Wincanton" provides evidence for the proposition that decentralized political systems are *more* corruptible, because the potential corrupter needs to influence only a segment of the government, and because in a fragmented system there are fewer centralized forces and agencies to enforce honesty. The "Wincanton" political system is formally and informally fragmented; neither parties nor interest groups (including the criminal syndicate) exercise overall coordination. The ample patronage and outright graft in "Wincanton" are not used as a means of centralization.[53] Indeed, governmental coordination clearly would not be in the interests of the private citizens there who benefit from corruption, or of the officials who take bribes. Attempts by reformers to stop graft or patronage often founder on the city's commission form of government, which is both the apotheosis of local governmental fragmentation and an hospitable environment for machine politics.

The conventional wisdom also holds that the machines' electioneering techniques are as obsolete as the social functions they used to perform. According to this interpretation, "the old politics" based its campaigns on

[52] Wolfinger and Field, "Political Ethos," pp. 314–316.

[53] Gardiner, *The Politics of Corruption*, pp. 8–12.

divisible promises and interpersonal persuasion, and these methods have been outdated by the mass media—particularly television, the growing importance of candidates' personalities, and the electorate's craving for ideological or at least programmatic promises.[54]

Like the other explanation of the machines' demise, this argument has serious factual and logical deficiencies. As we have seen, machine politics is an effective way of raising money for political purposes. There is no reason why the money "maced" from public employees or extracted from government contractors cannot be spent on motivational research, advertising copywriters, television spots, and all the other manifestations of mass media campaigns.

Similarly, there is no inconsistency between machine politics and outstanding candidates. Just as machine politicians can spend their money on public relations, so can they bestow their support on inspirational leaders who exude integrity and vitality. Many of the most famous "idealistic" politicians in American history owe their success to the sponsorship of machine politicians. Woodrow Wilson made his first venture into electoral politics as the gubernatorial candidate of an unsavory Democratic organization in New Jersey. (Once elected governor, Wilson promptly betrayed his sponsors.) In more recent times, such exemplars of dedicated public spirit as the elder Adlai Stevenson, Paul H. Douglas, and Chester Bowles were nominated for office as the candidates of the patronage-based party organizations in their several states.[55]

[54] Interviewing a number of party officials in New Jersey, Richard T. Frost found that "old-fashioned" techniques like door-to-door canvassing were considered more effective, and used more frequently, than newer methods like television advertising. See his "Stability and Change in Local Party Politics," *Public Opinion Quarterly,* **25** (Summer 1961), 221–235.

[55] Bowles is sometimes depicted as a high-minded victim of crasser and smaller men in the Connecticut Democratic party. The principal event presented as evidence for this viewpoint is his defeat by Thomas J. Dodd for the senatorial nomination at the 1958 state Democratic convention. Dodd had long been an opponent of the regular Democratic organization headed by then-Governor Abraham A. Ribicoff and state chairman John Bailey. Bowles, on the other hand, had been the organization's winning gubernatorial candidate in 1950. After his defeat for the senatorial nomination in 1958, he accepted the organization's offer of a congressional nomination and was elected to Congress in the fall. Ribicoff and Bailey thought that Bowles's popularity would help win the seat, then held by a Republican, and brushed aside the claims of the announced candidates for the Democratic nomination, who "voluntarily" withdrew their names from consideration by the convention.

One of the seconding speeches in support of Bowles's unsuccessful try for the senatorial nomination was by Arthur T. Barbieri, the New Haven town chairman (and later a close ally of Dodd's). It was devoted by praising Bowles's willingness, when governor, to accede to the party's wishes in matters involving patronage. The disciplined New Haven delegation voted unanimously for Bowles, a Yankee patrician. Dodd, an Irish Catholic, was the sentimental favorite of many delegates, but almost all of them were city employees or otherwise financially dependent on city hall.

Sayre and Kaufman explain this organization willingness to support blue-ribbon candidates: "They [machine politicians] have also learned the lesson of what retailers call the loss leader—that is, the item that may lose money for the storekeeper but which lures customers in and thereby leads to increases in purchases of profitable merchandise." [56] Generally, party regulars turn to blue-ribbon "loss leaders" when they think that their popularity is necessary to carry the ticket to victory. Otherwise, machine politicians eschew candidates with independent popular appeal, since popularity is an important bargaining resource in intraparty negotiating. Without it, an elected official is more dependent on organization politicians.

"The new politics" is an ambiguous term. It is used to describe increasing campaign emphasis on the mass media and professional public relations, and also is applied to popular participation in party affairs and direct contact with the voters by campaign workers. In the 1968 election "the new politics" was associated with peace advocates and the young enthusiasts who gave so much tone to Eugene McCarthy's presidential bid. Except for the age of the activists, there was little to distinguish this aspect of McCarthy's campaign from the idealistic appeal of such previous and diverse presidential candidates as Adlai Stevenson anad Barry Goldwater, both of whom projected to some people an image of altruism and reform that attracted legions of dedicated workers. "The new politics" seem to be one of those recurring features of American politics that political writers are always rediscovering. The trademark of "the new politics" is intense precinct work, one-to-one conversations with citizens, the same interpersonal style that machines have relied on for generations. As a Democratic organization politician in New York observed: "If the new politics teaches anything, it's that the old politics was pretty good. The McCarthy kids in New Hampshire rang doorbells, made the telephone calls, made the personal contact that people associate with the old-style machine." [57]

Both kinds of "new politics" have at least one thing in common: they tend to be found in elections that draw a great deal of attention and arouse strong emotions. State and local elections and party primaries (except presidential ones) rarely attain much visibility. Candidates for the city council, the state legislature, or the city or state under-ticket seldom attract much public attention. Even paid media advertising in such elections is not feasible because the voting jurisdiction for a single candidacy generally includes only a fraction of the reading or viewing audience of the most widely used media. An occasional mayoral or gubernatorial race may get a good deal of media space and arouse popular enthusiasm, but otherwise these elections do not present a high profile in most voters' perspectives. This is particularly true for local elections, which generally are not concurrent with

[56] Sayre and Kaufman, *Governing New York City,* p. 155.

[57] Quoted in the *New York Times,* June 1, 1970, p. 27.

national campaigns, as well as for party primaries and campaigns for any state office except the governorship. These low-salience contests are particularly amenable to the resources typical of machine politics. A New York state senator explained this point bluntly: "My best captains, in the primary, are the ones who are on the payroll. You can't get the average voter excited about who's going to be an Assemblyman or State Senator. I've got two dozen people who are going to work so much harder, because if I lose, they lose." [58] It is in elections of this type, where neither the mass media nor idealistic amateurs are likely to participate, that most of the spoils of machine politics are at stake. Since precinct work is effective in inverse relation to the salience of the election,[59] "old fashioned machines" do not seem very seriously threatened by either form of "the new politics."

Conclusions and Suggestions

To sum up my argument: Since an increasing proportion of urban populations is poor and uneducated, it is not persuasive to argue that growing prosperity and education are diminishing the constituency for machine politics. While governments now assume responsibility for a minimum level of welfare, other contemporary trends are not so inhospitable to machine politics. Various kinds of patronage still seem to be in reasonable supply, and are as attractive as ever to those people—by no means all poor—who benefit from them. The proliferation of government programs provides more opportunities for the exercise of favoritism. The continuing bureaucratization of modern government gives more scope for the machine's putative function of serving as a link between the citizen and the state.

These trends would seem to have expanded the need for the services the machines supposedly performed for the poor. Yet surviving machines apparently are not performing these functions, and machine politics has not flourished in many cities where the alleged need for these functions is just as great.

The potential constituency for political favoritism is not limited to the poor; many kinds of business and professional men can benefit from machine politics. They do in some cities but not in others. Again, it appears that the hypothesized conditions for machine politics are found in many places where machines are enfeebled or absent.

Real and imaginary changes in campaign techniques are not inconsistent with machines' capacities. In short, machines have not withered away

[58] Quoted in the *New York Times*, June 17, 1968, p. 30.

[59] Raymond E. Wolfinger, "The Influence of Precinct Work on Voting Behavior," *Public Opinion Quarterly*, **27** (Fall 1963), 387–398. Turnout in the primary to select the Democratic candidate for the Manhattan Surrogates' Court rarely reaches 100,000 voters and thus the outcome is more easily influenced by party organizations.

because the conditions that supposedly gave rise to them are still present. The problem with this answer is that the conditions are found in many places where machine politics does not exist.

Attempts to explain the growth and alleged decline of machine politics usually emphasize the importance of immigrants as a constituency for machines.[60] Yet many cities with large immigrant populations have never been dominated by machine politics, or were freed of this dominance generations ago.[61] Machine politics continues to flourish in some states like Indiana, where foreign-stock voters are relatively scarce. In other states, like Pennsylvania and Connecticut, machines seem to have been as successful with old stock American constituents as with immigrants.[62]

Far more interesting than differences in ethnicity or social class are regional or subregional variations in the practices of machine politics and in attitudes toward them.[63] Public acceptance of patronage, for example, appears to vary a good deal from place to place in patterns that are not explained by differences in population characteristics such as education, occupation, and ethnicity. Although systematic data on this subject are not available, it does seem that voters in parts of the East, the Ohio Valley, and the South are tolerant of practices that would scandalize most people in, say, the Pacific Coast states or the Upper Midwest. The residents of Indiana, for example, seem to accept calmly the remarkable mingling of public business and party profits in that state. One researcher notes that these practices have "not been an issue in recent campaigns." [64] Another student of midwestern politics reports that "Indiana is the only state studied where the governor and other important state officials described quite frankly and in detail the sources of the campaign funds. They were disarmingly frank because they saw nothing wrong in the techniques employed to raise funds,

[60] For a good statement of this position see Elmer E. Cornwell, Jr., "Bosses, Machines, and Ethnic Groups," *The Annals,* **353** (May 1964), 27–39.

[61] This is most obviously true of the large cities of the West Coast: San Francisco (44 per cent foreign stock in 1960), Los Angeles (33 per cent), and Seattle (31 per cent). These cities are equally or more ethnic than eastern and midwestern cities characterized by machine politics, e.g., Chicago (36 per cent), Philadelphia (29 per cent), and St. Louis (14 per cent).

[62] See the works by Frank J. Sorauf cited in notes 39 and 65 and Duane Lockard, *New England State Politics* (Princeton: Princeton University Press, 1959), pp. 245–251.

[63] Several studies show major regional or subregional variations in political preferences that cannot be accounted for by varying demographic characteristics. See, e.g., Irving Crespi, "The Structural Basis for Right-Wing Conservatism: The Goldwater Case," *Public Opinion Quarterly,* **29** (Winter 1965), 523–543; James W. Prothro and Charles M. Grigg, "Fundamental Principles of Democracy: Bases of Agreement and Disagreement," *Journal of Politics,* **22** (Spring 1960), 276–294; and Raymond E. Wolfinger and Fred I. Greenstein, "Comparing Political Regions: The Case of California," *American Political Science Review,* **63** (March 1969), 74–86.

[64] McNeill, *Democratic Campaign Financing,* p. 39.

and neither did the opposing political party nor the press nor, presumably, the citizenry."[65]

California provides a particularly useful contrast to the East Coast states and Indiana. While California has a cosmopolitan population and an urban, industrial economy, it also displays virtually no signs of machine politics. The Governor has about as many patronage jobs at his disposal as the Mayor of New Haven. Californians who worked in John F. Kennedy's presidential campaign report the bemusement of Kennedy organizers from the East who came to the state with thoughts of building their campaign organization around public employees. These and other practices that are widely accepted in the East are abhorred on the West Coast. Paying precinct workers in commonplace in eastern cities. But when Jess Unruh, a prominent California Democratic leader, hired some canvassers in the 1962 election, he was roundly denounced from all points of the political spectrum for importing such a sordid practice. The president of the California Democratic Council said that Unruh's action "smacked of ward politics" ("ward politics" is a common pejorative in California) and sternly announced, "I am firmly convinced that the expansion and development of the use of paid workers is unhealthy for the Democratic party in California."[66]

The reason for these marked geographical variations in political style are not easily found, but looking for them is a more promising approach to explaining the incidence of machine politics than the search for functions supposedly rooted in the socioeconomic composition of urban populations.[67]

[65] Fenton, *Midwest Politics*, p. 7. For an account of public acceptance of patronage in bucolic, native-stock Centre County, Pennsylvania, see Frank J. Sorauf, "Chairman and Superintendent," in *Cases in State and Local Government,* ed. by Richard T. Frost (Englewood Cliffs, N.J.: Prentice-Hall, Inc., 1961), pp. 109–119.

[66] *San Francisco Chronicle*, December 17, 1962, p. 10; and *CDC Newsletter*, December 1962.

[67] The study of regional variations in American political perspectives is still in its infancy. For a general discussion and survey of the literature see Samuel C. Patterson, "The Political Cultures of the American States," *Journal of Politics,* **30** (February 1968), 187–209.

For an interesting typology of three American political value systems that encompasses the regional differences concerning machine politics discussed here see Daniel J. Elazar, *American Federalism: A View from the States* (New York: Thomas Y. Crowell Company, 1966).

Jeffrey L. Pressman

Preconditions of Mayoral Leadership*

Policy making at the urban level has been distinguished for many years from that at the other two levels of government by the presence on the local scene of a supposedly politically sterile form of government, the council-manager plan. Indeed, the development of that plan is one of the proud boasts of American political practice.

But the emphasis in much of the study of urban policy making on the city manager and the emphasis on the urban policy arena as largely an administrative one which has accompanied the city manager form have served to detract attention from the mayor as a central figure in policy making.

Pressman here examines the potential and reality of the mayor as leader and forces us to reconsider his role in urban leadership.

Introduction: The Search for Mayoral Leadership

After reviewing the problems which constitute the contemporary "urban crisis," most observers come to the conclusion that urban political leadership—usually mayoral leadership—is a crucial ingredient in a city's

* This paper is based upon four years of participation in, and observation of, the mayor's office in Oakland. The research was conducted under the auspices of the Oakland Project at the University of California at Berkeley, headed by Aaron Wildavsky and funded by the Urban Institute. I would like to thank Professor Wildavsky, Robert Biller, William K. Muir, Jr., Bill Cavala, and Robert Nakamura for their comments.

Reprinted from *American Political Science Review*, **66**:511–24 (June 1972) by permission of the author and the publisher. Some descriptive and bibliographical footnotes have been omitted for considerations of space and textual format.

ability to deal with those problems. The President's Riot Commission was outspoken on this subject:

> Now, as never before, the American city has need for the personal qualities of strong democratic leadership. Given the difficulties and delays involved in administrative reorganization or institutional change, the best hope for the city in the short-run lies in this powerful instrument. In most cities the mayors will have the prime responsibility.

For the Commission, the role of the mayor is an awesome one:

> As leader and mediator, he must involve all those groups—employers, news media, unions, financial institutions and others—which only together can bridge the chasm now separating the racial ghetto from the community. His goal, in effect, must be to develop a new working concept of democracy within the city.[1]

Proponents of mayoral leadership readily admit that few mayors have formal authority and resources which are adequate to deal with the enormous task facing them. But this is not considered an insuperable obstacle. Alexander George has written that

> The pluralistic structure of dispersed, decentralized power requires a political leader who can accumulate personal influence to supplement his limited formal authority. Studies of successful leaders in urban systems have led to the formulation of a simple, but incisive model of the "political entrepreneur"—a political activist adept at accumulating a variety of political resources and using them to gain influence and additional resources.[2]

An alert mayor can view political fragmentation as providing numerous opportunities for the "brokerage" function—mediating disputes, serving as a line of communication, and suggesting integrative solutions in which diverse groups can all gain. And in performing this function, the mayor finds his own power increased. "To the political entrepreneur, who possesses skill and drive, the pluralistic dispersion and fragmentation of power in democratic systems offer unusual opportunities for pyramiding limited initial resources into a substantial political holding." [3] Thus, effective political leadership in a fragmented system is proclaimed to be a necessity in

[1] *Report of the National Advisory Commission on Civil Disorders* (New York: Bantam, 1968), p. 298.

[2] Alexander L. George, "Political Leadership and Social Change in American Cities," *Daedalus* (Fall 1968), p. 1197.

[3] George, p. 1197.

American cities. And political scientists have provided a model of the broker-entrepreneur who can fill that need.[4]

It is easy to advocate "mayoral leadership" and "political entrepreneurship." But what does successful "leadership" mean in a modern American city? Andrew McFarland has defined leadership in the following way:

> A *leader* may be defined as one who has unusual *influence*. Influence may be viewed as one's capacity to make people behave differently than they would have otherwise. A leader may also be defined as one who has unusual *power*. Here we view "power" as a person's capacity to make others do something that they would not do otherwise and that the person specifically wants or intends.[5]

According to this social causation definition, a mayor may be said to exercise leadership when he alters human behavior in ways that he himself desires. Thus, he must set goals and influence others to aid in the pursuit of those goals.

MODEL OF MAYORAL LEADERSHIP. For those who call for strong and progressive mayors, a model of effective mayoral leadership should include a specification of: (1) the goals toward which a mayor might strive; (2) those groups in his environment which he must influence in support of those goals; (3) the ways in which he may influence them; and (4) the resources required for an effective exercise of power.

The goals toward which a model mayor might devote his energies and lead his constituency are numerous, varied, and difficult to accomplish. Writers on urban affairs have listed numerous possible goals: effective law enforcement; redevelopment; relocation of those living in redeveloped areas; expansion of the tax base; construction of low-cost public housing; improvement of the schools; creation of jobs and job training programs. Besides these substantive goals, the ideal mayor might strive to maintain within the political system a process of constructive dialogue between diverse groups which would contribute to harmony in the city.

In pursuing his goals, a mayor would have to exercise control and direction over the city council and relevant city departments: schools, redevelopment, housing, police, etc. The successful mayor would attempt to stretch his "legal" jurisdiction as far as possible. Furthermore, he would

[4] See Robert A. Dahl, *Who Governs?* (New Haven: Yale University Press, 1961), pp. 225–227, 308; Edward C. Banfield, *Political Influence* (New York: Free Press, 1961), chap. 8 and pp. 17, 309, 312–313, 320–321; Aaron Wildavsky, *Leadership in a Small Town* (Totowa, N.J.: Bedminster Press, 1964), pp. 244–245, 248; H. H. Gerth and C. Wright Mills, *From Max Weber* (New York: Oxford University Press, 1946), p. 109; and Andrew S. McFarland, *Power and Leadership in Pluralist Systems* (Stanford, Calif.: Stanford University Press, 1969), pp. 153–219.

[5] McFarland, p. 154.

have to activate nongovernmental groups in the community to support his efforts by promising rewards and threatening sanctions. He would have to persuade businessmen to locate factories in his city and to initiate job training programs, and he would have to persuade labor unions to open places in apprenticeship programs to minority groups.

An ideal mayor would use his control of the mechanism of a political party to further his policy preferences, by supporting the nomination and election of candidates who were willing to support him. Furthermore, the model mayor would be willing to use publicity in order to appeal to the public to support him against opponents by voting in elections or by trying to influence recalcitrant groups.

In order to exercise leadership over these various groups—in order to make them do what they would otherwise *not* do—the ideal mayor would require various resources. They would include:

a. Sufficient financial and staff resources on the part of the city government;
b. City jurisdiction in social program areas—such as education, housing, redevelopment, job training, etc;
c. Mayoral jurisdiction within the city government in these policy fields;
d. A salary for the mayor which would enable him to spend full time on the job;
e. Sufficient staff support for the mayor—for policy planning, speechwriting, intergovernmental relations, and political work;
f. Ready vehicles for publicity, such as friendly newspapers or television stations;
g. Politically-oriented groups, including a political party, which the mayor could mobilize to help him achieve particular goals.

As this list suggests, the opportunities for mayoral leadership in a particular case may be limited by the political structure of a city (electoral system, parties, groups), by governmental structure, and by the lack of staff, jurisdictional and financial resources. Furthermore, the quality of mayoral leadership may be strongly influenced by the personality of the mayor himself. Although social forces and governmental structures set limits to what *any* man might be able to do as mayor in a particular city, personal variability should not be discounted. Thus in examining the quality of mayoral leadership, we must ask to what extent a given mayor's performance is influenced by social forces and government structure, and to what extent that performance is influenced by the mayor's personality.

Perhaps because of most mayors' lack of extensive governmental authority, observers of city politics have not concerned themselves with the problem of unrestrained mayoral leadership. But an enumeration of forces for restraint might include the mayor's dependence on independent groups for the attainment of his goals and the existence of competitive elections in the city.

This paper will explore the politics of mayoral leadership—or non-leadership—in a particular city: Oakland, California, under the administration of Mayor John H. Reading. The second part examines the often hostile environment in which the mayor works—the city of Oakland and its political structure, the city government, and the mayor's own office. The third part focuses on the personality of the mayor himself, using material drawn from speeches, interviews, newspaper articles, and personal observation. The last part analyzes the mayor's performance in light of the resources available (or potentially available) to him.

By examining mayoral leadership in a particular city, and by comparing that leadership to the model described above, this essay will suggest some of the difficulties surrounding urban leadership in an era of racial tension, confrontation, and insufficiency of urban resources. If we understand these difficulties, we will be better prepared to chart the preconditions for successful mayoral leadership.

Although some of the vital preconditions—financial resources, governmental authority, groups, etc.—may be missing, a mayor can still attempt to be a leader. But the style and consequences of his leadership depend to a large extent on the type of governmental and political system in which he operates; the concluding section of this paper will discuss some of the connections between political environment and leadership.

Environment

THE CITY. Oakland's population in 1970 was 361,561, of which 34.5 per cent was black. Studies have repeatedly shown that minority groups (blacks and Mexican-Americans) are heavily over-represented in both the poor and unemployed population of the city. And Oakland's overall unemployment rate has reached a level more than twice the national average. This is the kind of city which is discussed at length in the news media and in the growing "urban crisis" literature. It is characterized by an increasingly large minority population, by geographical separation and emotional tension between races, and by continuing problems of poverty and unemployment.

POLITICAL ENVIRONMENT: THE "NON-POLITICS" OF OAKLAND. One of the requirements postulated for successful mayoral leadership is the existence of "politically-oriented groups, including a political party, which the mayor can mobilize to help him achieve particular goals." Such groups and parties would give the mayor an opportunity to identify interests which had become aggregated by and articulated through organizations. Furthermore, groups and parties could perform the function of recruiting political leaders with whom the mayor could bargain. Finally, the mayor could use friendly groups as vehicles for political education in the goals toward which he was working and as organizing devices to bring citizens together in support of those goals.

In Oakland, a fundamental obstacle to mayoral leadership is the nature of the political environment itself. For this environment is characterized by a lack of interest in the electoral process and an absence of political parties and groups.

It often appears as though politics in Oakland does not exist. In 1969, when elections were held for mayor, city council, and the board of education, the candidate response was tepid at best. Two little-known men emerged to challenge Mayor Reading's attempt for reelection; two new candidates filed against two of the three incumbents on the school board; and all three city councilmen who were up for reelection were unopposed.

In a city marked by serious divisions, what causes the avoidance of electoral politics? Many answers have been suggested: the lack of resources and power in city government; the middle- and upper-class white bias of the at-large election system, which makes candidacies expensive and victories for nonwhites difficult to achieve; and, finally, the paltry salaries of elected officials.

Another reason for the anemia of Oakland's electoral process has been the noticeable absence of political party activity in municipal elections. This absence has, no doubt, been encouraged by the nonpartisan nature of the municipal ballot, which gives voters no indication of the party to which a candidate belongs. But formal nonpartisanship is not a sufficient explanation for party inaction; it has not prevented extensive activity by Democratic and Republican organizations in neighboring Berkeley and San Francisco.

A basic cause of party inactivity in Oakland has been the lack of organized politically interested groups in the city upon which a party or mayor could build. When an organization of high-school students tried to form a "coalition" in 1968 and 1969 to work for changes in school procedure and curriculum, they found, as one leader put it, "that there was no one to coalesce with." Labor has not played a significant role in city politics since the 1940s. And business groups, though formally endorsing certain nonpartisan causes like charter reform, have not heavily involved themselves in city politics.

The absence of active parties and groups, and of citywide politics itself, constitutes a grave limitation on mayoral leadership. Additional limitations are provided by the structure and process of the city government.

THE LIMITS OF CITY HALL CONTROL. It is important at the outset to understand the jurisdictional limits of city government in Oakland. For only a few of the problem areas that we usually associate with the "urban crisis" are directly under the control of the city council and city manager. The school system, for example, is completely independent of city hall, except for the provision that the city council may pass a 5 per cent "emergency tax" for the schools. Another powerful independent body is the Oakland Board of Port Commissioners, which has exclusive control over management of the massive Port of Oakland.

Although redevelopment and housing have been two of the most controversial policy areas in Oakland, the commissions that have jurisdiction in these areas are the autonomous Redevelopment Agency and Housing Authority. These two organizations have had strained relations with each other, as well as with the city government.

Finally, the local poverty agency, the Oakland Economic Development Council, Inc., has been militantly independent of city hall since 1967. This agency operates a host of OEO programs, as well as the Department of Labor's Concentrated Employment Program.

The implications of fragmentation for mayoral leadership are fairly serious. Without jurisdiction, a mayor may be powerless to control outcomes in policy areas which are important to him. In Oakland, the mayor has been disturbed both by the slow pace of renewal and by the lack of relocation opportunities caused by the slowness of progress in public housing. But he has encountered difficulties in communicating with the two autonomous agencies involved, let alone in forging a bond of cooperation between them. Although a charter revision in 1968 brought the parks, recreation, library, and museum commissions more closely under city hall's control, the critical agencies discussed above remained autonomous.

Now that we have considered some of those governmental bodies which are outside city hall, let us look more closely at the inside of city government itself.

THE SEPARATION OF POLITICS FROM ADMINISTRATION. In a seminal article which first appeared in 1887, Woodrow Wilson declared that "administration lies outside the proper sphere of *politics*. Administrative questions are not political questions. Although politics sets the tasks for administration, it should not be suffered to manipulate its offices."[6] Politicians should set policy, and scientific administrators should carry it out. This separation of politics from administration, a hallmark of the Progressive era in American politics, lies at the root of the council-manager

[6] Woodrow Wilson, "The Study of Administration," reprinted in *Political Science Quarterly*, **56** (December 1941), 494.

form of government. In Oakland, according to the city charter: "The Council shall be vested with all powers of legislation." The charter goes on to state, however, that the council "shall have no administrative powers."[7] These are reserved for the city manager, who has "administrative" power over city government departments—police, fire, street and engineering, parks, recreation, and so on.

As for the mayor, who is a member of the council, the charter makes his duties sound impressive:

> The Mayor shall be the chief elective officer of the City, responsible for providing leadership and taking issues to the people and marshalling public interest in and support for municipal activity. He shall recommend to the Council such legislation as he deems necessary and shall encourage programs for the physical, economic, social and cultural development of the City. He shall preside over meetings of the Council, shall be the ceremonial head of the City, and shall represent the City in intergovernmental relations as directed by the Council.[8]

In theory, the mayor leads public opinion, the council formulates policy, and the manager carries it out. But in practice, the relationship between politics and administration in Oakland is strongly affected by the personalities of the men holding city offices and by the wide disparity in the levels of resources available to the politicians on the one hand and the administrators on the other.

An examination of comparative resources helps to explain why there is a strong tendency in Oakland for administration to devour politics—for the mayor and council to follow the manager's lead in the policy-making process. Councilmen, who earn $3600 annually from the city and the mayor, who is paid $7500, find it financially difficult to spend much time at their jobs; the manager's annual salary of $38,940 permits him to do so. The entire city council is served by one secretary, and the mayor is not much better off with three secretaries and an administrative assistant. But the city manager, besides having three full-time staff assistants, is able to utilize the manpower and informational resources of all city departments under his control. As a result, the city manager tends to know more than anyone else about city government structure, processes, and substantive policy.

A potential monopoly on staff and informational resources is not, however, the only reason for city manager domination of the Oakland governmental process at the present time: Jerome Keithley, the current city manager, is a man who is unusually adept at dealing with the internal environment of city government. The city council's power to fire the city manager gives councilmen an ultimate trump card to play against the man-

[7] *Oakland City Charter,* Sec. 207.

[8] *Oakland City Charter,* Sec. 219.

ager, but Keithley's performance in his job has gained him the solid and enthusiastic support of the council. There are a number of reasons for this support.

First of all, Keithley shares the views of most councilmen about what the goals of city administration should be: efficiency, cost cutting, and thus lower taxes. The city manager defines his role as an inside administrator, avoiding ambitious social programs. Secondly, City Manager Keithley uses his access to departmental records to satisfy as quickly as possible councilmen's requests for information. And he permits councilmen to make decisions in areas in which they are particularly interested. For example, the city manager allows the council to have jurisdiction over the budget for "civic organizations" such as the Chamber of Commerce, the Elks Club, the Italian-American Federation, and the California Spring Garden and Home Show Committee. Finally, Keithley builds support on the council by being "one of the guys." He is a regular attender at city council dinners and at ball games at the Coliseum—events that the mayor often avoids.

Armed with his considerable advantages, the city manager defines "policy" and "administration" in such a way that "administration" turns out to bulk very large and "policy" very small. When Mayor Reading complained in July 1968 that the police chief's stringent restrictions on policemen's use of guns (a decision in which the city manager had concurred but about which the mayor had never been consulted) constituted a dangerous policy decision which should be overturned by the council, the city manager disagreed. The manager's reasoning was clear: "A policy decision would be that policemen in Oakland should carry guns. Administrative decisions would be when they should carry guns, where they should carry guns, and how they should use those guns."

The city manager's definition of policy and administration is usually supported by the city attorney, Edward Goggin, who is appointed by the council but who takes his lead from the city manager. Goggin has a penchant for defining the area of permissible action by the city government as extremely narrow; within the government, Goggin tends to rule against city council jurisdiction. When the mayor sought to investigate his supposed new powers under the Green Amendment to the poverty program, the city attorney advised him that the amendment—which allows city governments to take control of poverty programs—could not apply to Oakland. For the legislation provided that, in taking over the new jurisdiction, a city council would administer the program. And Goggin pointed out that the Oakland City Charter specifically prohibits the council from exercising administrative power.

THE TYPICALITY OF OAKLAND'S GOVERNMENTAL SYSTEM AND ELECTORAL RULES. Table 1 shows the form of city government for cities with more than 5000 population. For cities in Oakland's population

TABLE 1 *Form of Government in Cities Over 5,000 Population*

Population group	No. of cities reporting	Mayor-council		Council manager		Commission	
		No.	%	No.	%	No.	%
More than 500,000	27	22	81.5	5	18.5	—	—
250,000 to 500,000	27	11	40.7	13	48.2	3	11.1
100,000 to 250,000	93	33	35.5	50	53.8	10	10.7
50,000 to 100,000	215	83	38.6	116	54.0	16	7.4
25,000 to 50,000	439	166	38.2	233	53.6	40	9.2
10,000 to 25,000	1072	511	47.7	488	45.5	73	6.8
5,000 to 10,000	1112	686	61.7	378	34.0	48	4.3

Source: *The Municipal Year Book, 1968* (Washington, D.C.: International City Managers' Association), p. 54.

group (250,000–500,000), the council-manager system is the most popular form of government. This plan is particularly prevalent in states along the Pacific coast; 84.3 per cent of the cities (above 5000) in those states have adopted the council-manager plan.

As to electoral rules, Oakland's nonpartisan form of local elections is widely used by cities in its population group; 76 per cent of cities in that range do not list parties on the ballot. But in another respect, Oakland's electoral system is unique. Seven of the city's nine councilmen must reside in and run for office from particular geographical districts; one councilman may reside anywhere in the city; and the mayor, who may live anywhere in the city, is elected separately. But each council seat is voted on by the city at large. Oakland is the only city in its (250,000–500,000) population group to "nominate by wards and at large, elect at large."

THE CITY COUNCIL. The segment of the political environment closest to the mayor is the city council, of which he is a member. And the council is a critical element affecting the mayor's ability to exercise leadership. For if the mayor could persuade four councilmen to go along with him, he could direct the city manager and attorney to follow his policy leadership—or he could fire the city manager and hire a new man who would work toward his goals.

City council recruitment has not been closely linked to elections. "Appointment politics" has become a tradition in Oakland; of the present members of the council, 6 were originally appointed, and only 3 were elected. Table 2 shows that this pattern of council recruitment has been a popular one in the city.

Once on the council, incumbents tend to be able to survive subsequent

TABLE 2 *Prevalence of Appointment Politics in Oakland, 1953–1968*

Office	Number of changes	Originally appointed	Originally elected
Mayor	2	1	1
Councilman	17	9	8

Source: Oakland Citizens for Responsive Government, "Effect of Appointments Upon the Oakland Governmental Structure" (pamphlet published in June, 1969).

elections with ease. In the past 16 years, no "appointed incumbent" has lost the ensuing election. Overall, in the period between the spring elections of 1953 through the spring elections of 1969, only a handful of incumbents have lost. Table 3 shows the enviable electoral record of Oakland's incumbents.

Official city council meetings take place on Tuesday evenings and Thursday mornings, but most decisions are made at special "work sessions" before the council meetings—in the mayor's office on Thursdays and over dinner on Tuesday's. Although citizens' groups and the press have raised pointed questions about the secrecy of such meetings, both the mayor and council have felt that they can be more honest with each other at such sessions and also be shielded from pressure. The model of mayoral leadership specifies that the mayor must direct both the council and public groups, but the conflicts over secrecy have shown that it may be difficult to do both at the same time. For the mayor is well aware that closed meetings facilitate informal discussion and the forging of agreement among council members, but the nonpublic nature of those meetings makes it difficult to

TABLE 3 *Success of Incumbents in Oakland Politics, 1953–1969*

Office	Number of incumbents' campaigns	Number of incumbents' victories	Number of incumbents' defeats
Mayor	6	5	1
Councilman	34	29*	5

Source: Oakland Citizens for Responsive Government.

* 12 of these were unopposed.

generate either interest in or support for city policies among Oakland citizens.

RESPONSES TO CONFLICT: THE "SHRINKING VIOLET" OR "RETRENCHMENT" SYNDROME. On the whole, the social and political attitudes of the councilmen tend to be conservative; these men are distrustful of governmental action in social areas and disturbed by the growing militancy of black people. At times, the council seems to pretend that Oakland's problems do not exist. In July, 1968, the Coordinating Community Council (made up of 16 school-community councils) asked the city council to levy a 5 cent emergency tax to lease portable classrooms, so that 19 elementary schools could eliminate double sessions. The chairman of the council's Ways and Means Committee admitted that the city council had the right to levy such a tax, but he noted that "what constitutes an emergency is a matter of opinion." He pointed out that, historically, an emergency in the schools had meant a "fire or catastrophe." Overcrowding and double sessions were not in that category, and the council did not accede to the request.[9]

If there is one thing that Oakland city councilmen do not like, it is conflict. And they have become adept at conflict avoidance, a process which is discussed in the literature of organization theory. Anthony Downs describes the "shrinking violet syndrome," in which a bureau avoids conflict by narrowing its actions and affecting fewer external agents.[10] And Matthew Holden, Jr., in an article on "'Imperialism' in Bureaucracy," states:

> Perhaps the most neglected cases are those in which there is a clear disposition toward retrenchment or self-limitation. It is not merely that the agency adopts kid-glove tactics in order to maintain a cooperative relationship with a constituency, but that it actually denies its powers.[11]

In order to avoid the conflict, uncertainty, and turbulence of a hostile urban environment, the Oakland City Council goes beyond merely narrowing its actions and denying its powers. Indeed, the council follows a consistent policy of actively giving up jurisdiction in areas which it considers troublesome. After turning down the mayor's proposal to appoint an ombudsman for the city in 1967, the council hit upon a painless way to solve the problem of citizens' grievances. For the low price of $10,000, the

[9] *The Montclarion* (Oakland neighborhood newspaper), July 24, 1968.

[10] Anthony Downs, *Inside Bureaucracy* (Boston: Little, Brown and Company, 1967), p. 217.

[11] Matthew Holden, Jr., "'Imperialism' in Bureaucracy," *American Political Science Review,* **60** (December 1966), 945.

city was able to enter into an agreement with Alameda County whereby the county's (powerless) Human Relations Commission would add another member to its staff—with that member concentrating his efforts in Oakland. The city government was able to avoid responsibility for setting up grievance procedures; restrictions on the county commission's activity made it unlikely that any administrator would be embarrassed or threatened; and the cost to the city was only $10,000.

Avoidance of conflict should not be confused with passivity or openness to mayoral initiative. For some mayoral initiatives—for example, a move for greater control of the poverty program—would mean more conflict for council members. Furthermore, the council tends to resent any special privileges available to the mayor; council criticism of the mayor's staff has been common.

Even the mayor's own office in City Hall is not necessarily friendly terrain. When Mayor Reading discovered in the fall of 1967 that his receptionist was openly critical of him and his policies, the mayor decided to transfer her to another department. But the city manager, fearing the wrath of the employees' association, advised caution, and civil service moved slowly in arranging the transfer. It was not until the spring of 1969—a year and a half later—that the change was made.

Such an environment would test the mettle of any mayor. But what manner of man is John H. Reading? The next sections will examine Reading's personality and his use of resources. By comparing Reading's actions with those of his predecessor, John C. Houlihan, we can suggest how much difference personality makes in the Oakland mayor's office.

The Mayor Himself

John Reading's life has been marked by a number of significant successes. As an air force pilot in World War II, he rose to the rank of Lt. Colonel. As a businessman, he has greatly expanded his family's food processing business and has become one of the leading manufacturers of tamales in the country.

In 1961, Reading was appointed to the city council. Mayor Houlihan had noticed Reading's attendance at, and participation in, meetings concerned with various neighborhood and civic issues. Feeling that Reading's comments were sensible and that his enthusiasm for "civic involvement" was strong, Houlihan asked Reading if he would like to join the city council. Reading was reluctant at first, but he felt that his advocacy of civic involvement meant that he should take the responsibility. (The appointment of a man who was not active in party politics or political groups, but just an "interested citizen," is indicative of the nonpolitical, nonactive-group nature of the Oakland system.) In the spring of 1966, when Mayor Houlihan resigned in the wake of an embezzlement scandal arising out of his law practice, Reading was chosen by the council to be the new mayor. He was overwhelmingly reelected in 1967 and 1969.

A PRIVATE MAN IN A PUBLIC OFFICE. Discussing the "purist" style in American politics, Nelson Polsby and Aaron Wildavsky state that such a style "represents a virtually complete privatization of politics" in which

> the private conscience of the leader—rather than his public responsibilities—becomes the focal point of politics. Internal criteria—possession of, devotion to, and standing up for private principles—become the standards of political judgment. Constituents disappear, and we are left with a political leader determining policy on the basis of compatibility with his private principles.[12]

In John Reading's view standards of conduct which are applicable to man's behavior in private life, embodying values of truthfulness, etiquette, and respect, should be applicable to the public sphere. If absolute openness is desirable in private life, then it is also desirable in politics. When a black community leader agreed with Mayor Reading on certain issues in private and then attacked the mayor in a public meeting before a black constituency, the mayor felt constrained to remind the community leader—publicly—of all he had said in private meetings. After all, reasoned the mayor, there should be no dividing line between private and public.

Mayor Reading finds himself facing a fundamental dilemma: He is a political leader who does not like politics. Talking about his experience at the University of California and afterward, the mayor once remarked: "I was never interested in political science, or any aspect of the political arena at all. But I am interested in business and modern management techniques—you know, span of control and that kind of thing. I wanted to put business management in practice in government." But the going has not been easy; Reading confessed that "as mayor, I've found that there isn't enough information or control to run government like a business. All we can do is just muddle through." [13]

THE CONSEQUENCES OF A BUSINESSMAN'S APPROACH TO POLITICS. Mayor Reading's attempt to bring private and business standards into politics has had a number of consequences for his behavior as mayor. First of all, this approach has led him to try to simplify politics, to make governmental action clearer and more rational. He has consistently

[12] Nelson W. Polsby and Aaron Wildavsky, *Presidential Elections* (New York: Charles Scribner's Sons, 1968), p. 180.

[13] Informal remarks at meeting of San Francisco Bay Area Chapter of the American Society for Public Administration, Oakland, October 5, 1967.

argued for the formation of "superagencies" within the city government, which could "coordinate" the tasks of existing departments. Reading talks about coordination as a technical exercise; a more public mayor might recognize that, when different organizations have different preferences, "coordination" between them might mean that one wins and the other loses.

A second consequence of the mayor's private-business approach is his tendency to define public problems in economic terms:

> I am convinced that employment is a factor of economics much more than of civil rights. Granted there may be areas of discrimination directly or inadvertently and we should continue breaking barriers, urging realistic employment standards and emphasizing full opportunity. But in my experience many of the unemployed are just not adequately prepared to take advantage of those opportunities.[14]

In the mayor's view, education and employment, not political organizing, are the keys to ending poverty.

Another outgrowth of the mayor's private attitude to politics is his tendency to deal with political problems in a moralistic way. People who take nonmoral social actions should be punished for them. When City Manager Keithley discussed the possibility in 1969 of levying a bar drinker's tax to help pay the costs of additional policemen, the mayor responded: "That's only fair. This links the issues nicely! People who drink at bars should bear the costs for protection from crime."

On law and order the mayor is uncompromising. Responding harshly to demands for decentralization and community control of the Oakland Police Department, Mayor Reading declared:

> Some persons . . . talk of harassment and brutality by policemen who are sworn to defend and protect this community with their lives. They call for creation of locally elected police control commissions which would be empowered to patrol and control the police. What they really are asking is the elimination of the police, for the proponents of this plan obviously advocate anarchy.[15]

Although the mayor often defends the status quo, it should not be thought that he is insensitive to individuals' grievances against the government. In fact, his private-business orientation has led him to be suspicious of unrestrained governmental power. In an effort to protect individual rights, he has fought—unsuccessfully—for an ombudsman plan in Oakland.

[14] Remarks before U.S. Civil Rights Commission, May 6, 1967.
[15] Remarks at Oakland City Council Meeting, April 23, 1968.

RESPONSES TO CONFLICT. Like the city council, Mayor Reading dislikes conflict. "I'm thankful that there's no dissent on our council. When you look at Berkeley, there are enormous divisions." The question that naturally arises is why a man who operates so successfully in the competitive world of business finds it difficult to deal with conflict in politics. A possible explanation is that Reading's success in his food business has been caused in great part by his discovery of a method of manufacturing tamales that was significantly cheaper than his competitors'. Thus, he won a technological competition, not a conflictful interpersonal one.

Recognizing that differences of opinion do exist in public life, Mayor Reading tries to deal with them by using what might be called the "big round table" method. He believes that if people could just get together on a personal level, around a table, and talk over their differences, then everything could be settled. But a "public" mayor, one who wishes to exercise leadership in accordance with the model outlined in the first section, might have much to gain from a different view: a recognition of the fact that conflicts exist and may be taken advantage of by leaders. McFarland[16] views leadership in a pluralist system as an individual's response to multilateral conflict. When conflict increases, set expectations break down and the environment may be manipulated by the leader. A mayor may serve as mediator between conflicting groups; he may seek to "upgrade the common interest" (as Mayor Lee did in New Haven by creating an urban renewal program that unified otherwise conflicting interests); or he may take advantage of a conflict situation to support the party with whom he agrees. All of these strategies are impossible if the mayor does not recognize, face, and deal with conflict situations.

The problem of current city politics, according to Mayor Reading, is that certain groups—most notably black militants—will not agree to set aside their own selfish interests and work for the community interest. And the losers are inevitably the "large, inactive majority . . . who would like to see real, lasting, and reasonable solutions to our problems." These people "go about their business, raise their family, take their tax lumps" and are currently "taking a back seat" to the militants in public dialogue.[17] The mayor has particular sympathy for Oakland's old people, who are living on fixed incomes and worried by crime.

Confrontation politics, with threats, demands, and insults—which Reading felt as personal attacks—took a tremendous toll on the mayor during disputes about the poverty program, police, and model cities in 1968. Depressed, he tentatively decided not to seek re-election in 1969. But the passage of a new charter, the election of fellow-Republican Richard Nixon

16 McFarland, *Power and Leadership . . .*, pp. 177 ff.

17 Mayor's Inaugural Address, July 1, 1969.

to the Presidency, and, perhaps most important, "a look at the alternative candidates" convinced the mayor to run again. Civic responsibility had once again overcome personal predilection.

Now we must ask what Reading can do as mayor, and what a different kind of man might do in this difficult governmental and political structure.

RESOURCES. As we have seen, students of mayoral leadership have focused on the wise use and "pyramiding" of resources as ways in which an urban political leader can gain power. Dahl notes that

> Although the kinds and amounts of resources available to political man are always limited and at any given moment fixed, they are not . . . permanently fixed as to either kind or amount. Political man can use his resources to gain influence, and he can then use his influence to gain more resources. Political resources can be pyramided in much the same way that a man who starts out in business sometimes pyramids a small investment into a large corporate empire.[18]

Oakland seems to offer few opportunities for a mayor to pyramid political holdings. But a mayor of Oakland does have some resources, or at least potential resources. They are:

(1) *The mayor's position as president of the city council:* As mayor, Reading presides over public council meetings and private "work sessions." He also appoints council committees. Thus, he has an opportunity to exert a strong influence on the subjects that come up before the council and the ways in which they are discussed and decided.

Former Mayor Houlihan—an outspoken, gregarious lawyer who loves politics—enjoyed this power and exploited it. A careful counter of council votes, he set about to secure outcomes favorable to himself. Houlihan often dispensed favors to friendly councilmen; for example, he gave certain members of the council the opportunity to borrow the mayor's limousine. Once, in order to please a councilman whose chief interest lay in an airport golf course, the mayor created a Golf Course Committee and made the councilman its chairman and only member.

Unlike City Manager Keithley, who uses informal council gatherings to strengthen his position with that body, Mayor Reading avoids council dinners and trips with councilmen to ball games. He appoints council committees on the basis of interest and expertise, and he makes little attempt to influence their deliberations. The mayor is generous in his regulation of the council agenda. At a 1969 work session, Reading told the council that "committees should speak up when they have a report. I've heard com-

[18] Dahl, *Who Governs?* p. 227.

plaints that I haven't notified committees that they may give reports, but it's your initiative, and any time you have a report, just speak up." In sharp contrast, Mayor Houlihan's practice was to give councilmen specific assignments and call upon them for reports.

Further complicating the mayor's task in leading the council is his unwillingness to count votes and to persuade councilmen to see things his way. That would be "pressuring," an activity the mayor does not regard as legitimate. Though Mayor Reading enjoys considerable respect on the part of the council, his failure to influence committee work, control the agenda, and employ persuasion have led him to an underutilization of the political resource of his city council leadership.

(2) *Power appointment:* The mayor appoints (with the approval of a majority of the council) members of city boards and commissions—including the Housing Authority, Redevelopment Agency, and Port. But Reading has often appointed people he likes and admires personally—only to find out after their appointment that they do not share his policy preferences. And the mayor's unwillingness to "pressure" the city council has also restricted his influence in the appointment process. In July of 1968, the council refused to approve the mayor's reappointment of two members of the Planning Commission—one of them the chairman. At the same time, the mayor's move to replace an anti-Reading councilman's business associate as head of the Housing Authority failed when the man simply refused to leave his post and was backed up by some councilmen. In neither of these cases was Mayor Reading willing to fight on the council or in the newspapers for his appointments.

(3) *Prestige:* Describing the success of Mayor Lee of New Haven, Dahl shows how the mayor was able to use his personal popularity and prestige to extract concessions from political and business leaders.[19] Richard Neustadt says that "popular prestige" in the form of "public standing" is a source of influence for a President in his dealings with people in Washington. This is because political actors depend on the public for votes and support.[20]

Mayor Reading has had an enviable electoral record—amassing more than 80 per cent of the vote in 1967 and more than 63 per cent in 1969. The prestige that results from electoral success in the city's highest elective office might be turned into an important resource; Mayor Lee was certainly able to capitalize on his success at the polls. But in Oakland, the lack of interest in electoral politics renders this resource much less useful. Mayor Reading has been able to use the prestige of his office in certain instances:

[19] *Who Governs?* p. 309.

[20] Richard Neustadt, *Presidential Power* (New York: John Wiley and Sons, Inc., 1960), pp. 86 ff.

in organizing business leaders into a campaign for a school tax, in promoting support for a downtown hotel and convention center, and in leading the campaign for a new charter. But on the whole, the mayor has tended to underutilize this potential resource. For the existence of prestige without the willingness to use the next named resource, publicity, may not be sufficient to accomplish mayoral goals.

(4) *Publicity:* In a discussion of protest groups, Michael Lipsky has demonstrated how important publicity is to "low resource" political actors:

> The communications media are extremely powerful in city politics. In granting or withholding publicity, in determining what information most people will have on most issues, and what alternatives they will consider in response to issues, the media truly, as Norton Long has put it, "set . . . the civic agenda." Like the tree falling unheard in the forest, there is no protest unless protest is perceived and projected.[21]

Like Lipsky's protest groups, Mayor Reading lacks adequate money, staff, and organizational foundation. But he has certain important advantages: widespread respect, the forum of city hall, and a friendly newspaper in the *Oakland Tribune*.

These advantages are not useful unless capitalized upon, and the mayor's essentially private nature and preference for quiet, rational discussion make him less than eager to take his case on public matters to the people through the news media. In May 1969, when the school board disregarded its own biracial citizens' screening committee in selecting a new superintendent (who turned out to be involved in a conflict-of-interest case elsewhere), the community was in an uproar. Sensing public outrage, the mayor sought to persuade the board to cancel an upcoming school tax election and to initiate immediate negotiations with community groups to try to rectify the situaton. Although he was just one vote short, in a secret meeting, of influencing the school board to take his advice, the mayor adamantly refused to put the board on the spot by making any sort of public statement. The tax election ended in overwhelming defeat, and the mayor lost a golden opportunity to appear as a successful mediator.

Publicity is a resource which is not severely limited by considerations of formal structure and jurisdiction, and an enterprising mayor can make good use of the media. Mayor Houlihan had a 10-minute weekly radio program, through which he told listeners about his activities and current governmental issues in Oakland. When the city council refused to endorse a bond issue for Bay Area Rapid Transit, Houlihan came out publicly for

[21] Michael Lipsky, "Protest as a Political Resource," *American Political Science Review*, **62** (December 1968), 1151.

the issue anyway. The bond campaign was successful in a close election; a switch of 2,000 votes in Oakland would have defeated the issue. In this resource area, a "public" personality can make a difference.

UNDERUTILIZATION AND DISPERSION OF RESOURCES. Operating in a low resource environment, Mayor Reading has tended to underutilize the political resources he has. For example, the mayor's failure to use persuasion has caused him to gain less than full advantage from his role as president of the council. Instead of pyramiding resources, he often appears to be engaged in *resource dispersion,* failing to combine his resources with each other. Thus, his power of appointment has been blocked by his failure to lead the council and to use publicity; and the mayor's personal prestige has been underutilized because of his unwillingness to take issues to the public. Except for occasional pronouncements on law and order, the mayor's private style has led him to avoid the public spotlight. For a low resource political actor who enjoys considerable personal respect, such avoidance seems unwise.

PERSONAL OPPORTUNITIES IN SPITE OF STRUCTURE. Although governmental and political structures set limits on what any mayor can do, personality can make a difference. On the basis of Mayor Houlihan's experience and studies of successful leadership elsewhere, we can suggest some of the ways in which a more politically oriented mayor might use his leadership resources in Oakland. In *The Washington Community 1800–1828,* James S. Young describes a situation in the nation's capital at that time which appears remarkably similar to that in Oakland today: a lack of active groups; fragmented social subgroups formed around separate branches of government with a few integrating forces; weak congressional parties; an anti-political ideology, even among politicians; and an absence of presidental staff. Here, according to Young, the personality of the President made a difference. For "the President had to improvise out of wit and ingenuity, as his political talents, circumstances, statutes and good fortune permitted." [22] During the period studied, only Jefferson was successful enough at "statecraft" to be able to provide leadership. He utilized a combination of "social lobbying" (mainly intimate White House dinners), personal persuasion, and the newspaper forum provided by a publisher who was a friend of the President's.

A mayor of Oakland can also use "social lobbying" and personal persuasion as techniques to influence councilmen to follow his leadership. Mayor Houlihan, as we have seen, delighted in providing special favors for friendly councilmen, and City Manager Keithley uses dinners and sports

[22] New York: Columbia University Press, 1966.

events to good advantage. Social lobbying is not an activity Mayor Reading enjoys, and his distaste for "pressuring" councilmen leads him to avoid attempts at persuasion. But if the mayor did control a majority on the council, he could then direct the work of the city manager and attorney. When Mayor Houlihan was involved in drawing up a contract for Oakland participation in building the Coliseum Complex, he had the city attorney deliver legal opinions which supported the mayor's preferences.

Just as Jefferson used a friendly newspaper to present his program, so Houlihan used a radio program to publicize his point of view. When he could not get the council to go along with him—as in supporting rapid transit bonds—he took his case to the people. And when city resources are inadequate, a mayor can try to persuade outside bodies to help. Thus, Mayor Houlihan was able to convince the Alameda County Supervisors to grant $350,000 from county highway funds to build a tunnel under the new Oakland museum.

Faced with a lack of groups in the political environment, a mayor can act to stimulate the creation of groups. When Mills College trustees informed Mayor Houlihan that construction of the potentially noisy MacArthur Freeway would force the college out of Oakland, the mayor decided to forestall the college's move by seeking a ban on truck traffic on that freeway. He formed a citizens' committee to support such a ban and joined them in pressing the case in the state capital. The state government decided to ban trucks; Mills stayed in Oakland.

Although mayors in Oakland are limited both by governmental structure and political disorganization, there are still opportunities for an inventive political man to make the most of the situation—by social lobbying, persuasion, publicity, and the creation of groups which will support him. But, as James Young has noted, all this requires adroitness, ingenuity, and political expertise. Even given Oakland's constraining structure, personality can make a difference.

American cities are unlikely to find their revenue constraints greatly eased in the near future, and the jurisdictional fragmentation about which so many mayors complain is not likely to disappear. Thus, the techniques of low resource leadership described here appear to have wide applicability.

Conclusion: Mayoral Leadership and the Political System

Although calls for "mayoral leadership" fill the literature on city politics, an understanding of such leadership in any given city requires an examination of the political environment, the personalities involved, and the ways in which the mayor uses the resources available to him.

It is clear that the leadership exercised by Mayor John Reading of

Oakland does not closely approximate the model of leadership described in Section I—the model of a mayor who sets goals and then uses a wide variety of means to influence others to act according to the mayor's own preferences. This is due both to environmental and personal factors.

The introductory section listed seven environmental requirements for effective mayoral leadership, and it is obvious that the Oakland governmental and political structure provides little comfort for any mayor. Like most cities, Oakland faces a revenue strain and rising personnel costs—which means that it does not have (a) *sufficient financial resources* with which a mayor can launch innovative social programs. Nor does the city have (b) *jurisdiction* in the vital program areas of education, housing, redevelopment, and job training. Under the council-manager form of government, there are severe limits to (c) *mayoral jurisdiction within the city government.* And the mayor had neither (d) sufficient *salary* ($7500 per year) nor (e) adequate *staff* (one administrative assistant and three secretaries) to perform as a full time and well-informed official.

Although Oakland provides the mayor with (f) *a ready vehicle of publicity* in the *Oakland Tribune,* the rest of the political environment offers him little comfort. There are few (g) *politically-oriented groups* which can provide support for a mayoral program.

Without governmental jurisdiction, staff, and financial resources, it is hard for any mayor to direct, or even influence, the actions of others. But it is not true that mayoral leadership is impossible in Oakland. For the mayor does have certain resources (position as presiding officer; power of appointment; prestige; legitimacy), and an adept political man can pyramid those resources. John Houlihan, a man who enjoyed the turbulence of the public arena, was able to build on his meager mayoral resources. But John Reading, a private man with a distaste for conflict and a preference for private discussion, has consistently underutilized his political resources. In Oakland, a mayor's lot is not a happy one, but it is not a hopeless one, either.

As in other cities, the mayor of Oakland is in large measure the product of the political system. The nature of that system has a significant influence on the kinds of people who become mayor and the forms of leadership they can exercise. In the nongroup, nonpartisan, and nonelectoral political system of Oakland, it is entirely possible for a "nonpolitical" civic reformer like John Reading to attain the position of mayor without really trying for it. No groups, parties, or politicians could make an effective claim on the office. Even John Houlihan, who stands out among recent Oakland mayors as an ambitious politician, was promoted for the office by a loose coalition of citizens' groups representing many political views. Although Houlihan sought to be a full time mayor, the low salary forced him into deep financial trouble and hence led to his eventual downfall. Thus, the Oakland governmental system may be said to have penalized him for trying to exert sustained leadership.

In a governmental system in which a mayor lacks administrative authority, the leadership most often possible is hortatory in nature (encouraging voters to pass a bond issue, charter reform, etc.). And in a political system which is relatively amorphous, such leadership can also run the risk of being unconnected to public opinion. The lack of organized groups and parties deprives the mayor not only of potential support; it deprives him of information as well. As a result, mayoral leadership can be sharply divorced from the policy preferences of relevant constituencies. In the spring of 1970, when Mayor Reading suggested that National Guard troops be called to operate buses in the midst of a tension-filled transit strike, his proposal was sharply criticized by *both* labor and management.

It is important to recognize that hortatory leadership need not necessarily be an isolated public speaking exercise. If a political system contains active groups to whom a mayor can appeal and from whom he can gain information, then the mayor can urge those groups to help him in influencing others. Thus, the extent to which public exhortation can be used to supplement meager financial and jurisdictional resources will depend in part on the structuring of the mayor's audience.

Election campaigns can provide political actors an opportunity to appeal to the public. But if electoral competition is nonexistent, there is no incentive for groups of councilmen to join together in framing a program. If no boats are rocked, then no competition may surface. Contested elections, which can have the effect of defining alternatives and building support for those alternatives, might provide both a start and a direction for the victors.

Of course, a lack of leadership in the mayor's office does not mean that no leadership is being exerted in the urban political system. In Oakland, the city manager has certainly been a leader within the city bureaucracy. And the weakness of elected officials has doubtless helped Oakland's ghetto residents to increase their control over federal poverty programs and model cities programs. But leadership exerted by elected officials differs from that of city managers and poverty program administrators in being potentially subject to popular review at regular intervals. Although the absence of groups, parties, and electoral competition can severely limit the effectiveness of that review and dilute the influence of citizens on the government, the potential for popular control is not trivial. For elections can provide a vehicle for mobilizing the resource of numbers against other resources such as money or social standing or control of communications media. The lack of power on the part of elected officials may lead to greater power for those who presently hold these other resources.

A city manager or program administrator may be responsive to citizens' preferences because he deems it to be a wise policy to act in such a manner. But under conditions of electoral competition, an elected official has a more direct incentive to pay attention to public concerns. Furthermore, there is evidence that Americans *expect* their local elected leaders to be more responsive than nonelected administrators are. As Almond and Verba have shown, Americans—unlike Germans, Italians, or Mexicans—are much more likely to contact elected political leaders than administrators if they wish to influence their local government.[23]

Because of their visibility, and the expectation that they might stimulate and respond to the concerns of urban constituencies, mayors have been a natural focus of those who study political leadership in cities. Mayors who can exert leadership by successfully pyramiding political resources are to be admired, but the ability to pyramid resources is by no means universal. Furthermore, it is often the case that people—even those in public office—try to avoid the exercise of power. Oakland officials are not unique in their avoidance behavior. Young's study of the early Washington community shows a group of men at the pinnacle of national politics who had a strong distaste for power.[24] And William K. Muir has pointed out that policemen, reacting to their hostile environment and the potential costs of decisive action, often devise ways of escaping the exercise of power.[25]

Clearly, there is no substantial variability in opportunities for leadership and in public actors' willingness to exercise it. Therefore, we must continue to search for the preconditions of leadership. How do alternative governmental structures influence the ability of officials to direct policy? What personal characteristics are most strongly related to the ability—and the desire—to pyramid resources successfully? Finally, because the opportunities for leadership appear to be closely linked to characteristics of the political system, we should try to discover those factors that encourage—or inhibit—the building of politically interested groups in cities. We also need to know more about the kinds of leadership that are possible in low resource, unstructured political arenas. Only through an analysis of these environmental and personal factors can we understand the constraints on—and potential for—urban political leadership.

[23] Gabriel Almond and Sidney Verba, *The Civil Culture* (Boston: Little, Brown and Company, 1965), p. 148.

[24] Young, *The Washington Community.*

[25] William K. Muir, Jr., "The Development of Policemen" (Paper delivered at annual meeting of the American Political Science Association, Los Angeles, 1970).

SUGGESTED READINGS

Policy Making at the Urban Level

In recent years, few problems in American government have been given as much attention as the so-called "urban crisis," a catch-all term for a whole complex of issues involving the inadequacy of current welfare and public housing programs, the prevalence of racial tension, the rising crime rate, the urban transportation snarl, and many others. Naturally, the growing concern over the problems of the cities has focused increased attention on the institutions and policies of government in urban areas.

THE URBAN CRISIS: AN OVERVIEW

It has become increasingly difficult to separate analysis of urban policy making from the feeling of deep crisis and impending disaster in the condition of major American urban areas. Running counter to the crisis literature, Edward C. Banfield, in *The Unheavenly City* (Boston: Little, Brown, 1970), holds that the problems of cities, with the exception of the troubles of urban poor, have been much exaggerated. For a critical review of this very controversial book, see "The Unheavenly City: A Review Symposium," *Social Science Quarterly,* **51** (March 1971), 817–859.

For a comprehensive textbook approach to the government and problems of cities, see John H. Baker's *Urban Politics in America* (New York: Scribner, 1971); John C. Bollens and Henry J. Schmandt, *The Metropolis,* 2nd ed. (New York: Harper & Row, 1970); and Charles R. Adrian and Charles Press, *Governing Urban America,* 4th ed. (New York: McGraw-Hill, 1972).

The following list is merely suggestive of the wide literature on urban politics and problems. Also refer to the bibliographic references for separate problem areas.

"The City of the Future: Conceptual Dynamics of Change," *American Behavioral Scientist,* **14** (July–August 1971), entire issue.

Committee for Economic Development. *Reshaping Government for Metropolitan Areas.* New York: Committee for Economic Development, 1970.

Donaldson, Scott. *The Suburban Myth.* New York: Columbia University Press, 1969.

Dye, Thomas R., and Brett W. Hawkins, eds. *Politics in the Metropolis,* 2nd ed. Columbus, Ohio: Merrill, 1971.

Green, Constance McLaughlin. *The Rise of Urban America.* New York: Harper & Row, 1965.

Greer, Scott. *The Urbane View: Life and Politics in Metropolitan America.* New York: Oxford University Press, 1972.

Hadden, Jeffrey K., Louis H. Masotti, and Calvin J. Larson, eds. *Metropolis in Crisis: Social and Political Perspectives,* 2nd ed. Itasca, Ill.: F. E. Peacock, 1971.

Hawkins, Brett W. *Politics and Urban Problems.* Indianapolis: Bobbs-Merrill, 1971.

Mumford, Lewis. *The City in History.* New York: Harcourt, Brace & World, 1961.

Schnore, Leo F. *The Urban Scene.* New York: Free Press, 1965.

Seashore, Stanley E., and Robert J. MacNeill. *Management of the Urban Crisis: Government and the Behavioral Sciences.* Riverside, N.J.: Free Press, 1971.

Vernon, Raymond. *The Myth and Reality of Our Urban Problems.* Cambridge, Mass.: Harvard University Press, 1962.

White, Morton, and Lucia Whik. *The Intellectual Versus the City.* Cambridge, Mass.: Harvard University and the MIT Press, 1964.

Wilburn, York. *The Withering Away of the City.* University, Ala.: University of Alabama Press, 1964.

Wirth, Lewis. "Urbanism as a Way of Life," *American Journal of Sociology,* **44** (July 1938), 1–24.

POLITICAL MACHINES

Apart from the extensive antimachine literature of city reformers, social scientists and political analysts have devoted much space attempting to account for the causes underlying the growth of urban machines, the nature of machine operations, and the future of political machines. A perceptive and personal account of Richard Daley's Democratic machine in Chicago is Michael Royko's *Boss: Richard J. Daley of Chicago* (New York: Dutton, 1971). For a theoretical approach to the operation of political machines, see Robert K. Merton's "The Functions of the Political Machine," in *Social Theory and Social Structure* (New York: Free Press, 1957), 71–82. In addition, James C. Scott's "Corruption, Machine Politics, and Political Change," *American Political Science Review,* **63** (December 1969), 1142–1158, provides an excellent comparative view of political machines, relating their operation to patterns of corruption in developing countries.

Banfield, Edward C. *Big City Politics.* New York: Random House, 1965.

Banfield, Edward C., and James Q. Wilson. *City Politics.* Cambridge, Mass.: Harvard University Press, 1963.

Dorsett, Lyle W. *The Pendergast Machine.* New York: Oxford University Press, 1968.

Gardiner, John A. *The Politics of Corruption.* New York: Russell Sage Foundation, 1970.

Greene, Lee S., ed. "City Bosses and Political Machines," *Annals of the American Academy of Political and Social Science,* **353** (May 1964), entire issue.

Greenstone, J. David, and Paul E. Peterson. "Reformers, Machines, and the War on Poverty," in James Z. Wilson, ed., *City Politics and Public Policy.* New York: John Wiley, 1968, 267–292.

Key, V. O., Jr. *The Techniques of Political Graft in the United States.* Chicago: University of Chicago Libraries, 1936.

Mandelbaum, Seymour J. *Boss Tweed's New York.* New York: Wiley, 1965.

Stave, Bruce M. *The New Deal and the Last Hurrah: Pittsburgh Machine Politics.* Pittsburgh: University of Pittsburgh Press, 1971.

Wolfinger, Raymond E. *The Politics of Progress.* Englewood Cliffs, N.J.: Prentice–Hall, 1972.

MAYORAL LEADERSHIP AND EXECUTIVE ADMINISTRATION

Social scientists have, so far, given very little systematic attention to the function of executives in city government. A good starting point, however, is Leonard I. Ruchelman, ed., *Big City Mayors: The Crisis in Urban Politics* (Bloomington: Indiana University Press, 1970). Also see Robert H. Salisbury's description of the role of mayors in directing urban development in "Urban Politics: The New Convergence of Power," *Journal of Politics,* **26** (November 1964), 775–777. William F. Buckley's witty account of his bid for mayor in New York City, *The Unmaking of a Mayor* (New York: Viking Press, 1966), is also the source of some insightful observations on the problems of a big city mayor.

In addition to the following works, refer to the bibliographical listing under "Political Machines."

Banovetz, James M., ed. *Managing the Modern City.* Washington: International City Management Association, 1971.

Blackwood, George. "Boston Politics and Boston Politicians," in Murray B. Levin, ed., *The Alienated Voter: Politics in Boston.* New York: Holt, Rinehart and Winston, 1960.

Bromage, Arthur W. *Urban Policy Making: The Council-Manager Partnership.* Chicago: Public Administration Service, 1970.

Farkas, Suzanne. *Urban Lobbying: Mayors in the Federal Arena.* New York: New York University Press, 1971.

Loveridge, Ronald O. *City Manager in Legislative Politics.* Indianapolis: Bobbs-Merrill, 1971.

Lowi, Theodore J. *At the Pleasure of the Mayor.* New York: Free Press, 1964.

Maier, Henry W. *Challenge to the Cities: An Approach to a Theory of Urban Leadership.* New York: Random House, 1966.

Sayre, Wallace S., and Herbert Kaufman. *Governing New York City.* New York: Russell Sage Foundation, 1960.

Talbot, Allan R. *The Mayor's Game, Richard Lee of New Haven and the Politics of Change.* New York: Praeger, 1967.

Part IV

Problems and Controversies

State and local governments were for long relatively inactive in terms of program activities, so that what problems and controversies arose in their operation were more political than anything else. The post–World War II era, however, has seen increasing demands placed on states and localities for a wide variety of services needed by the citizenry, so that currently the key issues in state and local government revolve around how to raise money to answer demands for services on the one hand and what areas of service demand priority action on the other. American government has never provided an even approach to the provision of services to the American people, and modern federalism does not guarantee equality any more than its earlier counterparts. The important issues in state and local policy thus vary from place to place across the country. The issues dealt with here, however, are universally encountered at the state and local policy-making level: financial resources are nowhere entirely adequate; problems of race intrude not only in the South but across the nation; issues in education, crime control, and environmental improvement are unfortunately ubiquitous. Thus the readings in Part IV touch upon the sensitive nerve ends of state and local policy generally in the United States.

Dick Netzer

Financing Urban Government

The problems of metropolitan areas are numerous and diverse, encompassing welfare, overburdened transportation systems, inadequate law enforcement, and troubled educational programs. If one issue could be considered overriding, it would almost certainly be the crisis in urban finance. Professor Netzer here examines urban finance in relation to other urban problems and with a view toward reform.

Few state or local governments are without fiscal problems. The rapid and virtually universal increase in public expenditures in the past two decades and the frequency and ubiquity of tax rate increases afford ample evidence of this. But the problems seem most severe for local governments serving the larger and older metropolitan areas of the country—say, the two dozen or so metropolitan areas with populations of more than one million and central city populations (usually) of more than 500,000, located mostly but not entirely in the northeast and midwest.

Their problems are more severe, despite the fact that much of the country's income and wealth is concentrated in such areas, in part because they operate with diverse and fragmented structures of local government. In part, their difficulties reflect the concentration of the urban poverty and race problems in the large old central cities. Also, the very fact of age creates problems associated with physical and functional obsolescence. In addition, there are difficulties stemming from extremely rapid growth rates on their urbanizing fringes.

The existence of these difficulties and the national interest in solving them have been recognized in various pieces of Great Society legislation enacted or proposed in the past few years. But these federal actions by no means solve all the local fiscal problems (nor should they be expected to). This analysis is addressed to the fiscal problems of the larger, older metropolitan areas, especially their central cities. It is not universal coverage, but it does encompass quite a large segment of our urban population and it does suggest something about the future prospects for some of the smaller and newer urban areas.

Some Recent Trends

In recent years, as throughout the twenty years following World War II, local (and state government) public expenditures have been increasing substantially more rapidly than has the nation's total output and income. Public expenditures in urban areas have always been significantly higher, in relative terms than those in nonurban areas and recently have been increasing slightly faster, in dollar terms, within the urban areas. This difference is to be expected, since nearly all the nation's population growth has been occurring in urban areas. But urban population growth alone does not explain the rate of increase in public spending. Indeed, the increase in *per capita* local government expenditures in metropoliton areas has been more rapid than the increase in *aggregate* gross national product.

What is perhaps most striking, public expenditures in the larger central cities have been climbing steeply, despite their losses or slow growth in population. In the most recent seven-year period for which data are available, expenditures of municipal governments in the larger cities rose by 45 per cent about two thirds as rapidly as expenditures of all other local governments combined. Consider the twelve largest metropolitan areas (1964 population over 1.8 million). In the eight-year period, 1957 to 1965, property tax revenues (used here as a partial proxy for local expenditures) rose by 86 per cent for these entire areas. In their portions, property tax revenues rose by 69 per cent.[1] But there has been little population growth in the central portions—less than half the rate of the entire areas between 1960 and 1964.

To be sure, substantially more external aid to central cities in the provision of public services has been forthcoming in recent years. State and federal aid to central city governments has risen considerably more rapidly than have central city expenditures. Also, the *direct* role of state governments in the provision of public services in and for the central cities has expanded considerably. Since the passage of the Interstate Highway Act in 1956, the states have been far more active in the construction of central city highways than previously. In a growing number of states, the state govern-

[1] "Central portions" are the counties that include the central cities. In five of the twelve areas, the "central portions" and central cities are substantially identical. In 1960, the central cities' population was 74 per cent of that of the "central portions."

ment is directly involved in urban mass transportation, in park and open space activities, and in housing programs. In some states in the northeast, expansion of state higher education programs has had an important effect on central city populations. But despite all this, the taxes imposed by central city governments, collected from static populations and slowly growing central city economies, continue to rise sharply.

The Purposes of Urban Government

The explanation for rising public expenditures in urban areas is not hard to find. In the central cities, local-tax-financed outlays for services directly linked to poverty (in the health and welfare fields) have not been static; the central cities of the twelve largest metropolitan areas account for an eighth of the country's population, but nearly 40 per cent of health and welfare outlays are financed from local taxes. For central city governments, the problems associated with poverty and race are by far the most urgent of public problems.

Neither poverty nor racial disabilities can be eliminated solely by governmental action, and still less by action by local or state and local governments combined (that is, governments other than the federal government). But local governments do have a major responsibility to grapple with these problems and can make a major contribution toward their alleviation. In the American system of government, it is local governments that are responsible for providing educational services that over time will have a major bearing on the chances of the poor and racially disadvantaged to overcome their disadvantages. Local governments are also responsible for a wide range of health and welfare services, which are almost entirely oriented toward the poor in American cities. They have had, since the late forties, major responsibilities in connection with the housing of the poor. And, as far as the poor are concerned, local government recreational facilities are about the only recreational facilities available.

A second major set of problems confronting the older central cities lies in the fact that they have a huge legacy of obsolescence. Their stock of housing and other social capital—that is, public and quasi-public facilities of all kinds—is old, often physically deteriorated, and generally far from competitive with the newer parts of the same urban areas. It may be, as some have argued, that the best national policy would be to allow this obsolescence to continue and allow further deterioration of the older parts of the older cities. In this case, population would decline in these sections and, presumably at some stage, values would be so low that private renewal of such areas would become possible. Or, if desirable, public renewal could be undertaken, but on the basis of exceedingly low values.

Developments in recent years suggest that this obsolescence policy is hardly a likely course of action. For one thing, there is the plight of those who, because they are poor, or Negro, or both, have little chance to escape the deteriorating areas. Amelioration, for these hundreds of thousands of people, is both politically and morally necessary. Quite apart from moral issues, most cities and the federal government appear to have decided that it is necessary to replace obsolete social capital and to compete for residents and businesses in an atmosphere of rising expectations. That is, the cities feel they must offer an environment of public facilities services that, together with other attractions that the central locations may have, will offset the blandishments of the newer and presumably more modern sections of the metropolitan areas where standards of public services and amenity are high indeed.

In the newer sections of metropolitan areas—the new portions of central cities as well as the urbanizing fringes of the metropolitan area—the main governmental problem is the provision of the new social capital needed by a rising population, and a population that has peculiarly heavy demands for public services and facilities, notably schools.

In the aggregate, these urban problems have resulted in a diversion of resources from private to public uses via tax increases. But this relative expansion of the public sector is costly in another way. If local governments are to command resources, they must pay prices for these resources that are competitive with those prevailing in the economy, notably salaries of public employees. If they are to expand *more rapidly* than the private sector, they must bid away resources by paying even more, which largely explains the rapid increase in urban government salary levels, especially for occupational groups whose talents are in heavy demand in the private sector.

Ideal Solutions

This catalog of governmental problems suggests something about the nature of the solutions. Assume for the moment that we are free to devise a structure of local government that is ideal from both an administrative and a financial standpoint.

First, consider the governmental fiscal problems associated with poverty and race. It seems clear that, in an ideal world, the financial burden of public services that exist primarily to cope with these problems would not rest on particular local governments with small geographic coverage. Poor people tend to be concentrated in the central cities of metropolitan areas for good reasons. The supply of housing that they can afford is in such places, the kinds of jobs to which their skills give them access tend also to be located in these sections, and the variety of social services they require tend to be available only in central cities. Indeed, it is probably in the national interest that the poor be concentrated in central cities, for it is rather unlikely that their needs would ever be sufficiently attended to were they not so conspicuous.

Another factor in the geographic location of the poor, and even more in the geographic location of those in racial minority groups, is national in character. This society is a very mobile one and over the years it has undergone rapid economic changes. There have been, in response to these economic changes, massive migrations of people from rural areas to urban areas, from central cities of urban areas to the suburbs, from the urban areas of the north and midwest to the southwest and west. No individual central city has been known to put up billboards advertising its attractions for the poor, trying to recruit them from other parts of the country. They have migrated to the cities in response to pressures in their older locations and attractions in the newer locations, but all these have been essentially national economic and social forces. Such being the case, it seems appropriate that the costs of attending to the needs of such people should be spread over a fairly wide geographic area. And because it is the economics or, rather, the economic prosperity of the larger metropolitan areas that have been the attraction for the poor and the disadvantaged, it could be argued that the metropolitan areas as a whole ought to finance the poverty-linked social services.

There is a good case for this argument because the great bulk of the wealth and income of the country is concentrated in metropolitan areas. But almost nowhere is there a governmental structure such that taxes can be levied throughout the metropolitan area on the economic base of the entire metropolitan area for the support of such services. In some places, in states that are overwhelmingly urban and metropolitan in character, the state government may be a reasonable substitute for metropolitan area government. But this is not true of all states, and, moreover, some metropolitan areas straddle state boundary lines. Also, the migration of the poor among the states has not been an even, proportional movement; some states, like New York, have been the recipients of very large numbers of poor in-migrants because of accidents of geography (access to Puerto Rico) rather than economic strength. All this suggests that the national government is the proper source of support for the bulk of poverty-linked services provided in urban areas.

In addition, it could be argued that some of the poverty-linked services actually provided by urban local governments should be directly *provided* as well as *financed* by governments covering a wider area. One example of this is the suggested negative income tax, which would supplant state and local public assistance expenditures.

What about the rebuilding of the central cities and the provision of adequate amenities in the form of public services? In a broad sense, if a central city has sensible redevelopment policies and strategies, ones that actually provide a good pay-off in social terms relative to the funds invested, the cities themselves should be able to finance the costs fairly readily. That is, the additional public expenditures in time will improve the environment of the city sufficiently so that its tax base—broadly defined—will be enhanced considerably.

There are some exceptions to this. First, there is need for outside help to offset some biases and imperfections in present arrangements. For example, recent heavy investment in urban highway facilities, based on outside financial support, may make it rather difficult to finance investment in public transportation facilities from local resources. A second qualification is that the particular local tax devices used to finance these socially self-liquidating investments have side effects. High central city taxes on business activity may make the central cities much less attractive locations for business capable of operating elsewhere. Equally important, high taxes based on the value of real property can discourage private investment which raises real property values. In old cities full of obsolete private structures, an ideal fiscal solution would avoid taxes that defer private rebuilding. Instead, such a solution would involve taxes that either encourage the needed rebuilding or are neutral in their effect. And the most nearly neutral kind of tax that is widely used and produces much revenue at any level of government is the tax on individual income.

The newer parts of metropolitan areas in general are characterized by relatively high levels of personal income and wealth. This suggests that they should be able to finance themselves with a minimum of outside help, provided they have boundaries that make some sense from the standpoint of the nature of the services provided and that do not fragment the potential tax base into wildly unequal portions. Also, because a good part of the problem in the newer areas is provision for new public investment, the outer areas would be able to finance themselves adequately only if they are free to meet the bunched-up (in time) needs they now face. That is, they should be able to borrow rather freely to meet current needs for capital outlays and repay this over the useful lives of the facilities. At a later stage, their capital needs will be much lower.

The poverty-linked services aside, many of the public services provided by local governments are in many ways like those provided by public utility companies. That is, they are not provided uniformly to the entire population, but rather in distinguishable quantities and qualities to individual families in the population, who consume them in accord with their personal preferences. For example, not all families use the same amount of water, not all use the same amount of highway transportation, and so on. There is a strong case for financing such services in the same way public utility services are financed—that is, via user charges, which are like prices, rather than through general taxes.

If the purpose of providing the public service is to offer different consumers the services they want, and place some value on, then they ought to pay for such services in proportion to the costs. Otherwise, governments will be called upon to provide a great deal more of the service than people would be willing to consume if they did have to pay for it—a wasteful use of resources; or the service will be in such short supply that a form of non-price rationing will be employed to allocate the service among consumers. The outstanding example is street congestion in cities: users pay for highways in the aggregate but not for specific individual uses of the streets and therefore, not surprisingly, treat highways as a free good. The only deterrent to use of the streets at the most crowded times and in the most crowded places is the value one places on time; the rationing in effect then results in those who place a low value on time preempting the street space from those who place a high value on time. Ordinarily, in our society, rationing is on the basis of price. Somebody who values a service highly bids it away from someone who places a lower value on that service and would rather use his income for alternative kinds of consumption.

This has relevance for public services in both the newly developing parts of urban areas and the older cities themselves. To the extent that pricelike mechanisms are employed, there is likely to be a more sensible allocation of resources in urban areas. Moreover, prices are by definition neutral in their economic effects. People do not exchange money for services or goods unless they consider the value of the services or goods they receive at least equal to the money they surrender. Substituting neutral prices for unneutral taxes has much to commend it. Of course, there is a limit to the extent to which pricing devices can be used, but the general principle remains: where prices make sense at all, they should be utilized and not rejected simply because the services are organized under public rather than private auspices.

There is a further extension of the market analogy to urban government. People do differ in their preferences for various kinds of public and private goods and services. For some people, locally available recreational facilities—say, public parks and swimming pools—are exceedingly valuable services, but for others—those who prefer to travel long distances on vacation, for example—the value is much less. And such differences are not simply a matter of differences in income—people with similar incomes have different tastes.

Since tastes differ, it is entirely conceivable that one might find people of similar tastes—in this case similar preferences for public services—tending to move into particular sections of the metropolitan area. There are real advantages to such ordering of residential patterns based on differences in preferences for various kinds of public goods and services. Without this arrangement, some people would be taxed to provide services they do not desire, while others would find that there are services they desire and would be willing to pay more taxes for.

In an ideal urban governmental and fiscal structure, it would be desirable to try to provide some arrangements that foster this kind of expression of differences in tastes. One such arrangement would result in large numbers of small separate service areas for kinds of public services that are likely to have this character, such as recreational services.

Neither user-charge financing (as a principal source of support) nor individual-preference-oriented service areas are appropriate for welfare and health services or any other poverty-linked services, and user-charge financing is inappropriate for schools as well. All of these are services provided to the poorer members of the urban community despite their inability to pay for the services, indeed *because of* their inability to pay. The consensus is that the rest of the community is better off if the poor are not destitute (hence public assistance) and have some medical care (hence clinics and free hospital care), and if their children are educated. Indeed, we feel so strongly about education that we *require* people to send their children to schools and levy the taxes necessary to provide the school places. Such "meritorious wants" as minimal health and educational levels contrast sharply with society's indifference as to whether individual families own more or fewer water-using appliances or own one, two or three cars.

This description of ideal solutions has not mentioned a frequent source of controversy: suburban exploitation of the central city or central city exploitation of commuters. The poverty-linked services, as noted, do present a problem. Putting them to one side, it is entirely possible to develop a system in which there is no significant degree of exploitation of either set of residents and to do this without setting up any sort of a massive metropolitan governmental structure.

The truly needed metropolitan-area-wide governmental machinery is related to the nature of certain kinds of public services. Transportation, planning, water pollution, air pollution, and water supply are all services that, for the most part, cannot effectively be provided by small local governments and require fairly large geographic service areas. Although cost is one consideration, yet another is the provision of reasonably adequate standards of service. Where technology and geography dictate metropolitan governmental arrangements, they would exist in an ideal situation. Where technology does not dictate such arrangements, the real *metropolitan* governmental need is to ensure a wide area for financing the poverty-linked services.

The Real World of Urban Public Finance

How do present arrangements for financing urban local governments compare with this ideal? First, there *is* a substantial local tax burden due to the financing of poverty-linked services, a burden that exists for many local governments but is especially important in the older central cities.

Public assistance, for example, is the most obvious poverty-linked public service. The federal government provides substantial amounts of funds for this, roughly 55 per cent of the total spent in 1964. In most states in the United States, the remaining funds are provided entirely from state government sources, and indeed the state government administers public assistance programs itself. However, there are urban states with large *local* public assistance expenditures. They include California, Ohio, Indiana, Minnesota, Wisconsin, New York, New Jersey, and Massachusetts. In fact, in all except six of the metropolitan areas with a population of over one million, there are significant locally financed outlays for public assistance. For the country as a whole, roughly one sixth of the funds are provided from local financial resources.

Similarly, there are significant health expenditures (which in cities are primarily directed to the poor) and hospital expenditures financed from local tax funds. In 1964, the locally financed total of welfare expenditures, current expenditures for health purposes, and current expenditures for hospitals (net of charges received from hospital patients) was about $2 billion. Some idea of the relative importance of this amount can be seen by comparing it with the total of $20 billion that local governments received in that year from the local property tax. For the governments of the largest American cities (those with populations over 300,000), the ratio is much higher. Locally financed services that are fairly directly linked to poverty absorbed nearly one fourth of the big-city property tax revenues in 1964, or one sixth of their collections of taxes of all types. In a number of the larger metropolitan areas, if the local tax drain due to central city financing of social services were equalized over the entire area, central city tax loads would be well below those elsewhere in the metropolitan areas, rather than well above, which is the more usual case.[2]

Another aspect of the poverty-linked services fiscal problem relates to the financing of schools in the older central cities. Most programs of state aid to the local school districts in a state appear to be fair; typically, state aid programs are based on the numbers of children and the local property tax base per pupil. Big cities tend to have fewer school children per family in public schools than in other parts of a given state and also tend to have relatively high business property values. As a result, they receive relatively small amounts of state school aid.

But this apparent equity is misleading, because the assumption underlying almost all state aid programs is that the cost of providing a given quality of education is uniform throughout a state. There is much evidence

[2] Per capita property tax revenues are significantly higher in most large central cities than in their surrounding areas; see Dick Netzer, *Economics of the Property Tax* (Brookings, 1966), p. 118. Where they are not, it is usually because the central city relies heavily on local *nonproperty* taxes (New York, St. Louis, cities in Ohio, for example).

that it is not—to provide an education equivalent in quality to that received in the better suburban schools would cost enormously more in the slum schools in the big cities. One commentator, Christopher Jencks, recently estimated that this equivalent-quality education would cost approximately twice as much per pupil. The reason is obvious. The many disadvantages under which children in poverty and minority group families suffer at home and before they come to school mean that they require a great deal more in the way of special services, small classes, and the like to assure a performance in school equivalent to that of the suburban middle-class child. And state aid formulas generally do not recognize this.

The 1965 Federal Aid to Education Act is specifically addressed to the problem of children from poorer families. It thus provides a substantial aid for large central city schools and partially makes up for the inadequacies of the state aid formulas. This is all to the good, but big-city school systems now spend, from their own resources, several hundred million dollars for programs related to poverty. The ideal solution would call for such expenditures to be *entirely* financed from external funds. Moreover, if the problems of poverty and race are really to be attacked, big-city school expenditures probably will need to be increased at a very rapid rate indeed. Under present arrangements, they will be increased at a much slower rate than they should be and, moreover, even that slower rate will be a severe economic burden on the big cities themselves.

There are serious problems with the existing arrangements for financing the rebuilding and improvement of central cities, aside from the poverty problem. The principal difficulty is the choice of tax instruments for local fiscal support. The main problem is the extremely heavy taxation of housing, which works at cross-purposes with the desire to rebuild and renew central cities. In the United States, local property taxes on housing equal roughly 20 per cent of the rental value of housing. That is, they are equivalent to a 25 per cent excise tax on housing expenditures. In the larger metropolitan areas, particularly in the northeastern part of the United States, the excise tax is more like 30 per cent, and for some of the central cities well over 30 per cent. There is no other type of consumer product aside from liquor, tobacco, and gasoline, which is as heavily taxed in the United States today. The effect of this very heavy taxation, other things being equal, is to deter people from spending their incomes for better housing.

Note the "other things being equal" clause. In suburban communities, particularly bedroom suburbs, the public services that a family receives or has access to are very closely tied to the local taxes that the same family pays. Therefore, in a sense, the property tax in many suburbs is analogous to a general charge for the use of public services, or perhaps even to a local income tax. It is unlikely to be a deterent to consumption of housing, that is, to the expenditure of consumer income for housing. For the central cities, this is not the case. Central cities provide a wide variety of services and tax a wide variety of property types. Individuals cannot reasonably assume that the prices of housing confronting them include an identifiable tax component that is in effect a charge for a preferred package of public services. What they do observe is that housing is expensive in the central city. It may not be any more expensive in the central city than in the suburbs. But an effective city-rebuilding strategy requires that the central cities encourage more private expenditure for housing, and this may in turn require that housing be much cheaper in the central city than in the suburbs.

It may be argued that any tax paid by individuals and families in a central city will have some discouraging effect on their choice of the central city as a residence. This is true, as is the argument that any tax that reduces incomes will have some bearing on housing expenditure. However, a tax specifically related to housing expenditure is much more a deterrent to the needed rebuilding of the central cities than a tax on income in general would be.

Another element in the choice of tax strategy for central city programs concerns the taxation of businesses by the central city. It is clear that many types of business activity have been decentralizing away from the central cities of the larger metropolitan areas. If, to all the other disadvantages of congestion and lack of adequate space, and so on, the central city adds business taxes higher than those elsewhere in the area, it may very well spur the further migration of businesses. No doubt this has *not* been a serious problem in many areas, although in a few cases property taxes on business may have had a discouraging effect on economic activity. More often, the over-all effect of taxation of business property in the cities at differentially heavier rates is to depress land values, which is not necessarily the worst thing in the world.

However, it is worth noting New York City's experience.[3] The city has had, for many years, exceptionally heavy taxes on business activity and real property, including a unique (and heavy) tax on gross receipts and a sales tax far higher than in surrounding areas. The gross receipts tax was exceptionally burdensome to manufacturing and wholesale trade activities, which would have been migrating away from the city in any case. But there is evidence that the tax accelerated the rate of decline in these economic sectors. Similarly, there is evidence that the decentralization of retail trade was substantially speeded by the sales tax differential. Fortunately, the city has now shifted to a less oppressive form of business taxation and the sales tax differential has also been reduced.

[3] See Graduate School of Public Administration, New York University, *Financing Government in New York City,* Final Research Report to the Temporary Commission on City Finances (April 1966).

What about the newly developing parts of metropolitan areas? The major problem here is connected with boundary lines. The boundary lines of political subdivisions in the suburbs are those that have evolved over a long period. They have no necessary relationship to the natural areas for the performance of particular services or for grouping people of similar preferences, which is a less important consideration. Moreover, the tax base of the suburban areas tends to be so fragmented in some parts of the country that there are enormous disparities between needs and taxable resources, particularly in connection with financing the schools.

One consequence of this fragmentation has been what has been referred to as "fiscal zoning": controlling land use in newly developing areas in such a way as to minimize tax costs (have as few school children as possible) and maximize tax base (have nonresidential or very high value residential property rather than ordinary houses). It is easy to think of organizational arrangements that can offset this problem: governmental reorganization, additional state aid for particular functions such as schools, or some kind of second-tier local governmental structure—that is, some form of fiscal federation within metropolitan areas. The idea is to offer common access to the tax base of large parts of the metropolitan area and reduce the incentive to plan land use primarily from the standpoint of fiscal considerations, rather than from the standpoint of larger notions of the suitability of functional patterns in metropolitan areas.

Real world solutions also fall short of the ideal in connection with the application of user charges to finance particular public services. They are frequently not used at all in cases where they *can* be sensibly employed. They are also frequently used in a most inept fashion. Air and water pollution is an excellent example of failure to apply user charges where they clearly make sense. By and large, the construction and operation of sewerage systems and sewage treatment facilities is financed in the United States by local property taxes. Some places have sewer service charges of one kind or another, but they are by no means the majority. Yet here is a case where it is rather easy to identify the specific people who give rise to public costs. The benefits of water pollution control or air pollution control may be very broad, but the sources of the public costs are highly individual. Moreover, it is not impractical to apply charges that have some relationship to the costs occasioned. This has been done in the Ruhr basin in Germany for many years; there is an elaborate system of pollution charges designed to apportion the costs of treatment facilities among the industrial establishments that actually occasion those costs and also to deter firms from polluting.

As noted earlier, conventional highway financing illustrates the inept use of user charges. Gasoline taxes and licenses have some relationship to the amount of use of the highways by all users as a group and by individual users over long periods of time. But flat charges of this kind cannot possibly discourage people from freely using the very high cost roads at the very high cost periods. There is no discrimination among the parts of the road system depending on the cost to the public of those road systems, including the costs of congestion.

Another example of inept use of user charges is in connection with the common structure of transit fares in cities. The flat fare is a time-hallowed principle, although the structure of costs would dictate a substantially higher fare in the peak hours than in the off-peak hours, differentials between predominant and reverse direction riding, and perhaps differentials based on distance in the larger cities. The use of parking meters as a user charge is also rather inept in most cases. Flat, low charges are the most commonly found kind of arrangement with relatively little discrimination among locations and times of day. As a result, in most places in central business districts metered curb space is cheaper but harder to find than less convenient off-street parking facilities. Moreover, since many cities use parking meter revenues to subsidize their own off-street parking facilities, they are to some extent competing with themselves by inept parking meter charge policies.

Directions for Reform

This comparison of prevailing practice with one man's notions of what is ideal is, of course, not a practical program of reform. It suggests, for example, abolition of the property tax on housing in central cities, which is hardly an immediate possibility. But it does indicate one set of views as to the proper *directions* for reform—more outside aid for poverty-linked services (although 100 per cent outside financing may be years off); refraining from increases in taxes on housing in the cities (although reduction may be even further off) and the substitution of other tax forms, preferably used on an area-wide basis; governmental structural improvements such as many have urged for years; and wider and more sophisticated applications of the price mechanism in local government.

What are the policy alternatives? One is to call for substantially increased federal (and in some cases, state) aid for a long list of urban, especially central city, activities. Federal assistance in the provision of urban services, either via aid to local and state governments or via direct federal performance (for example, expansion of social insurance, like Medicare), has increased sharply in the past few years. This assistance can be viewed as a belated recognition of the national interest in the resolution of certain urban problems, notably those related to poverty and those that leap geographic boundaries (for example, water pollution), with the increase in the federal role likely to level off at a new higher plateau, much as it did between the late 1930's and the late 1950's. Or it can be viewed as no more than the beginning of a continuously expanding federal role. The historical evidence suggests the former interpretation, but this is prophecy, not scholarship.

A second alternative is to reaffirm the received truth, discovered decades ago, that the property tax is inherently a good tax for local governments, which can be relied upon even more heavily, if only the abominations that characterize its administration are eliminated. This view has numerous proponents, but it is possible to entertain doubts as to whether a tax based on so ephemeral a standard as the "true value of property" can ever be equitably administered. Moreover, the persistence of bad administration over so many years makes one wonder whether good administration is publicly acceptable, even if attainable. It is worth noting that the advocates of a strengthened role for the property tax generally have little patience with those who propose to mitigate its effects on central city housing by special exemptions and abatements for administratively preferred types of housing investment.

The alternatives to the property tax are not easy ones. Proliferation of local nonproperty taxes imposed by existing local government units raises not only administrative problems but, more important, economic ones for central cities. If central cities are where the fiscal difficulties bind, they will be the heavy users of nonproperty taxes; differentially heavy taxation by central cities can surely affect their economic future, at the margin. The prospect of nonproperty taxes imposed on a metropolitan-area-wide basis, which would wash out competitive fears, is not promising, since there are few precedents in this country. But it remains an attractive concept. Finally, wider and more sophisticated applications of user charges demand local government imagination, administrative skill, and political courage. This course, more than any other, can run aground on the inherent conservatism of local government, a universal characteristic.

There is, perhaps, more knowledge concerning the mechanisms for financing urban public services than there is about the services themselves —consumer-voter preferences for public expenditures, cost functions for the major activities, alternative methods of achieving public *objectives* via differing public service *inputs,* and the like. The lack of knowledge on the expenditure side is considerable. There is, in addition, a special problem of uncertainty for central cities. We know very little indeed about the effects of differences in the supply of public services on locational choice within metropolitan areas—by businesses and households alike—and only slightly more about the effects of tax differentials on locational choice. But, in local finance as elsewhere, policy must be made daily, in the face of uncertainty. And the very fact that local finance has so many pressing problems has revived scholarly interest in the field, after a long lull, which ensures that the dimensions of uncertainty will be gradually narrowed in the years ahead.

John Anderson, Jr.

Tax Policy and State Legislative Capabilities

State and local taxation policy is the outgrowth of years of uncoordinated legislation, often adopted in response to short-term revenue needs, with little attention given to the long-term impact of various taxation programs. State and local tax policy is often inconsistent, and, at its worst, creates the inequities described by former Kansas Governor John Anderson, Jr., in the following article.

Most observers would probably agree that the tax policy of the states has been pretty much business as usual except for changes to meet emergencies. But I think the straw is in the wind and tax revision now is not just an election year issue to be discussed and then put on the shelf. The problems are deep-seated and have been years in the making. Like cream rising in milk they have come to the top. They have reached the point in development and the rank among issues where they must be reckoned with.

Evidence of this is shown in the farmer taxpayer revolt in Wisconsin, the taxpayer leagues and groups formed in communities and state-side groups throughout the nation, the unrest made clear in the protest vote in the presidential preferential primaries.

But the hard proof that tax revision or tax reform is more than a political issue is to be found in the recent wave of court decisions they have held that the traditional method of supporting public schools, primarily through the local property tax, denies equal protection under the fourteenth amendment to the United States Constitution, invidiously discriminating against the poor. And that such a taxing system makes a poor child's education a function of the wealth of his parents and neighbors.

Reprinted from *National Tax Journal*, **25**:369–372 (September 1972) by permission of the publisher and the author.

The first of these decisions *Serrano v. Priest,* was handed down by California's highest court on August 30, 1971. Others followed. In Minnesota, the U.S. District Court in a unanimous decision (*Van Dusartz v. Hatfield,* October 12, 1971) held that the school financing scheme in Minnesota was unconstitutional; it said that "plainly put, the rule is that the level of spending for a child's education may not be a function of wealth other than the wealth of the state as a whole." The court further stated: "This is not the simple instance in which a poor man is injured by his lack of funds. Here the poverty is that of a governmental unit that the state itself has defined and commissioned . . ."

Next, on December 23, 1971, the United States District Court in San Antonio, Texas (*Rodrigues v. San Antonio*) held that the "current system of financing public education in Texas discriminates on the basis of wealth by permitting citizens of affluent districts to provide a higher quality education for their children while paying lower taxes," thus denying equal protection of the laws under the United States Constitution.

Then came *Robinson v. Cahill,* decided by the State Superior Court in New Jersey on January 19, 1972. This case was filed in 1970 attacking the "foundation program." The court held the old law and the new plan adopted during pendency of the suit to be inadequate, saying: "In most cases, rich districts spend more money per pupil than poor districts; rich districts spend more money on teachers' salaries per pupil; rich districts have more teachers and more professional staff per pupil; and rich districts manage this with tax rates that are lower than poor districts, despite equalizing aid." Summing up, the court said: "the state must finance a 'thorough and efficient' system of education out of *state* revenues raised by levies imposed uniformly on taxpayers of the same class. The present equalizing factors in the law are not sufficient to overcome inequalities in the distribution of school funds and tax burdens."

It is obvious these cases had been under consideration simultaneously for some time. There are cases presently pending in more than twenty states. Two cases have been filed in Kansas—one of them in the school district in which I live.

Now, for a moment let's look at the reason for this development.

The property tax as a means of raising revenue for governments, particularly for education, is as old as public education itself. Little or no change has been made throughout the years in this taxing system.

On the other hand, there has been considerable change in the educational systems of our society in the recent past. With the growth of population and mobility of the people, concentration of population in the cities and changing methods of school administration, the expenses of education have grown tremendously.

Let's look at some of the facts behind the decisions.

In the California case in fiscal 1970 the assessed valuation per unit of average daily attendance of elementary school children ranged from a low of $103.00 to $952,156, or a ratio of nearly 1 to 10,000.

The law provided for a minimum foundation level per pupil, and for equalization aid. But for the poor districts to obtain supplemental aid, they first had to vote upon themselves an extra local tax effort. The equalization aid tended to lessen some disparities but the basic aid served to widen other disparities.

The effect of the law was that the poor district of Baldwin Park spent $577.49 per pupil—with a tax levy of $5.48—while Beverly Hills spent $1,231.72 per child—with a tax levy of only $2.38. So the district that spent twice as much on school operation per child was taxed only half as much per $100.00 valuation.

In the Texas case, the market value of property per student within the seven school districts in San Antonio ranged from $5,429 to $45,095. Even where the property tax levy as a per cent of market values were highest in the poor district and lowest in the rich district, the poor district raised $21.00 per pupil while the rich district raised $543.00 per pupil.

The court said of this system: "For poor school districts educational financing in Texas is thus a tax-more-spend-less system."

Without resorting to factual data from any case in Kansas, some pertinent comparisons are of interest. A look at two school districts—one in populous Johnson County on the eastern border, and one in Hamilton County on the western side of the state—reveals the following:

> Shawnee Mission School District (Johnson County) has 43,667 pupils with operating expenditures of $664 and a valuation of $9,522 per pupil and a levy of 51 mills.
> Kendall School District (Hamilton County) has 92 pupils, operation expenditures of $1,573, a valuation per pupil of $79,672 and a levy of 14.71 mills.

These figures are school district wealth indicators. They relate only to the wealth in real property or ad valorem tax base. Arguments were made that other factors such as per capita income within a district should be considered. However, it is apparent that the attacks in court on the school financing foundation programs are largely concerned with the question of equal protection under the law when measured against the property tax facts where proof shows that the lion's share of financing comes from real property tax.

In California, educational revenues for 1968-69 came 55.7% from local property tax, 35.5% from state aid, 6.1% from federal funds, and 2.7% from miscellaneous funds. In 1970 in Kansas, approximately 65% of total educational revenues came from local property taxes; 30% came from state aid, and 5% came from federal aid.

Thus, with more than half school funding coming from property tax and with the disparities (as pointed out above) in the tax base and the tax levies, it is evident that the challenge to the system warrants consideration. However, these facts and past legal precedents did not turn the tide.

While the tax laws are in for some real changes, the rationale of the decisions is not one of striking down the real property tax law, nor is it a declaration that state government must soak the rich and help the poor.

The decisions, in effect, mandate that one child within a state has a constitutional right to equal educational opportunities with other children within the same state. And that this right must neither be denied nor conditional upon wealth.

The courts pointed out that education plays an indispensible role in our industrial state. It is a major determinant of an individual's chances for economic opportunity and social success in our modern society. And it works a unique influence on a child's development as a citizen and a participant in political and community life. Its pivotal position in American society is undeniable.

The courts relied upon the *Brown v. Board of Education* case and reiterated the statement "today, education is perhaps the most important function of state and local government—it is doubtful that any child may reasonably be expected to succeed in life if he is denied the opportunity of an education. Such an opportunity, where the state had undertaken to provide it, is a right which must be made available to all on equal terms."

Thus, treating education as a "fundamental interest," the court said the right was of such importance that discrimination could not be made on the basis of wealth.

The Texas court held: "This court cannot act as a 'super-legislature' but that it can declare an act of the legislature as violative of the constitution." The court said, "It is incumbent upon the defendants and the Texas Legislature to determine what new form of financing should be utilized to support public education."

The court then retained jurisdiction for a period of two years, saying "In the event the legislature fails to act within the time stated, the court is authorized to and will take such further steps as may be necessary to implement both the purposes and the spirit of this order."

We can recall that in recent times the courts have told both the legislative and executive departments of government that if they didn't act, the courts would. In the case of reapportionment, where the legislature didn't implement the one-man-one-vote order, the courts did it. And in the segregation cases, the problems of busing have been the result of orders to implement the principle of integration in the schools.

In our system of representative government, policy decisions should be made by the legislative branch of government. But when this fails and constitutional rights are being denied the courts have been resorted to and they have acted.

Some would argue that the problem is one of equality in education but in reality it is a problem of taxation.

All the states of the nation, except Hawaii, depend on the local property tax to fund public education. Across the nation the localities pay more than half of the cost of such education. The states fund about 40% and the federal government less than 10% of the cost of education.

Of the forty billion collected in local property tax in the nation, more than twenty-one billion is used for support of public schools.

Of the twenty-one billion in local property tax for schools, eight billion comes from single family homes, three billion from multi-family dwellings and ten billion from commercial and industrial property. While it may fairly be said the children live relatively close to the schools, there is no fixed pattern with reference to location of commercial and industrial property.

Within the past year in one county in my state the state-assessed properties (i.e. the public utilities, pipe lines, railroads and power plants) exceeded in value all the privately owned real properties. Many of these state-assessed properties are concentrated within certain school districts.

Now that we have identified the problems, what are the implications? Some predict an end to the property tax. Some say it is the beginning of state-wide school systems, and a change in state-local relations.

Although the cases have not reached the supreme court, it is clear that even if they are affirmed the answers are not apparent.* The decisions do not strike down the property tax; they bar discrimination in education by disparities in local taxation.

The President of the United States has spoken of the gathering crisis of school finance and property taxes. He has asked the Advisory Commission on Intergovernmental Relations (ACIR) to study the problem and make recommendations. If the federal government doubled the money it puts into education (less than 10% of the total cost) it might help but would not solve the problem. The Congress has been unable to agree on a revenue sharing program. And there is much concern that if the federal government goes heavily into school financing, there will be strings of control attached. Thus it is apparent the state legislatures will be faced with the ultimate problem.

What are the capabilities of the state legislatures?

We must take the position that the state legislatures have the capabilities of providing financing for the school system in the state. We cannot

* [*Editor's Note:* The U.S. Supreme Court has since considered the issue of financing local education out of property tax revenues and did not upset the existing pattern.]

admit failure for this would in reality admit a substantial failure of the federal system.

There are problems as to capability because of disparities under present systems. Under the present system, the states' share of cost of education comes largely from income tax and sales tax. Just 10 years ago, only 19 states imposed both personal income and sales taxes. Now, however, 36 states have both types of tax. Only one state, New Hampshire, imposes neither. That state would have to raise its revenue collection approximately 80% to finance 90% of the cost of education. In Nebraska where property tax was long the main basis of revenue, the state revenue would have to be increased by approximately 70 per cent to finance 90 per cent of the cost of education.

The requirement for financial support on a state level in such manner as to provide equal educational opportunity could, of course, mean that the real property tax be levied in a state-wide levy. This could bring considerable adjustments.

If a state were to try to raise state revenue largely from a base other than their property tax or in lieu of the local property tax, it would be a difficult task. In those states where the main support of education is still the local property tax, raising this kind of new revenue will be very difficult.

It takes more than determination. It takes political guts! And if there isn't enough of both, the job will have to be done in stages.

The Citizens Conference on State Legislatures, a nonprofit, nonpartisan organization, was formed in 1965, by a group of people who felt the state legislatures were the weak links in our federal system. Observers saw that the state legislatures had lagged behind the changes that had worked in the executive arm of government, and indeed, behind the developments in the private sector.

Too many state legislatures were still meeting only once every two years and then for only sixty or ninety days. Too many state legislatures were understaffed and did not have the research and technical help to back them up as lawmakers. Too many legislators were underpaid which resulted in inordinate turnovers, lost experience, and inefficiency. Too many legislatures were bound by constitutional limitations on their own procedures and on areas of substantive law, such as internal improvements and revenue measures.

We have seen change and progress within the last few years. More than thirty-five states now meet annually. Interim meetings of standing committees allow for work on a continuing basis. Pre-filing and carry-over of bills allow sufficient time for adequate consideration of legislation. All of these changes provide considerable protection against the traditional log-jam of bills at the end of a session.

In short, state legislatures are a long way from being tooled up or modernized (so to speak) to handle the problems of the American states in 1972. Much progress has been made in recent years, however, allowing more time, staff facilities and procedural changes. Some states are still lagging.

I would say the legislatures have the capability of meeting their tax problems if they can muster the courage and stay at work.

SUGGESTED READINGS

State and Urban Finance

The best general works on state and local finance are James A. Maxwell's *Financing State and Local Governments,* rev. ed. (Washington: Brookings Institution, 1969), and L. L. Ecker-Racz's *The Politics and Economics of State and Local Finance* (Englewood Cliffs, N.J.: Prentice-Hall, 1970). A sound and comprehensive analysis of urban finance is Wilbur Thompson's *A Preface to Urban Economics* (Baltimore: John Hopkins Press, 1965). Ira Sharkansky's *Spending in the American States* (Chicago: Rand McNally, 1968), and Alan K. Campbell and Seymour Sacks' *Metropolitan America* (New York: Collier-Macmillan, 1967) give considerable attention to the socioeconomic determinants of state and urban spending (respectively). With regard to fiscal relations among different levels of government, the major work is George F. Break, *Intergovernmental Fiscal Relations in the United States* (Washington: Brookings Institution, 1967).

Advisory Commission on Intergovernmental Relations. *State-Local Finances and Suggested Legislation.* Washington, D.C.: U.S. Government Printing Office, 1970.

Davies, David G. "Financing Urban Functions and Services," *Law and Contemporary Problems,* **30** (Winter 1965), 127–161.

Due, John F. *State and Local Sales Taxation: Structure and Administration.* Chicago: Public Administration Service, 1971.

Feinberg, Mordecai. "The Implications of Core-City Decline for the Fiscal Structure of the Core City," *National Tax Journal,* **17** (September 1964), 213–231.

Greenbaum, William (commentator). "Serrano v. Priest: Implications for Educational Equality," *Harvard Educational Review,* **41** (November 1971), 501–534.

Johnson, Harry L., ed. *State and Local Tax Problems.* Knoxville: University of Tennessee, 1969.

Netzer, Dick. *Economics of the Property Tax.* Washington, D.C.: Brookings Institution, 1966.

Nortman, Bernard. "State and Local Tax Reform," *Urban Affairs Quarterly,* **7** (September 1971), 41–60.

Penniman, Clara. "The Politics of Taxation," in Herbert Jacob and Kenneth N. Vines, eds. *Politics in the American States,* 2nd ed. Boston: Little, Brown, 1971, 520–555.

"A Symposium on Problems of State and Local Government Finance," *National Tax Journal,* **23** (March 1970), entire issue.

Thomas F. Pettigrew

When a Black Candidate Runs for Mayor: Race and Voting Behavior

The Fifteenth Amendment failed dismally to provide for the participation of black Americans in politics. It has only been in very recent years that either by voting or running for office blacks have begun to be active in the operation of American government.

Because there is no deep reservoir of experience from which to draw, studies of blacks in politics are necessarily few. This study is a forerunner of others which will attempt to apply the techniques of social psychology to the role of the black in electoral politics.

Introduction

November 7, 1967, witnessed the beginning of a new era in American politics, the beginning of significant black entry into the political decision-making of urban America. Democrat Carl Stokes, a black state legislator, defeated Republican Seth Taft by less than one per cent of the votes to become Mayor of Cleveland. And on the same day, Democrat Richard Hatcher, a black city councilor, defeated Republican Joseph Radigan by an equally narrow margin to become Mayor of Gary, Indiana.

Since that historic election day, Stokes won reelection in 1969, Kenneth Gibson became Mayor of Newark, New Jersey, in 1970, and Hatcher won reelection in Gary in 1971. Moreover, two other black candidates nar-

"When a Black Candidate runs for Mayor: Race and Voting Behavior," by Thomas F. Pettigrew in *Urban Affairs Annual Reviews*, Volume 6 (1972) Harlan Hahn (ed.), pp. 95–118, is reprinted by permission of the Publisher, Sage Publications, Inc., Beverly Hills, Calif. Some descriptive and bibliographical footnotes have been omitted for considerations of space and textual format.

rowly lost in mayoralty bids in major cities: Thomas Bradley in Los Angeles in 1969 and Richard Austin in Detroit in 1969. And there will be many more competent blacks running for mayor in major cities. Indeed, there are serious black bids being made for the top office in other cities such as Boston, Baltimore, and New Haven together with preparations for such bids in cities from Atlanta (Vice-Mayor Maynard Jackson in 1973) to Los Angeles (Bradley again in 1973). Clearly, the 1970s will be the decade of major racial progress in this area that was opened up in 1967.

These races offer ideal opportunities for research to students both of politics and race relations. There have now been enough of these critical elections, with the promise of many more to come, to warrant careful study. What uniformities emerge across these varied cities when a black candidate runs for mayor? Who are the whites who vote for a competent black for high office? And what are some of the political conditions that make it possible for a black aspirant to succeed?

Another feature of these mayoralty races makes them particularly attractive for research in race relations. The office of the mayor, like those of governor and President, involves being "the captain of the ship." This contrasts with the offices to which a disproportionate share of blacks have been so far elected (city council member, legislator, and lower executive posts) where blacks are either a minority in a larger body or in a lower post below the top executive position. Running for "captain of the ship" is obviously, then, a far more rigorous test of the white voter's racial prejudices and behavior.

Finally, social science must begin to study this phenomenon now if it is to learn about the racial and political dynamics that undergird its evolution. Before too many years have passed, the election of competent black mayors will have become normative; and the chance to gather baseline data and to observe its acceptance over time by initially threatened whites will have been lost. Witness the manner in which the election of President John F. Kennedy in 1960 practically removed the issue of membership in the Roman Catholic church as a dominant national political concern. Interestingly, the considerable discussion of various Democratic Party possibilities to run for President in 1972 has virtually ignored as irrelevant their religious affiliations.

Consequently, I initiated a research project in 1968 to study the campaigns of black mayoralty candidates throughout the nation. So far, this project has focused on the 1967 and 1971 races of Mayor Hatcher in Gary, the 1969 race of Mayor Stokes in Cleveland, the 1969 race of Bradley in Los Angeles, and the 1970 race of Mayor Gibson in Newark. Both precinct analyses and surveys of probability samples of registrants have been utilized in each of the four cities. This article presents the first preliminary overview of the project's work. First, brief descriptions and discussions of the elections will be provided. Then we shall explore in more detail a number of the uniformities and dynamics that have been uncovered so far across all of the elections.

Five Mayoralty Elections

GARY, 1967. The project began its work with extensive aggregate analyses of the vote by precinct for Richard Hatcher for Mayor of Gary in November 1967. Next we conducted during October of 1968 a survey of 257 white adult males who were registered to vote and who were representative of nine varied white precincts of Gary. The auspicious timing of this survey right before the 1968 presidential election allowed us to study simultaneously the support for Governor George Wallace in one of the northern communities where he ran strongest.

A year prior to our survey, Mayor Richard Hatcher had won a narrow victory over Joseph Radigan in a bitter contest that required U.S. Department of Justice intervention to ensure its being held fairly. Both our survey and aggregate data agree on the following election statistics:

1. in 1967, the black percentage of the total Gary electorate was between approximately 40 and 44%;
2. turnout for both whites and blacks was unusually large, with well over 80% of those registered of each race voting;
3. Hatcher received virtually all the black votes but only about 15% of the white votes (including Spanish-speaking voters who generally supported Hatcher);
4. since mayoralty elections in Gary are partisan, Hatcher was the nominee of the Democratic Party, and about 65% of the city's whites are registered Democrats, this 15% figure means that over three-fourths of the white Democrats in Gary in November 1967 voted against their party's nominee. In other words, for the vast majority, race overcame party identification. Of course, this phenomenon reflects the fact that the Lake County Democratic Committee—the local political machine which Hatcher opposed—openly supported the Republican candidate.

Who, then, were the rare white voters for Hatcher in 1967? In capsule form, they were disproportionately found among Jewish Americans and upper-status, college-educated Democrats. Not only were they significantly less anti-Negro, but they were far less concerned over "law and order" issues. As Table 1 shows, attitudes toward desegregation and concern over law and order are positively correlated, of course, but, surprisingly, each independently accounts for approximately equal percentages of the variance in voting for Hatcher in 1967. Note, for example, that at the under-

TABLE 1 *Attitudes Toward Desegregation and Law and Order and the 1967 White Gary Vote for Hatcher (in percentages)*

Anti-desegregation attitudes[a]	Low			Medium			High		
Concern over law and order[b]	Low	Medium	High	Low	Medium	High	Low	Medium	High
1967 Gary Mayoralty									
Vote For:									
Hatcher	77.8	20.0	0.0	18.2	14.3	12.9	0.0	18.2	0.0
Radigan	22.2	80.0	100.0	81.8	81.0	87.1	100.0	72.7	100.0
Don't know, did not vote, other	0.0	0.0	0.0	0.0	4.8	0.0	0.0	9.1	0.0
Total %	100.0	100.0	100.0	100.0	100.1	100.0	100.0	100.0	100.0
(n)	(18)	(20)	(13)	(11)	(21)	(31)	(6)	(11)	(47)

[a] "Anti-desegregation attitudes" are measured by responses to seven items such as: "Negroes shouldn't push themselves where they're not wanted" (agree); "White people have a right to keep Negroes out of their neighborhoods if they want to, and Negroes should respect that right" (agree); "Do you think white students and Negro students should go to the same schools or to separate schools" (separate schools).

[b] "Concern over law and order" is measured by responses to the following three items: "Buses aren't safe these days without policemen on them" (agree); "When looting occurs during a riot, police should shoot to kill" (agree); and "Safety on the streets is the most important issue facing America today" (agree).

lined extremes, 78% of the 18 respondents who both favor desegregation and are not concerned over "law and order" report having voted for Hatcher compared to none of the 47 respondents who oppose desegregation and are concerned over law and order.

This brief sketch of the 1968 Gary findings will be modified in detail by the more complex analyses now being prepared. But let one example serve here to illustrate the interesting complexities of the data. Annual family income does not relate to either the Hatcher or Wallace white votes in a linear fashion. Both our precinct and survey data reveal that the poorest whites vote slightly more for Hatcher and less for Wallace than the lower-middle-income white voters. Thus, those between $6,000 and $12,000 annual income form the core of Hatcher's opposition and Wallace's support in the Gary electorate (this is best expressed statistically as a quadratic function centered around $9,000 as follows: ($9,000–reported income) where the larger this squared discrepancy, the larger the Hatcher vote and the smaller the Wallace vote). Other findings from this early work in Gary are described below.

CLEVELAND. Mayor Carl Stokes, a former state legislator from a black district of Cleveland, first ran for mayor in 1965 as an Independent. He lost, though he received fully 11% of the white vote. In 1967, he ran again; this time, he nosed out the incumbent in the Democratic Party primary and went on to gain a narrow victory over the Republican nominee, Seth Taft, in November 1967. In the latter race, he received, by our calculations, about 19% of the white vote. With only a two-year term, he had to run for reelection in 1969 and again won in both the primary and the partisan election. In the latter race, he received about 22% of the white vote. In outline, then, the Stokes elections for mayor in 1967 and 1969 are characterized by the following statistics:

1. in 1967 and 1969, the black percentage of the total Cleveland electorate was between approximately 37 and 40%—slightly smaller than that of Gary, thus making Stokes somewhat more dependent upon white support than Hatcher;
2. turnout for both whites and blacks was unusually large—especially in 1967, with over 70% of those registered of each race voting;
3. Stokes received all but a scattering of the black votes in each election, while, as mentioned above, he slowly increased his white percentage from 11 to 19 to 22%. It should be noted, however, that Stokes lost a number of his key campaign staff members between 1967 and 1969, and this apparently explains some of the slight reduction in his black support in 1969. Yet his slightly greater white support made up the difference and set up his narrow victory margin in 1969;

4. just as in Gary, mayoralty elections in Cleveland are partisan; Stokes in 1967 and 1969 was the nominee of the Democratic Party, and a strong majority of the city's whites are registered Democrats. Yet once again the small percentages of 19 and 22 of the white vote indicate that most of the white Democrats in Cleveland in both November of 1967 and 1969 voted against their party's nominee. And just as in Gary, Stokes has been opposed by the local county Democratic committee—though not as openly as in Gary.

The profile of the white voter for Stokes resembles what we found in Gary. Our surveys in Cleveland were conducted with 488 white registrants and 400 black registrants in the late spring of 1969, with the same white respondents being reinterviewed in November and December of 1969 after the election (the retrieval rate was over 80% of the original white sample). Both surveys, togeher with the aggregate analyses of the voting pattern by precincts, found the upper-status, college-educated Democrats to typify the white support for Stokes. Few Jewish voters still reside in the central city, but those few Jewish respondents in our sample did tend to favor Stokes disproportionately.

Another difference with the Gary data concerns ethnicity. In the Indiana city, our survey revealed that those ethnic whites who did not live in ethnic enclaves were the most likely to reject Hatcher and accept Wallace—precisely counter to our theoretical expectations. But in the Ohio city, our expectations were verified; that is, Polish Americans, Hungarian Americans, Czech Americans, and so forth, were most likely to vote against Stokes and for Wallace in neighborhoods which were largely ethnic enclaves for one group. We are now testing for this effect in our Newark data. But what caused this reversal between Gary and Cleveland? We have one promising lead at present; and it concerns the lower-middle-class white voter again. Put simply, this class and income phenomenon of the greatest resistance to black candidates centering in the lower-middle-status ranks appears to be far more critical than the ethnic factor. Thus, in Gary the lower-middle-class whites center in mixed ethnic areas while in Cleveland they are largely found in the ethnic enclave—and this seems to have caused our reversal of ethnic findings between the two cities.

LOS ANGELES. In the spring of 1969, Thomas Bradley, a city council member, became the first serious black contender for Mayor of Los Angeles. In April 1969, he ran in the nonpartisan race against incumbent Mayor Samuel Yorty and over a half-dozen other candidates of widely varying positions and characteristics. Bradley led this first race with an impressive 42% of the total vote, and entered the runoff against Yorty, who came in second with 28% of the total vote. In June, however, Bradley could not significantly increase his percentage and lost to Yorty by a decisive

55,000 vote margin (52.1 to 47.9%). We conducted two surveys during this period, the first of 300 white registrants between the two elections and the second following the runoff involving the reinterviewing of the same respondents (again our follow-up response rate was 80%). The vast size of Los Angeles, however, necessitated one change in the sampling design from the studies conducted in Gary and Cleveland: namely, the sampled precincts were drawn exclusively from two areas of the sprawling metropolis—West Los Angeles and the northern half of the San Fernando Valley area, which included heavily Jewish strongholds of Bradley's support as well as areas of largely lower-middle status where Bradley tended to run weakest.

Drawing upon aggregate and survey data, . . . we believe the Bradley-Yorty runoff election in 1969 is characterized by the following statistics:

1. in 1969, the black percentage of the total Los Angeles electorate was only about 15 to 18%—a situation qualitatively different from the three other cities studies;
2. turnout for both whites and blacks was unusually large in the runoff —as in Gary and Cleveland—with over 70% of those registered of each race voting. The total voting percentage of 76% set a city record for mayoralty elections;
3. Bradley received all but a scattering of the black votes in each election, while securing in the runoff a white percentage of roughly 38 to 41% (including Spanish speakers, a majority of whom voted for Yorty)—the highest degree of white support yet obtained by a black candidate for mayor of a major city. Our data suggests that this result largely reflects in order of importance: (a) widespread discontent with the Yorty administration of the previous eight years; (b) qualitatively less anti-Negro prejudice and perceived racial threat in Los Angeles; (c) Bradley's success with Jewish-American voters, whose concentration in Los Angeles is second only to that of New York City; and (d) a well administered and financed campaign by Bradley;
4. mayoralty elections in Los Angeles are technically nonpartisan and both Yorty and Bradley are identified as members of the Democratic Party. Bradley, however, ran to some extent as a Democrat, while Yorty's widely publicized breaks with the Democratic party made him most popular among white Republicans. Our surveys suggest the whites of Los Angeles are split almost evenly between the two major parties. Bradley led slightly among white Democrats but trailed almost one to three among white Republicans: his greatest strength among Democrats were those who labeled themselves "liberals," roughly four-fifths of whom indicated support of Bradley in our survey.

The question thus becomes: what happened to Bradley's white voting base between the two elections? The black vote remained solidly behind Bradley and significantly increased in turnout in June from the earlier April race. But the white vote increased even more between the two elections, and this suggests that part of our answer lies in the "out-from-under-the-rocks" phenomenon. That is, many whites who do not routinely vote in civic elections—and did not in fact vote in the April 1969 election—were attracted to the polls in June 1969 and voted overwhelmingly for Samuel Yorty. Similar instances of this phenomenon have been noted by this project in the Boston races of Mrs. Louise Hicks and the presidential races of Governor George Wallace. And it is consistent with a vast political research literature on nonvoters who are repeatedly found to be more conservative, authoritarian, and anti-Negro as a group than voters.

But the "out-from-under-the-rocks" appearance at the polls of whites who typically do not vote is only part of the explanation of Mayor Yorty's triumph. A detailed analysis of our post-runoff interviews reveals that many of the whites who initially favored Bradley were in fact more anti-Yorty than pro-Bradley. The election placed them in a harsh avoidance-avoidance conflict between a Mayor they did not like and a challenger whose race presented a threat. Moreover, those whites who did shift from Bradley to Yorty were especially upset over campus unrest, a revealing survey fact that coincides with the student violence at UCLA and San Fernando State College on the weekend immediately before the June election on Tuesday. It is tempting to speculate, then, that Bradley's 52 to 48% defeat can also be attributed in part to these campus disturbances which harmonized so completely with the Mayor's campaign charges against Bradley as "one of *them* who cannot control *them*" and as a leader who would unnecessarily restrain the important operations of the Los Angeles Police Department. At any rate, we know that there were many "undecided" white voters late in the campaign, that there was a white voter shift toward Yorty late in the campaign not unlike the Truman-Dewey presidential race of 1948, and that only the last survey made (by the Field Organization) detected this trend in a telephone survey.

Finally, the profile of the white voter for Bradley is one that the Gary and Cleveland results had prepared us to expect. Jewish voters were over twice as likely to favor the black candidate as other white voters; those who identified themselves as either Democrats or Independents were over twice as likely to favor Bradley as Republicans; the young (21–40) were twice as likely to favor Bradley as the old (51+); and those with some college training were twice as likely to favor Bradley as those with a limited education (11 years or less). Unlike Gary and Cleveland interviewees, respondents in Los Angeles of all types did not typically evince the more blatant forms of racism; thus, they overwhelmingly rejected notions of biological inferiority, of sanctioned racial discrimination and segregation, and of the fairness of treatment of Negroes in America today. But the somewhat more subtle and symbolic forms of racism—"most Negroes who receive welfare . . . could get along without it if they tried"—is reflected in our Los Angeles data and does differentiate between Bradley and Yorty supporters, a critical point to which we shall return.

NEWARK. In many ways, Newark and its black-white mayoralty election resembles Gary and its 1967 election: in the shadow of a powerful metropolis, it is a rundown city with a large black population, profound social problems, and a history of ethnic machine politics. Kenneth Gibson, a former city council member and an unsuccessful candidate for mayor in 1966, wrote civic history by becoming the first black mayor in 1970. After leading comfortably in the initial nonpartisan contest in April, he ran up an impressive 56% to 44% victory over the entrenched incumbent, Hugh Addonizio. In addition to aggregate analyses of precinct votes, we conducted four surveys in Newark: 300 whites and 200 blacks were interviewed prior to the first election, and 240 of the same whites (an 80% retrieval rate again) and 200 different blacks were interviewed in May 1970 between the initial election and the runoff. Our data suggest the following electoral statistics:

1. in 1970, the black percentage of the total Newark electorate was approximately 45 to 48%;
2. turnout for both whites and blacks was high for Newark in the June runoff election, though our estimate of 58% of the registered Negroes voting is by far the lowest black turnout of our four cities;
3. in the final race, Gibson received about 97% of the black vote, though Addonizio had been expected by local observers to attract from 8 to 10% (mostly the families of city workers, and the like). But Gibson received only about 16 to 17% of the white vote. This figure seems to be the crude order of magnitude a black candidate, not running as a "machine man," can expect in white support in a city such as Gary, Cleveland, and Newark where anti-Negro feelings are relatively high and no serious challenge for mayor has previously been made by a black candidate. Moreover, this figure holds up in this instance even when the white incumbent is undergoing trial and conviction for civic corruption;
4. in broader perspective, the Gibson campaign constitutes the opposite extreme from the highly financed and polished campaign of Bradley in Los Angeles. Gibson did not make the all-out effort for white votes made by Bradley and Stokes nor did he mobilize the black community in the fashion of the other three candidates. But he benefited enormously from the federal trial against his opponent held during the campaign as well as from the active campaigning in the

white areas of the former fire chief and defeated white candidate for mayor, John Caufield (after election, Gibson reappointed the popular Caufield as fire chief). And, not incidentally, Gibson entered the race with the highest black registration percentage of any of the four black aspirants.

Our preliminary analysis of the two white surveys suggests that their results replicated the previous studies on who are the white voters for a black mayoralty candidate. Virtually all of Newark's previously extensive Jewish community have now departed the city. But Gibson's white support came disproportionately from the ranks of the young, the college-educated, the higher-income respondents, Democrats, and the least racially bigoted.

GARY, 1971. Two years after our initial study of Gary in October of 1968, the project returned to the city to investigate the mayoralty election shaping up for 1971 in which incumbent Mayor Richard Hatcher would try to win reelection. Two surveys were conducted, one of a probability sample of 192 black registrants and the other of a probability sample of 291 white registrants.

Hatcher faced two serious challengers: City Council President John Armenta and Lake County Coroner Alexander Williams. Armenta is a Mexican-American with some following throughout the city. Dr. Williams is a well-known black politician and physician who was generally regarded as the candidate of the local "machine"—the Lake County Democratic Committee. The mass media took considerable interest in Gary's mayoralty primary, held on May 4, 1971, largely because Mayor Hatcher's major rival was another black. Some media observers mistakenly thought that the Mayor was in serious trouble, that Williams would effectively split the black vote and make it possible for either Williams or Armenta to upset the incumbent.

The surveys painted a different picture. And unlike Los Angeles, there were no sharp shifts in sentiment at the close of the primary campaign so that our electoral predictions proved accurate. The surveys indicated that the overwhelming majority of black voters would continue to support Hatcher; and that Hatcher would keep or increase his modest 1967 white support while the entry of white candidates into the race would sharply erode the white support of Williams. The primary returns gave Hatcher a decisive 58% of the vote with Williams a distant second and the other candidates out of the running. The survey data together with the precinct data from the election suggest the following statistics:

1. by 1971, the black percentage of the total Gary electorate had risen from 1967 several percentage points to approximately 42 to 46%. But in a Democratic Party primary, the registered blacks of Gary may slightly outnumber registered whites;

2. the black turnout was again large, though it may not have reached the remarkable record of 1967. White turnout, however, was down in many areas, unlike 1967. It appears that for a sizable minority of whites an avoidance-avoidance conflict provided by two black candidates led to withdrawal despite the efforts of the machine to achieve a major white turnout for Williams;
3. Hatcher probably received more than 90% of the black votes, with precinct totals in the black areas of 518–55 and 471–7 not uncommon. His white support increased from about 15% in the 1967 final election to about 22% in this 1971 primary. These results are close to what the project's surveys indicated five months earlier;
4. Hatcher's black following is so extensive that few demographic distinctions can be made, though the survey of blacks suggested his greatest black strength is found among those with characteristics similar to Hatcher himself: males, the well educated, home owners, and those born in or near Gary. His limited white following is concentrated among males, the well educated, English-Scots and Germans, and those residing in their neighborhoods for less than three years. Not surprisingly, too, the Mayor's white voters are more liberal than other Gary whites on a wide range of issues.

In choosing three adjectives to describe Mayor Hatcher, his supporters —both black and white—see him as "intelligent, honest, and progressive." Anti-Hatcher whites see him as "intelligent, out-for-himself, and prejudiced." This last description—"prejudiced"—is one that occurs often in the four cities when resistant whites describe their black mayoralty candidate. It refers to the fear that many whites share that powerful blacks in high office will prove antiwhite and openly discriminate against whites in jobs, services, and taxes. Some observers might see in this phenomenon a simple case of projection. Yet it is a genuine and widespread fear that aspiring black candidates throughout the country will have to face. One might expect this fear to recede in time, particularly when the black mayor proves effective and provides little or no validity to the fear. Yet in the two years between the 1968 and 1970 Gary surveys, we detect scant reduction of this particular racial anxiety in spite of Hatcher's able leadership.

Blacks in Gary share similar racial attitudes with other urban blacks in the North. They overwhelmingly reject violence, support integrated schools, and favor liberal governmental policies in general. They are unusual in one interesting respect: presumably as a result of Hatcher's electoral successes and administration, they appear to believe in the political system as a principal means for needed racial change somewhat more than comparable blacks in other cities.

Whites in Gary, however, express an extreme degree of racial animosity, even when compared with such other predominantly lower-middle-class cities as Cleveland and Newark. Furthermore, this racial prejudice is directly related to attitudes toward and voting for Hatcher in both 1967 and 1971 (as shown in Table 1). This severely limits the degree of electoral penetration the Mayor can achieve in the city's white community.

Nevertheless, the black and white voters of Gary have a surprising degree of consensus regarding the major local issues. Leading the list by far is concern over crime followed by attention to sanitation, street repairs, and parks and recreational facilities. High levels of dissatisfaction are recorded among both races over present police protection and recreational facilities, among whites over the public schools, and among blacks over garbage collection. This considerable overlap in interests across the races gives the black candidate the opportunity to seek white and black votes with the same platform. And it provides him the opportunity to emphasize issues which many whites place over racism in importance—a point which we shall emphasize in the next section.

Tentative Answers to Initial Questions

Data on these mayoralty races shed light on two sets of initial questions; one set focuses specifically upon fundamental issues in American race relations, the other upon fundamental issues in social psychology. The mayoralty elections per se, then, provide a salient, real-life situation in which to pursue these matters.

ISSUES IN AMERICAN RACE RELATIONS

How salient will "race" be in mayoralty elections? Is racial bigotry (or "individual white racism" in today's fashionable parlance) operating in a relative vacuum apart from a person's other values and beliefs? Is there a pattern among white voters across cities of the greatest support of and greatest resistance to competent black mayoralty candidates?

Not surprisingly, our data reveal that "race" has been extremely salient in all of the elections studied. Indeed, the fact that a leading candidate for mayor is Negro becomes a dominant feature for both white and black voters, overwhelming in importance political party identification in Gary and Cleveland and scandals in incumbent administrations in Los Angeles and Newark. Thus, the voting turnouts were unusually high for mayoralty races in all four cities (save for whites in Gary in 1971 when the leading opponent was also black); respondents spoke freely of the influence of race on their voting intentions; and our survey measures of prejudiced attitudes related highly and consistently with voting for the white candidates. We have already seen in Table 1 the predictive value of anti-Negro attitudes in the 1967 mayoralty race in Gary.

Yet the salience of race in these political contests cannot be interpreted as evidence for the widely voiced assumption that "white racism" is almost impossible to combat because it operates in a virtual personality vacuum. Said in this manner, of course, this assumption appears psychologically absurd; accordingly, this project has utilized as a guiding hypothesis that racist attitudes are in constant interaction with other attitudes and values and must take their place in a dynamic hierarchy of what is most important to the individual. We believe our data fully support this hypothesis, though the hypothesis directly challenges much of the loose popular analysis of racial prejudice which followed the Kerner Commission Report on Civil Disorders in 1968.

Consider responses to such an open-ended query as: "Is there anything that Mayor Hatcher could do that would cause you seriously to consider voting for him in the next election?" Among the Gary respondents who would not vote for Hatcher for mayor as of October 1968, only about 30% were unable to suggest reasonable actions. Interestingly, most of these respondents were supporters of George Wallace for President; they were, in short, racists who tended to put their anti-Negro beliefs high up in their value hierarchy. But 70% did supply reasonable actions they cared about, most of them local matters that touched their daily lives directly. "If Hatcher would close that stinking city dump at the end of the street," blurted out one interviewee, "then I'd vote for him even if he is black." Or, in our terms, he is stating: "Though I am a racist, I value the closing of the local dump more than I do my racial beliefs." Similarly, two lower-status white precincts in Cleveland which had given Stokes only minimal support in 1967 became pro-Stokes in 1969 after he had opened a much desired playground in the area. We believe this phenomenon is critical to an understanding of American race relations and its future, and we plan to explore it further in future analyses and studies. One theoretical application of it has already been made to the general problem of racism and mental health. . . .

Our brief review of results of the elections in the four cities has already indicated the tentative answer to our third race relations question: consistent patterns emerge across Gary, Cleveland, Los Angeles, and Newark of where the chief support for and resistance to competent black mayoralty candidates lie within the white electorate. Where there are significant concentrations of Jewish voters, as in Gary and Los Angeles, they are especially conspicuous among the supporters. And in all the cities, the college-educated, the young, the least prejudiced, and the least concerned about student unrest and crime in the streets tend to be disproportionately found among white supporters. It also appears that Democrats are more likely to favor black candidates than Republicans; but this finding is rendered ambiguous by the fact that all four black candidates are highly identified Democrats.

The source of greatest white opposition to black political aspirations appears even more clearly. It is not centered among the poorest and least educated, but rather among the lower-middle class. This pattern is sharpest for Wallace support, but it is also to be found in the white votes against all four black mayoralty candidates. One of the dynamics we have uncovered which undergirds this special resistance of the urban lower-middle class is a keen sense of deprivation relative to both blacks and white-collar workers. We shall probe this social psychological phenomenon in the next section.

No other subject has so dominated the attention of the discipline of social psychology as attitude change. Yet much of the research literature on this subject has at least three glaring weaknesses. First, the attitudes influenced in experiments seldom involve deeply rooted, emotionally charged sentiments that typify racial bigotry among white Americans. Second, these experiments have rarely linked the changed attitudes to non-verbal, concrete acts of behavior. And, third, these experiments have generally treated attitudes as simply responses to a particular object (e.g., "Negroes") rather than toward an object in the context of a particular situation (e.g., a particular Negro as the mayor of my city). Seen from this perspective, then, our studies present a unique opportunity for testing attitude change in a real-life situation that corrects for all three of these weaknesses in the present research literature in social psychology.

The discussion above of racial attitudes not existing in a psychological vacuum is, of course, directly relevant to these concerns. In addition, the success of Mayor Yorty's campaign to communicate a message which effectively aroused white fears of a black mayor is of prime importance to social-psychological theories of attitude change. Since neither the Mayor personally nor his fear-provoking message were "popular" among most white voters in Los Angeles, this example neatly illustrates a widely recognized phenomenon in the laboratory: namely, the effectiveness over time of a salient message from a deprecated source. We plan to explore in more detail our before-and-after survey data relevant to this point both within this theoretical context and that of the avoidance-avoidance paradigm.

Also important to social-psychological theory are the effects upon individual whites and blacks of having personally voted for a black mayor who goes on to win the office. We predict for whites, especially if they publicly discuss their vote with others, that this act will lead to more positive racial views in the classic manner of salient behavioral commitment. This notion requires more detailed analysis of our survey data; but the aggregate data are reassuringly consistent. Thus, Mayor Stokes' white total rose slowly with every race from 11% to 19% and 22%. And Mayor Hatcher's white vote also appears to have risen somewhat between 1967 and 1971.

The project has given most of its attention to date, however, on the general theoretical area of social evaluation theory. This theoretical area is built on the basic notion that human beings learn about themselves largely through comparisons with others. A wide range of molecular theories and concepts can be subsumed under this more general theory, such as Festinger's social comparison theory, Hyman and Merton's reference group theory, Lenski's status inconsistency theory, Thibaut and Kelly's concept of comparison level, Homans' concept of distributive justice, and Stouffer's concept of relative deprivation. It is this last concept, relative deprivation, that has proven unusually useful in our analyses of white voters. . . .

We have developed over the course of our twelve surveys an elaborate battery of measures of relative deprivation, the fullest we believe yet attempted in survey research. Eight basic questions are asked requiring 49 different responses; and though this sounds complex, even poorly educated respondents typically had no trouble supplying meaningful data. In addition to the standard Cantril . . . self-anchoring ladder items, we ask about the respondent's economic gains over the past five years and his satisfaction with them. More important, we obtain comparative ratings of his economic gains relative to eight critical groups: white-collar workers, blue-collar workers, Negroes, professionals, whites, unskilled laborers, people in this neighborhood, and people in the suburbs.

Two general trends across the two races and all four cities are of interest. First, the average ratings assigned the economic gains of the eight groups by our respondents are quite accurate. This suggests that the social science dogma that Americans are relatively unaware of their social class structure deserves serious questioning. Second, there exists a broad resentment in these cities of the economic gains of white-collar workers in general and professionals in particular. Large numbers of the respondents of varying background from Newark to Los Angeles believe, for instance, that "professionals in America today have gained more economically in the past five years than they are entitled to."

Our interest in the role of relative deprivation in racial voting was initiated by an array of amazingly consistent relationships noted between a single relative deprivation item and support for Governor George Wallace in Gary in 1968.

Table 2 shows how agreement with the straightforward statement—"In spite of what some say, the lot of the average man is getting worse, not better"—predicted Wallace voting intentions within a number of relevant social controls. Moreover, as Table 3 indicates, the item's predictive value is independent of anti-Negro prejudice despite their positive relationship.

Once we measured relative deprivation with a battery of items beginning with the Cleveland surveys, we soon learned that the most effective approach was through use of the scheme shown in Table 4. This scheme builds on the theoretical analysis of relative deprivation advanced by

TABLE 2 *Relative Deprivation and Wallace Support, Gary, 1968 (in percentages)*

	Supporters			
	Wallace	Nixon	Humphrey	Total
"In spite of what some people say, the lot of the average man is getting worse, not better."				
Agree (118)	41.5	33.1	25.4	100
Disagree (122)	18.9	49.2	32.0	100
Union Members				
Agree (76)	47.3	30.2	22.5	100
Disagree (63)	27.0	33.3	39.7	100
Nonmembers				
Agree (40)	27.5	40.0	32.5	100
Disagree (59)	10.2	66.1	23.7	100
Religion				
Protestants				
Agree (53)	50.9	34.0	15.1	100
Disagree (45)	22.2	53.7	24.1	100
Roman Catholics				
Agree (53)	34.0	34.0	32.1	100
Disagree (51)	17.6	43.1	39.2	100
Social-class Identification				
Close to the working class				
Agree (49)	57.1	18.4	24.5	100
Disagree (36)	25.0	47.2	27.8	100
Not close to the working class				
Agree (25)	36.0	36.0	28.0	100
Disagree (20)	30.0	20.0	50.0	100
Close to the middle class				
Agree (27)	25.9	44.4	29.6	100
Disagree (40)	7.5	60.0	32.5	100
Not close to the middle class				
Agree (15)	26.7	60.0	13.3	100
Disagree (23)	21.7	56.5	21.7	100
Total sample (245)	29.8	42.0	28.2	100

Runciman on the basis of his social class studies in the United Kingdom. Table 4 is formed with two pieces of information: how each respondent views his own economic gains over the past five years in relation (1) to his ingroup (his class or racial category) and (2) to the relevant outgroup (e.g., white-collar workers for the blue-collar respondent, or blacks for the white respondent). Type A respondents are *doubly gratified,* for they feel they

TABLE 3 *Anti-Negro Prejudice, Relative Deprivation, and Wallace Support, Gary, 1968 (in percentages)*

	Supporters			
	Wallace	Nixon	Humphrey	Total
"The lot of the average man is getting worse."				
High Anti-Negro Prejudice				
Agree (59)	52.5	20.3	27.1	100
Disagree (34)	23.0	42.3	34.7	100
Moderate Anti-Negro Prejudice				
Agree (38)	36.8	44.7	18.5	100
Disagree (38)	26.3	44.7	28.9	100
Low Anti-Negro Prejudice				
Agree (18)	27.7	44.6	27.7	100
Disagree (58)	12.1	55.2	32.8	100
Total sample (245)	29.8	42.0	28.2	100

have been doing as well or better than both their ingroup and outgroup. Type B are the critical respondents, for they feel *fraternally deprived.* This is Runciman's term for his key group in British class-deprivation research. They feel they have kept up with or even surpassed the gains of their own group but that they have slipped behind those of their outgroup. Consequently, their deprivation is fraternal in that it is their group as a whole which is seen as losing ground in comparison with the outgroup, and they are likely to perceive this situation as unfair.

TABLE 4 *Four Types of Relative Deprivation and Gratification*

		Personal economic gains compared to outgroup ("white-collar workers" or "Negroes")	
		Equal or greater than	Less than
Personal economic gains compared to ingroup ("blue-collar workers" or "whites")	Equal or greater than	A. doubly gratified	B. fraternally deprived
	Less than	C. egoistically deprived	D. doubly deprived

TABLE 5 *Class Deprivation and 1968 Wallace Vote in Cleveland (in percentages)*

	Class deprivation type			
	A. Doubly gratified	B. Fraternally deprived	C. Egoistically deprived	D. Doubly deprived
Entire Cleveland sample[a] (n = 301)	16	31	15	13
Just those who identify themselves with "working class"[a] (n = 154)	11	41	23	15

[a] Those who did not vote in the 1968 presidential election are omitted.

TABLE 6 *Class Deprivation and 1972 Wallace Preference in Gary, 1970 (in percentages)*

	Class deprivation type			
	A. Doubly gratified	B. Fraternally deprived	C. Egoistically deprived	D. Doubly deprived
Entire Gary sample (n = 288)	12	24	15	17
Non-Democratic party identifiers subsample only (n = 92)	9	47	13	18

By contrast, Type C consists of individuals who sense their gains to have been less than those of their ingroup but at least equal to those of their outgroup; they are therefore termed by Runciman as the *egoistically deprived.* Finally, and least interesting, are the *doubly deprived* respondents of Type D who feel they have lost ground to both their ingroup and outgroup. These individuals are typically older and often retired; their fixed incomes probably have in fact been surpassed by younger groups generally.

Both social class and racial comparisons, using the scheme of Table 4, have been found to be particularly important. The class comparisons contrast blue-collar versus white-collar workers; and since our respondents are largely blue-collar themselves, this means blue-collar workers form the ingroup and white-collar workers the outgroup for our purposes. The racial comparisons, of course, contrast whites versus blacks in economic gains.

Tables 5 and 6 demonstrate how *one* of these two types of comparisons operates differently as a predictor of Wallace support in Cleveland and

Gary. Fraternal *class* deprivations relate to Wallace voting or preferences in both cities, especially for such meaningful subsamples as working-class identifiers and non-Democrats (Tables 5 and 6). Some, but not all, of these differences, however, are traceable to background differences of the four class-deprivation types. Whites who feel fraternally deprived in class terms are disproportionately concentrated among those of medium income and education who are younger, full-time, working-class members of labor unions. These respondents, of course, are precisely the ones we have isolated in other analyses as especially prone to being pro-Wallace and against black candidates. Yet controls for these factors, as in the earlier Gary analysis of Table 3, reduce but do not remove the predictive value of the relative class-deprivation measures. This fact strongly implies that fraternal class deprivation acts as a mediator of some, though not all, of the special lower-middle-class component of the Wallace phenomenon in the North. In sharp contrast, fraternal race deprivations do not effectively predict Wallace leanings in either city. This suggests . . . that the Wallace appeal in northern cities had a strong populist as well as racist flavor.

Perceived racial deprivations become important, however, for predicting white support of black mayoralty candidates. Table 7 provides these consistent and dramatic results across the four cities. Note that the fraternally deprived on race report less willingness to vote for, and a more negative image of, the black candidate in every instance. The background differences among the four racial-deprivation types are similar to those among the four class-deprivation types noted above, though they are less extensive. Controls for these background variables do not substantially affect the relationships shown in Table 7.

Conclusion

Despite the wide variations in political systems, political personalities, and urban contexts, a number of important phenomena appear to be replicated across cities when a black candidate runs for mayor. It is not surprising in the United States of the late twentieth century that racial considerations become paramount in these contests. And public opinion survey data over the years prepare us for the findings on which white voters are most likely to support the black candidate: Jewish Americans, the young, the college-educated, and the self-designated "liberals."

The base of major resistance in the white electorate to black aspirants, however, is more subtle. As with the "George Wallace" phenomenon in the North, the lower-middle-class whites are conspicuous in their opposition even in comparison with lower-class whites. This phenomenon has been much discussed and distorted in popular analysis, and variously labeled "the backlash of the ethnics," "the revolt of the silent majority," and other catchy but largely meaningless phrases. Initial analyses of the data de-

TABLE 7 *Racial Deprivation and the Reactions of Whites to Black Mayoralty Candidates (in percentages)*

	Racial-deprivation type			
	A. Doubly gratified	B. Fraternally deprived	C. Egoistically deprived	D. Doubly deprived
MAYORALTY VOTING				
For Stokes vesus Perk, Cleveland, 1969[a]	31	12	49	29
For Bradley versus Yorty,				
LA primary vote, 1969	26	17	34	30
Runoff preference, 1969	51	30	46	46
Runoff vote, 1969	35	21	52	42
For Gibson versus Addonizio, Newark, 1970	19	14	29	20
For Hatcher versus Williams, etc., Gary primary, 1971	17	7	30	15
CANDIDATE IMAGE (% FAVORABLE)[b]				
Stokes, 1969	57	33	64	50
Bradley, 1969	65	44	71	49
Gibson, 1970	25	18	27	36
Hatcher, 1970	35	17	36	29

[a] For Democrats only, since this was a partisan final election.

[b] The respondents were each presented a printed card with 12 adjectives from which three were chosen as the most descriptive of the black candidate. Half the adjectives were favorable in tone (e.g., intelligent, honest) and half were unfavorable (e.g., out-for-himself, prejudiced). The favorable percentages provided here represent those whites who chose 3 favorable adjectives in the cases of Stokes and Gibson, and 2 or 3 favorable adjectives in the cases of Bradley and Hatcher.

scribed in this chapter point to a specific social-psychological condition that appears to be an important motivational source of this phenomenon. Fraternal relative deprivation as perceived by workers themselves acts in these data as both a cause and mediator of lower-middle-class white anger directed at blacks in northern cities. It is relative deprivation and not absolute deprivation; and it is relative to the perceived gains of black Americans as a group compared to those of white Americans as a group. By no means is this social-psychological factor a complete explanation of the larger lower-middle-class phenomenon of special resistance to racial change. But fraternal relative deprivation does seem to attain an importance that cannot be ignored in any broader explanation.

SUGGESTED READINGS

Race

Hanes Waltons, Jr.'s work *Black Politics: A Theoretical and Structural Analysis* (Philadelphia: Lippincott, 1972) provides a useful starting point for the consideration of racial issues in American society. The examination of black voting patterns, local interest groups, urban blacks, and the characteristics of black elected officials results in an almost complete survey of black political participation in American politics. Expressions of political ideology by black leaders are contained in works such as Malcolm X, *The Autobiography of Malcolm X* (New York: Grove Press, 1964); Stokely Carmichael and Charles Hamilton, *Black Power: The Politics of Liberation in America* (New York: Vintage Books, 1967); Eldridge Cleaver, *Soul on Ice* (New York: McGraw-Hill, 1968); and H. Rap Brown, *Die Nigger Die!* (New York: Dial Press, 1969). Theodore Draper views black consciousness in the broader context of nationalism in his book *The Rediscovery of Black Nationalism* (New York: Viking Press, 1970). *The Black Politician: His Search for Power* (North Scituate, Mass.: Duxbury, 1971), edited by Mervyn Dymally, surveys the problems faced by black leaders competing in the political arena.

Other suggested works include:

Altshuler, Alan. *Community Control: The Black Demand for Participation in Large American Cities.* Indianapolis: Pegasus, 1970.

Bartley, Numan V. *The Rise of Massive Resistance.* Baton Rouge: Louisiana State University Press, 1970.

Bell, Carolyn S. *The Economics of the Ghetto.* Indianapolis: Pegasus, 1970.

Bellush, Jewel, and Stephen M. David, eds. *Race and Politics in New York City.* New York: Praeger, 1971.

Marx, Gary T. *Protest and Prejudice: A Study of Belief in the Black Community.* New York: Harper & Row, 1967.

Matthews, Donald R., and James W. Prothro. *Negro Political Participation in the South.* New York: Harcourt, Brace & World, 1966.

Matthews, Donald R., and James W. Prothro. *Negroes and the New Southern Politics.* New York: Harcourt, Brace & World, 1966.

Orleans, Peter, and William Ellis, eds. *Race, Change, and Urban Society.* Beverly Hills, Calif.: Sage Publications, 1971.

Silverman, Sandra, ed. *The Black Revolt and Democratic Politics.* Lexington, Mass.: Heath, 1970.

Tabb, William. *The Political Economy of the Black Ghetto.* New York: Norton, 1970.

Wilson, James Q. *Negro Politics: The Search for Leadership.* New York: Free Press, 1960.

Wirt, Frederick M. *Politics of Southern Equality: Law and Social Change in a Mississippi County.* Chicago: Aldine, 1970.

Woodward, C. Vann. *The Strange Career of Jim Crow,* 2nd rev. ed., New York: Oxford University Press, 1966.

Young, Richard P., ed. *Roots of Rebellion.* New York: Harper & Row, 1970.

Carol Crowther

Crimes, Penalties, and Legislatures

One of the most pervasive problems of modern society is how to cope with the rising crime rate. For the most part, attention has been devoted to improving apprehension methods and providing a more efficient trial process. Little attention has been paid, on the other hand, to the general assumption that penalties deter crime and to legislative responsibility for action on the matter. Carol Crowther's approach is thus distinctive, both because of its relevance to crime control and because of its suggestion for reform of the present criminal justice system in the states. Her evidence suggests that the criminal-penalties system at present in use in California (and everywhere else in the Union) neither deters nor rehabilitates effectively and ought to be replaced by a less arbitrary and less costly parole system.

In 1967 the California Legislature requested the Assembly Office of Research to study the deterrent effects of criminal penalties and to design future research on other aspects of the crime-control problem. The study resulted in the publication of a report, *Crime and Penalties in California*.[1] Some of the findings of this study are presented here, together with a discussion of their implications.

Experience had already shown that social research undertaken to meet legislative needs can have a rapid and significant impact on lawmaking. A

[1] California, Assembly, Committee on Criminal Procedure, *Crime and Penalties in California*, prepared by Robin L. Lamson and Carol Crowther (Sacramento, 1968).

Reprinted from "Crimes, Penalties, and Legislatures" by Carol Crowther in volume no. 381 (January 1969) of *The Annals* of the American Academy of Political and Social Science. Some descriptive and bibliographical footnotes have been omitted for considerations of space and textual format.

case in point was an earlier study of mental health facilities and services conducted by the staff which later became the nucleus of the Assembly Office of Research.[2] This study formed the basis of legislation which abolished the involuntary and indefinite mental commitment system. Under the new system, involuntary commitment can only be authorized as a last resort and for specific time periods, usually very short.

The *Crime and Penalties* study closely resembled the investigation of the mental health system. Both studies were evaluations of public service systems. In both studies, we followed a plan of action somewhat along these lines:

1. Search of the literature for expert opinions relevant to decision needs.
2. Development of unambiguous statistical support of those opinions —often these opinions were proffered, it was found, without such support.
3. Commissioning of original research where needed.
4. Application of findings to cost-benefit analysis of existing government programs.

The rehabilitative value of the systems examined was found to be minimal at best. No solid evidence could be found that institutionalization improved the social competence of the majority of mental patients or prison inmates. Therefore, the studies could have an immediate budgetary impact: an ineffective program could be drastically reformed or cancelled, thus freeing public funds for diversion into existing alternative programs known to produce better results.

These studies illustrate the important difference between purely academic research and legislative-oriented research. Major legislative policy changes can be made on the basis of available date *before* the question of *why* one program works better than another, the proper concern of social scientists, is answered in detail.

However, legislative research can produce ideas of use to both academicians and legislators. Clearer and more humane perspectives on changes can be made on the basis of available data *before* the question of social processes can emerge from gross consideration of the cost-effectiveness of government systems. An example of such an attempt at reformulation—a distinction between "primary" and "secondary" penalties—is presented at the end of this essay.

[2] California, Assembly, Committee on Ways and Means, Subcommittee on Mental Health Services, *The Dilemma of Mental Commitments in California—A Background Document*, 1966.

General Conclusions Based on Gross Statistics

Penal legislation in California has been based on the belief that more severe penalties (longer sentences and longer time served in prison) deter the general population from committing crimes, and protect the community from criminals. The consequences of this legislative trend and its influence upon parole policy have been expensive. The median stay in California prisons is thirty months, second highest of the twelve largest states in the United States, and the number of state prisoners per 100,000 population is the highest of the large states.

The implicit assumptions have been: The more time served, the more deterrence, the more rehabilitation, the more community protection.

We found no solid evidence that these assumptions are correct, and substantial evidence that they are wrong.

If lengthy incarceration operated as a deterrent, crime rates should be lowest in states where the time served by convicts is highest. They are not. The median time served in the fifty states runs from nine months in New Hampshire to thirty-nine months in Hawaii. High and low crime rates are found at both ends of the scale of median time served. Further, the states which annually support the greatest number of prisoners (per 100,000 population) show no lower crime rates than the states which support the smallest number. The same lack of relation between crime and penalties holds for the twelve largest states, where urbanization might be assumed to have some special effects on crime and government response to it.

The assumption that those who have experienced severe felony penalties will be deterred from future crime is especially resilient. It also appears to be incorrect.

Allowing for discrepancies in parole policies and reporting systems, recidivism rates in all states are generally constant. Webster defines "recidivism" as the habitual or chronic tendency to relapse into crime or antisocial behavior patterns. Parole authorities use the term to cover anything from trivial misbehavior (subjectively judged by parole agents to warrant return to prison) to recommitment for new felony convictions. Return-to-prison rates vary 10 to 15 per cent from year to year, but these fluctuations show no relation to differences in median time served. Total return-to-prison rates appear to be functions of administrative decisions rather than of parolee behavior. Recommitments for new felonies are the most solid statistics available.

Because many states, including California, have increased the use of probation and other noninstitutional devices, it is probable that the most serious and habitual offenders are now concentrated in state prisons. Even this trend has not clearly affected the regularity of recidivism rates.

For any large state in the nation, whether median stay is long or short, it is safe to predict that about 35 per cent of persons paroled from state prisons will return in a few years because of a technical parole violation or a new felony conviction. Another 15 per cent will be fined or jailed for minor offenses. Returns with a new commitment—including the commission of another felony—are considerably lower. Since 1958 in California, these rates (one to two years after release) have varied from 13 to 19 per cent. These returns seem to be typical of the national picture. Whether "recidivism," with its varying definitions, or "returns with new commitment" are accepted as the measurement of institutional effectiveness, no evidence can be found to support extended incarceration as a determinate element in the deterrence of crime among former convicts.

The crime-rate data are, of course, defective and reflect on the validity of the conclusions. But the legislative value of the findings is still high. The crime rates used were those published by the Federal Bureau of Investigation for the twelve states containing 62 per cent of the United States population. No more comprehensive facts are available.

If the various discrepancies in the classification and reporting of crime and recidivism are assumed to cancel each other out in at least some large states, then the true crime and recidivism rates for large states are similar, while the median times served vary greatly. Our expensive policy of severe penalties is therefore not justified on grounds of effective deterrence.

On the other hand, if the crime and recidivism rates are assumed to be so inaccurate as to be meaningless, then we have no comprehensive facts about the frequency of crimes. Our expensive policy of severe penalties, therefore, cannot be said to have objective evidence to justify it.

Specific Analyses Supporting the General Conclusions

ATTACKS ON POLICE OFFICERS

In the city of Los Angeles (which contains one seventh of the population of California) the rate of attacks on police went from 2.5 per 100 policemen in 1952, to 15.8 in 1966—an increase of 528 per cent. In 1961 the first special penalties for attacks on the police were enacted by the Legislature, and such penalties were further increased in the sessions of 1963 and 1965.

Before 1961, a person who committed assault with a deadly weapon could receive a fine up to $5,000 and/or up to one year in jail, or up to ten years in a state prison. By 1966, all sentences for attacks on peace officers *required* commitment to the state prison, and persons using a deadly weapon received a mandatory sentence—ranging in extent from five years to life—of commitment to a state prison. The state of California has thus experienced more than five years of increased penalties for attacks on law enforcement officers. During this same period, 1961 to 1966, the rate of attacks on Los Angeles policemen went from 8.4 to 15.8 per 100 officers per year, an increase of 90 per cent.

After five years of increasing penalties, a Los Angeles policeman was almost twice as likely to be attacked as he was before the increases.

MARIJUANA OFFENSES

In 1961 the California Legislature removed the sentence of 0 to 12 months in the county jail as an *optional* penalty for the possession of marijuana and *required* that possessors serve 1 to 10 years in the state prison. Penalties for the sale of marijuana and for offenders with prior convictions were also increased.

In 1961, 3,500 persons were arrested for marijuana offenses; in 1967 over 37,000 persons were arrested for marijuana offenses.

BAD-CHECK WRITING: A "TYPICAL" CRIME

An exhaustive study of this offense in Nebraska, where bad checks over $35 establish a felony, found that in some counties, the felony provisions of law were rarely invoked, while in other counties, there was a high incidence of criminal sentences for bad-check offenses. But no correlation between felony sentences and the number of bad checks written per capita in the various counties was found. No evidence that felony provisions deter bad-check writing.

Research in Colorado, where the offense is only a misdemeanor, also demonstrated no correlation between the strictness of the penalties actually imposed and the number of bad checks per capita. Comparison of four counties of Nebraska with four Colorado counties matched for similar social and economic conditions also indicated no significant difference in bad-check-writing rates. In Colorado, where penalties were more lenient, there were fewer short-check losses.

EFFECTS OF REDUCTION OF PENALTIES ON RECIDIVISM

Examples range from the extraordinary early-release situation created by the *Gideon* v. *Wainwright* decision in the Supreme Court, to the experience of the states of Washington and California when administrative decisions were made to reduce incarceration time. In all these cases, no significant increase in recidivism rates was found. In some cases, a decrease in recidivism accompanied the reduction of time served.

EFFECTS OF INCARCERATION

Since 95 per cent of the men now in California prisons will eventually be returned to the community, the problem of rehabilitation (often designated in the literature as the custody-versus-treatment dilemma) is urgent.

Official opinion (for example, the American Bar Association and the President's Commission on Law Enforcement and Administration of

Justice) and numerous individual criminologists have emphasized the actively destructive potential of most penal institutions. Incarceration breaks a man's constructive ties with the community, educates him in crime, deprives him of his skills and of the employment contacts needed to regain his place in society, and requires that he learn to conform to abnormal social patterns enforced by both official and inmate codes of behavior. In such prison situations, rehabilitative programs are not likely to be effective.

These conclusions are difficult to prove statistically because most studies of the beneficial effects of probation as a substitute for incarceration, for example, involve comparisons of populations already screened for lesser "criminal potential." It is usually argued that only lesser offenders will be placed on probation or granted early release to parole and that, therefore, lower recidivism rates are to be expected for these groups.

However, some empirical evidence of the destructive nature of institutions is available. For example, a comparison of the recidivism rates of early and late releases to parole provides statistical evidence on the effects of imprisonment.

In February 1968, the Assembly Office of Research requested from the California Department of Corrections information on the relation of time served to parole outcome. In May the office received an analysis of differences in recidivism for matched pairs of men who had served more or less than the median time for first- and second-degree robbery and first- and second-degree burglary.

> In comparisons of parole outcome within three follow-up periods [one half year, one year, and two years] there were differences in outcome between the male felons paroled in 1965 who served less than the median months, and who served more than the median time for robbery and burglary commitment offenses.
>
> To minimize the effect on outcome of the factors affecting parole, matched samples were selected in each offense category—controlling on age [Base Expectancy Score—which includes previous criminal history], ethnic group, parole region, and type of parole unit.
>
> For all offense categories and in all follow-up periods the per cent of favorable outcome among the men who served less than the median was greater than among those who served more than the median. Almost half of the testable comparisons showed statistically significant differences.[3]

The populations concerned were large enough to permit the selection

[3] California, Department of Corrections, Research Division, *Parole Outcome and Time Served for First Releases*, 1968. This study was received too late for inclusion in *Crime and Penalties*.

of 139 matched pairs for first-degree robbery and 240 pairs for second-degree burglary. After two years, favorable outcome (as defined by the parole agency) for men serving less than the median for first-degree robbery was 73 per cent; for men serving more than the median, 48 per cent. Second-degree burglars scored 53 per cent and 43 per cent.

Facts such as these tend to refute the notion that the temporary protection of the community bought by the temporary incarceration of a particular offender contributes to long-range public safety.

Subjective accounts of prison experience provide another kind of evidence of destructiveness of prisons. The following letter from a young inmate, reproduced verbatim, was recently received by a sociologist. It exemplifies both the illicit, organized violence that can control behavior within a prison system and the grotesque decisions that an inmate may feel he has to make in order to survive in that environment.

> Dear Sir:
>
> I delayed this letter purposely because I've been engaged in mental combat with my peers for almost two months now, figuring on a drastic change. Well the change came! ! !
>
> But now I'm almost afraid to pass on the happening because it could very easily confuse you. However, on the contrary, I feel I must let you share this with me, you being my only link to the outside besides my mother.
>
> Sir, the first day I came to the Mainline [a California State Prison] from R.G.C. [Reception-Guidance Center] I knew I wasn't in the right frame of mind to wage war on my peers and programmers [the prison staff] alike. One has to be hard, evil and self-centered in order to make it here.
>
> It all started when a pal of mine told me he was being pressured for his canteen [his ration of cigarettes, etc.]. By my being fair size and having plenty status from old timers, I took it upon myself to try and help the pal. Anyway, I asked the main party involved in the little scheme to give the guy a chance and not to jump on him in a mass, after which I was thoroughly beaten and hospitalized.
>
> Upon my release, I was promptly tagged as "fink" and had to lock up to avoid further engagement in combat. The problem of getting in protective custody was easy. I told the programmer I was a homosexual. It seems my problems have just begun.
>
> Sir, in all seriousness, I am losing my faith in people.
>
> I hope the programmer returned your check. You see, personal checks are taboo. Thanks anyway. I dig the feeling more than the money.
>
> Peace, Sir

THE IMPACT AND CONSISTENCY OF THE CRIMINAL-JUSTICE SYSTEM

More than 400,000 felonies were reported in California in 1966. Of the 57,000 crimes of personal violence, 51 per cent (more than half committed by family members or other persons previously known to the victims) were reported cleared by arrest or other means, and 21 per cent of the 362,000 property crimes were cleared in like manner. In the end, only five thousand offenders were committed to state institutions.

The regional inconsistencies in the application of penalties are remarkable. Filing of felony complaints against those arrested for felonies ranged from 29 to 90 per cent among the 58 counties of California in 1966. Imposition of prison sentences ranged from 0 to 63 per cent of convicted felony defendants in 1964. Among the larger counties, the range was 18 to 44 per cent in that year. Whether or not severe penalties are statutory, the minimal impact and the inconsistencies of the criminal-justice system probably undermine the credibility of both penalties and justice for the population most concerned: the criminals.

DETERRENTS OTHER THAN PENALTIES

A special survey of public knowledge of penalties,[4] commissioned through the Assembly Office of Research, revealed that the public knew little about penalties for common felonies and that convicts and the criminally oriented, who knew much more, appeared primarily deterred by fear of apprehension and the practical consequences of conviction, that is, external controls.[5]

A variety of physical deterrents to crime, such as improved automobile and building security, have been tested which definitely reduce crime (though to what ultimate degree is not known).

Increasing the numbers and visibility of policemen as a crime-prevention measure, and improving the technical capability of police agencies to increase the certainty of apprehension of serious criminals, obviously would enhance the degree of prevention and control of crime at the first

[4] Social Psychiatry Research Associates, *Survey of Knowledge of Criminal Penalties,* A report to the California State Assembly Committee on Criminal Procedure, February 1968.

[5] There is also evidence that strongly suggests that critical deterrents differ according to type of *offense* as well as type of individual. A recent article on this subject concludes from empirical data that the legal system may be operating very ineffectively: "It punishes most severely those persons and crimes that are least deterrable, and it punishes least severely those persons and crimes that are most deterrable." See William J. Chambliss, "Types of Deviance and the Effectiveness of Legal Sanctions," *Wisconsin Law Review,* No. 3, 1967.

level of contact between the criminally inclined and the criminal-justice system.

However, given the faults in our crime-control system, the ultimate effects of generally increasing the number of contacts between police and citizens can be rather paradoxical. Increased community *protection* amounts to increased community *surveillance,* and the results could be great increases in arrests for crimes without a victim, such as the use of marijuana, or great increases in incidents of reciprocal provocation between police and juveniles.

Not enough comprehensive studies of the relation between law enforcement capability and crime rates have been made, but some evidence is available.

In 1954, New York City increased the number of police by 125 per cent in one ethnically mixed precinct of 120,000 people. In a four-month period, the felony-crime rate in that area was reduced by 55 per cent. Robberies, burglaries, grand larceny, and auto theft decreased approximately 70 per cent. Of further importance, felonies cleared by arrest rose from 20 per cent to 66 per cent.

A study of response-time and arrest rates in Los Angeles further supports external factors, in this case, technical capability, as significant controls. A one-month study in Los Angeles, in 1966, of 4,704 incidents (of which 1,905 were "reported crimes") demonstrated a close relation between speed of police response and effective enforcement. When response-time (by the police) was one minute, 62 per cent of reported crimes ended in arrest. When all cases with response-time up to fourteen minutes were grouped together, only 44 per cent led to arrest.

Legislative Policy Implications

Severe penalties do not deter more effectively than the less severe. Prisons do not rehabilitate. The criminal-justice system is inconsistent and has little quantitative impact upon the mass of offenders and offenses. Most crime is property crime. The criminals who commit it are in the community, and not in prison, and it is highly probable that the prison population represents the least skillful criminals.[6]

Therefore, it seems clear that both the crime problem and the best rehabilitative possibilities are in the community—that investment of more thought and money in control of criminal-community interaction will be more productive than continuing reliance on the isolation of offenders in prisons as an effective crime-control measure.

[6] According to the California Department of Corrections, the median educational level of state prisoners is the seventh-grade level. In 1967, about 6 per cent were illiterate.

COST-EFFECTIVENESS OF PRESENT ALLOCATION IN CALIFORNIA

The 1966–1967 budget of the institutional portion of the state corrections system was approximately $100 million. In that year, 31 per cent of the adult felon population in California prisons had been committed for property offenses: burglary, auto theft, other kinds of theft, and forgery and checks. Sixteen per cent had been committed for drug offenses—a group whose proportion of serious "criminality" is not known. This group, convicted for crimes connected with property and drugs, consists of more than 10,000 persons—maintained by the state at an institutional cost of more than $26 million each year.

The cost of maintaining one adult prisoner in 1966–1967 was $2,628, including all institutional costs, excluding capital outlay. The average parole cost in that year was $572 per parolee. The average policeman in that year was paid $7,500–$8,500.

For every five lesser offenders released to payrole one year before the present median time served (thirty months) one policeman could be added to local law enforcement, or several could be trained to higher levels of effectiveness.

These facts indicate that state-prison incarceration, especially lengthy incarceration, for many offenders is a misuse of public funds which would be better allocated to local rehabilitation programs and local law enforcement agencies.

Proposals to increase funds available to local law enforcement agencies are controversial, given the present degree of dissension over the propriety and effectiveness of police behavior. However, improvements in the prevention and control of crime and in community police relations will certainly never occur unless innovative programs are funded.

PROBLEMS OF REALLOCATION

At present, whole classes of offenders are retained at unnecessarily close and expensive levels of confinement and supervision because the various decision-makers involved are required to make predictions about the future behavior of offenders which cannot, given the present state of social science, be made. "Social and psychological history," "changes in attitude," estimates of "institutional progress," and "anticipation of constructive response to parole supervision" [7] are particularly useless as evaluative criteria in the disposition of offenders because such subjective evaluations are rooted in the attitudes of the appraiser and in the conservative tendencies of bureaucracies.

In California, the result has been that while probation is used exten-

[7] These are actual examples of official disposition criteria.

sively (probably chiefly because institutions are overcrowded), parole board policy has become increasingly cautious and expensive. In California, the Adult Authority, an administrative body, determines (within the legislated limits for the offense) the length of sentence and the parole-release time of the convicted offender. Median time served by those released from prison has increased from twenty-four months in 1960 to thirty months in 1967. No technical or legal justifications have been offered. Although the initial choice between probation and commitment to prison is often arbitrary, the offender thus committed tends to remain incarcerated.

Because the absence of a *clear, positive,* and *legislatively authorized* parole policy is a fundamental obstacle to the reallocation of funds, and because the decision problems involved are repeated at each level of the correctional system, *Crime and Penalities in California* focused on the parole problem.

PROPOSED LEGISLATION

The model legislation presented in the report* required that offenders committed to prison be automatically released to parole at expiration of the statutory minimum parole-eligible period (often only six months under present law), unless their individual histories contained substantial evidence of past serious violence.

The resulting institutional savings were to be devoted chiefly to improved parole services and subsidies for improvements in local law enforcement agencies.

Although it is known that certain types of violent offenders are those *least* likely to recidivate, it was believed that a first politically feasible step in decreasing unnecessary and wasteful confinement in California state institutions would be to relieve the parole authorities, who are vulnerable to a variety of political pressures, of their heavy and unfulfillable responsibility for *prediction* of parole behavior, at least for nonviolent offenders. The known high recidivists, check-forgers, for example, would receive early release under this act, but the supporting logic is that nonviolent repeaters should be dealt with locally, and not by the expensive *state* correctional system.

The basic intent of the act was to substitute clearly defined *statutory ineligibility for release* criteria based on the past *actions* of offenders for the present *administratively defined eligibility* criteria that necessarily rely on "predictive" data of highly questionable validity. By requiring the early release of any offender not shown to be clearly ineligible, the act would essentially remove responsibility for the disposition of doubtful cases from the parole authorities and return it to the courts.

The negative criteria, while imperfect, represent an attempt to give

* Introduced as A. B. 1269, 1968 Session, California State Assembly.

substance to the American Bar Association's recommendation that "no confinement is to be preferred to partial or total confinement, in the absence of affirmative reasons to the contrary.[8] This concept of negative criteria, developed to expedite the early release of nonviolent prisoners from state prisons, could obviously be further refined and applied to other decision points in the criminal-justice process.[9]

At present, many officials are, in effect, required to show reasons for retaining offenders at the lowest levels of supervision or confinement. The establishment of negative criteria would require officials to establish evidence of serious criminality in order to justify placing any offender *above* minimal levels of supervision or confinement, thus countering the institutionalizing tendencies of most components of the present system.

. . .

Reformulation: Primary and Secondary Penalties

Research on the crime problem continued after the report was issued. Evidence regarding the cost-effectiveness of present probation and parole programs as supervisory (community protection) and rehabilitative systems was collected. The tentative conclusion was that the intensity—thus, expense—of supervision was unrelated to recidivism rates among probationers and parolees. Community-based treatment facilities designed to fit local circumstances and individual offenders seem the only exceptions. The less punitive quality of such programs, as well as the reward elements generated by work-furlough programs (wages and the social approval of the job-holder), appeared to be among the elements determining their greater success.

The destructive aspects of conviction and confinement have been discussed at length by many criminologists. However, the cumulative injurious impact of criminal processing has eluded clear delineation and measurement.

Each separate step of intake into the criminal justice and corrections process imposes handicaps on the offender. The severity of these penalties may be far more significant than has been or can be measured. Besides the obvious primary penalty of loss of freedom, a number of secondary penalties are automatically incurred by some arrests, and by any conviction, which can have permanent effects, inappropriate to the gravity of the

[8] American Bar Association, *Sentencing Alternatives and Procedures,* December 1967, p. 64.

[9] For example, the disposition of a multiple-offense criminal does not, at present, usually seem to be affected by whether his history demonstrates an increase or decrease in his "criminality."

offense or uncontrollably severe (hence unjust). These secondary penalties are an extreme handicap to the individual and, consequently, result in some amount, often great, of public cost.

The following outline of system actions and individual and social consequences attempts to clarify the structured, yet indiscriminate and costly, punitiveness of the present system. The subject matter is extremely condensed in order that the complex effects of system actions may be appreciated, and that specific *minimum* dollar costs of offender intake may be emphasized.

Studies of negotiated justice and the great variations in prison commitments from different court jurisdictions indicate that the choice between misdemeanor or felony charge and conviction is also essentially a lottery. Thus, the discrepancy between total misdemeanor-penalty range and total felony-penalty range is a costly and crucial defect in our justice and corrections system. It is especially critical that severe secondary penalties can be the same for lesser and greater felony offenders. The wide range of debilitating punishment available in the system can be intentionally or accidentally applied to lesser offenders or to those whose crimes, however serious, are not likely to be repeated.

System Actions, Primary Penalties, Secondary Penalties, and Public Costs

Action	Primary penalty range	Secondary penalty range	Public costs
Arrest	Possible short confinement	Possible stigma, job loss, bail payment	Possible lost income (hence tax revenue), possible court costs
Serious Misdemeanor Conviction	Possible six to twelve months in county jail	Stigma (often transferred to family) Job loss Reduced job opportunities	Lost income (hence tax revenue Court costs Jail costs $1,150/ yr./prisoner, if family goes on welfare; $2,057/ yr./average family[a]

[a] In California, approximately $17,000,000 is expended each year in public assistance for families who need support because the father is in prison or in jail, according to the Assembly Social Welfare Committee.

Systems Actions, Primary Penalties, Secondary Penalties, and Public Costs (continued)

Action	Primary penalty range	Secondary penalty range	Public costs
Felony Conviction	Probation status (often includes up to one year in jail) State imprisonment time served (California median)[b] murder (2nd): 63 months marijuana: 30 months burglary (2nd): 21 months auto theft: 19 months Parole supervision and restriction	Stigma (often transferred to family) Job loss if incarcerated Reduced job opportunities Voting rights (statutory) Public office (statutory) Barred from most public employment or military service Social ostracism Possible official harassment Exposure to dangerous criminals if incarcerated Sequential penalties: increased probability of arrest and more severe penalties if conviction	Lost income (hence tax revenue) Court costs Probation-supervision $270/yr./probationer If jail a condition of probation, $1,150/yr./prisoner State imprisonment $2,700/yr./prisoner plus education in crime and/or enforced participation in pathological prison system Parole supervision $528/yr./parolee

[b] Actual times served for various offenses are included in this outline to call attention to the apparent imbalance of primary penalties.

There is substantial evidence that the present criminal-justice system cannot administer justice consistently,[10] and that the deterrent or social effectiveness of the degree of punishment or treatment of the majority of persons entering the system is far less than the costs of (1) supervision of offenders (including confinement), (2) the handicaps—imposed upon per-

[10] Some extraordinary increase in court process expenditure might, of course, improve the quality of justice. However, the total cost of the California criminal-justice system is approaching $800 million per year, of which court, district-attorney, and public-defender costs alone amount to $90 million.

sons by identification as criminals and/or by intake into the penal system, and (3) the long-range public service burdens incurred by the system's production of persons so handicapped.

Furthermore, because the deviant of questionable criminality, the poor, and the least competent are the most likely to be taken into this system, the areas of behavior proscribed as "criminal" should be reduced, and constructive alternatives to arrest and intake into any *large* system should be developed immediately.

SUGGESTED READINGS

Crime

The area of crime and corrections is a major problem of state and local governments, but there has not been much work done with an eye toward linking the governmental systems with the treatment of the problem. There is a tendency to treat the police and correction officials as separate from the rest of the policy-making structures of government. Perhaps these are examples of those bureaucracies that stay the same regardless of the leadership at the top. However, such a proposition is doubtful and one suspects that police departments are more political than they seem.

The same is true of the treatment of crime. It is seen as divorced from politics. But on closer look, there are political questions that need to be answered. How much money will be allocated to fight crime? Who will get the money? Who will get arrested? How harsh will sentences be for certain crimes? What will the parole and probation policy be? Who will get paroled? What will be the overall correctional policy? And an array of other questions demand political answers.

There have been several national commissions established in recent years to examine various aspects of crime and violence. The best known, the National Commission on the Causes and Prevention of Violence, has published numerous reports. A lesser known one, the President's Commission on Law Enforcement and Administration of Justice, has also done extensive work. One of its most recent publications is a two-volume report by Albert J. Reiss, *Studies in Crime and Law Enforcement in Major Metropolitan Areas.* In addition, there are innumerable Congressional hearings and reports on the subject.

There is a good body of literature on the machinery of the administration of justice. In his *An Introduction to the Legal System,* Jay A. Sigler discusses the role of lawyers, the juries, the probation officers, and other participants in the system. An insight into a crucial aspect of trials is given by Harry Kalven and Harris Zeisel in *The American Jury.* There has been some work done on the question of sentencing. Edward Green, "Judicial Attitudes in Sentencing," in Glendon Schubert, ed., *Judicial Behavior,* argues that judges do not allow their prejudices to govern their sentencing as much as has been generally thought. Another article on the subject is "The Ethnic Factor in Criminal Sentencing," by A. D. Castbery, in the September 1971 issue of the *Western Political Quarterly.*

Other recommended works in the area include:

Glaser, Daniel, comp. *Crime in the City.* New York: Harper & Row, 1970.

Glaser, Daniel. *The Effectiveness of a Prison and Parole System.* Indianapolis: Bobbs-Merrill, 1969.

McLennan, Barbara, N., ed. *Crime in Urban Society.* New York: Dunellen, 1970.

Preiss, J. J., and H. J. Ehrlich. *An Examination of Role Theory: The Case of the State Police.* Lincoln: University of Nebraska Press, 1966.

Westley, William A. *Violence and the Police: A Sociological Study of Law, Custom, and Morality.* Cambridge, Mass.: MIT Press, 1971.

Marilyn Gittell

Education: The Decentralization-Community Control Controversy

A dominant trend in school administration and local government generally in recent years has been consolidation. Consolidation has recommended itself as offering economy of scale and thus permitting the employment of better and more efficient techniques in education and government. However, certain values are lost in any centralizing move, and difficult questions of minority representation are raised. In an effort to counteract some of the disadvantages of consolidation, a program of decentralization, to permit some degree of community control, was begun in New York in the 1960s. Much has been written about that experimental program; Gittell has provided the best overall examination and analysis of it to date.

City institutions have yet to adjust to the changing character of the city population. Pressing needs have been met with limited responses. Although, over the last three decades, cities have increased their services—and, as one result, city bureaucracies have doubled in size—such expansion has not been paralleled by any fundamental change in structure and environment. Urban school systems are typical of this situation.

Throughout this century, and particularly since World War II, economy and efficiency, civil service reform, professionalism, and centralization have characterized the major movements in urban government. All these factors have contributed to the development of a remote, static bureaucratic structure, ill equipped to handle the demands of the new population

Reprinted from *Race and Politics in New York: Five Studies in Policy-Making* (pp. 134–161), edited by Jewell Bellush and Stephen M. David. Some descriptive and bibliographical footnotes have been omitted for considerations of space and textual format.

that has flowed into most of the nation's urban centers. The old mechanism for immigrant entry to the city's political structure is gone: The political party no longer serves as the community welfare agency, as a major channel for achieving status or power. Today, government jobs are restricted by professional standards and examination procedures; the poor nonwhite, newly arrived and badly educated, is shut out of the system.

With the expansion of the nonwhite population in the cities, segregation in housing has intensified. The increased isolation produced by this pattern has made communication and meaningful contact between black and white less possible now than during previous periods. And, while black and white grow further apart, the expectations and demands of the deprived now far exceed what present programs, set up to correct past inequities, can offer. The result is that the already existing feelings of isolation, neglect, and political impotence are exacerbated. As with other ethnic minorities in earlier times, the only source of power for the black ghetto community is racial solidarity, but, because of the changes in city administration, voting provides only a minor outlet for the effective use of such solidarity. Within the ghetto, there is increasing belief that only the kind of redistribution of power that assures the ghetto community a greater role in the policy process will be acceptable. The survival of America's urban communities will depend upon their ability to respond to these pressures; somehow they must make the adjustments necessary to accommodate these demands.

One of the first areas of attack has been the city school system because it represents so essential a part of the total structure and so important a link to mobility in American society. Moreover, the movements of middle-class whites to the suburbs and lower-class nonwhites to the cities have effected radical changes in the school population; in many of our large cities, a majority of the lower-school population is now nonwhite.

Of the nonwhite school children, many are first-generation urban dwellers and a large proportion of these are still rurally oriented; their cultural traditions differ significantly from the standard middle-class values embedded in the city school system and professed by teachers and school administrators. It is understandable, therefore, that the rate of failure of these children within the system is high. In the ghetto communities, parents are now asking whether it is the children or the system that is failing. One can take the position that the school system should subtract out black and Puerto Rican children—in New York City, over 51 per cent of the student population—from the standard measurements of performance, since the socio-economic background of these students is the cause of their failure. Placing responsibility on the larger society may appear realistic, yet it also leads to a deterministic position in regard to failure. Thus, such children will fail until society does something about their socio-economic status, but their very failure will keep them in that status. This position not only locks these children into a rigid pattern of lifetime failure; it also shifts responsibility from the school system. If one assumes, however, that the test of an educational system is its ability to educate all its children, analysis must necessarily turn to the institution itself rather than to the clientele or the larger society. For one, this might make it possible to take the first realistic steps in breaking the deterministic pattern. From this latter perspective, it is clear that the New York City school system, and urban school systems generally, have failed to meet their responsibility. Though the American public school system was founded on reform—the public school was seen by school reformers as a utilitarian tool to combat poverty, much as it is viewed by such reformers today—it is questionable whether this egalitarian ideal was ever really accomplished. No hard evidence is available on how competently the pubilc school system educated its clients—in particular, those from immigrant families—fifty years ago. Even in regard to the record of the poor in the two most education-minded immigrant groups—Jews and Chinese—There are no dropout statistics and testing data proving their performance in the public schools was as good fifty years ago as that of their middle-class counterparts today. The suspicion is that the public school system never fully succeeded in educating its poor.

If vast changes in population are integral to this failure, it is the lack of institutional adjustment to those changes that must be the subject of concern. Using New York as a case in point, we may ask what then the nature of power is in the school system and how it influences the decisions that are or are not made to accomplish educational goals.

The findings of this author's 1967 study of power distribution in urban school systems emphasized that, in the previous two decades, education in New York City had become amazingly insulated from public control.[1] What is described is an abandonment of public education by key forces of potential power within the city. Bureaucratization and professionalization were contributing factors: Weber's theory of the emergence of a specialized bureaucracy, monopolizing power through its control of expertise, accurately described the role of the education bureaucracy in New York City.

[1] Marilyn Gittell, *Participants and Participation* (New York: Praeger, 1967), pp. 23–41.

In analyzing school policy in New York City, five areas of decision-making in education were used; these were selected to take in the widest possible range of participation by those involved in education and to prove relevance of the policy selected to the over-all education function. Chosen for intensive study were: (1) selection of the superintendent, (2) increases in teachers' salaries, (3) budgeting, (4) school integration, and (5) curriculum development. Other areas of policy were reviewed in a more cursory way, to broaden the scope of the analysis.

The claim that only the professionals can make competent judgments had been accepted, and contributing to, and perhaps growing out of, this attitude was the change in the mayor's role to one of noninvolvement. Civic and interest groups—other than the specialized education groups such as the United Parents Association (UPA) and the Public Education Association (PEA)—responded ambivalently to education issues; on the one hand, they accepted the notion of the professional competence of the bureaucracy, and, on the other, they recognized the need for reform but expressed a hopelessness regarding their ability to change the system. The result was narrow or closed participation in large areas of decision-making. Effective influence in these areas was restricted to an inside core of top supervisory personnel in the headquarters staff of the Board of Education and the United Federation of Teachers. Together, these two groups of professionals were responsible for major policy decisions affecting education in New York City. Policy alternatives were rarely discussed or offered, and the inclination to support the *status quo* was reinforced.

The circumstances surrounding the school decentralization movement in New York City from 1966 through 1969 provides a meaningful basis for reanalysis of the power structure as defined in that 1967 study. With some few additions brought in because the policy decision was taken to the state level, the actors are the same.

THE ACTORS

Within any school system, the potential participants in the policy-making process are essentially the same. Legal power is usually divided between a board of education and a superintendent. The bureaucracy breaks down into a central administrative corps, field administrators, top supervisory staff and middle management. Organizations representing supervisors are common in the larger school districts. Teachers, parents, and their respective organizations are also potential participants. Specialized education-interest groups may also be active and, at times, vitally effective. In the general community, there are other potential participants —local, state, and federal officials, civic groups, the press, business organizations, and individual entrepreneurs seeking the rewards of the school system.

The Board of Education

The Board of Education in New York City is the official policy-making body for the school system, and its members are responsible for long-range educational planning. Prior to 1961, the mayor directly appointed the members, and his appointments traditionally reflected careful consideration of local interests. A screening-panel procedure instituted in 1961 strengthened the role of the civic groups (who obtained representation on the screening panel), thereby reducing the influence of the mayor.[2]

The Board's role has largely been one of balancing conflicting pressures and interests. Essentially, it is a mediator rather than an initiator of policy. As the spokesman for official policy, the Board nominally participates in all major decisions. Though it spends a great deal of its time on sensitive issues, the balance of power in the Board generally fails to produce the consensus necessary for it to act in concert. These issues, though sensitive, are not necessarily major areas of policy; boards have rarely been involved in long-range planning. A major problem for the Board is its lack of an independent staff. This has greatly limited the level and character of Board decision-making. Without such a staff, the Board cannot realistically challenge or review the program of the administrative bureaucracy.

The Superintendent

The highest ranking schoolman in New York City is the superintendent of schools. Appointed by the Board of Education for a six-year term, the superintendent lacks the most essential power of a strong executive—the power of appointment and removal. The system's supervisory staff is developed completely through promotion from the ranks, allowing the superintendent little flexibility in appointments. For example, all assistant superintendents receive tenure after a three-year probationary period. The superintendent's position is further weakened by his dependency on the Board of Examiners, which sets up and administers the machinery for promotions. It is not uncommon for the Board of Examiners to delay examination and approval of candidates for assistant superintendent whom the superintendent may wish to appoint to his own staff. Because he cannot freely develop his own advisory staff and is encumbered by the appointments and promotions made by his predecessors, no superintendent can rely on having his own team of trusted advisers. No superintendent can expect to avoid having to cope with the potentially competing interests of his own supervisory bureaucracy. No superintendent can be sure that directives and policy statements he issues on key policies won't in fact be

[2] From 1961 to 1968, the Board of Education had nine appointed members; in April, 1968, the Board size was increased under state law to fourteen. The 1969 decentralization law completely revised the selection procedures for Board members. An interim board of five appointed by the borough presidents was to hold office until July, 1970. They were to be replaced by a seven-man Board, five of whom were to be elected on a borough-wide basis with two additional members appointed by the mayor. In 1970, the interim board was given another year of life.

attacked by his own supervisory staff, both by that staff's external professional organizations, and, internally, by the organized committees on which the staff members sit.

The Bureaucracy

The education bureaucracy in New York City breaks down into two separate categories: (1) the headquarters staff and (2) the operational field staff. A precise figure on the size of the headquarters staff is difficult to determine, but it is estimated to be somewhere around 4,000. At least 400 to 500 people working at the headquarters do not appear in its budget; although serving as full-time headquarters personnel, they are paid out of local school budgets. The operational field staff includes some 2,200 principals and assistant principals, 31 district superintendents, and 740 department chairmen.

A core supervisory group that holds much of the decision-making power includes some thirty headquarters-staff-members, among them, the executive deputy superintendent, the deputy superintendent in charge of instruction and curriculum, the Board of Examiners, twenty of the thirty assistant superintendents, and a few active directors of special bureaus.

With rare exceptions, members of the core supervisory group come from within the New York City school system—many as principals, almost all with long experience at headquarters. A review of the background of the twenty-six top supervisory staff members in 1965 revealed that their careers followed a general pattern. Having served as principals or assistant principals, they were brought into headquarters on special assignment and/or had served on special committees (usually as a result of contacts already established at headquarters). A . . . study of school principals [has] verified their general commitment to the *status quo* and their resistance to innovation in the system.[3] (As of 1970, there were six permanent black principals and one black district superintendent in the city.)

Supervisory Personnel Associations

The Council of Supervisory Associations (CSA), organized in 1962, is a professional organization made up of the various individual supervisory associations, including those for high school principals, junior high school principals, elementary school principals, assistant principals, high school department chairmen, the Board of Examiners, assistant superintendents,

[3] Arthur J. Vidich and Charles W. McReynolds, "Study of New York City High School Principals Presented to U.S. Office of Education," *New York Post,* October 27, 1969.

and associate superintendents. The council has more than 3,000 members. Through the individual associations and, jointly, through the council (even though it has no formal position in the school system), the vested interests of the supervisory staff exert a strong influence in forming education policy. The council has openly opposed decentralization, a 1969 change in the student suspension policy, students rights proposals, school busing, the comprehensive high school plan, school pairing, and the dropping of IQ examinations—*after* these were adopted as official policy by the Board of Education and by the superintendent.

The Teachers and the Union

Because of its base of power in collective bargaining, the United Federation of Teachers is one of the school system's major policy-makers. The UFT, whose membership in New York City totals more than 40,000, is the official bargaining agent for the city's teachers, and the union contract determines an ever widening area of school policy. To a great extent, it determines the allocation of all education resources, because salaries and teachers' benefits represent close to half the total education budget; as a result, the union is of necessity directly involved in matters of over-all fiscal policy. In the last few years, the union has laid claim to other policy areas, such as those affecting school organization and governance, personnel practices, student behavior, and curriculum. Establishing the More Effective Schools (MES) program in their 1967 contract was the union's first major thrust into broad educational policy; the 1969 contract made further inroads into this area. In addition to the power exercised through the contract, the union wields considerable influence through the city-wide labor federation, the Central Labor Council. The UFT conducts extensive city and state lobbying activity through its own representatives and in association with this general labor lobby.[4]

Local Specialized Education Interest Groups

Two specialized interest groups in New York City have traditionally shared the responsibility for overseeing public education policy: the United Parents Association and the Public Education Association. For many years, board memberships in both organizations overlapped, and their professional staffs worked closely together. Lately, because the PEA has supported stronger decentralization legislation, some disagreement has been evident.

The UPA is a central, city-wide organization made up of delegates

[4] It was reported that, in 1969, the UFT spent over $60,000 in Albany to defeat decentralization. *The New York Times*, February 1, 1970.

elected by local-school parent associations that have chosen to join the central city agency. Its leadership has generally been drawn from the Jewish community. Its general membership is largely made up of middle-class white parents, who are primarily concerned with local school problems and facilities. Accordingly, the UPA has directed much of its attention to individual school matters. In recent years, site-selection controversies and school integration problems have occupied much of its time. The UPA speaks for parents and concerns itself with the immediate effects of policy on local school situations, although it has at times taken general policy positions on key issues. When possible, it makes use of direct influence on Board of Education members: Over the years, members of the city Board were often officers of the association; for example, the association's former executive director is now secretary to the Board. The association has at times supported appointments of supervisory staff, and it continues to maintain viable contacts within the bureaucracy. Although it is unlikely that the UPA could stimulate city-wide support for certain policies, it has effectively used this threat to influence staff and Board decisions. By and large, however, the association supports current school policy and offers little in the way of alternatives.

The PEA is a composite organization; its board is composed of the representatives of other interest groups and organizations active in the city. Its membership is generally drawn from the upper-middle class, although an effort has been made to attract the leadership of black and Puerto Rican groups to the organization. PEA's activities have centered on the broader and more long-range educational aspects of school policy. Its strategy has been to study special problems and to make public recommendations based on its analyses.

The Mayor

In almost every New York City administration since the 1940's, complaints of undue "political interference" have resulted in the delegation of increased responsibility to the Board of Education and the reduction of the role of the mayor. Mayoral noninvolvement is in part a result of public deference to professionalism. The institution of a strict merit system and internal controls over promotions and transfers has further limited the role of the mayor. Mayor Lindsay, however, chose to use educational reform to promote his image as a reformer. Lacking a base of support in the major-party structure, minor-party mayors are more likely to gamble on such issues to build their own constituencies, especially if they intend to move up the political ladder. Lindsay's experience on the decentralization–school-reform issue may well reinforce the view that mayors are not likely to gain political advantage from school issues.

Civil Rights Groups and the Demonstration Districts

Primarily as a result of the 1954 Supreme Court decision on school desegregation, civil rights groups became involved in school issues in most large cities. In New York City, the NAACP, CORE, and EQUAL were the leading organizations in the struggle for school integration. Some local groups were organized in individual schools and neighborhoods around specific controversies, but they were short-lived. Unsuccessful in achieving school integration, these groups became the basis of a public challenge to the governance of large city school systems. All they had learned about the failure of city schools was rechanneled into an effort to achieve fundamental reform of a system that was incapable of reforming itself.

The three demonstration school districts in New York City—IS (Intermediate School) 201, Ocean Hill–Brownsville, and Two Bridges—were an outgrowth of that civil rights—school integration movement. In each of the three districts selected for the experimentation with greater community involvement, demands for local control had already been made. In Brooklyn's Ocean Hill–Brownsville, a rump local school board had been established; in the IS 201 area in Harlem, a ten-day parent boycott had overturned the appointment of a principal; and, in the Two Bridges area on the Lower East Side, local groups had named their own district superintendent. In establishing the three districts, the Board of Education was responding to the continuing pressure from areas that included what were probably the most actively engaged communities in New York City. The districts, their elected parent- and community-resident boards, administrators and their organizations were to become important participants (as well as political targets) in the city-wide struggle over school decentralization.

The plan for the creation of the districts was a product of meetings between the union, the Superintendent of Schools, and community groups. Ford Foundation representatives, who had been called in by Mayor Lindsay when difficulties first developed in IS 201, were also involved in the negotiations over the establishment of the districts. This was Ford's first involvement with the New York City school system; eventually, it agreed to fund the summer planning phase of the experiment.

In the poverty area known as Ocean Hill–Brownsville, public education had been failing at an alarming rate. By the fall of 1966, an aroused Ocean Hill–Brownsville community formed its own local school board. (The particular issue that sparked this action concerned the selection of personnel to staff a new intermediate school—IS 55—in the community.) By April, 1967, the Board of Education designated Ocean Hill–Brownsville, consisting of eight schools, as one of the three experimental demonstration districts.

The IS 201 complex in Harlem, made up of five schools, also had its seeds in a controversy over a new intermediate school—IS 201—in the area. At issue, however, was the site selected: The community saw the official site as a means of continuing *de facto* school segregation. When efforts to gain a site that could aid in integration failed, the community responded by demanding that a black principal be brought in and eventually by advocating total community control of the school within an experimental school district. The 201 complex was so designated in April, 1967.

Located on the Lower East Side of Manhattan and made up of five schools, the Two Bridges district emerged through the community's Parent Development Program, which had been designed to involve the poor in the education of their children. In the spring of 1967, a committee composed of representatives from the program, from the Two Bridges Neighborhood Council, and from one of the community's churches approached the Ford Foundation for a grant. (The Foundation had already granted planning funds to the IS 201 district.) Ford's selection of Two Bridges was based on its belief that the area had a substantial enough middle-class population to make it a test of decentralization in a middle-class community.

By spring, 1967, these three communities were officially designated by the Board of Education as demonstration school districts. Each had its special problems and each had somewhat different beginnings; yet all three had the same goal of demonstrating that a decentralized school district responsible to the community would improve the quality of education being offered to the children in the public schools of New York.

The districts moved quickly, electing their own local boards, appointing district administrators and staff, and setting out to take over education in their communities. But, from the outset, they faced enormous ambiguities concerning the limits and extent of their authority. This ambiguity was, in large part, the result of the fact that the motives and objectives of those who created the districts were in conflict: The Superintendent sought a relaxation of tensions in troublesome areas; the union hoped to get additional MES schools in each of the districts; and community leaders aimed at obtaining a power base for achieving change in the system.

The challenge the community presented to the entrenched power interests in education was immediate; so were the responses. Clearly, a community district that sought independent status would not be satisfied to have decisions made for it by the central staff, and these districts moved immediately to appoint their own administration and principals. By the fall of 1967, the UFT and the CSA, recognizing the threat, had entered into a joint court action to enjoin local appointment of demonstration school principals. At the same time, the UFT called a strike action to support its contract negotiations, which centered on salaries, the "disruptive child" issue, and the MES program. The demonstration districts, in part responding to the "disruptive child" issue, which many considered racially instigated, and, in part, seeing the union demands for a more direct role in educational policy-making via the contract as contrary to their own interests, refused support. In the three demonstration districts, all schools remained open during the strike, and relations between the communities and the union polarized further.[5]

The State Level

The decentralization controversy was ultimately to hit the state level before a settlement would be reached. On that level, two sets of actors were involved: the professional set, centered in the State Board of Regents and the State Commissioner of Education; and the political set, ranging from the Governor's office to the State Legislature.

Of the first, the State Board of Regents is the governing body for all public education in the state. The state commissioner of education is appointed by the Regents with the approval of the governor. Normally, the state department of education does not directly intervene in the city's educational affairs. Of course, legal and discrete relationships exist between the state and local school districts, resulting from the fact that education is a state function. The state education department did become involved in the decentralization controversy, since city education authorities seemed unable to resolve the issues. Because state officials were removed from the local warfare, it was hoped that some constructive resolution would be possible on the state level. In addition, Commissioner James E. Allen had indicated support for decentralization and worked diligently with the Regents to come up with a viable bill.

The second set of actors on the state level was led by the Governor's office and the leadership of the State Legislature. Here the power and influence of the UFT-CSA were apparent. Despite the fact that the Governor had indicated early support for decentralizatoin, he was soon to withdraw from any direct role, although one piece of legislation was proposed by the Regents and the State Commissioner. A prounion Republican Governor and a Republican-dominated legislative leadership were deciding a thorny issue. Their sentiments on decentralization were ambivalent, and they were not pressured by any constituency able to compete with the influence of the UFT-CSA. The Democratic caucus of the State Legislature, largely influenced by the UFT, opposed all of the stronger legislation.

The scenario for decentralization was operational on two political levels, state and local, and the state actors were instrumental in the final outcome.

[5] The education directors of the poverty corporations in New York City and the boards of each local corporation were also potentially important participants in the decentralization movement, but, except for support at rallies and meetings, they proved to be of minor significance in influencing the outcome of the struggle.

THE EVENTS: PHASE 1

Pinpointing the beginning of a political or social movement is always a difficult task, because the roots often reach far back in time and may extend to parallel issues and groups. In the case of the decentralization issue, this is particularly true. Much of the impetus for reform came from the frustrations of the school integration forces, who turned to community control as a policy alternative when integration efforts failed. In this sense, one can say that the IS 201 site-selection controversy ended one era in school reform and began another. Significantly, most of the coalition (with few notable exceptions) of poverty workers, parents, and ministers that demanded control over the school looked upon community control as a consolation prize: Still wedded to the school integration battles of the 1950's, the group initially demanded that IS 201 be integrated; only if integration could not be assured, would they take total community control.

The community control adherents had reason to anticipate that integration was a hopeless cause. Increasingly, schools were becoming more segregated in the large cities of the North. New York City school segregation had doubled in the five years preceding the IS 201 controversy. Other cities were experiencing similar changes. Almost all efforts at integration had failed after a long and arduous struggle, and there is no longer any question that the education bureaucracy played a large role in obstructing implementation of Board policy. The pro-integration forces were unable to secure any meaningful action on any of the proposed plans.

There should have been little doubt of the future thrust of ghetto parents for community control of the schools. One broadsheet circulated in Harlem warned that "the present structure of the New York City school system, not responsible or accountable to the minority community, is guilty of educational genocide." In the neighboring borough of Queens, the predominantly black Federation of Parent's Clubs demanded that teachers be rated according to the standardized test scores their students achieve. Between 1963 and 1967, over a dozen parent boycotts occurred at various ghetto schools. At one point, a self-styled People's Board of Education—which included a Catholic priest, a protestant minister, and a black former school-integration leader—proclaiming itself the true Board of Education, staged a sit-in in the Board members' seats, holding out for two days, until they were arrested. All these demonstrations had a common theme: Parents wanted a say in the running of the schools. "What the parents are asking for is a revolution," Superintendent of Schools Bernard Donovan remarked, "and that doesn't happen overnight."

By mid-winter of 1967, the politics of school decentralization was in full swing. Mayor Lindsay, convinced that the public schools had to show "demonstrably better results" for the city's billion-dollar investment, had openly entered the picture. For the first time since Fiorello LaGuardia, a mayor of the city was openly involving himself as a participant in school politics. In 1967, during the parent boycott of PS 125, the Mayor had let it be known that, in principle, he believed parents should have a voice in selection of the principals and should be given the right to interview candidates for such supervisory posts as principals and district superintendents. Still, the Mayor possessed little leverage for change, his major educational function was to appoint members of the city Board of Education, and, since 1961, the choice was made from a list supplied by a screening panel composed of civic group representatives.

Departing from tradition, Lindsay committed himself to school reform. In the spring of 1967, he succeeded in getting a green light from the New York State Legislature to reshape the city's public school system into five school districts. Bypassing both the city Board of Education and the State Education Department, the Mayor had obtained a mandate to redesign the public school system. In one sense, the law Lindsay obtained was a clever maneuver aimed at getting the city a larger proportion of funding, for, if for educational purposes, the city was considered a conglomerate of five school districts rather than a single school district, it stood to gain an additional $108 million in aid. But, in another sense, the 1967 law went beyond the simple designation of five school districts for the purpose of securing additional money. It was a mandate to the Mayor, stating that:

> Increased community awareness and participation in the educational process is essential to the furtherance of educational innovation and excellence in the public school system within the city of New York. . . . The legislature . . . declares that the creation of educational policy for the public schools within such districts will afford members of the community an opportunity to take a more active and meaningful role in the development of educational policy closely related to the diverse needs and aspirations of the community.[6]

The Mayor was instructed to present a plan to the legislature by December 1, 1967. He appointed a blue-ribbon six-member committee headed by Ford Foundation President McGeorge Bundy to draw up a reorganization plan. The membership of the panel included none of the obvious holders of power in the school system (for example, the UFT, CSA, or UPA), which later proved to be of significance in the failure of the panel's recommendations.

Initially, the new law evoked an angry chorus of protest from the city's educational establishment because it empowered the Mayor, rather than the Board of Education, to prepare the study. The PEA decried the "destruction of the city school system," feeling that, "badly as the city's schools need funds, [the law] was too high a price to pay to get them"; State Commissioner of Education Allen's immediate reaction was that the Mayor had exerted a "measure of political control"; the Association of Assistant Prin-

[6] New York State Legislation, 1967 Session, Col. 484 of the Sessions Laws of 1967.

cipals thought schoolchildren would now be "political pawns"; the Congress of Parents and Teachers feared that "every politician in the city [will now decide] on how our children will be educated"; and *The New York Times* found an "outrageous element in the act of legislative blackmail" that will signal a "forceful reassertion of political fiat as a controlling factor in the schools."

Despite the outcry, no hard lines had yet formed. At that point, educational and civic groups reacted out of surprise, fearing the new law gave political control of the schools to city hall. Lindsay, however, moved quickly to placate these fears; holding forth at a special meeting, which took place in the offices of the Public Education Association and included every educational interest, he assured his audience that he had not the slightest intention of running New York's school system. During this same period, the Board of Education sanctioned the experimental districts, and, coming when it did, their action gave the impression that the city Board favored reorganization along decentralized lines.

Yet, even before the Bundy panel released its decentralization recommendations, alliances were forming. Black school-activists, academicians, some of the more radical, white educational groups, and the Mayor shouldered the greater burden of pressing for school decentralization. On the other side, the professional educational organizations (the CSA and UFT) and the Board of Education submerged their traditional internecine bickering and united in opposition to the growing demand for community control of the schools. If the decentralization alliance united the city's upper class, who had long despaired of the school system and long been leaders in school reform movements, with the city's underclass, who had, as clients, little faith in the schools, the antidecentralization forces largely reflected in a coalition between the newly emergent middle-class white civil servants and the labor unions. Ironically, the prospect of school decentralization brought the UFT into collaboration with its past rhetorical foe, the CSA. Although, in union terms, the CSA was an arm of management, on the decentralization issue the protection of professional status made for a common cause.

The Bundy plan, presented to the Mayor in the fall of 1967, crystallized these developing alignments. Essentially, it recommended that the New York City school system be subdivided into from thirty to sixty autonomous school districts, each with elected school boards having assigned powers over budget, personnel, and curriculum. Following the lead of previous studies, the plan recommended abolition of the anachronistic system by which civil service personnel were certified and the replacement of it with a more equitable examination procedure, similar to current state certification, that would admit more minority-group members into teaching and supervisory positions. As to the structure of the local boards, the plan recommended that the majority of members on each be elected by parents of children in the schools.

New York City schoolmen were alarmed. The President of the Board of Education—the sole dissenting member on the Bundy panel—sharply criticized the report: "Serious problems must arise in recasting, in one single stroke, the largest educational system in the world." The professional groups charged that thirty to sixty independent districts would "balkanize" the city system and that local control would impede school integration.

Once the Mayor's version of the plan went, as directed, to the State Legislature, neither the UFT nor the CSA spared any expense in defeating the passage of a decentralization bill based on it. During the 1968 legislative session, the UFT reportedly spent somewhere between $125,000 and $500,000 in a public relations campaign that included hundreds of school meetings, newspaper ads, and radio spots.

On the other hand, the prodecentralization forces split on the degree of decentralization each supported and, lacking tight organizational direction and unlimited funds, were hampered in their attempts to press for a meaningful bill. The two most influential civic educational organizations—the UPA and the PEA—presented their own drafts of a decentralization bill, it departed significantly from the Bundy model by minimizing the delegation of power to the local districts. The net effect of the various ideological differences among black and white reform groups was to enfeeble their collective strength. An umbrella coalition—the Citizens' Committee for Decentralization of the Public Schools—was finally formed in early spring, 1968. Nominally under the chairmanship of Radio Corporation of America President Robert Sarnoff, it was set up to lobby for the Mayor's version of the Bundy plan.

In the effort to develop more broad-based support prior to and during the legislative session, the lack of city-wide leadership was significant. The Mayor did not play as forceful a role in pushing for passage of his bill as he had indicated he would. The Citizens' Committee headed by Sarnoff provided little financial or institutional muscle; Sarnoff served as chairman of the committee but removed himself from any direct role, the committee lacked funds, and the campaign never got off the ground. (The PEA supplied the only meaningful commitment to the Citizens' Committee, and its staff director—who later resigned to work for the Board of Education—undermined the movement in his public statements and speeches.)

As discussion meetings were set up throughout the city, the UFT and the CSA organized their large membership to cover every one, both on the platform and in the audience. Their approach was blunt: They raised fears about the abolition of the merit system and about black racism, and they quite suddenly became concerned with the terrible problem ghetto districts would have in securing personnel—having previously squashed every plan set up to effect this. Supporters of decentralization were poorly organized and lacked sufficient speakers to cover meetings. Their own differences in point of view and commitment also reduced their effectiveness. They made no dent in public opinion and, by and large, allowed public discussion to deteriorate to the level of charges and countercharges. Although there was some recognition of the need to convince white parents that their interests were also to be served by school reform, the meetings and propaganda were not effective in gaining such support. In large part, this failure was a result of the opposition's setting of the stage along explosive racial lines.

In the spring of 1968, a more moderate bill was worked out by State Commissioner of Education Allen and the Board of Regents. It looked for a while as if a compromise bill, with elements of the Regents' plan and the Mayor's plan, could be enacted. The Governor, leaders of the legislature, the State Commissioner of Education, and the Regents supported this more moderate plan for decentralization, though there was legislative backing for the Mayor's version. The more liberal city Democrats in the legislature, and especially the reformers from New York's upper West Side and the few black legislators formed a small coalition operating for passage of stronger legislation. Most state legislators, ill informed on decentralization and viewing it as a city issue, were especially susceptible to pressure from political leaders, colleagues, and the various groups lobbying in the capital. During a two-day period prior to the arrival of the UFT delegation in Albany, it seemed that a compromise would be reached; the issue had narrowed to consideration of central structure—whether to expand the existing Board or to create a new three-man education commission to be appointed by the mayor. Legislative demands that commission appointments would have to be approved by the City Council were rejected by Lindsay, and the controversy delayed agreement long enough to allow the opposition to muster increased forces for the defeat of the legislation.

Although the Governor had indicated his support for the bill both in private and in public, he made no effort to move it through the legislature during the 1968 session. Possibly his generally unfriendly relationship with the Mayor was the reason; possibly his commitment was limited; certainly his inaction was an important element in the failure to secure passage. The Mayor's strategy seemed to be designed to limit his leadership in the undertaking. Staff commitments to the effort were left to the Education Liaison Officer who, though appointed by the Mayor, had almost no contact with him and little knowledge of state or local politics. In fact, the supporting coalition lacked any decisive leadership, and confusion and differences of point of view were constantly evident. At one point, the city coalition (comprised of the more militant city groups, including representatives of the three demonstration districts, with the Reverend Milton Galamison as chairman) sent a telegram to leaders in Albany indicating that they did not support the Regents' plan; yet Galamison was in the capital at that very moment lobbying for that plan as a member of the Citizens Committee. The Bundy panel was virtually nonfunctioning: Panel members had moved on to other activities and were largely inactive in the political arena. Had the panel continued to function, it could have been a source of significant political influence.

In its legislative campaign, the UFT successfully used the threat of political reprisals. As a result, the legislators, all up for re-election in the fall, postponed action for a year, empowering the city school board to draw up another decentralization plan. In order to placate the prodecentralization forces, the legislature increased the membership of the nine-member city Board of Education to thirteen, thus opening the way for the Mayor to gain a more decentralization-minded Board.

THE EVENTS: PHASE 2

Although the legislative battle was postponed to the 1969 session, a second phase in the campaign was waged in the fall of 1968, when the city school system was struck for thirty-six days. The decision by the UFT to escalate their battle against decentralization, with Ocean Hill–Brownsville as the target, was probably made in the previous spring, when the district ordered the involuntary transfer of nineteen educators. At a meeting of the Education Committee of the Urban Coalition held that spring, UFT President Albert Shanker allegedly proclaimed that he would destroy the Ocean Hill–Brownsville Governing Board and its administrator, Rhody McCoy. During the spring, the union had struck only the Ocean Hill–Brownsville district, with 350 teachers boycotting the district's schools. By September, the union decided that a city-wide strike was the only way to satisfy its demands. It was not until the middle of October, 1968, however, at a tense point in the city-wide strike action, that the UFT announced openly that the cost of settlement of the strike would be abolition of the Brownsville district. Certainly, the union leadership must be given credit for realizing that their newly gained power over policy, won in the 1967 contract, was threatened by the local districts. Tactically, however, all of the UFT's early publicity claimed that the issue in the strike was "due process" for the nineteen teachers who had been transferred—or, as the union put it, fired without adequate charges. (Through the union contract, the UFT had obtained guaranteed job security under a system whereby teachers were to be transferred only with their approval, or in negotiation with the union. An involuntary transfer would be subject to the grievance machinery as stipulated in the contract.) Despite this claim, each union maneuver seemed directed at securing a confrontation with the opposition. In the meantime, between the spring and fall union actions, the Ocean Hill–Brownsville district had, with headquarters approval, replaced many of the staff people who had boycotted the schools.

The union successfully used the levers of fear and intimidation to arouse its own membership and the middle-class white population of the city. A heavy-handed CSA-UFT campaign, charging racial extremism and anti-Semitism in Brownsville, proved extremely successful. Leaflets and flyers, distributed throughout the city by the UFT and the CSA, quoted from materials purported to have been circulating throughout the Ocean Hill–Brownsville district. Some of the content later proved to be false; little of it ever was proven to have come from the district. Nonetheless, mass circulation of the propaganda fed the fuel of existing fears and latent racism, as the atmosphere in the city became more charged with each day of the strike. The Jewish community, in particular, became militant in its demands for redress.[7] Jewish leadership in the city either joined the UFT and CSA in their inflammation of the conflict or sat tight, providing no opposition or rational evaluation of the circumstances. The Board of Rabbis, a rather politically conservative body, became the spokesman for what was accepted as Jewish opinion. At meetings, attended by a wide range of the city's political leaders, the concern of Jewish organizations was voiced.

When the Board of Education directed that schools be opened, even if this meant breaking in (custodians were supporting the strike), the racial split was further intensified. Black parents throughout the city, along with small groups of white parents and teachers, opened schools; generally, however, white parents joined the picket lines. In some areas, "freedom schools" were held for white children, while black children were in the public schools. Reports indicated that UFT militants shouted racial epithets and, in some cases, were violent in their abuse of parents and teachers who crossed the picket lines. Black militants were accused of similar actions.

Although the Mayor attempted to balance the interests of both sides during the strike, he was personally committed to the preservation of the Ocean Hill–Brownsville district and to school decentralization. This pitted him against the UFT-CSA and led to a political stalemate because of the commitment of the professional groups to abolition of the district. The solid alignment of labor in support of the UFT was an additional and important element in the controversy. In fact, the Central Labor Council threatened at one point to call a general strike, according to reports from the Mayor's office. Forced to make various concessions to the union, Lindsay appeared to have no political leverage in dealing with it. His influence was effective only on the Ocean Hill–Brownsville board, and he used it to force them to accept the teachers back as a part of the strike settlement. There is no doubt that many of the participants, including the Mayor, underestimated the strength of the union—greatly enhanced by Shanker's leadership ability; equally underestimated was the full extent of latent racist feeling that was aroused in the white community. Nor was there any

[7] In a voter profile of the November, 1969, city election, a high percentage of Jewish voters indicated that they were voting against community control of the schools in voting against Lindsay.

question of the mass support for the union: A city-wide prodecentralization rally produced a crowd of 5,000 to 6,000 people while, two days later, a UFT rally marched 40,000 people around City Hall.

The illegal opening of schools, parent sleep-ins, and teacher opposition to the UFT position did produce a new base of support for decentralization, but the numbers were comparatively small and largely confined to elements in the black community that had not been actively involved in school affairs before the strike. Aside from this, efforts to develop institutional muscle for decentralization through the Committee to Save Decentralization and Community Control (the Reverend Donald Harrington was chairman) were slow in getting off the ground, although several new sources, particularly church groups, were successfully tapped.

Most interpretations of the school strike tend to isolate the events of that period from the total struggle for school reform and demands for a redistribution of power in the system. The action of the Ocean Hill–Brownsville Governing Board in transferring nineteen teachers out of the district was an attempt to establish local discretion and to define district power over school resources (in this instance, jobs)—both poorly defined at the time the board was set up. The action or inaction of the local board and its administration was based on their desire to establish independence from the central Board and to challenge the power of the professionals in the UFT and the CSA.

For the most part, the local board was not included in the city negotiations to end the strike. Early in the strike, the board had agreed to take the nineteen teachers back to the district but not to assign them to schools. Later, it supported the creation of a state trusteeship of the district under the Commissioner of Education, because it viewed the state as more friendly to its cause than the city. But any open compromise on the board's powers was viewed as a capitulation.

The strike settlement indicated that the usual power sources had maintained their position. The professional coalition of teachers and supervisory staff succeeded in negotiating a trusteeship status for the district, if not in killing it outright. The Ocean Hill–Brownsville Governing Board and the unit administrator were suspended, and, pending negotiation, involuntary transfers were in future to be covered by arbitration machinery.

THE EVENTS: PHASE 3

The third phase of the politics of school decentralization was played out in the 1969 legislative session. Although it followed the pattern of 1968, there was a clearer indication throughout of the polarization of forces that had taken place during the protracted strike. The manifestation of school policy-making power was more obvious. The lines of battle had been drawn in public. No longer could anyone question the role of the UFT, the CSA, and the Central Labor Council. Support for strong legislation (with delegation of personnel and curriculum powers to local districts) was, once again, weakened by disagreements among the prodecentralization groups. The demonstration districts had become the nucleus of the grass-roots movement for community control, and their experience had led them to a more extreme position. Decentralization no longer seemed adequate to their needs and interests. The Ocean Hill–Brownsville confrontation had indicated that only more complete community control over local resources (jobs and contracts) would provide sufficient power to influence school policy in a meaningful way. City-wide cohesiveness was undermined, however, by concerns community leaders had for their own districts. This reduced their interest in, and commitment to, city-wide decentralization. Supportive community groups throughout the city were unable to organize with the demonstration districts to provide a united front in the black and Puerto Rican communities. Milton Galamison, who had formerly served as the spokesman for those groups, had been appointed to the Board of Education in September, 1968, and was its vice-chairman. It is noteworthy that the demonstration districts and the grass-roots organizations lobbied infrequently—and ineffectively—in the capital. In fact, Senator Waldaba Stewart (representing an area that included Ocean Hill) was a major instrument in the passage of a weak bill. The failure of the districts to play the legislative game was probably a central factor in allowing the 1969 legislative session to go as far as it did in destroying the districts.

The community groups' lack of knowledge of legislative politics explains in part why effective pressure was not brought to bear even when it could have produced some minimal results. It would be naïve, however, to assume that, even given this knowledge and a will to play the game, the groups could have exerted strong influence. These groups did not have the financial resources or political influence to impress legislators. Certainly, events during the 1969 session indicated that the elected state and city officials were extremely responsive to such vested school interests as the unions and the school professionals. Union financial support for election campaigns was not an unimportant factor in their decisions. Only the more radical Reform Democrats from the Manhattan's upper West Side and the Harlem legislators remained a solid force for effective legislation. Early in the legislative session, the Republican leadership was prepared to lend its support to a strong bill but was soon swayed by the regular city Democrats who had begun to talk about the need to compromise with the UFT. Stanley Steingut, the Brooklyn Democratic Party leader, led the downstate opposition to the stronger bill. Many of the opponents of decentralization now had larger stakes in the political struggle—the defeat of Mayor Lindsay in the upcoming election. A resounding defeat of both his board and his decentralization plan would embarrass him and could block his re-election.

The proponents of decentralization repeated their 1968 roles. The Mayor again chose to moderate his position; obviously, he was now also concerned about how developments would influence his re-election. Perhaps he had begun to appreciate why urban mayors had removed themselves from the educational arena. The Governor seemed unwilling to enter the controversy; he wanted a bill, but its content seemed unimportant. He was finally accused by community groups of buying off the Harlem delegation with the legislation creating a Harlem Hospital community board: CORE leaders were informed about the hospital concession in a private meeting with the Governor before he signed the weak bill, and, apparently as a result, CORE agreed not to criticize the Governor's action on decentralization.

The policy output of the three-year period of the politics of decentralization came in the 1969 legislation. The legislation passed in the last day of an extended 1969 session accomplished for the UFT-CSA what they were unable to achieve by a thirty-six-day city-wide strike. The bill not only abolished the three demonstration school districts; it provided a new series of protective devices to guarantee centralization and professionalism. It also removed the first prodecentralization city Board of Education, adding to the total success of the recentralization forces. That Board was replaced with an interim Board, whose members were appointed by the Borough Presidents; they were to remain in office for fourteen months.[8] But, in 1970, the legislature amended the law to allow the Board to remain in office another year. The interim Board was to set school-district boundaries and thus could determine who would control local district boards. School population data indicate that black and Puerto Rican populations represent a majority in eighteen of the thirty-one districts. Shrewd gerrymandering can reduce that control to five or six districts.

Further evidence of the *status quo* aspects of the law can be found in the restrictive provisions regarding personnel appointments. Local boards will have virtually no control over personnel. For example, although many cities have used the "merged list" as a means of increasing the appointment of black administrators, the new law prohibits such lists for principals.[9] It is likely that the legislation now virtually closes off appointments

[8] The five borough appointments provided the city with a rather conservative political body. Borough presidents in New York City are of a more conservative cast than city-wide officials. They must be more responsive to local party machinery. Traditionally, borough-wide elections tend to underrepresent minority groups and reform voting because of the distribution of population in the individual boroughs.

[9] Under this procedure, new exams are given to qualify larger numbers of minority-group supervisors; their names are then added to existing accredited lists, and they can be assigned jobs immediately. If existing lists must, by law, be used first, there is no way to expand the number of potential candidates and increase minority-group appointments.

to blacks for at least five years, because current lists, which must be used first, include few blacks. The bill further provides that any future list of eligibles must be exhausted before new lists are prepared. The impact of this provision is disastrous for the city, especially if there were any plans for breaking new ground in this area.

The assignment of all personnel who are no longer needed at headquarters to local districts by action of the interim Board will further reduce local options for a considerable time to come. Local districts will not have the chance to elect their local boards until after these assignments are completed. Under the legislation, transfers of personnel are generally more difficult to accomplish than previously, because restrictive provisions are now written into law and appeals machinery is more intricate and detailed. The community superintendent can no longer transfer personnel within his own district, unless certain school utilization criteria are in question. Under the law's procedures, transfers are made at the request of the district superintendent. This provision in itself violates the essence of decentralization and community control: It will be impossible for communities to transfer personnel internally or externally.

The only concession on personnel relates to the possibility of certain districts (those in which reading scores fall in the lowest 40 per cent) appointing teachers who have passed the National Teachers Examination and scored within the average grade of the five largest cities. With this exception alone, the city teachers' examination remain intact, and central assignment of teachers is otherwise retained. Discretion in the assignment of teachers, as noted, is severely limited. The Board of Examiners retains its major role of qualifying teachers; the only change in that procedure is that the chancellor (the new title for the superintendent of schools) now becomes a member of that body.

Budget powers for the community boards as outlined in the legislation, are advisory only. The local boards are, however, to be consulted on budget requests, and their unamended requests are to be submitted with the central budget to the mayor for review. A $250,000 local fund for repairs and maintenance remains controlled by closed competitive city bidding procedures for all contracts over $2,500. The advisory role of local community boards on site selection and expense and capital budgets has been expanded; however, full discretion remains in the hands of the central city Board and the Planning Commission.

The election procedures established for the city-wide Board and the local boards contrast sharply and indicate the political manipulation encouraged by legislation. With borough-wide elections (all registered voters) for each central Board member, the role of minority groups is completely undermined. The majority of the city's school population is now black and Puerto Rican, yet these groups cannot effectively exercise political power in borough elections—and this limiting of their power is, undoubtedly, an intention of the bill. Financing of the elections is unrestricted, which should provide the UFT with carte blanche to underwrite campaigns and influence the very people with whom they must negotiate their contract. In fact, in the contract negotiated by the interim Board, the UFT was—several Board members admitted—able to secure all of its demands.

In contrast to the city-wide procedure, the local election procedure provided for in the bill is highly complex and virtually guarantees local minority-group conflict. It requires that only registered voters can vote; parents who are not registered voters must preregister. Voters must be residents of the city for ninety days and be twenty-one years of age. The complexities of the proportional representation system established by the law are extremely difficult to translate to the poor and may well account, in part, for the poor turnout at the first election in the spring of 1970. The most politically astute will have no difficulty in controlling the results of the local board elections. The bill also calls for petitions signed only by registered voters, which seems to exclude parents who are not yet registered as voters. No local resident can serve as a board member if he or she is employed by the district. Thus, all community people working as paraprofessionals in the schools are eliminated as potential candidates. A restrictive clause automatically removes board members who miss three successive local board meetings. It should be noted that no such provision is prescribed for the central Board or any other board in the city.

The support and protection of centralization by the legislation is further reflected in the lack of flexibility of action given to local boards. The law guarantees that no power will be delegated to those boards. In reaction to Ford Foundation financial support to the experimental districts, all outside funding must now be centrally approved, and funds are to be channeled through the central agency and the comptroller's office, thus limiting local control over the power resources of jobs and funds. Textbooks must be chosen from a centrally approved list. All local decisions on instructional materials—and, therefore, on curriculum—must have central approval. Examinations are centrally prepared and evaluated. The central office can change or install new programs in the local district at any time. They can arbitrarily adjust local boundaries and remove local personnel. The legislation is careful to state in several places that the local district is not to be considered a local educational agency; it is, rather, a subdivision of the central agency. While local boards presumably are allowed to operate cafeterias and social and recreational centers in the schools, funds are centrally controlled, and the local board's discretion is, therefore, limited, if not meaningless.

Throughout the legislation, all local district personnel are designated as city Board personnel, an attempt to guarantee their loyalty and obligation to the central agency. Only the community superintendent is appointed by the local board. All personnel are assigned by the chancellor and appointed by the local board. The legislation, however, encourages the chancellor to be responsible to local requests for staff.

The establishment of uniform districts of 20,000 minimum school population creates a further limit on experimentation and local prerogative. Decentralization as outlined in the Bundy plan called for districts of different size in order to achieve diversity and competition; thirty uniform districts denies this goal. The provision limiting size was aimed at abolishing the three demonstration school districts. Ocean Hill–Brownsville, the largest district of the three, has a student population of less than 10,000. All of the programs and personnel appointed by the three demonstration districts have been abolished under the legislation without consideration of their value or accomplishment. Perhaps this indicates most clearly the threat the districts presented to those who hold power in the school system; nothing short of abolition would satisfy their interests.

WHO GOVERNS?

It should be evident from this description of school politics that the actors, their roles, and the final policy output all reflect an enormous concentration of power in the hands of the school professionals. It also suggests their wider influence on other power sources in the city and state, and the lengths to which these groups will go to retain their power interests in the system. The complete insensitivity to the demands of the black and Puerto Rican communities and the unwillingness to compromise suggest a continuing and perhaps intensified struggle between these forces. Racial polarization has become more overt and more pronounced.

One should not ignore that city-wide decentralization was initially supported by the Mayor (albeit a reform Mayor with no party support), the Governor, civil rights and grass-roots minority organizations, the PEA, and the Ford Foundation. The Superintendent of Schools was also mildly supportive of the movement. Many a student of politics would predict that there was enough clout in that combination to effect the goal. Instead, not only was decentralization soundly defeated, but the defeat was extended to the political and personal status of the issue's proponents. The Mayor's defeat in the Republican primary election and Ford's retrenchment on its direct ghetto aid policy were by products of the battle. The extended coalition of the labor unions, the Jewish organizations, and the school professionals demonstrated their enormous power in the city and state political arena. The Mayor, attempting to gain a compromise from among the various forces, found himself faced with a no-compromise issue. One could presumably argue that the decentralization bill did represent a compromise of the various interests—it does create elected local governing boards. On the contrary, however, the centralization forces were served in every aspect of the policy—the larger districts, the creation of the more powerful chancellorship, the restrictions on transfer of personnel, and the complete failure to allocate control of any resources to the local districts. It is clear that the Mayor was not the instrument of compromise, although he attempted to play that role.

In *Participants and Participation* (1967), I predicted that the UFT and the CSA would oppose any decentralization movement, because it would endanger their place in the system. I greatly underestimated, however, the power of the union, its willingness to use any and all tactics to achieve its ends, and the extent that latent racism and fear could be played upon. These were the elements that finally dealt a resounding defeat to school reform and reinforced the *status quo* politics of the system.

In school politics, the insulation of the professionals effectively closes off new power sources. The limited roles and lack of access to power of the new population, which comprises over 50 per cent of the system's clients, has resulted in far more serious consequences. The resistance to change in urban institutions has produced an enormous gap between demands and needs, and policy output.

SUGGESTED READINGS

Education

In recent years scholars have done considerable research in the volatile field of politics and education. One of the leading writers has been Marilyn Gittell in the field of urban education, one of whose studies appears in Part IV. Other than those works she refers to therein, she is the author of:

Berube, Maurice, and Marilyn Gittell, eds. *Confrontation at Ocean Hill–Brownsville.* New York: Praeger, 1969.

Gittell, Marilyn, ed. *Educating an Urban Population.* Beverly Hills: Sage, 1967.

Gittell, Marilyn. *Participants and Participation: A Study of School Policy in New York City.* New York: Praeger, 1969.

Gittell, Marilyn, and Alan G. Hevesi, eds. *The Politics of Urban Education.* New York: Praeger, 1968.

Gittell, Marilyn, and T. Edward Hollander. *Six Urban School Districts.* New York: Praeger, 1968.

Charles S. Benson's *The Economics of Public Education, Second Edition* (Boston: Houghton Mifflin, 1968) is a comprehensive look at school finance. New York City school politics is the subject of David Rogers' *110 Livingston Street* (New York: Random House, 1968). In *Rich Schools, Poor Schools* (Chicago: University of Chicago Press, 1968), Arthur Wise examines the monetary disparities between school districts and their implications.

ADDITIONAL SUGGESTED READING

Crain, Robert L. *Politics of School Desegregation: Comparative Case Studies of Community Structure and Policy-Making.* Chicago: Aldine-Atherton, 1968.

Edwards, T. Bentley, and Frederick M. Writ, eds. *School Desegregation in the North.* San Francisco: Chandler, 1968.

Greenbaum, William N., editor and commentator. "Serrano v. Priest: Implications for Educational Equality," *Harvard Educational Review,* **41** (November 1971), 501–534.

Iannaccone, Lawrence. *Politics, Power and Policy: The Governing of Local School Districts.* Columbus, Ohio: Merrill, 1970.

Kirst, Michael W., ed. *State, School and Politics: Research Directions.* Lexington, Mass.: Heath, 1972.

Salisbury, Robert H. "State Politics and Education," in Herbert Jacob, and Kenneth N. Vines, eds. *Politics in the American States, Second Edition.* Boston: Little, Brown, 1971.

Wirt, Frederick M., and Michael W. Kirst. *The Political Web of American Schools.* Boston: Little, Brown, 1972.

Matthew A. Crenson

Political Parties and the Pollution Issue

Air pollution presents a good example of decision- and nondecision-making in a specific policy field. This is a study of the party aspects of the formation of air pollution control efforts in Gary and East Chicago as compared with other U.S. cities. The air pollution data used therein is based on findings of the National Air Sampling Network. A note on Crenson's methodology appears as an appendix to the reading itself.

Industry's reputation for power has proved to be a useful explanatory variable, but a mysterious one. We know that it can help to make political inaction a more comprehensible phenomenon, but industry's reputation for power itself remains fundamentally incomprehensible. Perceived industrial influence in the pollution field does not grow, as one would expect, from industry's actions in this area. For that reason, it may be argued, there is something arbitrary or unjustified in the informants' perceptions of industrial influence. To say that the life chances of the dirty air issue are dependent upon industry's power reputation may mean only that they are related in a systematic way to the random imaginings of our respondents.

Yet these imaginings do have tangible political effects, and it would be a mistake to dismiss them as phantoms. What is more, they are not random. Certain kinds of cities appear to provide especially congenial environments for industrial power reputations. Where local elections are partisan, for example, industry is more likely to qualify as highly influential on the pollution issue than in towns where they are non-partisan $(r = +.33)$.

Reprinted from *The Un-Politics of Air Pollution: A Study of Non-Decisionmaking in the Cities*, pp. 135–158; pp. 31–32. Some descriptive and bibliographical footnotes have been omitted for considerations of space and textual format.
[*Editor's Note:* The appended section "A Note on Methodology" is reprinted from pp. 31–32.]

Cities without civil service regulations also appear to be hospitable breeding grounds for industrial power reputations. Where major municipal employee groups remain outside the coverage of civil service laws, industry is more likely to be regarded as highly influential than in towns where city bureaucrats are civil service employees ($r = +.33$). In short, industry's reputation for power tends to flourish where local government bears some of the formal earmarks of traditional machine politics—where local candidates for office carry partisan labels and municipal jobs are legally available for distribution as patronage.[1]

There are several possible explanations for this affinity between industrial influence and the characteristic signs of machine politics. Industrial influence, we might argue, is likely to be substantial where industrial operations are extensive. Such operations presuppose a local labor force that is largely blue-collar, and blue-collar populations have traditionally been inclined toward machine politics—hence the relationship between industrial influence and the formal trappings of the machine.

The trouble with this plausible explanation is that the data do not support it. It is true that industrial influence and blue-collar populations tend to go together. The larger the blue-collar fraction of a town's labor force, the greater the likelihood that industry will be highly influential on the pollution issue, but the connection is so weak ($r = +.08$) that it cannot carry the weight of our argument. It is necessary to look for some alternative explanations.

Alternative explanations are not hard to find, but they suffer from old age. More than fifty years ago Lincoln Steffens, Moise Ostrogorski,[2] and other observers of American urban affairs perceived that there was a symbiotic relationship between big business and the political machine. Businessmen, it was argued, sought special privileges from local governments—low tax assessments, franchises, licenses, and favors of all sorts. Of course, they were not unique in this respect. Most organized groups seek concessions of some kind from governmental authorities. What distinguished the businessmen were the large monetary rewards which they could offer for the fulfillment of their political desires. In effect, these capitalists sought to extend the incentive system of business to politics, and the appearance of the political machine signaled their success. Its distinguishing characteristic as a political organization was its extensive use of specific, material incen-

[1] It should be pointed out that partisanship and patronage are not the only manifestations of machine politics. A third characteristic of the machine is its ability to control the party primary (see Edward C. Banfield and James Q. Wilson, *City Politics* (Cambridge, Mass.: Harvard University Press, 1963), p. 117). Unfortunately, it was not possible to collect sufficient primary election data to test for machine control of the primaries.

[2] Lincoln Steffens, *Autobiography* (New York: Harcourt, Brace, 1931), chap. 27; Moise Ostrogorski, *Democracy and the Party System in the United States* (New York: Macmillan, Inc., 1921), pp. 268–280.

tives to maintain the reliability of its employees.[3] Private business organizations provided the wherewithal to sustain the machine; the machine used these resources to secure control of government; the businessmen were repaid with the privileges that they desired.

Under such an arrangement, the incentive system of the machine would make the polity particularly responsive to the wishes of business. In the field of pollution control, for example, the machine polity would be especially receptive to the demands of local industry, and this special receptivity might account for the fact that industrial influence in the pollution field and the formal traits of machine politics tend to appear in tandem. This, at least, is the explanation that Steffens or Ostrogorski would probably have favored.

But the conclusions of Steffens and Ostrogorski are founded upon the observation of urban political institutions as they existed more than half a century ago, and, by all accounts, urban affairs have undergone a substantial change since then. Today, it is held, businessmen rarely distribute their riches among local politicians. In fact, many who built their enterprises with the assistance of the machine subsequently became the backers of local reform movements, attracted by the prospect of a stable, predictable, and professional municipal bureaucracy.[4] The view is widely held that the old connection between local business and the machine has been weakened substantially, if not severed; it is therefore peculiar that we should continue to find some fairly strong hints that the old pattern of deference still persists. Perhaps what we have found is only a cultural vestige of a bygone political arrangement: the material connection between business and the machine may have withered, but the political perceptions that it engendered have survived. There is reason to believe, however, that the deference of machine politics to industrial interests is based on something more substantial than a memory, at least where the air pollution issue is concerned. It is not the cash contribution of the industrialist that maintains this deference but the party organization's way of doing business and the nature of that business. In order to understand why this is the case, it is necessary to give these matters rather extensive consideration.

The Political Party as a Brokerage Operation

In spite of its abuse, the traditional machine performed an important political function. In order to provide his businessmen-clients with the privileges and protection that they demanded, the political boss had to establish control over the city government. In most cities the formal apparatus of government was (and still is) a rather disjointed affair, some-

[3] Banfield and Wilson, *City Politics,* p. 115.

[4] Ibid., p. 265.

times paralyzed by the constitutional decentralization of formal authority. The boss and his machine overcame this fragmentation. Behind a constitutional façade they attempted to establish a more centralized, orderly, and informal government, and urban party organizations are still engaged in this task.

Neither the traditional machine nor its modern counterpart have attempted to achieve the desired consolidation of influence by lining up adherents behind a charismatic leader or a popular ideology. They proceed more quietly, by "purchasing" small pieces of influence and authority from the people who own them. These purchases are often made with no specific use, no policy or ideological commitment, in mind. The party boss, according to Banfield and Wilson, is merely a broker in the power business, and "much of what the political broker gathers up is on speculation: he does not know exactly how it will be used, but he is confident that someone will need a large block of power."[5] Someone is sure to find that the fractionation of local authority obstructs the achievement of a desired objective.

The boss obviously needs resources to make such purchases of power. In the heyday of the machine he seems to have relied heavily on cash and patronage, but it is generally acknowledged that municipal reform and the loss of businessmen-clients have cause a considerable shrinkage in his supply of these inducements. Today, he must acquire his purchasing power from alternative sources, and it is public policy that generates the new political currency. The party leader uses the costs and benefits of public policy to purchase bits of influence.[6]

Not all public policies have an equal exchange value for the party leader. Their worth will naturally vary with the magnitude of the costs and benefits that they create. But it is also important to take account of the nature of those costs and benefits. In general, "collective" benefits will be less valuable to the party leader than "specific" benefits. Clean air is an excellent example of a collective benefit, collective because there is no way to control or restrict its distribution among the residents of a city. If the local Democrats get clean air, they cannot deny its use to Republicans or

[5] Ibid., p. 104.

[6] One interesting possibility that arises from these considerations is that the federal government, through its urban grant and subsidy programs, may be providing a large part of the resources that now sustain the operations of party politicians. These federally funded programs, though they seldom yield much in the way of traditional patronage, may supply politicians with reservoirs of policy costs and benefits, which can be used to "purchase" bits of influence. Of course, a broker can purchase power only from people who already have it. If left to his own devices, he is therefore likely to dispense federal largesse to those who are already influential in his community. He is not likely to use federal programs to achieve any significant redistribution of local political power.

Independents. Collective benefits are indivisible and cannot be captured by any social grouping whose membership does not include the whole community. The distinguishing quality of these benefits is that "they must be available to everyone if they are available to anyone."[7]

There are two reasons why control over collective benefits does not give the influence broker as much purchasing power as control over specific benefits. Because collective benefits must be available to everyone in a community, there is no way to restrict their distribution to people who have paid for them. It is understandable that many people—perhaps most people—would like to be included among those who receive without paying. People who own pieces of influence, therefore, will not readily exchange them for collective benefits. It is more profitable to be a freeloader. Nevertheless, there are some people who ignore narrow considerations of personal profit and willingly pay for the enjoyment of collective benefits. In return for a promise of clean air, for example, they may voluntarily surrender their time, energy, votes, money, or influence. Their willingness to make these sacrifices in return for a collective good, as Mancur Olson has pointed out,[8] cannot be attributed to the desire for material profit alone. Devotion to principle, program, ideology, or a sense of public obligation probably plays some part in the behavior of most clean air advocates. Their precise motivations need not concern us for the present. The important thing to note is that they surrender the influence that they possess in return for a combination of material benefits (clean air) and non-material inducements (moral or ideological gratifications). An influence broker might conceivably buy the influence of these program- or principle-oriented people by simply committing himself to their "collective" objective, thus giving them the ideological or moral gratifications that they desire in addition to the material benefit of clean air. But influence that is purchased in this way is not the kind that is likely to be most useful to an influence broker. It must certainly be counted as a political asset, but it is not an especially fluid asset because the broker's title to it is likely to be encumbered with non-material commitments.

The second reason why collective benefits are not especially useful to influence brokers, then, is that they are not fluid. Fluid assets are essential to a brokerage operation. Resources acquired in one transaction must be used in other transactions to acquire still more valuable resources. The influence broker overcomes the fragmentation of local influence by assembling bits and pieces of power that he has purchased in a variety of political transactions and applying them to a single political objective. A politician

[7] Mancur Olson, *The Logic of Collective Action* (Cambridge, Mass.: Harvard University Press, 1965), p. 14.

[8] Ibid., pp. 10–11.

who extends a favor in the field of urban renewal, for example, may demand repayment in the form of support for a municipal bond issue. In this way, he makes himself useful to those who have a stake in the achievement of a political objective and "purchases" their labor and support for any subsequent political enterprises which he may undertake.

Influence purchased with collective benefits will not exhibit the kind of fluidity that is essential for these transactions. It will tend to be tied to a relatively restricted range of principles, policies, or objectives.[9] Outside this range, the influence sellers will not receive the moral or ideological gratifications that were part of the original purchase price. Once these inducements are withdrawn, the sales contract is broken, and the sellers are likely to withdraw their support. A political leader whose assets are tied down by moral or ideological commitments will therefore find it difficult to behave like an influence broker, and a leader who "purchases" support with collective benefits is likely to find himself in just such a situation.

A leader who dispenses specific benefits in exchange for pieces of influence is much more likely to maintain the fluidity of his political holdings. His title to these assets is likely to be less encumbered because the people who surrender their influence in return for specific benefits need not be paid off with non-material inducements such as programmatic or ideological commitments. A desire for personal profit is sufficient to make people respond to specific benefits, and this is why influence purchased with these benefits is a more fluid political asset than influence purchased with collective benefits. It can be applied to political projects in which the seller has no interest or commitment. The practice of log-rolling depends on this kind of fluidity and provides a good illustration of what it means for political assets to be fluid. A log-roller creates political obligations by bestowing specific benefits on other political actors. Later, he can call in these political debts on behalf of enterprises to which the influence sellers may be completely indifferent or even antagonistic. Log-rolling is an operation that maximizes the convertibility of political assets. It tends to prevail, as some observers have noted, where the political stakes are highly specific, and this is probably no accident.[10]

Because specific benefits have greater purchasing power than collective benefits and because they yield more fluid political assets, they are likely to be attractive to people who are influence brokers—in American cities, usually the party politician. The preference for specific benefits probably has much to do with his behavior. It may explain, for example, why he usually purchases influence in bits and pieces rather than in wholesale

[9] James Q. Wilson and Peter Clark, "Incentive Systems: A Theory of Organization," *Administrative Science Quarterly,* **6** (1960), 129–166.

[10] Theodore Lowi, "American Business, Public Policy, Case-Studies and Political Theory," *World Politics,* **16** (1964), 677–715.

lots.[11] It may help to account for some of the policy preferences of party men. It has been noted, for instance, that politicians tend to be antagonistic toward urban planning because "the politician's way at the municipal level seems to be usually slanted toward segmental approaches and special interests." [12] The segmental bias is certainly more congenial to a specific than to a collective incentive system.

The same kind of bias may be responsible for the connection that we have observed between perceived industrial influence on the air pollution issue and the formal characteristics of the machine. Because party organizations are not inclined toward collective benefits, we can expect that political machines will be relatively uninterested in the benefits of pollution control policy. Clean air, a collective benefit, will not add much to the resources that party influence brokers require to sustain their political operations. On the other hand, the costs of pollution control—its negative benefits—are clearly not of the collective variety. It is not the case that if these costs fall on anyone, they must fall on everyone. A large portion of them can be "captured" by a group whose membership is quite limited. In short, the costs of pollution control constitute a specific, negative benefit of public policy that might be used to carry on the operations of a political brokerage. These costs fall most noticeably on local industry, and it is for that reason, perhaps, that a machine polity is more likely than others to turn toward industry where the air pollution issue is concerned. It is there that the politician's entrepreneurial opportunities lie. By manipulating the costs of pollution control, he may be able to purchase the kind of influence that is most useful in overcoming the formal fragmentation of urban authority.

The inclination toward industry is evident not only in machine politics, but among party men generally. The findings reported in Table V–1 show political party chairmen more likely than most other informants to perceive that industry would have an essential role in any local anti-pollution efforts. It can be argued that this result reflects the interest of the party politician in maintaining or enhancing the brokerage operations of his organization. He turns toward industry in the matter of pollution control because it is there that he can use specific inducements to acquire relatively fluid political assets. Of course the "brokerage" interpretation is not the only one that might be offered to account for the political perception of party men or for the conjunction of perceived industrial influence with machine politics. What makes this interpretation a particularly attractive one is the fact that it is consistent with both of these findings and with others as well. Because

[11] Edward C .Banfield, *Political Influence* (New York: Free Press, 1961), pp. 241–242.

[12] David Wallace, "Renaissancemenship," *American Institute of Planners Journal,* **26** (1960), 174.

TABLE V–1 *Perceptions of Industrial Influence on Air Pollution Control*

Group	Industrial support is "essential"
	%
Labor council presidents	58.5
	(46)
Political party chairmen	55.9
	(92)
Newspaper editors	51.1
	(47)
Chamber of Commerce presidents	47.9
	(48)
Bar association presidents	37.2
	(43)
Bank presidents	35.0
	(48)

Note: Numbers in parentheses represent respondents in each category; total respondents, 336, of which 12 were n.a.

it lends coherence to many bits of evidence, it is useful, and probably correct.

Many characteristics of pollution politics in Gary and East Chicago can be understood in terms of the party politician's preference for specific rather than for collective policy benefits. It is probably significant, for example, that the promoters of pollution control proposals in both towns were not party organization men. The advocates of clean air appeared outside the party organizations because the party incentive systems, relying as they did on specific benefits, were probably not congenial to men who sought collective goods.

The behavior of party politicians during the course of the dirty air debate may also reflect the bias of the party system. Local politicians seldom intervened in local discussions of the pollution problem, but when they did, it was often to represent the interests of industrial corporations. Mayor Migas, at the request of some East Chicago industrial executives, delayed the introduction of Loyd Cohen's dirty air ordinance. Mayor Chacharis, when he spoke out on the pollution problem, counseled caution in the campaign against dirty air lest an excessively strict regulation of industrial emissions do damage to the economic interests of U.S. Steel and perhaps to the economic well-being of Gary. It may be that these kindnesses to local manufacturers represented attempts to manipulate the costs of pollution control and thereby purchase bits of industrial influence.

Parties and the Life Chances of the Pollution Issue

Because of the nature of his political operations, the broker-politician will probably respond more readily to requests for specific benefits than he will to requests for collective benefits. Where he is a prominent figure, his favoritism can be expected to have some effect upon the kinds of demands that rise to the surface of local politics. "Collective" demands will tend to be filtered out of the political system because they cannot be made to serve his purposes so easily as specific demands. In politics dominated by party organizations, then, we can expect that the demands for clean air will tend to be shunted aside, and pollution politics in Gary and East Chicago provide a possible illustration of this phenomenon.

In East Chicago during the late 1940's the local Democratic Party organization was torn by factional rivalries. Mayor Frank Migas, the party chairman, was under political siege. He could not attract a majority vote in the primaries, and it was not long before an opposition faction ejected him, first from the party chairmanship and later from the mayor's office as well. It was during this period of party debilitation that Loyd Cohen successfully mobilized East Chicagoans for the campaign against dirty air and managed, with no great difficulty, to place the air pollution problem on the community's political agenda.

There may have been more than a coincidental connection between the temporary confusion in East Chicago's dominant party and Cohen's success. Cohen did not feel obliged to take his anti-pollution proposals to the party politicians, and his effectiveness, one might argue, depended in part upon his circumvention of these broker-politicians. He did not rely on political middlemen to assemble the bits of influence that were needed for his project: he himself secured the acquiescence of local industrialists; he activated public support for his anti-pollution campaign. He was his own political broker, and his political self-reliance meant that the dirty air issue, in its rise to prominence, would skirt the party organization and the organizational bias which inclines politicians toward policies that generate specific benefits.

The Democratic Party . . . was probably more powerful and tightly organized in Gary during the late 1950's than it was in East Chicago during the late 1940's. When Milton Roth raised the dirty air issue with Mayor Mandich, Gary's Democratic organization was in the midst of a political consolidation, and by the time that Albert Gavit attempted to reopen the dirty air debate, the consolidation appears to have been complete. Mayor Chacharis had been able to command more than 80 per cent of the vote in the Democratic primary of 1959. The robust condition of the party may have been one of the factors that obstructed the emergence of the air pollution issue. If obstruction did occur, it was not the result of any active attempt to suppress the issue. Party leaders were simply uninterested in it, perhaps because it originated with political outsiders like Albert Gavit and Milton Roth, possibly because the issue did not seem to be particularly profitable. Their disinteret was a crucial factor in the progress of the pollution issue because Gary's pollution activists, unlike Loyd Cohen, seem to have thought it necessary to turn to them for assistance. Albert Gavit was especially sensitive to this need: his anti-pollution efforts were designed, for the most part, to activate party politicians on behalf of clean air. When the party men remained unmoved after his repeated attempts to mobilize them, Gavis finally gave up. He believed that the anti-pollution campaign was a hopeless effort so long as it did not number them among its backers.

In East Chicago, then, where the party organization was temporarily disorganized and pollution activists did not rely on its brokerage services, the dirty air issue flourished. In Gary, where the party organization was strong and pollution activists turned to it for assistance, the issue floundered. It was not until Mayor Chacharis went to jail, and the party hierarchy was momentarily disorganized, that the pollution issue began to rise toward a position of prominence on Gary's political agenda. This coincidence and others like it suggest that where local party organizations are strong and unified, the life chances of the pollution issue will be diminished. Clean air, we might argue, simply does not yield the kinds of political assets that party organizations are likely to find attractive, and its irrelevance to party interests is sufficient to diminish the force of demands for pollution control in cities where parties monopolize the political initiatives of their communities.

If this is an accurate analysis of pollution politics in Gary and East Chicago, then we ought to find some support for it in other cities of our sample. We ought to find that where members of local political strata turn to political parties for a solution to the dirty air problem, the size of the pollution issue is diminished. People who "turn to the parties" are those who believe that party support is essential to the success of a local pollution control program. . . . For the time being, no distinction will be made between Republican and Democratic influence. The party influence measurement combines reputational votes for both parties in a single index. Political parties in a city qualify as highly influential on the air pollution issue if their joint share of the "essential" votes on this issue is greater than the median two-party share.

The nature of political party operations and the evidence from Gary and East Chicago lead us to expect that, among towns with similar pollution levels, there will be a negative relationship between party influence in the matter and the life chances of the pollution issue. The findings reported in Table V–2 do not support these expectations: after controlling for variations in local pollution levels, there is only a weak and uneven association between the power reputation of local parties and the various indicators of positiontaking on dirty air.

TABLE V–2 *Perceived Party Influence and the Issue-ness of Air Pollution, Controlling for Suspended Particulate Level*

	Issue-ness scale item			
	Newspaper	Chamber of Commerce	Labor council	Political parties
Party influence on air pollution	−.19* (45)	−.02 (46)	+.02 (44)	+.11 (45)

* Partial correlation coefficients.

There are, however, some local conditions that accentuate the impact of party influence upon the survival and growth prospects of the pollution issue. As in the case of industrial influence, the operation of perceived party power appears to be affected by the local pollution level. In low-pollution towns party influence does seem to inhibit the early growth of the issue; in high-pollution towns it does not. The finding is an understandable one. In low-pollution towns, the prospective benefits of pollution control are relatively small. The party's need for specific inducements can therefore be expected to override the need for pollution abatement. In high-pollution towns, on the other hand, the benefits of pollution abatement are relatively large, and the dirty air issue can therefore be expected to overcome the party bias against "collective" policies.

Low pollution is not the only condition that appears to activate the deterrent capacity of perceived party influence. Another and more important catalytic factor is the absence of perceived industrial power. The operation of this factor is notable not only because it accentuates the impact of party influence but because it most effectively reveals the nature of the political party's organizational bias. It has been argued here that this bias inclines the party toward public policies that are likely to generate specific, capturable benefits because control over such benefits enables the party organization to sustain itself as a political brokerage. Control over collective benefits, on the other hand, is not likely to provide the party with the kind of purchasing power that it needs to acquire the fluid political assets that are essential to a brokerage operation. This is why the benefits of pollution abatement policy fail to arouse the interest of broker-politicians. They are collective benefits. But the costs of pollution control policy may well stimulate the party politician's entrepreneurial appetite. These negative benefits of public policy are relatively specific. They fall heavily upon a social grouping whose membership is limited—the local industrial community. Because this is the case, they may provide the party politician with the sorts of inducements that he needs to carry on his brokerage activities. He may manipulate the costs of pollution control in order to purchase useful bits of industrial influence, provided, of course, that industry is perceived to have influence to sell. In towns where industry enjoys a reputation for power, therefore, we should find that perceived party influence operates to enhance the life chances of the pollution issue because the dirty air debate will appear to offer entrepreneurial opportunities to political parties.

Where industry does not enjoy a reputation for power, the pollution issue can supply the party politician with little that is useful to his organization. We can therefore expect that party influence will operate to inhibit the emergence of the dirty air issue. That is precisely what we find. The results in Table V–3 show that among cities where industry does not enjoy a reputation for power in the pollution field, perceived party influence is negatively associated with most of the indicators of issue-ness. Here, the party's influence appears to reduce the life chances of the pollution issue. Among cities where industry does enjoy a reputation for power, however, party influence seems to operate to enhance the life chances of the dirty air debate.

It was found earlier that the air pollution issue tends not to flourish in cities where industry enjoys a reputation for power. These new findings suggest, in addition, that where industry does enjoy that reputation, the life chances of the air pollution issue will be greater in cities where political parties are influential than where they are not. This finding, like several of the previous ones, can be subsumed under the "brokerage" interpretation of political party operations. It seems to reflect the interest that party organizations have in using the air pollution issue to "purchase" industrial influence—when that influence is available.

The impact of party influence could not be explained away by referring

TABLE V–3 *Perceived Influence and the Issue-ness of Air Pollution, Controlling for Perceived Industrial Influence and Suspended Particulate Level*

		Issue-ness scale item			
		Newspaper	Chamber of Commerce	Labor council	Political parties
Perceived party influence	High industrial influence	—.06 (19)	+.13 (20)	+.48 (19)	+.40 (20)
	Low industrial influence	—.44 (26)	—.20 (26)	—.20 (25)	+.01 (25)

to local population characteristics like median age, educational level, income, or racial composition—factors that were previously found to affect the level of public concern about dirty air. It is likely, then, that the workings of party influence do not simply reflect public preferences in the matter of air pollution. They represent a response to organizational, not just popular, demands. The consideration of local population characteristics therefore fails to alter the assessment that party influence can have an important effect upon the penetrability of community political systems.

Nor is this assessment much altered when a distinction is made between Democratic and Republican parties. Both parties appear to affect the life chances of the pollution issue in roughly the same way, as Tables V–4 and V–5 indicate. They show that Democratic Party influence and Republican Party influence both operate according to the "brokerage" pattern. They promote the emergence of the pollution issue in those cities where industry has a reputation for power—where it is perceived to have

TABLE V–4 *Perceived Democratic Party Influence and the Issue-ness of Air Pollution, Controlling for Perceived Industrial Influence and Suspended Particulate Level*

		Issue-ness scale item			
		Newspaper	Chamber of Commerce	Labor council	Political parties
Perceived Democratic influence	High industrial influence	+.23 (19)	+.18 (20)	+.56 (19)	+.14 (20)
	Low industrial influence	−.44 (26)	−.20 (26)	−.20 (25)	−.01 (25)

TABLE V–5 *Perceived Republican Party Influence and the Issue-ness of Air Pollution, Controlling for Perceived Industrial Influence and Suspended Particulate Level*

		Issue-ness scale item			
		Newspaper	Chamber of Commerce	Labor council	Political parties
Perceived Republican influence	High industrial influence	−.16 (19)	+.08 (20)	+.53 (19)	+.38 (20)
	Low industrial influence	−.27 (26)	−.01 (26)	−.21 (25)	−.18 (25)

influence to sell; they inhibit the emergence of the issue in towns where industry does not enjoy a reputation for power and does not have influence to sell. The small differences that do appear between the effects of Democratic and Republican influence suggest that the operation of Democratic Party influence may adhere somewhat more consistently to the "brokerage" pattern than Republican Party influence.

The Nature of Party Influence

It should not be difficult to understand how the built-in biases of the political party may affect the treatment that the pollution issue receives at the hands of party organizations. However, it remains unclear just why party bias should also affect the responsiveness to the pollution problem of local newspapers, Chambers of Commerce, and labor organizations. We do not know how perceived party influence is brought to bear on these organizations nor why they respond to it. The survey data do not provide clear answers to either of these questions. It is uncertain, in the first place, whether the party exercises its influence through observable political actions or whether its "unjustified" reputation for influence affects the behavior of other organizations—in other words, whether the party's influence is direct or indirect.

The problem here is to discover whether or not perceived party influence in the pollution field is based on party behavior in the area. . . . The weight of the evidence is divided about evenly between the conclusion that party influence is direct and the conclusion that it is indirect. It is probable, therefore, that it is a mixture of both.

We can only speculate about the ways in which the two kinds of party influence manage to affect the behavior of civic activists, but the speculations are supported at some points by bits of evidence. For example, the findings from Gary and East Chicago suggest that, if party support is thought to be essential to a pollution control campaign, then the expressed disinterest of party politicians in the pollution problem could have a decisive effect upon the career of the issue. Local pollution activists might abandon their efforts on behalf of clean air and turn their attention to projects that appear to have more favorable political prospects. Few people like to waste their effort on enterprises that seem doomed to failure.

The prospect of failure seems to have had something to do with the slow development of Gary's dirty air debate. Party politicians were able to influence the growth of the anti-pollution campaign by diminishing the optimism of some pollution activists. Because the politicians were thought to be essential to the anti-pollution effort, their actions in this matter were critical signs of the chances for success. The cues that they gave to other political actors could influence the distribution of energy and attention among alternative civic enterprises.

The party's reputation for power, however, is probably not the only thing that may induce a civic activist to take his cues from party politicians. The politician, after all, has traditionally been regarded as expert in the evaluation of political possibilities, and it is understandable that people should rely on his judgment where questions of political success and failure are involved. As a political broker, it is his business to know which political projects are likely to yield a return on investment and which ones are not. His evaluation of a civic enterprise can therefore make it more or less attractive to other political actors. Its stock may rise or fall according to his judgment. Of course, if he is not regarded as an effective influence broker, his judgments will probably carry little weight with other political actors, but where he has a reputation for power, there is an especially good chance that it will be accompanied by a reputation for political expertise.

There is another, more indirect avenue of party influence which may also help to carry the party's organizational bias into the activities of newspapers, labor organizations, and Chambers of Commerce. The connection between the party and these other organizations may be an "ecological" one such as Norton Long describes when he suggests that communities may be regarded as an ecology of games.[13] The ecological interpretation of urban affairs emphasizes the interconnectedness of various local institutions and organizations. Like the plants and animals in a natural ecological system, the elements of a local organizational ecology use one another in order to maintain themselves. The fruits of one organization provide other organizations with sustenance.

The ecological approach to local politics calls attention to these interdependent relationships and to the continuous mutual adjustments that they are likely to entail. Organizations, like the creatures of a natural ecological system, modify their life habits so as to make use of the resources generated by their neighbors, and an ecological system that includes a strong party organization is likely to be characterized by modifications of a particular sort. We have seen that the resources that a strong party typically makes available to its organizational neighbors will adjust their incentive systems so that, in their own efforts to keep and attract members or adherents, they can make use of the inducements that the party provides. These adjustments are likely to have a visible impact upon organizational behavior. The nature of an organization's incentive system . . . is likely to be reflected in the character of organizational strategy, in the configurations of organizational conflicts, and in leadership behavior. It is also likely to have some effect upon the kinds of political demands that an organization generates or nurtures. If its incentive system is fueled by specific benefits, it will tend to make relatively few collective demands because collective

[13] Norton Long, "The Local Community as an Ecology of Games," *American Journal of Sociology*, **64** (1958), 251–261.

benefits will not effectively serve its own maintenance and enhancement interests.

Political parties, therefore, may influence the activities of other organizations by affecting the character of the organizational resources that happen to be available within a local community. The very existence of a strong party organization may induce other local groups to shift their survival strategies and their political behavior. For example, Chambers of Commerce in strong party towns will probably differ in a systematic way from Chambers in weak party towns. In a strong party town we would expect the Chamber to stress "specific" services to its members. In a weak party town we would expect the Chamber to concentrate on more diffuse, intangible inducements, like appeals to the spirit of civic boosterism or local pride.[14]

The adaptation of its organizational neighbors to the existence of the party is something like the adaptation of giraffes to the existence of tall trees. In both cases the adaptation functions to enhance growth and survival prospects, and in both cases the adaptors acquire a limited resemblance to the objects that have induced their adjustments. Party indifference to clean air and to collective benefits generally is likely to be transferred to other organizations within its environment. This hypothesis might explain why, under certain conditions, perceived party influence seems to deter local newspapers, Chambers of Commerce, and labor organizations from taking positions on the dirty air issue. The party's influence may operate to create or reinforce organizational incentive systems that are inhospitable to such collective benefits.

But there are also some situations in which party influence seems to have just the opposite effect. In towns where industry enjoys a reputation for power, perceived party influence operates to enhance the survival prospects of the pollution issue. This result, as has been pointed out, is quite consistent with the organizational needs of political parties, reflecting their interest in using specific policy benefits (in this case, negative benefits) to purchase bits of industrial influence. In towns where industry has influence to sell, it is understandable that parties themselves might attempt to promote the pollution issue. But it is not quite understandable why, in these

[14] An "ecological" explanation of this sort seems to provide the most promising way to account for James Q. Wilson's findings that the organization of Negro politics in a community generally comes to resemble the organization of white politics. Negro political organization is heavily influenced by the organizational resources available, and the nature of those resources is influenced, in turn, by the character of white political organizations. Chicago provides a good illustration of the ecological relationship that may exist between white and Negro political organizations. Here, it appears, the emergence of the Dawson machine within the black ghetto was in large part a response to the availability of organizational resources that were generated by Chicago's white machine, chiefly patronage, favors, and cash [see James Q. Wilson, *Negro Politics* (New York: Free Press, 1960), pp. 22–24, 48–76].

same towns, party influence should induce other organizations to promote the issue. The "ecological" bias that strong parties engender would presumably diminish the interest of these other organizations in the quest for collective benefits like clean air. How can party influence operate to reverse this bias?

A partial answer is that the party does not uniformly succeed in doing so. A look at the top row of Table V–3 shows that local newspapers and Chambers of Commerce are not especially responsive to party influence in towns where industry enjoys a reputation for power. Only local labor organizations seem to be sensitive to their influence, and it is a notable coincidence that only in the case of labor organizations can we conclude that the operation of party influence is largely direct rather than indirect. The responsiveness of labor councils to party influence can be explained in terms of observable party action in the matter of dirty air.[15]

This coincidence suggests that we may be able to describe the operations of party influence like this: where the pollution issue is irrelevant to the party's organizational interests, the party's indirect, "ecological" influence will operate to diminish the life chances of the issue. Where it is advantageous for the party to promote the debate, it must exercise its influence directly in order to overcome the community bias that it has created indirectly: it must take some positive action if the issue is to develop. The party organization can then bargain about it with local industrial influence by making concessions to industrial interests.

Two points concerning this description ought to be kept in mind. First, it is highly tentative, though it is occasionally supported by uncertain hints in the survey data or in the case study materials. Second, even if the speculative nature of the description is discounted, it must be recognized that the portrayal is onesided. It attempts to reveal the ways in which a strong party organization may affect the behavior of its organizational neighbors but neglects to take account of the reciprocal influence that neighboring organizations may exert upon the operations of a political party. The possibility of mutual adaptation, not just onesided adjustment, is implied by the ecological analogy used here.

The debut of the political machine, which was discussed earlier, provides a good illustration of the way in which the party may adjust to its organizational neighbors. If the classic account is reliable, the appearance of the machine can be regarded as the party's response to the emergence of large-scale, capitalist enterprise. Party organizations adapted their operations and their incentive systems so that they could make use of the

[15] Specifically, there is a positive relationship between perceived party power and the occurrence of dirty air discussions between labor council officials and party officials ($r = +.28$) and another positive association between the occurrence of these discussions and positiontaking by labor on the issue ($r = +.40$).

resources that local capitalists were able to provide. The growth of the machine represented an "ecological" adjustment of the party to other organizations in its environment.

Another sign of party adjustment is the impact of reputedly powerful manufacturing firms upon the operation of party influence. The presence of these industrial corporations seems to make a difference in the way the party works, and community newspapers appear to have a somewhat similar capacity to affect party operations. Newspapers, like industrial corporations, are profitmaking organizations, but in the newspaper business "profit" will very probably include diffuse, intangible rewards as well as hard cash. If publishers were singlemindedly devoted to financial advancement, they would probably not be in the newspaper business. Among the intangible returns that help to sustain the newspaper as a community oranization, moral and ideological gratifications figure prominently. Newspapermen like to think of themselves as public crusaders or as guardians of the public welfare, and the fact that the newspaper claims the public in general as its constituency, and things in general as its field of competence, reinforces these self-conceptions. It is, as Norton Long points out, one of the few local institutions with a long-term interest in the community as a whole.[16]

The newspaper's claim to represent the whole community will probably incline it, more than other local organizations, toward public policies whose benefits accrue to the whole community. Its advocacy of collective causes may help to justify its institutional pretensions and to strengthen its ability to employ moral or ideological inducements to maintain itself and its following. We should therefore expect to find local newspapers among the leading advocates of collective benefits such as clean air. . . . We might also anticipate that the presence of an influential newspaper within a community would affect the operations of local political parties. The newspaper is probably less responsive than most other local organizations to specific inducements, the broker-politician's stock in trade, so that where the newspaper is influential, the party politician may have to change his way of doing business. In order to purchase newspaper support for his civic enterprises or to forestall its opposition, the politician may find it necessary to employ non-material or collective incentives. In doing so, he would of course depart from the normal operating procedures of an influence broker.

Perhaps more important than newspaper influence itself is what newspaper prominence reveals about the character of a community and its residents. Where newspapers enjoy a reputation for power, it is likely that a large segment of the local population is responsive to the moral or ideological inducements that newspapers can employ. When this is the case, the party politician will find it difficult to play the role of an influence broker.

[16] Long, "The Local Community as an Ecology of Games," pp. 259–61.

He will frequently discover that specific policy benefits do not provide him with much purchasing power because the sellers of influence demand moral or ideological gratifications in exchange for their support or cooperation. To the extent that the politician meets those demands, he leaves the influence brokerage business.

In short, newspaper influence and the things that go with it could conceivably modify the operations of political party organizations in a way that might be significant for the life chances of the pollution issue. In the presence of a reputedly powerful newspaper, the party bias against clean air might dissolve. This change could be brought about in much the same way that industrial influence can induce a shift in the party's treatment of the pollution issue. Where newspapers are perceived to be powerful, party politicians may see some profit in promoting the dirty air issue. They can use the benefits of pollution control to purchase newspaper influence, which they can then use to sustain their own operations. Where newspaper are not perceived to be powerful, however, the air pollution issue will not present these entrepreneurial advantages. An uninfluential newspaper has nothing of political value to offer in exchange for the benefits of pollution control. In such a situation, the party's organizational biases will not be softened, and party influence will operate to diminish the force of clean air campaigns.

Unfortunately, the data do not bear out these reasonable expectations. The power reputations of local newspapers have no consistent effect upon the operation of party influence. Newspaper prominance is reflected less in the operation than in the level of perceived party power, and there is a good reason for this result. Newspaper influence tends, as suggested above, to be encumbered with moral or ideological commitments and is not an especially fluid political asset. This is not to say that it is completely irrelevant to the dealings of a party influence broker, however. It is significant that party organizations do not thrive on the kind of influence that they can buy from newspapers or their adherents. Newspapers do not contribute much to their sustenance. Where newspapers occupy a prominent place in the local ecology of organizations, we can therefore expect that political parties will find it relatively difficult to collect the kind of political influence which makes them grow strong. Newspapers and political parties tend not to flourish as influential actors within the same ecological system; that, at least, is the implication of the findings presented in Table V–6.[17] The table

[17] The associations between newspaper power in one issue-area and party power in that issue-area have been purposely omitted from Table V–6. The reason, briefly, is that the influence measures for the two kinds of local organizations are based upon each organization's share of the reputational votes cast within particular issue-areas. The larger the newspaper's share of the votes within an issue-area, the smaller the party's share is likely to be, and vice versa. In other words, there will tend to be an artificially induced negative relationship between the index of party influence in an issue-area and the index of newspaper

TABLE V–6 *Perceived Newspaper Influence and Perceived Party Influence*

		Newspaper influence in				
		Air pollution	Municipal bond referenda	Urban renewal	School board appoint-ments	Mayoral elections
Party influence in	Air pollution		—.19	—.26	—.14	—.19
	Municipal bond referenda	—.20		—.38	—.15	—.38
	Urban renewal	—.35	—.29		—.05	—.18
	School board appoint-ments	—.31	—.21	—.22		—.31
	Mayoral elections	—.13	—.22	—.40	—.10	

shows that perceived newspaper influence in any issue-area is negatively associated with perceived party power in any other issue-area. The relationship between these two local institutions appears to be competitive, not symbolic.

Conclusion

Edward Banfield has argued that local political issues grow out of the maintenance and enhancement needs of a city's large formal organizations.[18] . . . The argument, in effect, is that the neglect of potential political issues can be traced to their incompatibility with the maintenance and enhancement needs of large organizations.

Where industry is powerful, for example, the life chances of the pollution issue are diminished, and it is not difficult to understand why. Industrial corporations are sustained by profits, and the pollution issue poses a possible threat to profits. Industrial influence therefore operates

---

influence within that issue-area. This artificial association tends to inflate the negative correlation between perceived party power and perceived newspaper power. The same problem does not exist when we compare perceived party influence in one issue-area with perceived newspaper influence in another issue-area. In this case, the two local organizations would be drawing on different pools of reputational votes.

[18] Banfield, *Political Influence*, p. 263.

to inhibit the growth of the dirty air issue. The impact of political parties is somewhat more subtle. Parties maintain themselves by exchanging specific benefits for pieces of influence, and there are some circumstances in which the pollution issue fails to generate benefits that can be employed in these exchanges. In such situations, party influence operates to obstruct the entry of the issue into local politics.

In a sense, the source of this obstruction is not the political party itself, but political pluralism. The party's operating procedures, as well as its organizational biases, are derived from the need to do business in politics where a variety of independent political elites hold the power to frustrate successful political action. Were it not for this fractionation of influence, there would be little demand for the brokerage services that American political parties have traditionally provided, and were it not for the imperatives of its brokerage operations, the political party would probably not have maintained its indifference toward collective goods. In pluralism, it appears, there is a built-in potential for political bias, and influential party organizations help to realize that potential. The bias is quite similar to the one that seems to have roused muckrakers fifty years ago to complain that American politics and politicians accorded special advantages to "special interests." Some of the muckraking journalists, like Lincoln Steffens, went on to point out that this inclination toward special interests did not originate in the moral degeneracy of party politicians but was built into the business of American politics. The preference for specific benefits has a similar kind of origin, and perhaps it is a descendant or a continuation of the political bias that Steffens and others perceived. At any rate, it may constitute an important limitation upon the alleged openness of pluralistic political systems, tending to obstruct the expression of collective interests and the political progress of collective issues.

In general, a political issue tends to be ignored if there is a mis-match between the kinds of benefits that it is likely to create and the kinds of inducements that influential community organizations need in order to survive and grow. This elementary generalization, however, leaves some important things unsaid. It suggests that the life chances of a political issue will depend in part upon the kinds of policy benefits that are at stake in it, but the proposition says nothing about the criteria that might be used to distinguish one kind of benefit from another. It would not be hard to assemble a long list of ways in which we might classify policy benefits. The problem is to identify those dimensions of variability that are worthy of attention, and it is to that problem, among others, that recent investigations in "policy theory" have addressed themselves. The one element common to most of these efforts is the distinction, presented under various labels, between collective and specific benefits. Theodore Lowi, for example, has called attention to the "disaggregability" of public policies—the divisibility of the costs and benefits that they entail. Lewis Froman, relying on the work of Lowi and others, has drawn a distinction between "segmental" and "areal" policies—policies that affect particular groups within a community vs. policies that affect the whole local population.[19]

The same kind of distinction has occasionally been employed by organization theorists in their efforts to classify organizational incentive systems. Something like the collective-specific dimensions appears to underlie the division that Wilson and Clark make between organizations with purpose-oriented incentive systems, on the one hand, and organizations with solidary or material incentive systems on the other. The difference between collective and specific also seems to be one element in Amitai Etzioni's distinction between "expressive" and "utilitarian" organizations.[20] Organizational incentives, like policy benefits, can be arranged on the continuum from collective to specific. More important, the location of an organization's incentive system on this continuum has something to do with organizational practices and propensities. The classificatory efforts of the organization theorists would have been wasted if they did not show that the character of an organization's incentive system makes a difference in its behavior.

In the present effort to relate the maintenance and enhancement needs of organizations to the costs and benefits of political issues, the attempt has been made to capitalize upon the analytic tendencies that are shared by both organization theory and policy theory and to merge the categories implicit in organizational analysis with the categories of policy analysis. Collective organizations, it is argued, will tend to attach themselves to collective issues, specific organizations to specific issues. The fortunes of a political issue can be expected to vary with the prominence of its organizational patrons.

Policy theory and organization theory are drawn together by more than the similarity that exists between their respective classification schemes. There is also some resemblance between the ways in which these two enterprises use the classification systems that they have developed. Policy theorists seek not only to categorize policy characteristics but to relate these characteristics to patterns of political activity—to uncover the connection between the substance of policy and the process of policymaking. That has been one concern here as well. In . . . an attempt . . . to find out whether the air pollution issue regularly evoked some distinctive pattern of political activity, it was [found] that, where dirty air was concerned, different cities tend to move toward a single pattern of political decision-making. The costs and benefits that are at stake in the pollution issue are

[19] Lowi, "American Business, Public Policy"; Lewis A. Froman, Jr., "An Analysis of Public Policies in Cities," *Journal of Politics,* **29** (1967), 94–108.

[20] Wilson and Clark, "Incentive Systems"; Amitai Etzioni, *A Comparative Analysis of Complex Organizations* (New York: Free Press, 1961).

everywhere similar, and this similarity in the political stakes is responsible for inter-city similarities in the political process. The line of reasoning here is quite similar to the one that Wilson and Clark follow in their attempt to relate organizational behavior to organizational incentive systems. Like the policy theorists, they hope to discover some systematic relationship between patterns of activity and the types of inducements which stimulate and sustain those activities. In this respect, policy theory and organization theory seem to run parallel. In fact, the phenomena themselves, as well as the analytic approaches to them, exhibit some notable similarities.

Issues and policies are not simply pieces of political subject matter. To say that an issue has arisen is to announce the emergence of an informal organization, a body of would-be decisionmakers who interact with one another in their efforts to deal with some common concern. Political issues, then, have an organizational aspect. When policy theorists try to relate the characteristics of a policy to the pattern of political activity which it has generated, they are attempting, in effect, to establish a connection between the kinds of inducements that are distributed by an informal organization and the internal practices of that organization. We have been looking at issues as organizations, but we have been less concerned with their internal operations than with their external relations. As organizations, issues are dependent upon their environments for the fulfillment of their maintenance and enhancement needs. They are elements in the same local ecological systems which contain Chambers of Commerce or political parties.

What has been said about the local ecology or organizations suggests that a certain kind of coherence or unity will tend to develop within such a system. To the extent that it is possible, groups will adapt their operations so as to make use of the resources that are provided by other, influential groups. When such adaptations are not consistent with the maintenance and enhancement needs of an organization, its prominence can be expected to decline. This seems to be the fate of a political party that finds itself confronted with a highly influential newspaper. The end result of all these organizational adjustments is a degree of consistency among the operations and inclinations of organizations that are locally influential. In this way, organizational biases may be translated into a general community bias.

As members of the local ecological system, issues and issue-areas can be expected to partake of this bias. This means that we may expect to find some consistency or unity among the political issues that flourish in a community, just as we would expect to find a similar consistency among the influential organizations of a town. In part, this common tie among issues may reflect the consistency which has been presumed to exist among the inclinations of locally influential organizations. In part, it may be the result of "ecological" interactions among the issues themselves.

. . .

A Note on Methodology

The information about urban political issues and activities contained in this study comes from a survey, conducted by the National Opinion Research Center during late 1966 and early 1967, of formal leaders in fifty-one American cities, ranging in population from 50,000 to 750,000.[21] The leaders (ten from each city) are the heads of organizations and institutions which are likely to be found in almost any urban area: mayors, Chamber of Commerce presidents, presidents of local bar associations, chairmen of local Democratic and Republican Party organizations, city or county health commissioners, municipal planning or urban renewal directors, local labor council presidents, editors of leading community newspapers, and the president of the largest bank in each of the cities surveyed. These formal leaders provide most of the testimony on which "issue-ness" of air pollution is gauged and the political characteristics of the fifty-one towns determined.

The reliability of the leaders' testimony obviously depends in part upon the kinds of information that they have been asked to supply. Past community research has shown, not surprisingly, that respondents are most accurate as informants when they are answering questions about their own activities or about occurrences in which they have been directly involved.[22] Questions of this kind were relied upon in order to gather the information necessary for measuring the "issue-ness" of air pollution. The respondents were asked, for example, whether their organizations had ever taken positions on the matter of air pollution. They were also asked to describe any organizational activities related to air pollution or pollution control—special meetings on the subject, studies conducted, publicity campaigns, and so on. Their answers to these questions were used to construct an index of the "issue-ness" of air pollution.

In effect, the assumption was made that the local panels of organizational leaders could serve as human yardsticks for estimating the level and nature of decisionmaking activity in each of the cities under study. They serve in this capacity not because they themselves are sure to stand in the path of influence and decisionmaking. Their formal authority is likely to make them essential in the formulation and execution of local policy decisions. From the strategic vantage points which they occupy, we can scan various policymaking regions for signs of activity. They themselves are likely to reflect the policymaking concerns of their communities in their own organizational activities. These activities will almost never tell the

[21] For a description of this survey, see Peter Rossi and Robert Crain, "The NORC Permanent Community Sample."

[22] Raymond Wolfinger, "A Plea for a Decent Burial," *American Sociological Review*, **27** (1962), 842.

whole story about any decisionmaking episode, but they will indicate what kinds of issues have engaged the attention of the local political stratum. The bigger the issue, the more activity we can expect to find among the members of our panel.

SUGGESTED READINGS

Environment

The numerous scholarly studies produced in response to the environmental problems confronting the states and urban areas are as varied as the problems the studies attempt to explore. Lynton Caldwell's book Environment: *A Challenge to Modern Society* (Garden City, N.Y.: The Natural History Press, 1970) surveys the scope of the environmental issue by classifying the problem of a social issue with an emphasis upon the policy and technological complications inherent on the solution process. *Pollution, Property and Prices* (Toronto: University of Toronto Press, 1968) by J. H. Dales illustrates the technique of economic analysis of environmental issues and its application to policy determination and implementation. Clarence Davies in his book *The Politics of Pollution* (New York: Pegasus, 1970) includes a survey of the political background of pollution problems and policies in the context of federal pollution programs. Neil Fabricant's and Robert Hallman's work *Toward a Rational Power Policy: Energy, Politics and Pollution* (New York: Braziller, 1971) focuses on one basic environmental concern, the energy needs of the public, in the context of the specific needs of the New York metropolitan area.

Other works include:

Anderson, Walt, ed. *Politics and Environment: A Reader in Ecological Crisis.* Pacific Palisades, Calif.: Goodyear Publishing Company, 1970.

Campbell, Rex R., and Jerry Wade. *Society and Environment: The Coming Collision.* Boston: Allyn & Bacon, 1972.

Cooley, Richard A., and G. Wandes Forde Smith, eds. *Congress and the Environment.* Seattle: University of Washington Press, 1970.

Goldman, Marshall I., ed. *Ecology and Economics: Controlling Pollution in the 70's.* Englewood Cliffs, N.J.: Prentice–Hall, 1972.

Grad, Frank P., G. W. Rathjens, and A. J. Rosenthal. *Environmental Control: Priorities, Policies, and the Law.* New York: Columbia University Press, 1971.

Johnson, Huey, ed. *No Deposit—No Return: Man and His Environment.* Reading, Mass.: Addison-Wesley, 1970.

Jones, Charles O. "From Gold to Garbage: A Bibliographic Essay on Politics and the Environment," *American Political Science Review,* **66** (June 1972), 588–595.

Kneese, Allen V., R. V. Ayres, and Ralph C. d'Arge. *Economics and the Environment: A Materials Balance Approach.* Baltimore: Johns Hopkins Press, 1971.

Page, James K., ed. *Law and the Environment.* New York: Walker & Company, 1970.

Roos, Leslie L., Jr., ed. *The Politics of Ecosuicide.* New York: Holt, Rinehart and Winston, 1971.

Wrlght, Deil S. *Intergovernmental Action on Environmental Policy: The Role of the States.* Bloomingdale: Institute of Public Administration Indiana University, 1967.